JUSTICE AND ETHICS IN TOURISM

This is the first book to look at justice and ethics in tourism in one volume, bringing theoretical perspectives into conversation with tourism, development and the environment.

The book explores some key ethical perspectives and approaches to justice, including building capabilities, distributive justice, recognition, representation, and democracy. Human rights, integral in the context of tourism, are discussed throughout. Space is also given to structurally embedded injustices (including those related to historical racism and colonialism), responsibility toward justice, justice within and beyond borders, and justice in the context of sustainability, governance, policy, and planning.

A variety of international case studies contributed by researchers and experts from around the globe illustrate these concepts and facilitate understanding and practical application. Comprehensive and accessible, this is essential reading for students and researchers in tourism studies and will be of interest to students of geography, development studies, business and hospitality management, cultural studies, anthropology, sociology, urban planning, heritage conservation, international relations and environmental studies. The range of insights offered make this valuable reading for planners, policymakers, business managers and civil society organizations as well.

Tazim Jamal is a Professor in the Department of Recreation, Park and Tourism Sciences at Texas A&M University, Texas, USA.

Tourism, Environment and Development Series

Edited by Richard Sharpley, School of Sport, Tourism & The Outdoors, University of Central Lancashire, UK

Editorial Board: Chris Cooper, Oxford Brookes University, UK; Andrew Holden, University of Bedfordshire, UK; Bob McKercher, Hong Kong Polytechnic University; Chris Ryan, University of Waikato, New Zealand; David Telfer, Brock University, Canada

Tourism, Development and the Environment: Beyond Sustainability?
Richard Sharpley

Tourism and Poverty Reduction: Pathways to Prosperity
Jonathan Mitchell and Caroline Ashley

Slow Travel and Tourism
Janet Dickinson and Les Lumsdon

Sustainable Tourism in Island Destinations
Sonya Graci and Rachel Dodds

Climate Change and Tourism
Susanne Becken and John Hay

Justice and Ethics in Tourism
Tazim Jamal

For more information about this series, please visit: https://www.routledge.com/Tourism-Environment-and-Development/book-series/ECTED

JUSTICE AND ETHICS IN TOURISM

Tazim Jamal

LONDON AND NEW YORK

First published 2019
by Routledge
2 Park Square, Milton Park, Abingdon, Oxon OX14 4RN

and by Routledge
52 Vanderbilt Avenue, New York, NY 10017

Routledge is an imprint of the Taylor & Francis Group, an informa business

© 2019 Tazim Jamal

The right of Tazim Jamal to be identified as author of this work has been asserted by her in accordance with sections 77 and 78 of the Copyright, Designs and Patents Act 1988.

All rights reserved. No part of this book may be reprinted or reproduced or utilised in any form or by any electronic, mechanical, or other means, now known or hereafter invented, including photocopying and recording, or in any information storage or retrieval system, without permission in writing from the publishers.

Trademark notice: Product or corporate names may be trademarks or registered trademarks, and are used only for identification and explanation without intent to infringe.

British Library Cataloguing-in-Publication Data
A catalogue record for this book is available from the British Library

Library of Congress Cataloging-in-Publication Data
A catalog record has been requested for this book

ISBN: 978-1-138-06070-8 (hbk)
ISBN: 978-1-138-06071-5 (pbk)
ISBN: 978-1-315-16294-2 (ebk)

Typeset in Bembo
by Integra Software Services Pvt. Ltd.

CONTENTS

List of Illustrations	*vi*
List of Case Studies	*viii*
List of Contributors	*xi*
Preface and Acknowledgements	*xv*

1	The Landscape of Travel and Tourism	1
2	Equity and Justice	25
3	Diversity and Recognition	62
4	Responsibility and Care	102
5	Sustainability and Conservation	146
6	Democracy and Governance	195
7	Toward Good and Just Tourism?	233

Index	*255*

ILLUSTRATIONS

Photos

1.1	Tourist on golden staircase in Copenhagen, Denmark	3
1.2	The Little Mermaid's wistful pose, Copenhagen harbor	3
2.1.1	Visitor preparing for a Husky Safari tour in Muonio, Lapland	43
2.2.1	*Cozumel: Heaven on Earth* 2010 campaign sample ads, Mexico	57
3.1.1	Palenquera selling fruits to tourists in Cartagena, Colombia	73
3.1.2	Palenquera figurines sold in souvenir shops in Cartagena	74
3.1.3	Palenquera in the 2017 national tourism campaign "Colombia the Land of Sabrosura"	74
3.1.4	A Palenquera fruit stand displaying: "To take a picture with us collaborate by purchasing a fruit or leaving a tip"	76
3.2.1	A family of four international visitors at the Taj Mahal, India	88
3.3.1	Native American Memorial at Little Bighorn Battlefield National Monument, USA	96
3.3.2	Cavalry obelisk at Little Bighorn Battlefield National Monument, USA	96
4.1.1	View of the Hiroshima Peace Memorial Park and the A-bomb Dome	118
4.1.2	Hiroshima Peace Memorial (Genbaku Dome; A-Bomb Dome), Japan	118
4.1.3	Band playing in the Hiroshima Peace Memorial Park	119
4.1.4	High school girls collecting signatures to abolish nuclear weapons	119
4.2.1	Burial scene at the African Burial Ground National Monument Visitor Center, USA	126
4.3.1	Students and faculty members from Aalborg University, Copenhagen, being led by Street Voices guide	131

4.4.1	Representatives of UNDP visiting a San Ramón community, Nicaragua	137
4.4.2	Bienvenidos. Welcome sign in front of a home offering accommodation in San Ramón	137
5.3.1	Galápagos Islands, Ecuador	165
5.3.2	An iconic Galápagos inhabitant	165
5.5.1	Shijia Hutong Museum front entrance, Beijing	177
5.5.2	Model of alleyways and courtyard houses in Shijia Hutong neighborhood, Beijing	178
5.5.3	Famous residents of Shijia Hutong during the Republic of China era	179
5.6.1	Puppy Stairs repaired, Alcatraz Island, USA	186
5.6.2	Art Exhibition sign and Water Tower with restored Native American Graffiti in the background, Alcatraz Island	187
6.2.1	Youngshin Haengcha Street Parade at the Gangneung Danoje Festival, Korea	207
6.2.2	A masked couple dancing at the Gwanno Mask Dance at the Gangneung Danoje Festival	208
6.3.1	Fishers tend to their nets at the Jaffa port, Tel Aviv-Jaffa	212
6.4.1	Role Playing Game Board	219
6.5.1	Children's University Tasmania graduation ceremony, Hobart, Tasmania	226
7.1.1	The Arctic Circle is getting hotter	237
7.2.1	The Lynton and Barnstaple Railway: Southbound train behind a restored 1915 locomotive, N. Devon, UK	249
7.2.2	The Lynton and Barnstaple Railway with Exmoor National Park landscape in background, N. Devon, UK	250

Figures

1.1	An illustration of the "tourism system"	14
1.2	A Venn diagram to look at tourism's "impacts"	16
5.1.1	Percentage of CO_2 emissions by world population	150
6.5.1	Children's University Australia: Passport to Learning	225

Tables

| 2.2.1 | Key Tourism Statistics: Quintana Roo 2016 | 52 |
| 2.2.2 | Approved Marketing Funds for Key Destinations in Quintana Roo from 2010–2016 | 54 |

CASE STUDIES

1.1 Amsterdam's Burgeoning Tourism Growth 5
Tazim Jamal

1.2 Sustainability and Spiritual Well-Being in Bhutan 10
Tazim Jamal

2.1 Worker Protection, Entrepreneurship and Loopholes: New Challenges for Finnish Trade Unions 41
Johan R. Edelheim

2.2 Mayan Cultural Tourism in Quintana Roo, Mexico 51
Blanca Alejandra Camargo

3.1 Palenqueras in Colombia: A Case of Cultural Injustice in Tourism 72
Blanca Alejandra Camargo

3.2 "A Teardrop on the Cheek of Time" in Agra, India 87
Tazim Jamal

3.3 Commemoration and Contestation: The Little Bighorn Battlefield National Monument, USA 92
Jeff Wahl

4.1 Japan: Resilience through Conservation and Tourism 116
Carolina Manrique

4.2 Roots-Seeking and Belonging in the African Diaspora 123
Linda Lelo Enoh

4.3 Street Voices, Copenhagen, Denmark 129
Dianne Dredge and Eóin Meehan

4.4 Responsible Tourism Development in San Ramón, Nicaragua 134
Emily Höckert

5.1 Climate Justice and the Challenge to Global Tourism 149
Noel Healy and Tony Weis

5.2 Sea Level Rise Planning Initiative, Matanzas Basin, Florida 155
Dawn Jourdan

Case Studies **ix**

5.3	Ecotourism in the Galápagos Islands	165
	John Dirck Friebele	
5.4	Is Sustainable Tourism Really the Key to More Ethical Forms of Tourism?	170
	Bernard Lane	
5.5	Diversity and Inclusiveness in Community Museums: Shijia Hutong Museum, Beijing, China	175
	Mingqian Liu	
5.6	Cultural Resilience, Heritage Conservation and Tourism: Alcatraz Island, California	182
	Carolina Manrique	
6.1	Youth Participation in Governance: Juliana v. U.S.	199
	Dawn Jourdan	
6.2	Democratization of Tourism Policy in Korea: Gangneung Danoje Festival	205
	Jiyoung Choi and Songyi Kim	
6.3	The Jaffa Port Redevelopment Process, Tel Aviv-Jaffa, Israel	211
	Nufar Avni	
6.4	Indigenous Planning and Game Changing Perspective: Water Resource Planning in the Chickasaw Nation, Ardmore, Oklahoma, USA	217
	Dawn Jourdan	
6.5	The Children's University Tasmania: The Transformative Power of Tourism	222
	Can-Seng Ooi and Becky Shelley	
7.1	Smell the Melting Arctic Ice	236
	Emily Höckert	
7.2	Tourism and Conserving the Past: Addressing Ethical and Justice Issues in Heritage Tourism	247
	Bernard Lane	

Cases by Country/Region

CONTRIBUTORS

Nufar Avni, PhD, is an urban geographer and planner. She earned her PhD at the School of Urban Planning at McGill University. She currently holds a Marie Sklodowska Curie Fellowship (2018–2020) at The Hebrew University of Jerusalem. Her main research interests are the role of justice and equity in planning policies, urban redevelopment, and planning in spaces of ethnic conflict.

Blanca Alejandra Camargo is Associate Professor of tourism in the Business School at Universidad de Monterrey, Mexico. She received her doctoral degree from Texas A&M University and her research is oriented toward sustainable tourism with a focus on ethics and justice in tourism development, marketing and management. She is also interested in examining aspects of cultural relationships with nature, corporate social responsibility, and sustainable tourism and ethics pedagogy. Since 2012 she is a member of Mexico National System of Researchers.

Jiyoung Choi is a doctoral student in the Department of Recreation, Park and Tourism Sciences, Texas A&M University, USA. Her research interests include tourism planning and policy for sustainable tourism, community participation and governance, and heritage tourism.

Dianne Dredge is Professor in the Department of Culture and Global Studies, Aalborg University, Denmark. Her research focuses on tourism as an agent of change in multiscalar contexts wherein she employs story-telling, policy ethnographies, policy network analysis, and social learning approaches. Dianne is currently Chair of the Tourism Education Futures Initiative (TEFI) and a member of the International Academy for the Study of Tourism.

xii Contributors

Johan R. Edelheim looks at society and events with a purpose to highlight inequality in order to bring issues to common awareness. These matters of inequality can be found in all fields of studies and a conscious use of different theoretical lenses allows him to investigate matters in novel ways. The majority of his studies focus in different ways on tourism, hospitality, leisure, education and society—quite often using different popular culture sources as his data collection sites.

Linda Lelo Enoh, PhD, as a college professor, has taught courses ranging from Impacts of Tourism to Event Management. Her academic research focused on Heritage Tourism, with a specific emphasis on the representation of the "difficult" past like wars and slavery and how people can make sense of this past in a positive and uplifting way. Now as a consultant, her work is focused on tourism and marketing support for organizations and small businesses.

John Dirck Friebele is a Master's student in the Department of Recreation, Park and Tourism Sciences at Texas A&M University, with a focus in sustainable tourism of coastal destinations. He is the recipient of the Gene Phillips Memorial Scholarship and the Robert B. Ditton Endowed Scholarship. In addition, he is Vice President of Sales and Marketing for Experience Bryan College Station. John lives in Bryan, Texas with his wife, Mary Beth, daughter, Bailey, and their golden retriever, Gus.

Noel Healy is Associate Professor of Geography at Salem State University. His research focuses on responses to the climate crisis and normative dimensions of rapid climate change mitigation. Key research interests include: fossil fuel politics, climate policy, energy justice, and the link between academic knowledge, political activism, and policymaking. He has published in journals such as *Energy Policy, Local Environment, Journal of Environmental Policy & Planning, Society and Natural Resources, Tourism Management*, and *Marine Policy*.

Emily Höckert is a Postdoctoral fellow in tourism studies at the Linnaeus University in Sweden in the Department of Organisation and Entrepreneurship. At the broadest level, her research is driven by curiosity about how hosts and guests welcome each other in responsible tourism encounters. Emily is the author of *Negotiating Hospitality* (2018) and co-author of *Disruptive Tourism and Its Untidy Guests* (2014), which both discuss questions of hospitality and ethics in tourism settings.

Tazim Jamal is a Professor in the Department of Recreation, Park and Tourism Sciences at Texas A&M University, Texas, USA. Her primary research areas are sustainable tourism, collaborative tourism planning, and cultural heritage management. She also addresses methodological issues in tourism, with particular interest in critical and interpretive research. She is the co-editor of *The SAGE Handbook of Tourism Studies* (2009). For more on her research, see: https://scholar.google.ca/citations?user=Zuaq0fsAAAAJ&hl=en&oi=ao.

Contributors **xiii**

Dawn Jourdan is the Executive Associate Dean for the College of Architecture at Texas A&M University. She is a professor of Urban Planning in the Department of Landscape Architecture and Urban Planning. She teaches courses in: land use law, growth management; citizen participation; affordable housing; and planning history and theory, among others. Dawn conducts research in these areas with a special focus on the legal aspects of planning.

Songyi Kim is a researcher at Korea Culture and Tourism Institute, Seoul, South Korea, and she is a doctoral student at the Department of Recreation, Park and Tourism Sciences, Texas A&M University, USA. Her research interests lie in sustainable tourism, with particular interest in social and environmental issues in tourist destinations.

Bernard Lane is a consultant, writer and lecturer working on sustainable tourism, rural regeneration, and heritage conservation. He is an Associate of Red Kite Environment (www.redkite-environment.co.uk), a consultancy specializing in the management and sustainable development of heritage sites, protected areas, and rural regions. He was the founding editor of the Journal of Sustainable Tourism which he edited for 25 years. He is now working with Anna Scuttari at EURAC Research, Bolzano, in the South Tyrol (Italy) on heritage railways and slow tourism corridors. They plan to create a global research group on those subjects.

Mingqian Liu is a doctoral student in the Department of Architecture at Texas A&M University. Her research interests include architectural and urban history, historic preservation, heritage tourism, and public education in museums. She has worked in various museums and cultural institutions in China and the United States. She holds an M.A. in History of Art and Architecture from Boston University and a B.A. in International Studies from the University of Iowa.

Carolina Manrique (cmanrique@uidaho.edu) is an Assistant Professor at University of Idaho, USA. She holds a PhD in Architecture from Texas A&M University, USA. Her dissertation aimed toward an integrated approach between heritage conservation and heritage tourism. Topics included causes and consequences of preservation material decisions in cultural and heritage sites. She is an architect with a master's degree in building technology, and an advanced Master's degree in structural analysis of monuments and historical constructions. Her current research focuses on developing the notion of resilience in architecture, and the relationship between structures and architectural design.

Eóin Meehan is a researcher in tourism in the Department of Culture and Global Studies, Aalborg University, Denmark. His research interests include social entrepreneurship and tourism, the tourism–migration nexus, and the collaborative economy. Recent research has centered on the socioeconomic transformations

xiv Contributors

occurring as a result of Industry 4.0 expansion and impacts on work, labor and wellbeing in the services sector. In his research, focus is given to the co-production of policy responses between public, private and third sector actors for responding to tourism challenges.

Can-Seng Ooi is a sociologist and Professor of Cultural and Heritage Tourism at the University of Tasmania. For more than two decades, he conducted investigations on tourism and society issues such as tourism and cultural development, heritage tourism and nation-building, destination branding and social engineering, and politics in stakeholder collaboration. After Singapore, Denmark, Malaysia, the Czech Republic, Slovakia and China, he now delves into tourism development issues in Australia. His personal website is www.cansengooi.com.

Becky Shelley is a political scientist. She worked in social policy and programming for many years before she joined the Peter Underwood Centre at the University of Tasmania in 2016 as their Deputy Director (Aspiration and Attainment). Becky has sustained success in the field of novel social policy and social programs. Her personal website is www.beckyshelley.com.

Jeff Wahl is a PhD student in the Department of Recreation, Parks, and Tourism Sciences at Texas A&M University. His current research is focused on issues of justice and cultural representation in heritage tourism. His research interests include sustainable tourism, heritage tourism, and community and cultural issues.

Tony Weis is an Associate Professor in Geography at Western University. His research and teaching are broadly located in the field of political ecology, with a focus on agriculture and food systems. He is the author of *The Ecological Hoofprint: The Global Burden of Industrial Livestock* (2013) and *The Global Food Economy: The Battle for the Future of Farming* (2007), and co-editor of *A Line in the Tar Sands: Struggles for Environmental Justice* (2014).

PREFACE AND ACKNOWLEDGEMENTS

This book is not what you think it is. At least it is not as heavy as the title suggests. The title may even be a bit "unjust" for it sounds like a heavy, pedantic, typically "academic" text awaits you. Yet, as you turn the pages, a storied landscape emerges, exploring facets of travel and tourism from a few different perspectives on justice and ethics. A narrative style calls the reader to join this quest, which draws on my own work and experiences as well as the voices and research of other contributors from around the world. A treasure trove of photos accompanies their insights to make the subject come alive. After all, in exploring what appears to be such a daunting topic, we cannot forget the magic of travels elsewhere! There is, too, responsibility, sustainability, and relationships with others, human and nonhuman, that are constant companions calling us to care and attention. And so, this book's journey includes them, too, in search of new ways and courage (hope?) to tackle some of the complex challenges we face in the current landscape of the 21st century.

What is the subject that inspired this effort? Justice? Ethics? Both, actually, for it is quite difficult to separate the two, as will soon become evident. One important driver was the frustration at the plethora of principles that engulf tourism researchers attempting to study "sustainable tourism," "responsible tourism," or any notion of "good tourism." For those interested in theory building, empirical research *and* practice, something appears to be missing. Does justice not play a role, perhaps an even bigger role than we first envision? Too little has been written or conceptualized in tourism studies on this subject and sobering events since Fall 2016 send a wake-up call to seek new understandings and new directions on the right thing to do, seeking both *justice* and the *good* of tourism. Unfortunately, or perhaps fortunately, ours is not the period of Antiquity when, for the ancient Greek philosophers, these two aspects (justice and the good) seemed to go hand in hand. They appear to be decoupled in 20th-century notions of justice in the "west," making the task even tougher. So,

xvi Preface and Acknowledgements

where to start? Our lens into this here is via the problems and potential of this thing called tourism.

Fortunately, theoretical conversations related to justice and tourism have been started by David Fennell, Mick Smith and Rosaline Duffy, among various other scholars referenced in the following chapters. They are acknowledged here for helping this book's journey, along with apologies to those I was unable to draw upon or cite. This is not a book on laws and legal matters related to tourism. It is not theoretically ambitious and does not aim to do a review or analysis of the early research stage of justice and ethics in tourism. Rather than a dense, theoretical text, the book aspires to be widely accessible to those interested in the study and practice of tourism. A justice-oriented lens offers a glimpse of potential new avenues to better understand and address a variety of challenges related to tourism development, marketing and management. The view here is partial and broad, offering several justice perspectives from the "west," incorporating a bit from the Global South, extending an invitation to all worldwide to join and contribute diverse knowledge, understandings, practices, and approaches to justice in the context of tourism (which extends into travel, hospitality, etc.).

Starting with a look at the landscape of travel and tourism in Chapter 1, and how to approach the study of tourism and its "impacts" in this book, Chapters 2–6 take up a range of issues and approaches to justice from the local to the global. Among the approaches to justice discussed are distributive justice (redistribution as Nancy Fraser puts it), the capability approach, recognition (including recognition of difference), representation and democracy. Human rights arise throughout as it is integral in the context of tourism. There is more, too, like structural injustices (including structurally embedded injustices related to historical racism and colonialism), responsibility toward justice, justice within and beyond borders, and justice in the context of sustainability, governance, policy, and planning. Ethical issues abound in relation to these (hence the title of the book—it is difficult to separate justice and ethics clearly). The title of each chapter subsequent to Chapter 1 is indicative of principles being addressed within it, but note that the chapters are interrelated and should be read *holistically*. Later chapters build on earlier ones and a picture of a *pluralistic* approach to justice emerges. Several characteristics and principles related to this are summarized in the final Chapter 7. Websites noted within the text and the references offer some helpful information on various topics.

The approaches and issues raised here are richly informed by diverse cases of varying lengths provided by contributors from around the world. Each of Chapters 2–7 closes with a longer case. Shorter cases are included within the chapters. They are integral to understanding each contributor's perspective and how justice appears to be playing out in practice. Instead of following a particular definition of justice, the contributors were asked to address justice as they felt it spoke to them with respect to their case. Given the paucity of empirical and theoretical research on this subject in tourism studies, it enabled a freer exploration, producing synergistic insights that flowed with the approaches to justice discussed in the upcoming chapters. But this is just a start. A deeper and more thorough examination of the approaches raised here is needed. Much is left out; many other philosophical and theoretical approaches await attention. Some may criticize the lack of preoccupation to "define," argue, or elaborate on the various perspectives presented here. The hope is that the approaches to justice discussed here, complemented by numerous cases and stories, are helpful to (i) direct attention to some concerns that are under-addressed or merit greater attention, (ii) encourage learning and future research, (iii) inform practice and inspire collaborative efforts among public, private, and nonprofit participants (including academia).

In June 2018, the U.S. Supreme Court ruled on the third travel ban executive order signed by President Trump. The first two versions had encountered fierce criticism as targeting people from the Muslim-majority countries listed in each, and also looked like they contravened basic principles of freedom and equality enshrined in the U.S. constitution. It matters. I still eat sushi from time to time (being a sliding vegetarian), and have been accused more than once of "agonizing" over my ethical choices. It matters too. There are calls to conscience and *conscientization* (Paolo Freire's term) that fall alike on individuals, educators, and academics. If the book provokes thought and reflection, as well as good actions in tourism, research, and practice, then it will make my brother happy. He read every line, dotted every "i" and crossed every "t." This book is dedicated to him, with deep appreciation to all who supported me along the way, friends, relatives, and the Department of Recreation, Park and Tourism Sciences (Department Head Dr. Scott Shafer) at Texas A&M University. Thanks, too, to Brian Smith, tourism analyst and desktop expert, whose call to excellence in formatting and presentation was perhaps the hardest to heed! Last but not least, I wish to thank the many willing case and note contributors who shared their knowledge and time to enrich this exploration of justice and ethics in tourism.

1

THE LANDSCAPE OF TRAVEL AND TOURISM

Introduction

What a marvelous thing it is to be able to embark on a journey elsewhere, on holiday especially, filled with anticipation, enthusiasm, and perhaps trepidation if it's the first visit to a different land. You are looking forward to encountering a different language, experiences that call on all the senses, whether it's walking around your dream city (which one is that?) or gazing at the Milky Way from an equatorial ecolodge, encountering hospitality, a gesture of kindness as you walk into a café, exhausted and famished. Then there are all those souvenirs you bring back, that bring recollections of the trip, or perhaps they're a conversation piece attracting the attention of your dinner guests. You may even be wearing the souvenir—a bracelet, a T-shirt, or sandals bought in a bazaar teeming with color and life. They act as powerful memory receptacles of the place; you might remember the shopkeeper, the artisan, or the bargaining you might have done (hopefully having checked first if it was an acceptable practice there, as one might with tipping). There's the joy of new conversations, possibly making new friends, and hopefully benefiting local economies rather than exploiting them (buy local!). But it is a chimera, this thing called tourism. It can offer fun, joy, rich existential experiences, ways to contribute constructively to conservation and to individual as well as social well-being. Yet there are also possibilities to wreak thoughtless harm on the destination, the environment, and those who inhabit them.

This chapter looks at the local to global landscape that we will be exploring in future chapters. The "impacts" of tourism are complex, and disguise many issues related to justice and ethics that one might not even think are related to it. To engage in "good tourism" requires, among other things, being able to identify and address injustices that arise in relation to tourism, directly or indirectly, and for this a holistic view as described further below is important. It applies to every approach and form of

2 The Landscape of Travel and Tourism

tourism that aspires toward being responsible, just, and "sustainable." In fact, an exploration of justice and ethics (the two are not easily separable) in tourism shows that justice, responsibility, and sustainability are close companions, and they are accompanied by several other important principles. The goal in future chapters is to examine a range of justice-related issues, and to identify and explore some principles that can help to redress injustices and enable good actions in tourism. A related goal is to look at some theoretical approaches to justice that can assist with this task. Note, however, that this is not a legalist book—tourism law is not the focus. The journey into justice here is a holistic one to help advance insight and understanding of this subject and its contribution to "good tourism." While only a few theoretical perspectives related to justice are raised in the limited space of this book, the range of issues and insights that emerge will hopefully tempt you to embark on new journeys to advance research and practice in this important area. But before we get too far, let us take a quick trip around the world and develop a joint understanding of the landscape of travel and tourism that we will be entering in future chapters and how to view tourism's "impacts."

Travels in the 21st Century

Most of the time, you're not traveling alone. Accompanying you, aside from your fellow travelers, are many accouterments of modern travel—your cell phone, iPad or other mobile device that enables you to post pictures on Facebook, Instagram, Snapchat, etc., and almost instantaneously hear from friends and family. Use your phone apps to get more information on a museum exhibit, a historic site, an upcoming event, the weather; Siri or Alexa will help direct you if you're lost or hungry! As the critical geographer David Harvey put it, we live in a world of "time-space compression" (Harvey, 1990). Time has speeded up and space has shrunk under rapid mobilities, images, and news from a globalized media. The global culture industries are gathering and spreading world music, film, and literature. You are traveling through Europe but you are connecting with your friends ten thousand miles away through social media—they love your Instagram post of this beautiful leaning church tower in Copenhagen (see the brave modern tourist-warrior in Photo 1.1). If you're afraid of heights, you could wander instead to Copenhagen harbor and take a Selfie with the bronze statue of the "Little Mermaid" (Photo 1.2) to post on your favorite social media site... but, wait a minute, do you actually know the story of this iconic little mermaid from Hans Christian Andersen's fairy tale? How many times do you think she has been vandalized?[1]

Traveling offers marvelous opportunities to enjoy, learn, relax, and connect with these "elsewhere" places. Virtual tourism and augmented reality experiences, "Smart Tourism" or "Smart Hospitality," are opening new worlds and new tastes—your GPS and Google Maps will guide you through a maze of streets and alleys to locate restaurants to match your foodie tastes. Actually, Franklin and Crang (2001) argue in the first edition of the journal *Tourist Studies* that we can also have tourist-like

PHOTO 1.1 Tourist posing on the golden staircase of the baroque Church of Our Savior in Copenhagen, Denmark. Her tourist friend from Australia posted a similar photo of herself and the spectacular setting on Instagram, and a dozen friends responded within minutes.
Photo credit: Deni Valentina

PHOTO 1.2 The Little Mermaid's wistful pose under the tourist gaze in Copenhagen harbor
Photo credit: T. Jamal

4 The Landscape of Travel and Tourism

experiences without stepping outside our increasingly cosmopolitan home world—we may be fortunate and live in an urban city where foods from around the world can be found, interior decorations from indigenous to modern can be easily sourced, diverse cultural festivals, world music, and sporting events fill local arenas, and so on.

Of course, along with all the technological advances has come the ability for increased surveillance of human movements, consumer behavior and activities, e.g., through monitoring your social media activities, online purchases, and web searches. Much is known of your travel choices and consumption profile, and entertainment companies like Disney are experts at designing experiences to match your profile in order to offer a good (marketers would say satisfactory) leisure experience...and to shape your understanding, behavior, and preferences with well-designed interpretive materials.[2] New innovations and mobilities of work and travel, however, bring increased governance challenges in both virtual and physical spaces. Many who labor in the sharing economy (e.g., Airbnb) and on-demand platforms like Uber, for instance, are in those in-between spaces of governance where contentious issues of workers' rights and sexual abuse have arisen due to lack of clear oversight and regulation (see, for example, Duan, 2018; Schmitt, 2017). Is the new collaborative economy (sharing/on-demand/gig economy) a less than fair "taking economy"? A closer look at this mobile landscape is merited to identify the opportunities and challenges facing travel and tourism in the 21st century.

Growth, Mobilities, and Action Agendas

The World Travel and Tourism Council (WTTC) is a global organization engaged in awareness raising and advocacy for tourism. It points out that tourism is a multi-billion dollar industry, employing over 100 million people directly, and generating about 10% of global GDP (https://www.wttc.org/mission/). In addition to facilitating travel across borders and seeking to ensure that the "growth of our sector is managed responsibly, finding the balance between people, planet, and profits," it "informs governments about ways to implement policies that ensure the business environment is conducive to the growth of Travel & Tourism" (https://www.wttc.org/mission/). Note the discourse of "growth" in the WTTC's statements above and that of another supranational organization, the United Nations World Tourism Organization (UNWTO). The UNWTO confirms that international tourism demand and growth was robust in 2016 despite various challenges. International tourist arrivals grew by 3.9% to 1,235 million, according to the latest UNWTO World Tourism Barometer. It was the seventh consecutive year of sustained growth since the 2009 global economic and financial crisis. At least 300 million more international tourists traveled the world in 2016 compared to the pre-crisis record in 2008 (international tourism receipts grew at a similar pace in this time period), and 46 million more tourists (overnight visitors) traveled internationally in 2016 compared to 2015 (UNWTO, 2017).

The Landscape of Travel and Tourism **5**

"Tourism has shown extraordinary strength and resilience in recent years, despite many challenges, particularly those related to safety and security. Yet, international travel continues to grow strongly and contribute to job creation and the wellbeing of communities around the world," said UNWTO Secretary-General Taleb Rifai (UNWTO, 2017).

Take a look at how this long-standing discourse of "growth" has been experienced in popular urban destinations like Amsterdam. Case 1.1 illustrates some mass tourism issues that you might find in a tourism impacts textbook, but it is a current, live challenge for the city and its residents.

Case 1.1: Amsterdam's Burgeoning Tourism Growth

Tazim Jamal

As part of their education, young wealthy Europeans in the 18th century would often embark on a "Grand Tour" of great cultural cities in Europe, like Venice, Rome, Paris, and London, to gain cultural experiences and learning. Today, these cities are inundated with international and regional visitors, causing immense stress on infrastructure and local residents. Some like Amsterdam are experiencing even higher inflows due to incoming business expatriate work. The city recently won a contest to be the new home of the European Medical Agency (EMA), which was seeking to relocate from London after Britain leaves the EU. While Dutch politicians celebrated this Brexit gift, for it would bring economic gain from 900 new white-collar workers, local residents felt it just added more stress. These high-income expats were just another group of strangers who would drive up property prices and rent (Sterling, 2017).

The city of 850,000 residents and its historic 17th-century city center are already stressed by high numbers of visitors and remarkably inappropriate behaviors. One autumn weekend (in 2017), resident Els Iping discovered a bunch of drunk male tourists tearing up the shrub in front of her house, which didn't surprise her: "These kind of things happen all the time," she says matter-of-factly. "It's worse when they throw up in your plant boxes, because you can't rinse it away—you have to scoop it out" (van der Zee, 2017). Over the past ten years, visitation has grown from 11 million in 2005 to almost 18 million in 2016, and at the current rate of growth the city is expected to attract 23 million by 2030. Iping's picturesque downtown neighborhood has changed, with screaming, drunk visitors starting to revel on Thursday into the weekend, leaving behind an immense amount of rubbish, she said. Meanwhile, the small businesses she knew, the chemist, fishmonger, hairdresser, even the shoe shop, had disappeared, replaced by tourist-oriented services, including ice cream shops and cannabis seed vendors (van der Zee, 2017).

Bern Nap, a 59-year-old French teacher and writer, also sees the loss of neighborhood identity, social cohesion and overall deterioration in his part of town, near the red-light district where he has lived for more than 40 years. Many tourists indulged in wild partying and behaviors they would not exhibit at home, he felt, in part because Amsterdam had always portrayed the image that everything was possible there. As he said: "I have nothing against guided tours through my neighborhood. But it's a different thing when 40 people block the entrance to your house while listening to a guide who's giving a loud, 20-minute performance that looks more like a standup comedy act than a guided tour" (van der Zee, 2017). Much of the growth stemmed from the money the city pumped into tourism after the 2008 financial crisis, in order to help the economy. Sebastiaan Meijer, the council's spokesperson for economic affairs, said: "For years we have actively stimulated property developers to build hotels in the city, and our marketing organization travelled around the world promoting Amsterdam as a tourist destination." Their marketing policy then was targeted to make Amsterdam a visitation choice, but now they want to convey a new message: "'come to Amsterdam, but please behave'" (van der Zee, 2017).

Critics argue that the economic benefits of jobs and revenue tend to mostly benefit large companies and do not match the social and financial costs; estimates indicate tourism costs the city €71m a year, which is well above the €64m raised in tourism taxes (*Dutch News*, 2017). City officials are working hard to manage the effects. The beer bicycle (a vehicle serving beer to about a dozen tourists) has been banned (aided by local residents' efforts), new hotel construction is being curbed in the city center, tourist taxes are being raised. The city is also negotiating with Airbnb to address a range of issues of concern to local residents. Airbnb is the largest among short-stay rental platforms; around 22,000 rooms and flats are offered for rent annually, and one in six homeowners rent out a room or flat on Airbnb in the more popular neighborhoods (van der Zee, 2016).

Local movements have also arisen to counter mass tourism's problems. Resident Sito Veracruz, an urban planner concerned about the distortions to rent and real estate prices (already very high in the city) caused by Airbnb, is attempting to set up an alternative short-stay platform, FairBnB, where hosts are registered with the council and more socially responsible. "I am talking about a platform that really complies with the principles of a fair, non-extractive and collaborative economy," Veracruz says. "We would like to encourage visitors to stay in areas where they are not a disturbance, but could add something to the neighborhood" (van der Zee, 2016). The FairBnB website opens with the banner "A smart and fair solution for community power tourism" offering this ethical alternative (FairBnB.coop, 2017):

> FairBnB is first and foremost a community of activists, coders, researchers and designers that aims to address this challenge by putting the "share" back into the sharing economy. We want to offer a community-

centered alternative that prioritizes people over profit and facilitates authentic, sustainable and intimate travel experiences.

References

Dutch News (2017). Economic benefits of Amsterdam tourism are over-estimated: researchers. Retrieved December 21, 2017, from https://www.dutch news.nl/news/2017/05/economic-benefits-of-amsterdam-tourism-are-over-estimated-researchers/

FairBnB.coop (2017, April). FairBnB: a smart and fair solution for community powered tourism. Retrieved December 21, 2017, from https://fairbnb.coop/

Sterling, T. (2017). "Expats go home": Amsterdam's visitor boom angers locals. Retrieved December 21, 2017, from https://in.reuters.com/article/us-netherlands-amsterdam-tourists/expats-go-home-amsterdams-visitor-boom-angers-locals-idINKBN1DY1Y7

van der Zee, R. (2016). The "Airbnb effect": is it real, and what is it doing to a city like Amsterdam? Retrieved December 21, 2017, from https://www.theguardian.com/cities/2016/oct/06/the-airbnb-effect-amsterdam-fairbnb-property-prices-communities

van der Zee, R. (2017). Amsterdammers v tourists: "It's worst when they throw up in your plant box." Retrieved December 21, 2017, from https://www.theguardian.com/cities/2017/nov/01/amsterdam-tourists-worst

Amsterdam reflects some typical challenges of mass tourism and the strain on local residents. Workers are mobile, tourists are mobile, expatriates and second-home owners are mobile. So are finance, capital, and trade, aided by globalization and transnational corporations that appear to float through borders with little oversight and regulation; see, for example, Wood (2000) on the dovetailing of neoliberalism and globalization in international cruising. Joining these mobilities are migrant workers in the growing tourism industry and other sectors, as well as refugees seeking a safe home. Europe has been dealing with the influx of migrant labor and refugees from adjacent regions for decades, but political and social backlashes are rising. Over the past couple of years, once-porous borders within the European Union are being controlled more rigorously or simply slamming shut amidst growing concerns about the strain on local economies from settling refugees and, lurking behind this, fear of terrorism (recall Brexit and Britain's pending departure from the EU, based on the outcome of a national referendum on June 23, 2016).

Like the UK, France has stoically weathered a series of terrorist attacks but it has continued to welcome visitors. During Bastille Day celebrations in 2016, 86 people died when a lorry driven by a Tunisian French resident believed to be affiliated with the Islamic State ploughed into a crowded promenade in Nice on the French Riviera. The massacre in November 2015 of concert-goers at the Bataclan, plus

8 The Landscape of Travel and Tourism

attacks in various restaurants and bars across Paris, resulted in 130 lives lost. Tourism accounts for about 9% of GDP earnings in France, and the government made a concerted attempt to court and reassure visitors, resulting in a robust rebound in 2017 of this leading destination in Europe—visitor numbers hit a ten-year high in the first half of 2017 with increased international visitation from the US, Japan, and China, as well as European countries (Willsher, 2017). International tourism in the non-West has not been as resilient to terrorism as Paris. Across the globe, tourist resorts and cultural venues have also become specific targets of terrorism, e.g., nightclub, airport, and historic district attacks in Turkey (2016), at the Bardo National Museum in Tunisia (March 2015), on the beach outside the five-star Imperial Marhaba hotel in Sousse, Tunisia (2015), the Bali nightclub attack (2002), attacks over the years at resorts, hotels, and tourist attractions in Egypt, and at public spaces and events in England and the US (see Crawford, 2012; Grierson, 2017; Hayden, 2017; The Associated Press, 2017).

Meanwhile, the new US president elected in November 2016 launched an "America First" slogan alongside attempts to implement a highly controversial and contested travel ban. The third version of President Trump's travel ban is currently in effect as the Supreme Court upheld its constitutionality in June 2018. It imposes a range of travel restrictions on Iran, Libya, Syria, Yemen, Somalia, Venezuela, and North Korea (Chad was dropped from the original list in the third travel ban). Five of these are predominantly Muslim countries. In addition, travel restrictions to Cuba have been initiated again under President Trump, subsequent to the Obama administration's efforts to loosen the decades long travel and trade embargo (Zanona & Fabian, 2017). What is the right thing to do? What a difficult question in such a complicated terrain, but perhaps exploring some issues and approaches to justice over the next few chapters can help guide ongoing conversations and identify good actions in the local–global landscape of travel and tourism.

The Climate Agenda

Local to global action will also be needed to address a growing number of environmental risks, of which some are related to global mobilities (e.g. the spread of diseases and invasive species with trans-border travel) and many are due to human impacts. The 21st century ushers in the era of the Anthropocene, a popular (not geological) term for a period marked by significant human-induced impacts on the climate and on the natural environment. With the US walking away from the Paris Accord in 2017, new players are arising from the local to the state and regional levels to act on climate change. Aging infrastructure will need to be made more resilient to withstand extreme weather events as wildfires, record rainfalls, and storms are expected continue to magnify, while sea-level rise threaten low-lying island and coastal destinations and cultural sites worldwide. The Caribbean saw two catastrophic Category 5 hurricanes in September 2017, while the US received a record three Category 4 landfalls in 2017 (Maria, Harvey, and Irma). Puerto Rico will need to rebuild its entire tourism infrastructure with this in mind (tourism was its main income-generator). Its aging infrastructure and power grids were ill-equipped and desperately needed upgrading before Maria's devastation. Yet tourism hummed on, the airlines and tourists they carried seeming oblivious or uncaring of the preparedness of the destinations for known risks such as hurricanes during hurricane season. Let's not forget, too, the cost to their governments and citizens to bail them out during extreme weather emergencies, along with the airlines that had flown them in. Are there issues of justice and ethics involved here? How best to identify and address these? A justice-oriented lens is a good start, and since justice and ethics are not easily separable, related ethical issues also come under scrutiny.

Of course, climate change further impacts the resilience of major ecosystems, species, and habitats already under threat from various pressures. For example, back-to-back coral bleaching events in 2016 and 2017 has severely affected over 70% of the Great Barrier Reef (a World Heritage Site) and other stresses on the reef, like the effect of cyclones and the invasive Crown of Thorns starfish, compound the damage. Australia's Minister for the Environment and Energy, Josh Frydenberg, said that climate change was the "number one threat" to the Great Barrier Reef (Cummins & Westcott, 2017). Programs like Seafood Watch offer a wealth of information on responsible seafood choices and on some restaurants that follow these, as well as noting the human rights abuses in the marine industry and importance of protecting people and the environment (Conservation & Science Programs for Businesses and Consumers, n.d.). Note Seafood Watch's call to action to us here, where it says it is working with human rights experts and various organizations (e.g., Fair Trade USA) to "to better identify abuses and what you can do": http://www.seafoodwatch.org/resources/human-rights-resources (accessed December 21, 2017). Would tourists so easily enjoy unsustainably caught seared-tuna salad at a four-star hotel on their tour route if they understood the ecological cost, or the possible human costs (e.g. labor exploitation) that might have been associated with it? How would they know? How many of the tourists who flood Venice annually understand its plight or that of many other destinations and ecosystems being affected by warming oceans, sea-level rise and other effects of climate change, environmental degradation, and various forms of environmental and social injustices to workers and residents? Action on climate change is a crucial global agenda in the 21st century and we will explore some aspects related to this in future chapters.

Good Actions in Tourism

Fortunately, we have made hopeful advances toward sustainability and social justice with approaches like "sustainable tourism," as well as "responsible tourism" and "pro-poor tourism" which are especially attentive to vulnerable populations and poverty alleviation, both crucial concerns in global sustainability agendas. See, for example, the Sustainable Development Goals put forward by the United Nations in 2016 to build on the Millennium Development Goals that expired in 2015: https://sustainabledevelopment.un.org/post2015/transformingourworld (accessed

10 The Landscape of Travel and Tourism

December 21, 2017). Alternatives to mass tourism have arisen in the forms of "good" tourism types like ecotourism, volunteer tourism, fair trade tourism, slow tourism, and community-based tourism (CBT), as well as a range of certification and accreditation schemes to show their good practices. Of course, many such schemes are voluntary, not regulated, and corporate greenwashing is one of several concerns (see Fennell, 2016; Mowforth & Munt, 2016).

Some destinations are also making concerted attempts to actively address the world we are leaving to "future generations" (a concept embedded in the notion of sustainable development forwarded by the Brundtland Commission's report *Our Common Future* (World Commission on Environment and Development, 1987). This report is a must-read, as it has been widely spread and sedimented in the sustainability lexicon, but be cognizant of criticisms leveled at it and its near relative, sustainable tourism (e.g., Smith & Duffy, 2003). Costa Rica, long a proponent of sustainable tourism, not only aims to be carbon-neutral by 2021, it also aspires to be the first country to get rid of single-use plastics. This will require concerted, collaborative action among multiple stakeholders, including its government, private sector, and civil society, and technical and financial assistance from the United Nations Development Program (Gutierrez, Anchía, & Shackelford, 2017). Their aspiration for environmental conservation, justice, and fairness in development and use is reflected well here (bold in original):

> We must continue to move towards sustainable production and consumption systems that also generate development opportunities, particularly for at-risk communities suffering the consequences while not causing water pollution. This entails a comprehensive system **that cares for people's health, ensures fair wages and equal opportunities for women and men, while taking care of forests and wetlands** (Gutierrez et al., 2017).

And while popular urban cities like Amsterdam struggle with controlling mass tourism, others like Bhutan in Case 1.2 below have been proactive rather than reactive in controlling visitation and planning for tourism and sustainable development.

Case 1.2: Sustainability and Spiritual Well-Being in Bhutan

Tazim Jamal

Nestled in the Himalayas, Bhutan implements careful tourism policies in order to protect the Buddhist traditions and spiritual well-being of its population, within its mandate for sustainable development and Gross National Happiness (GNH). GNH is Bhutan's alternative, human-centered approach to development. This moral concept was enshrined historically within Bhutan's legal code and became the guiding principle to manage the effects of globalization and modernization on Bhutan, and ensure the collective well-being and happiness of its people (Verma, 2017). The Royal Government of Bhutan's tourism policy situates GNH as the central guiding principle for tourism (Tourism Council of Bhutan, n.d.). It represents a proactive approach to guiding the robust growth of tourism in this small mountain nation. As the Bhutan Tourism Monitor 2016 report states (Tourism Council of Bhutan, 2017, Foreword):

> Bhutan's tourism industry continued to grow in 2016 contributing significantly towards socio-economic development through revenue and foreign currency generation and employment creation amongst others. A total of 209,570 foreign individuals visited Bhutan in 2016 which is an increase of 35% over 2015. International arrivals grew by 9.10% to 62,773 over 2015 while arrivals from the regional market grew by 50%. A total of 54,600 international leisure arrivals was recorded in 2016 which represents a growth of 11.9% over the previous year.

As indicated in the report, sustainability is at the core of Bhutan's development agenda, and it will seek greater benefits for its people through sustainable tourism. Its visitor management and other interventions seek sustainable growth, enhance visitor experience and help to spread tourism benefits across wider sections of its population, regions and seasons. Take a break now and listen to this TED talk by Bhutan's Prime Minister Tshering Tobgay. As you watch it, think about visitors, too, learning about Bhutan's history, culture and sustainability approach. As the Prime Minister says, "we're in it together" (access the TED talk in the References: TED, 2016).

References

TED (2016, April 1). This country isn't just carbon neutral—it's carbon negative: Tshering Tobgay [video file]. Retrieved from https://youtu.be/7Lc_dlVrg5M

Tourism Council of Bhutan (n.d.). Tourism policy. Retrieved December 14, 2017, from https://www.tourism.gov.bt/about-us/tourism-policy

Tourism Council of Bhutan (2017). *Bhutan Tourism Monitor: Annual Report 2016*. Thimphu, Bhutan. Retrieved from http://tcb.img.ebizity.bt/attachments/tcb_041217_bhutan-tourism-monitor-2016.pdf

Verma, R. (2017). Gross National Happiness: meaning, measure and degrowth in a living development alternative. Special Section of the *Journal of Political Ecology*, 24, 425–666. Retrieved from http://jpe.library.arizona.edu/volume_24/Verma.pdf

Examples like that of Bhutan, worldwide efforts by many places such as Costa Rica, and over five decades of tourism research and textbooks on tourism planning and managing impacts would suggest that we have many tools to address issues and

12 The Landscape of Travel and Tourism

challenges in tourism development and governance of issues such as Amsterdam has faced. Globalization and technological advances have facilitated ease of travel and the ability of small businesses to access knowledge and advertise to visitor markets, and the democratization of information and action has also empowered consumers in many ways. Lightning speed information and images shared on social media sites make service providers and policymakers more watchful of their reputation and behavior. Consider how easily you can now evaluate goods and services on the Internet (e.g., on sites like Trip Advisor, Yelp, and directly on the websites of various service providers like those in the collaborative economy), participate in online and on-the-ground social movements that can form quickly thanks to social media, and obtain travel and tour information online (including responsible/sustainable travel). And if you have access to the Internet, you can even learn about and join boycotts of tourism destinations and international events that are called by concerned tour operators and human rights advocates. The following are two well-known examples of how tourists and tourism service providers (foreign and domestic) influence injustices at the destination level:

1. On November 4, 2010, Burma Campaign UK ended its call for tourists not to visit Burma after Burma's National League for Democracy (NLD) led by Aung San Suu Kyi softened its 15-year-long call for a tourism boycott of targeted package tours only (Burma Campaign UK, 2010). The military dictatorship in place then had launched "Visit Myanmar Year" in 1996 and benefited from packaged tours and foreign currency it generated. Human rights abuses were also linked with tourism, such as tourist facilities using forced labor (Burma Campaign UK, 2010). The Lonely Planet Guide was entered into Burma Campaign UK's "Dirty List" for continuing to promote tourism during the stricter boycott, while other guidebooks like The Rough Guide and travel marketing and booking platforms like Responsible Travel had abstained. Responsible Travel had also supported the boycott on Burma/ Myanmar for over ten years.[3]
2. China's crackdown on Tibetan demonstrators in the capital city of Lhasa in March 2008 provoked widespread condemnation and calls for boycotting the upcoming 2008 Beijing Olympics (see Eimer, 2008, for some tourist accounts of the bloody clampdown they witnessed in Lhasa). In the recent *Cultural Genocide in Tibet* report (Tibet Policy Institute, 2017), Dr Lobsang Sangay, president of the Central Tibetan Administration, reported that cultural genocide was being committed by the Chinese through policies in four vital areas: religion, language, forceful removal of Tibetan nomads, and ongoing transfer of the Chinese Han population onto the Tibetan Plateau. These policies have been relentlessly carried out against the minority Tibetan Buddhist population; human rights are being violated, cultural heritage and traditional way of life are being severely impacted, and their cultural survival is at stake. The report is being brought before the international community, Dr. Lobsang Sangay said:

The Landscape of Travel and Tourism   **13**

because the cultural genocide that is going on is the collective experience of the Tibetan people. It is also because those of us living in free societies have the moral responsibility to speak up for the Tibetans in Tibet whose collective voice has been effectively silenced. (Tibet Policy Institute, 2017, p. iii) (The report can be accessed at: http://tibetpolicy.net/wp-content/uploads/2017/10/Tibetocide.pdf)

Of course you can read the report, or leisurely google airline fares for places on your bucket list of "must do" trips if you are lucky enough to have ease of access to the Internet. About 48% of the total population of independent states (104 countries) use the Internet; gender wise, the proportion of women users is 12% lower than men worldwide, and 25% lower in Africa (International Telecommunications Union, 2017). Of all Internet users, 71% are youth, with youth from the least developed countries (LDCs) being the fastest growing segment among all young users. But nine out ten youths in Africa don't use the Internet and only 15% of households in the LDCs have Internet at home compared to 43% in the developing countries, and 84% in the developed ones (International Telecommunications Union, 2017).

All is not as equal as it seems. Many issues related to ethnicity, gender equity, diversity, human rights, and vulnerable populations intersect with tourism, and new challenges lie ahead with respect to sustainability and responsibility in this complex domain. Do we have adequate tools and understandings to face these? How do we visualize and study this thing called "tourism"? The next section explores some viewpoints to adopt as you progress into the following chapters.

Approaching the Study of Tourism

The 21st-century landscape of travel and tourism is fascinating and challenging. Immense technological advances are continuing to transform how we live, work, and travel. International tourism is robust despite some of the significant global issues noted above. Mass tourism continues its discourse of "growth," while technological innovations and the rise of new collaborative economies and on-demand services like Uber increase the challenge of managing various "impacts" that arise not just at the destination but also between the visitor generating place and the visitor receiving place. Figure 1.1 shows one version of the "tourism system" that you may find in a general tourism textbook, with examples of various flows (goods, services, travelers) between the place of origin and the destination.

A good textbook will also clarify that terms like "tourism," "tourists," and "the tourism industry" have been the source of much debate and redefinitions over time. As you can see, the UNWTO definitions below attempt to define tourism, the visitor, and the tourist in a way that can capture the *economic* impacts of tourism.[4]

Tourism is a social, cultural and economic phenomenon which entails the movement of people to countries or places outside their usual environment for personal or business/professional purposes. These people are called

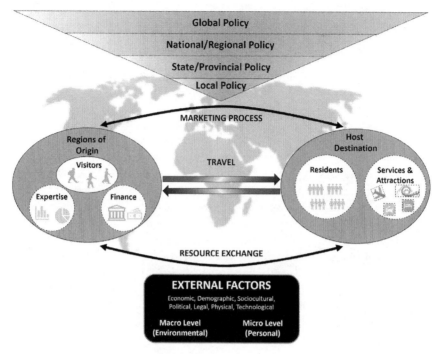

FIGURE 1.1 An illustration of the "tourism system"

visitors (which may be either tourists or excursionists; residents or non-residents) and tourism has to do with their activities, some of which involve tourism expenditure.

A visitor is a traveler taking a trip to a main destination outside his/her usual environment, for less than a year, for any main purpose (business, leisure or other personal purpose) other than to be employed by a resident entity in the country or place visited (IRTS, 2008, 2.9).

A visitor (domestic, inbound or outbound) is classified as a tourist (or overnight visitor), if his/her trip includes an overnight stay, or as a same-day visitor (or excursionist) otherwise (IRTS, 2008, 2.13).

An important clarification to think about in relation to the above is that tourism involves voluntary travel elsewhere and returning home after a temporary stay at the destination (the visitor receiving place). This helps to distinguish it from migrations in search of new domiciles. As Hall and Lew (2009, p. 6) explain, a migration "represents a form of voluntary one-way human mobility, tourism can be referred to as a type of voluntary return mobility." However, look carefully through the UNWTO glossary and statistics document (referenced in UNWTO, 2010) and note that the main purpose of a personal trip can include attending funerals or family-

The Landscape of Travel and Tourism **15**

related events like short-term caring for the sick or old, etc., as noted in the "visiting friends and relatives" (VFR) category (UNWTO, 2010, p. 25). Detailed definitions and descriptions such as the ones UNWTO provides are geared to be able to help capture economic measures of tourism, providing valuable statistics for tourism satellite accounts, policymakers, destination managers, and other stakeholders. But try to use them to see the non-economic impacts of tourism and you may face some headwinds. You can measure number of visitors, length of stay, visitor expenditures, various tax revenues such as those from hotel and motel tax – but consider other hard-to-quantify aspects. What about the travel *experience*—is there a role for this important aspect in defining tourism, or the purpose of tourism, or the tourist? Sebastian Meijer says in the Amsterdam case above that the focus there was on attracting visitors, seeking tourism growth and expenditures. Seeking positive economic impacts based on a growth-driven vision is problematic, and tools such as cost–benefit analysis based on quantification and valuation of positive and negative impacts of tourism need to be approached cautiously. Are they so easy to box and categorize?

You can indeed quite easily identify positive and negative impacts of tourism from the Amsterdam case. Basic textbooks in tourism and tourism impacts offer a good guide to identifying such types of impacts. An early classic was Mathieson and Wall's *Tourism: Economic, Physical and Social Impacts* (1982). You can find in such texts discussions of "positive impacts" like jobs, economic diversification, revenues and foreign exchange, new services (e.g., restaurants), and facilities (e.g., for events, recreation), and social benefits like increase in community pride and tolerance. And of "negative impacts" like low-paying jobs (rather than a living wage) and limited career advances, gentrification, seasonality challenges (where peak visitation periods can place immense stress on environmental and human resources), as well as commodification of culture. These can be easily categorized under environmental, social, cultural (related to social, but separated here to show its importance), economic, and political impacts. You can even build separate lists for positive and negative impacts under each category. Of course, that makes it easy to see them as static, isolated events rather than as dynamic, interconnected, and spread over time.

A Venn diagram like Figure 1.2 with overlapping circles may help to show different effects or "impacts" of tourism that arise over time in a destination. Areas of overlap in Figure 1.2 are a signal to examine the relationships between various aspects. For example, revenues from tourist expenditures in Case 1.1 on Amsterdam is a positive economic benefit of tourism growth, but just look at the social costs (and environmental too—note the rubbish mentioned!). The large outer circle represents the natural and physical environment within which the other circles are embedded in Figure 1.2. It is meant to suggest that the social, cultural, economic, and political aspects of tourism are intricately related with the natural and physical environment.

So, if we can identify and group all the measurable impacts that occur at the destination and the related impacts in the wider tourism system, and carry out a "cost-benefit analysis," then we'd really know how to manage the impacts to

16 The Landscape of Travel and Tourism

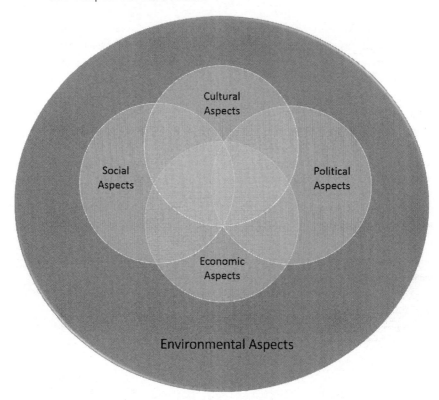

FIGURE 1.2 A Venn diagram to look at tourism's "impacts"

increase the positive impacts and minimize the negative ones—a good, scientific way to manage tourism impacts! Or not. What issues can you envision in such an approach? You might point out that that some things are hard to measure, like the tourist experience. Yes, indeed, and think about how many marketing surveys try to capture this through questions related to tourist "satisfaction." To use an ecotourism example:

- How satisfied are you with your ecotourism experience in Costa Rica?
- What did you like most/least?
- What could be improved?

You're on the right track if you are questioning this, but it is only the tip of the iceberg (bad metaphor perhaps, it's melting!). Consider the following:

- One can identify many types of tourism "impacts" which are easily grouped under categories like economic, social, cultural, political, and environmental impacts. But while such broad categories are helpful to guide discussion, there are many aspects that are not easily identified or measurable, like

The Landscape of Travel and Tourism **17**

spiritual well-being (consider the example of Bhutan above), or the psychological effects of travel, whether to the backcountry, or to holocaust sites, or war memorials, or in search of one's heritage/roots, or other. Or, to use another example, the democratic empowerment of consumers who can search for information, provide feedback, or reprimand service providers online, and share images, news, and stories of places and travel experiences at lightning speed through multiple media and social networking sites.

- Some aspects of travel and tourism are easier to identify and quantify than others. Things like the number of visitors and length of stay are popular statistical items compared to other more difficult to measure, intangible and longer-term effects. Consider, for instance, how the *commodification* of places and people as things to be purchased or "consumed" affects human–environmental relationships (e.g. sacred indigenous relationships with the land, or the relationship of local residents with their place). What has changed when, instead of the daily routine of walking onto the veranda with a cup of coffee to watch the sunrise define the soft edges of fields and hedges shrouded in early morning mist, the rural farmer now checks to see if anyone has booked the bed and breakfast accommodation set up to support a struggling agricultural livelihood? There could be a booking from around the state or even overseas, for some lucky visitor to discover this hidden gem of frontier heritage and hospitality—nothing beats Texas barbeque and chicken fried steak (unless you're vegetarian or vegan!). The sun will have risen by the time the farmer frees up from this task and it may be too late to sit on the verandah anyway.

- Picture this as a *complex* local–global tourism system (Farrell & Twining-Ward, 2004, refer to it as a complex adaptive system), where travel and tourism impacts are interrelated and can have local to global consequences. They may be tangible and easy to quantify, or intangible and hard to measure. There are multiple stakeholders with varying degrees of influence and power, ranging from local residents (permanent, temporary, second-home owners, etc.) to businesses, non-profit organizations, and different governmental bodies (national, regional, local). Regulation and governance of the local to global reach of tourism continues to be problematic. Who controls the way Cozumel is marketed to cruise visitors or Hawai'i to honeymooners or as a winter getaway? It is an interrelated local–global space. Tour operators from very far away can affect the kind of experience being delivered to its customers—you may have to change from jeans to your native Maasai dress when these international tours are coming to your *boma* (dwelling) in southern Kenya! But you can also share your cultural traditions and dances with pride, sell souvenirs, craft, and ethnic food . . .that is if you're not fed up, unable to control the number of visitors or have meaningful interactions with your guests, because you are only a fleeting curiosity to them in their busy tour itinerary.

- Cultural and environmental changes through tourism can take a long time to manifest and need to be thought about *contextually* in terms of place and space, in relation to the past, present, and future. In other words, see them as spatially and

18 The Landscape of Travel and Tourism

temporally situated. Hall and Lew (2009) concur that the term "impacts" is rather misleading, but it is a helpful term and we can use it with a clear understanding of what it means. As they explain, rather than seeing tourism as *causing* impacts (e.g., in the way billiard ball A impacts or strikes billiard ball B at a point in time), see it as effecting change over time. Seeing "impacts" this way becomes even clearer when we use a *relational* perspective (a key principle). Effects arise over time and space in relations, through dialogue, actions, and interactions among people, and between people, events, and things. Some actions and relationships may be just and equitable, as when destinations care for their vulnerable populations, support women's empowerment, gender equity, and fair wages in tourism services, etc. Injustices can arise through unethical actions and behaviors, such as unethical procuring of organs for transplant patients in medical tourism, sexual abuse in the workplace, violation of labor rights, etc. The key point here is *relationality*, to think of impacts as effects arising over time and space (an interrelated local–global space as noted above), in relations among people and between people and other living and non-living things.

- It is important to view tourism-related impacts relationally, not merely within the tourism system but also as interrelated with other systems (environmental, social, cultural, political, economic, etc.) locally to globally (a local–global view). Figure 1.1 is meant to be a helpful illustration but could easily be mistaken as an independent system in which tourism operates, not showing its externalities as it draws on public resources like public transportation and common pool resources that affect local residents. For example, extensive study of water consumption by the rapidly growing number of tourists in the 1980s and 1990s in the Bay Islands, Honduras, showed immense stress on the island's environmental resources, inequitable water supply, and increasing hardships for vulnerable groups, particularly the poor. Water quality deteriorated and availability of safe potable water was disproportionately skewed toward affluent foreign residents and elite local families as well as upscale tourist hotels (Stonich, 1998). This was an inequitable relationship and unfair to the rest of the island's less well-off residents. We simply miss "the good, the bad and the ugly" of tourism if we see it in a disembodied and disembedded way, rather than intimately and deeply imbricated with society, everyday life, and the people and things in them. The local affects the global and the global affects the local in deeply interrelated ways, as we shall see in the upcoming chapters.

Venturing Forth to Seek the "Good" of Tourism

> We cannot solve problems by using the same kind of thinking we used when we created them. —Albert Einstein

The above quote is commonly attributed to Einstein. We, too, need new thinking and new ways to approach the globalized landscape of travel and tourism in the 21st century and the kinds of issues described above. It may mean adopting a more critical lens that you may be comfortable with, for instance, tackling neoliberalism or troublesome issues related to race, capitalism, and colonialism. One of the aims of this book is to become more cognizant of western liberal beliefs and modernist values that have shaped much of the knowledge base in tourism studies and many textbooks. An important task lies ahead to better understand the sociopolitical landscape in which tourism plays out, and where other diverse worldviews deserve fair consideration. For this, a spatially and temporally situated perspective is needed, where social processes and cultural changes can be traced back historically from the past into the present and future. In other words, identifying injustices and harms to individual and social well-being, as well as to the well-being of nonhuman others, requires careful assessment of the *context* in which they arise. The context includes tourism's interrelatedness with other ecological, social-cultural, political, and economic systems and spaces. Among other things, perceiving a more relational world of tourism (of which we are a part) in the forthcoming chapters will help to identify injustices as well as opportunities, and good actions to redress them and to work toward "good tourism."

So why are both "justice" and "ethics" in the title in the book? It looks like a lot to chew on. Do a quick Google Scholar search using search terms "justice" and "tourism" and you will find "equity" and "inequality" as well as "human rights" as dominant themes. Dig a bit further (add "ethics" to the search terms), and familiar topics like sex tourism, gender and women, disabilities and tourism, ethical issues in medical tourism (organ transplants being one contentious area) arise. You will also find descriptive and case study research; see, for example, Cole and Morgan (2010). And there are efforts to forward some theoretical perspectives on ethics and a few notions of justice, such as Fennell, (2017), Lovelock and Lovelock (2013), Smith and Duffy (2003). As these illustrate, justice and ethics are closely related. Hultsman (1995, p. 561), an early proponent of "just tourism," ties it closely to ethical behavior in the service industry: "just tourism" counsels service providers "to act in a manner that reflects ethicality." Like Fennell (2017), Holden (2018) calls attention to environmental ethics, and raises concern about continued anthropocentric behavior among tourism stakeholders to see nature in terms of utility (instrumental value) rather than for its intrinsic value (i.e., adopting an ecocentric ethic). Interpreting Hultsman's efforts, Holden (2018) states:

> Hultsman (1995) called for consideration of the application of Leopold's (1949) seminal "land-ethic" to tourism as a useful model as a general ethic for a "just" tourism, i.e. one that is ethical, encouraging the development of tourism as a moral agent for the benefit of the wider community that extends beyond humankind to encompass nature.

While ecological justice is not taken up in this book, the perspective adopted here sees human beings as part of "social-ecological systems" where human beings are

20 The Landscape of Travel and Tourism

interrelated with the wider ecological community (in human–environmental relationships, human–animal bonds, etc.). Keeping the above in mind, the exploration of justice and ethics in the forthcoming chapters does not make a sharp demarcation between the "just" and the "good." It does not focus on legalistic aspects and matters of law and distributive concerns that have dominated the subject of justice in the 20th century (see Chapter 2). Rather, it is oriented toward the "good" of tourism. "Good tourism" is tourism that is guided by principle of justice, responsibility, sustainability, and an ethic of care, among other principles. Development and governance for good tourism strives to be "just," democratic, and contribute actively to the conservation and sustainability of planet Earth, and to the *well-being* of its human and nonhuman inhabitants (the notion of well-being will be examined further). Practicing good tourism involves being engaged in the social and environmental well-being of the destination place and space, and being able to exercise good judgment and virtues in the conduct and practice of tourism (Jamal, 2004). Looking at the kaleidoscope of tourism activities, events, and issues, as well as the characteristics of tourism "impacts" above, reveals a complex landscape of travel and tourism. It will hopefully become evident as chapters unfold that greater attention to justice and ethics is needed to guide good tourism in the 21st century.

Summary and Further Considerations

Global tourism is robust, with increasing opportunities to travel and experience different cultures and landscapes, natural areas and heritage places, but new challenges have arisen. There was a time before 9/11, before Brexit (2016), before the travel bans and restrictions imposed by the US, before the Paris Accord was informed of USA withdrawing as a member, when the world of travel and tourism appeared much safer. And tourism seemed a much simpler concept to study and "manage" in traditional textbooks filled with principles and instructions for managing tourism "impacts." But, alas, it is no longer simple. As this chapter shows:

- The scale and scope of tourism is vast. Activities and processes at the micro-level are interrelated with the macro-level in the local–global tourism system, which itself is interrelated with other systems and processes (social, environmental, political, economic, etc.).
- There are multiple stakeholders and interests at play, creating a fragmented tourism domain in which planning, coordination, and control over development and growth are immensely difficult. Rapidly evolving ICTs create both opportunities and new challenges in this complex domain.
- Adding to the challenge are environmental and social risks from climate change and increased mobilities, as well as political risks (e.g., domestic and global terrorism), among other issues including poverty alleviation, environmental health and conservation, and neoliberal globalization (see Sharpley, 2009).

The Landscape of Travel and Tourism **21**

- In addition to tangible, easily identifiable and measurable impacts related to economic growth and visitor numbers, there are invisible, intangible human-environmental and other cultural and sociopolitical relationships and values which are difficult to discern and monitor, but are vital to understand.

"Tourism" is clearly difficult to define, but we will continue to use the term despite its ambiguity and the difficulty of defining it. It is a useful term, just like "impacts." The characteristics and principles described in this chapter should help guide understanding and use of these concepts. Tourism is a powerful phenomenon, with potential for providing pleasure and joy, and facilitating peace and well-being. It offers opportunities for economic diversification and environmental conservation (e.g., via ecotourism), but can also threaten ecological and social as well as cultural well-being. Tourism is also highly political. The 20th century landscape of travel and tourism reveals new forms of terrorism arising, populations are mobile, and new questions of identity and belonging accompany them. Ideologies and worldviews are being shaped and reshaped through new technologies and what some have called tourism's powerful ability for "worldmaking" (Hollinshead, Ateljevic, & Ali, 2009). Meanwhile, a new period referred to as the Anthropocene has arrived.

We need new understandings and new approaches to understand and address the increasingly challenging landscape of travel and tourism in the 21st century. A key perspective to adopt moving forward is that issues and impacts arise in *relations* between individuals, things, events, etc., situated in a spatial and temporal matrix—*context* is important. Look back at the center of the intersecting circles in Figure 1.2, where all types of "impacts" seem to be present. Where the four circles intersect is a space offering a valuable standpoint from which to see all aspects of tourism (environmental, social, cultural, political, and economic) from a holistic perspective.

We must, however, be very clear about the limitations and potential of this book. It cannot give answers. This book is not a western colonial dominating view. It seeks to open conversations, share the rich stories and learnings of numerous case contributors, and encourage new approaches guided by justice and ethics to address the problems and potentials of this wonderful, powerful thing called "tourism." Several approaches are described in the upcoming chapters, but many more wait to be explored. Join in now as we journey through the chapters: Equity and Justice (Chapter 2), Diversity and Recognition (Chapter 3), Responsibility and Care (Chapter 4), Sustainability and Conservation (Chapter 5), Democracy and Governance (Chapter 6). The chapter titles reflect important principles, but they are not mutually exclusive; all the chapters should be examined in relation to each other. While Chapter 7 summarizes some of the perspectives and principles that have arisen along the way, it is not an offer of another fixed framework of principles. It should rather be seen as a dynamic, pluralistic, and interrelated approach to justice and ethics in tourism. Let the journey begin—read on!

22 The Landscape of Travel and Tourism

Questions for Further Reflection

1. What were the main drivers of Amsterdam's growth-related problems in tourism?
2. What do you think of Gross National Happiness (GNH), Bhutan's alternative, human-centered approach to development? Should it be used to guide tourism in this small mountain country? If yes, why, if no, why not?
3. Why is it important to carefully examine the *context* of tourism development and governance at the destination? Provide examples from the chapter to support your answer (Hint: Recall that GNH arises from a moral concept that was enshrined historically to Bhutan's legal code, and the country's population is primarily...?)
4. What does a *relational* approach to tourism mean? Why is it important?
5. Can you define tourism differently than the traditional views described in Chapter 1?

Notes

1 See the Little Mermaid's tumultuous existence as the most photographed tourist object in Denmark: https://www.visitdenmark.com/denmark/little-mermaid-denmarks-most-photographed-statue. See: http://www.bbc.com/news/world-europe-40293396. Accessed April 22, 2018.
2 See Hollinshead's review of *Vinyl Leaves: Walt Disney World and America* (Hollinshead, 1998), written by Stephen J. Fjellman (1992). See also the interesting analysis of Seaworld by Davis (1996).
3 For more on the debate about whether Burma/Myanmar should have been marketed by tour operators and guidebooks (think about the rights to publish versus the moral imperative related to human rights and democratic freedom), see: http://www2.irra waddy.com/article.php?art_id=6863&page=1. Accessed December 21, 2017. For Responsible Travel's perspective on the pros and cons of tourism boycotts, see: https://www.responsibletravel.com/copy/boycotts-and-tourism. Accessed December 21, 2017.
4 Source: http://statistics.unwto.org/sites/all/files/docpdf/glossaryterms.pdf. Accessed December 20, 2017. Source of IRTS 2008 within the quote (UNWTO, 2010) is in this report online: https://unstats.un.org/unsd/publication/Seriesm/SeriesM_83 rev1e.pdf#page=2. Accessed December 21, 2017.

References

Burma Campaign UK. (2010, November 4). Burma Tourism Boycott Now Targeted At Package Tours. Retrieved December 21, 2017, from http://burmacampaign.org.uk/burma-tourism-boycott-now-targeted-at-package-tours/

Cole, S., & Morgan, N. (2010). Introduction: Tourism and inequalities. In S. Cole & N. Morgan (Eds.), *Tourism and inequality: Problems and prospects* (pp. 15–24). http://doi.org/10.1079/9781845936624.A

Conservation & Science Programs for Businesses and Consumers: Seafood Watch. (n.d.). Retrieved December 21, 2017, from http://www.montereybayaquarium.org/conservation-and-science/our-programs/seafood-watch

Crawford, D. (2012). Recovering from terror: The Egyptian and Balinese experiences. *Worldwide Hospitality and Tourism Themes*, 4(1), 91–97. http://doi.org/10.1108/17554211211198615

Cummins, A., & Westcott, B. (2017, April 15). Great Barrier Reef "cooking and dying" as seas heat up, warn scientists. Retrieved July 2, 2018, from https://www.cnn.com/2017/04/10/asia/great-barrier-reef-coral-bleaching/index.html

Davis, S. (1996). Touch the magic. In W. Cronon (Ed.), *Uncommon ground: Rethinking the human place in nature* (pp. 204–217). New York: W.W. Norton & Co.

Duan, N. (2018). Desegregating the home-sharing economy. Retrieved May 9, 2018, from https://ssir.org/articles/entry/desegregating_the_home_sharing_economy

Eimer, D. (2008, March 16). Dalai Lama condemns China's "cultural genocide" of Tibet. Retrieved December 23, 2017, from https://www.telegraph.co.uk/news/worldnews/1581875/Dalai-Lama-condemns-Chinas-cultural-genocide-of-Tibet.html

Farrell, B. H., & Twining-Ward, L. (2004). Reconceptualizing tourism. *Annals of Tourism Research*, *31*(2), 274–295. http://doi.org/10.1016/j.annals.2003.12.002

Fennell, D. A. (2016). *Tourism ethics* (2nd ed.). Bristol, United Kingdom: Channel View Publications Ltd.

Fennell, D. A. (2017). *Tourism ethics* (2nd ed.). Bristol, United Kingdom: Channel View Publications. Retrieved from https://www.world-of-digitals.com/en/fennell-tourism-ethics-ebook-pdf

Fjellman, S. M. (1992). *Vinyl leaves: Walt Disney World and America.*

Franklin, A., & Crang, M. (2001). The trouble with tourism and travel theory? *Tourist Studies*, *1*(1), 5–22. http://doi.org/10.1177/146879760100100101

Grierson, J. (2017, February 28). Tunisia attack: How a man with a parasol could murder 38 people on the beach. Retrieved July 2, 2018, from https://www.theguardian.com/world/2017/feb/28/tunisia-attack-how-a-man-with-a-parasol-could-38-people-on-the-beach

Gutierrez, E., Anchía, M. E., & Shackelford, A. (2017, July 14). Costa Rica paves the way to end single-use plastics. Retrieved December 21, 2017, from http://www.undp.org/content/undp/en/home/blog/2017/7/14/Costa-Rica-abre-el-camino-hacia-el-fin-de-los-pl-sticos-de-un-solo-uso.html

Hall, C. M., & Lew, A. (2009). *Understanding and managing tourism impacts: An integrated approach.* London, UK: Routledge. http://doi.org/10.4324/9780203875872

Harvey, D. (1990). *The condition of postmodernity.* Cambridge, MA: Blackwell.

Hayden, M. E. (2017, September 15). Terror in the UK: A timeline of recent attacks. Retrieved July 2, 2018, from https://abcnews.go.com/International/terror-uk-timeline-recent-attacks/story?id=47579860

Holden, A. (2018). Environmental ethics for tourism- The state of the art. *Tourism Review.* http://doi.org/10.1108/TR-03-2017-0066

Hollinshead, K. (1998). Disney and commodity aesthetics: A critique of Fjellman's analysis of "distory" and the "historicide" of the past. *Current Issues in Tourism*, *1*(1), 58–119. http://doi.org/10.1080/13683509808667833

Hollinshead, K., Ateljevic, I., & Ali, N. (2009). Worldmaking agency–worldmaking authority: The sovereign constitutive role of tourism. *Tourism Geographies*, *11*(4), 427–443. http://doi.org/10.1080/14616680903262562

Hultsman, J. (1995). Just tourism: An ethical framework. *Annals of Tourism Research*, *22*(3), 553–567. http://doi.org/10.1016/0160-7383(95)00011-T

International Telecommunications Union. (2017). *Facts and figures.* Geneva, Switzerland. Retrieved from http://www.itu.int/en/ITU-D/Statistics/Documents/facts/ICTFactsFigures2017.pdf

Jamal, T. B. (2004). Virtue ethics and sustainable tourism pedagogy: Phronesis, principles and practice. *Journal of Sustainable Tourism*, *12*(6), 530–545. http://doi.org/10.1080/09669580408667252

Leopold, A. (1949). *A sand count almanac and sketches here and there.* Oxford, UK: Oxford University Press.

Lovelock, B., & Lovelock, K. (2013). *The ethics of tourism: Critical and applied perspectives.* Abingdon, Oxford, UK: Routledge.

Mathieson, A., & Wall, G. (1982). *Tourism – economic, physical and social impacts.* Longman. Retrieved from https://books.google.ca/books?id=5nnftwAACAAJ

Mowforth, M., & Munt, I. (2016). *Tourism and sustainability: Development, globalisation and new tourism in the Third World* (4th ed.). New York, NY: Routledge.

Schmitt, R. (2017). The sharing economy: Can the law keep pace with innovation? Retrieved May 9, 2018, from https://law.stanford.edu/stanford-lawyer/articles/the-sharing-economy-can-the-law-keep-pace-with-innovation/

Sharpley, R. (2009). *Tourism development and the environment: Beyond sustainability?* London: Earthscan.

Smith, M., & Duffy, R. (2003). *The ethics of tourism development.* New York, NY: Routledge.

Stonich, S. (1998). Political ecology of tourism. *Annals of Tourism Research, 25*(1), 25–54. http://doi.org/10.1016/S0160-7383(97)00037-6

The Associated Press. (2017, January 7). Turkey's tourism drops after spate of terror attacks. Retrieved July 2, 2018, from https://www.ctvnews.ca/world/turkey-s-tourism-drops-after-spate-of-terror-attacks-1.3231712

Tibet Policy Institute. (2017). *Cultural genocide in Tibet: A report.*

UNWTO. (2010). *International recommendations for tourism statistics 2008.* New York: United Nations.

UNWTO. (2017, January 17). Sustained growth in international tourism despite challenges. http://doi.org/10.18111/9789284418145

Willsher, K. (2017, August 27). Tourists defy Trump to return to Paris in record numbers after terror attacks. Retrieved December 21, 2017, from https://www.theguardian.com/world/2017/aug/27/tourists-defy-trump-paris-record-numbers-after-terror-attacks

Wood, R. E. (2000). Caribbean cruise tourism: Globalization at sea. *Annals of Tourism Research, 27*(2), 345–370. http://doi.org/10.1016/S0160-7383(99)00073-0

World Commission on Environment and Development. (1987). *Our common future.* Oxford, UK: Oxford University Press.

Zanona, M., & Fabian, J. (2017, November 8). Trump tightens limits on personal travel, business ties to Cuba. Retrieved December 21, 2017, from http://thehill.com/homenews/administration/359354-trumps-cuba-policy-allows-airbnb-stays-for-americans

2

EQUITY AND JUSTICE

Introduction

Pablo was a tour guide in Cozumel whom I encountered several years ago. He was patiently standing on the promenade near the ferry dock, inviting tourists to a tour around the island on his scooter. With trepidation, I agreed, for the helmet he offered me looked unlikely to protect my head in an accident. But there was no public transit to this important cultural site, so I hung on to his portly middle for dear life as we set off on bumpy roads to visit the Mayan ruins of San Gervasio. Protected and administered by INAH (the National Institute of Anthropology and History), it was an ancient sanctuary for the worship of the goddess Ixchel. Many Mayan women made a pilgrimage once in their lifetime to pay homage to this deity of fertility and childbirth. Interpretive plaques at the site were in three languages, English, Spanish and Mayan. His two children, explained Pablo, spoke Spanish and were learning English in order to get a job in the dominant tourism industry that Cozumel depended on. Like most of their friends, they were more interested in American music and culture than their own customs and traditions, he said.

It turned out that Pablo's family was among the minority Maya population in Cozumel and the state of Quintana Roo. He said he took his two children to the Yucatán to visit their *abuelos* (grandparents) on the *milpa* (farm) and learn a bit of Maya from them, but he could not afford to do this much. Neither could he afford to take them to the large theme park called Xcaret on the coast near Playa del Carmen, it was too expensive. But Xcaret is a popular tourist destination, it provides rich experiences of Mexico's cultural traditions, food, music, dance, enactments of rituals, etc. (starting prices of tickets are towards US $100, see http://www.xcaret.com/world-heritage.php). Though Pablo struggled to make ends meet, he was grateful that tourism provided him income, and enabled the government to provide the concrete house that he and his wife and two children lived in. At his invitation, we

26 Equity and Justice

stopped there on the way back. It had one main room, just large enough for four colorful Yucateca hammocks, a tiny open kitchen across the back of the room, plus a teeny toilet/washing area. Wooden slats made up the shutters on the two tiny windows. I peeked into a hammock, and was startled to find it occupied. His two children were lying in their hammocks, it was siesta time. The concrete house had protected them from Hurricane Wilma when the eye of the hurricane sat over Cozumel for 72 hours, said Pablo.

Pablo's story reflects some of the benefits and challenges that destinations dominated by tourism face. The island's dependency on tourism (which is driven strongly by powerful external actors including international tour promoters, cruise industry, etc.) combined with economic downturns and travel warnings due to increasing drug-related violence have been hard on local Cozumelinos like Pablo. While Cozumel is a popular cruise destination, most cruise passenger spending in Cozumel is lost due to economic leakage (much of the revenue flows back to external operators and service providers). The costs and benefits of cruising are *inequitably* distributed, with the destination and the natural environment bearing the greater burden of the social and ecological costs. The cruising industry is a major beneficiary in terms of capital accumulation and profit. Cruising at sea fits the model of *neoliberal globalization,* where corporate power transcends borders through free trade and deregulatory policies while the ability of governments and international organizations to govern and monitor the practices of international tourism operators is gravely constrained (Wood, 2009). Cruise visitors appear generally unaware of what proceeds in the deep "back stage" of tourism.

What choice does Pablo have? Tourism is the principle provider of income and foreign exchange for Cozumel. Like many other Cozumelinos who depend on it, Pablo receives a small bit of the "trickle down" effects of tourism. But even in good times, what he earns is barely enough to sustain his family, and certainly not enough to enable him and his family more than an occasional visit to the *abuelos* in the Yucatán. While we can talk about two-tier pricing of attractions as a way to enable affordability and access for local residents, touristic sites like Xcaret would need to be almost free for Pablo to take his children there to experience and learn about Mexico's rich and diverse cultural heritage, including their own. Mayan rituals and traditions are demonstrated on sites, there are even some Mayan ruins at Xcaret. At the time of my visit a decade ago, tourists were wandering over them, posing for photographs and unaware of the ancient history they were standing on or the physical damage they were causing (contributing to degradation and erosion of the ruins). Would it contribute, too, to erasing their memories of the long history and presence of the Maya in this region?

There are several inequalities that can be identified in the story above (note that the name Pablo is a pseudonym to protect his identity). Abundant case studies and critical analyses in the field of tourism studies reveal many other social justice issues in tourism destinations, such as inequalities related to women and gender, sex tourism, labor rights and wage issues, e.g., rights to parental leave, a living wage, etc. (see, for example, Burns & Novelli, 2008; Cole & Morgan, 2010;

Mowforth & Munt, 2016). The task here is neither to repeat diverse examples of inequalities and injustices already published in tourism studies, nor to wade through the plethora of principles attached (rather mysteriously sometimes, it seems) to "sustainable tourism," "responsible tourism," "ecotourism," etc. Rather, the aim here is to:

- Discuss the idea of justice, some helpful ways to approach the study of justice, and identify some persistent issues that will arise in future chapters. How to deal with general principles of justice that may not fit particular circumstances and groups?
- Commence to explore two social justice perspectives: distributive justice and the capability approach. These are many conceptions of justice, and the ones raised here offer a start to the discussion. They can shed interesting light on approaches like "pro-poor tourism" and "community-based tourism" development.
- Explore some issues in the context of social justice and well-being at the destination level and look at the activities and actions of some stakeholders in the tourism domain. The examples discussed illustrate the importance of examining history and context, and the social systems and institutional structures in which tourism plays out (another recurrent theme in future chapters).

By the end of Chapter 2, an important insight arises that will be delved into in subsequent chapters, which is that the idea of justice in the context of tourism may require a *pluralistic* approach, i.e., more than one approach to justice. The case study by Blanca Camargo at the end of the chapter offers an interesting study of distributive justice challenges in the Costa Maya, Mexico, and the importance of considering other approaches to justice that may be at play here. Moreover, as the case of Finnish trade unions by Johan Edelheim shows, there is a tension between the general and the particular level in which issues of justice play out. This tension is a recurrent aspect to grapple with (resolve?) in subsequent chapters.

Approaching the Study of Justice

Pause for a second and think of tourism, all the places it touches, the people involved in it, the kinds of goods and services used by the traveler. Think, too, of your expectations and experiences of traveling somewhere else. If you were short-changed in an exchange somewhere, felt overcharged for a mediocre meal (you didn't speak the language or didn't want to cause a fuss, or offend anyone by complaining), you might have felt a sense of injustice. Or you might have felt a strong sense of discomfort while on a tour because a donkey and cart with two local residents in it chased your tour bus after seeing a tourist taking photos from the open bus window while going through a very poor neighborhood or slum district. I was on tour with other participants attending a "sustainable tourism" conference in Johannesburg, we were just driving through Soweto when the

28 Equity and Justice

person next to me pulled out his expensive camera with a very large zoom lens and proceeded to take photos. A fruitless chase ensued. It was discomforting to know that we were returning to a four-star hotel (not a "green" one) and soon headed to a luxury eco-resort near Kruger National Park. What is this sense of unease that one feels in such situations, when something just does not feel quite right, is there something unethical or unjust about the situation? Is it merely a worry about disrespect or offending someone by taking a picture of them, or is there more?

Justice, it turns out, is a complicated notion. It's not even easy to separate it from ethics. Justice is not an abstract notion for contemplation, it is closely related to people's lives, their well-being, their homes, their communities, their work, the places they travel to, and the journeys they undertake. For us, our reflections on justice are with tourism in mind, but as inhabitants in an interconnected local-global tourism system, we are also challenged to explore our own ethical presuppositions, actions, and practices in everyday life as much as in travel. They are not mutually exclusive. Some clarification of terms and concepts below may be helpful to start our travels in justice.

Ethics: Think of ethics in our personal lives as how to live well. But what does this mean? Some might say it is how to live a life of dignity, a life where we can exercise opportunities to become who we want to be. The term "quality of life" might come to mind here. For example, responsible tourism "recognizes the importance of cultural integrity, ethics, equity, solidarity, and mutual respect, placing quality of life at its core" (Goodwin, 2011, p. 16). Quality of life could mean a number of things and the notion of **well-being** may be useful to contemplate here. One way to think of human well-being is "what makes life good for the individual living that life" (Crisp, 2017). As he explains, there are many different ways to understand this, ranging from subjective perceptions, (e.g., a life of pleasure, fulfillment, or satisfaction of desires) to objective standards to measure quality of life. For philosophers in Antiquity like Aristotle, a good life is a life lived in accordance with virtue, towards the end of happiness or flourishing (*eudaimonia*), as he describes in the *Nicomachean Ethics* (1999). Contemporary philosophers Amartya Sen (1999) and Martha Nussbaum (2011) address well-being from a human development approach, specifically, a capability approach. The United Nations Human Development Index (HDI) attempts to capture the notion of well-being via a series of indicators including longevity, knowledge and standard of living (for more, see: http://hdr.undp.org/en/content/energy-and-human-well-being). A rich notion of well-being is very much part of justice for ancient philosophers like Aristotle and contemporary ones like Sen and Nussbaum, but modern philosophers like Rawls take a different approach to justice, as described further below.

Morality: Another related term, morality, refers to codes of conduct that are provided by a group or society and which individuals might use to guide their behavior (e.g., being courteous and helpful to visitors, extending hospitality).

However, as Gert and Gert (2017) further explain, morality can also be used in a normative sense, referring to a code of conduct that applies to all human beings. A well-cited example in tourism studies of such a universal norm is Immanuel Kant's maxim to treat people as an end in themselves, to respect them for their intrinsic value, rather than to treat them solely based on instrumental value (i.e., simply as a means to an end). This formulation of what is known as Kant's Categorical Imperative goes as follows:

> Act in such a way that you treat humanity, whether in your own person or in the person of another, always at the same time as an end and never simply as a means (Kant, 1998, p. 4:432).

Conceptions of justice: A theory of justice may be grounded in a comprehensive moral doctrine, or it may be a political conception of justice that comports with the public political culture of the society. An example of a comprehensive moral doctrine, for instance, is justice based on the moral theory of Utilitarianism, which seeks the greatest good for the greatest number (see Sandel, 1998, for a more nuanced discussion of this). Policy makers may favor this approach in seeking to maximize benefits to the majority of their constituents, but what if you fall into the minority who don't benefit from the policy passed? A Kantian view would call for members of a society to be regarded as free and equal moral persons; each have a right to equal respect and should not be used as a means to an end, as noted above (Kant, 1998).

By contrast, both John Rawls's theory of justice as fairness and Martha Nussbaum's Capabilities Approach (2011), for instance, are political conceptions of justice. They are not derived from any specific comprehensive moral doctrine. Members of a society can follow their own comprehensive moral doctrine (e.g., their own worldview or religion) *and* be able to endorse a political conception of justice that they might be willing to abide by. However, Rawls and Nussbaum offer two different approaches to social justice. Both offer much to think about for the distribution of income, opportunities, and other societal goods in the context of tourism. Some preparation prior to diving into these new worlds may be helpful, both in terms of openness to new possibilities and with respect to gaining familiarity with the subject matter.

Approaching the Study of Justice in Tourism

Justice is a complex notion and there are many ethical theories and theories of justice that will need to be carefully assessed with an open mind and much fortitude. Development theorist Amartya Sen said we must scrutinize our understandings and attitudes, and ask ourselves what kind of reasoning should count in assessing ethical and political concepts about justice and injustice. He calls for rationality and impartial scrutiny, engaging with reasoned argument with oneself and others so that what we end up will be the result of reasoning, not the absence

30 Equity and Justice

of it (Sen, 2009). Such scrutiny and reasoned judgment in the study of justice is critical, for what we may encounter in engaging with moral theories may not comport with our own value systems and beliefs. It requires being mindful and open to testing them against what we believe and experience in moral journeys, whether in theory or in travel and everyday life. Additionally, some background reading and familiarization with the literature is necessary for a successful foray into justice and ethics in tourism.

In the context of tourism, David Fennell's *Tourism Ethics* (2017) offers a good introduction and describes terms such as rights, equity, justice, that readers unfamiliar with these concepts are highly encouraged to read. Smith and Duffy (2003) provide short theoretical introductions to some perspectives and critique the ethics of tourism development (see also Mowforth & Munt, 2016). Lovelock and Lovelock (2013) also draw on a range of ethical perspectives to explore various issues in tourism, e.g., human rights, medical tourism, sex tourism, tourism and disability, climate change, nature-based tourism, as well as hospitality and marketing ethics. Lieberman and Nissen (2008) introduce and apply some ethical theories specifically to the hospitality ethics. Connell (2011) discusses some types of inequalities and injustices that can arise in medical tourism, and research is growing in this particular area of ethics. In addition, there are a number of researchers who have published on specific topics such as justice tourism (see, for example, Higgins-Desbiolles, 2009; Scheyvens, 2002).

Justice crosses many academic areas and one must quickly become an inter-disciplinary explorer across the social sciences and the humanities. Harvard professor and political philosopher Michael Sandel offers an accessible introduction to the study of justice (Sandel, 2009), including a helpful anthology of readings that illustrate competing conceptions of justice (Sandel, 2007). It is important to read primary sources (original works) and becoming familiar with the theorists of justice and ethics. Their theories don't give answers, but they provide ways of recognizing and identifying unjust as well as just actions and practices. They alert us to ways of thinking about how justice is being approached and served by governments, groups, and societies. Through many centuries, these kinds of ideas "animate civil life—justice and rights, obligations and consent, honor and virtue, morality and law" (Sandel, 2009, p. 29). Let us then look at the idea of justice, going on from there to discuss notions of distributive justice, equity, and rights. Examples and applications to tourism are included along the way.

The Idea of Justice

At a core level, as Miller (2017) explains, justice has to do with how individual people are treated ("to each his due" is one way to look at it). Conflict over the distribution of goods (e.g., freedoms, resources, opportunities) and the claims made to them may be resolved by calling on justice to determine what people are properly entitled to have. It is also possible to think about justice for groups, for example, with respect to the distribution of state resources among various groups of residents (distributive justice). "Justice here requires that the resources available to the distributor be shared according to some relevant criterion, such as equality, desert, or need" (Miller, 2017). However, there is more to justice than distributive justice.

What is your conception of justice? Are you thinking about justice in a legal sense, perhaps how the law is being invoked to fine or punish a tourist that has stolen a valuable artifact from a heritage site? Consider then the notion of *retributive justice*, which is oriented towards blame and punishment in the criminal justice system. Or is it a social concern such as for populations and groups within the state or country? If so, then one would have to be very careful to identify theories of justice that apply at the *societal* level. John Rawls's theory of justice as fairness (Rawls, 1971) cannot be applied to talk about organizational justice in the private sector; he is concerned about just distributions in society (his is one of several theories of *distributive justice*).[1] But what if residents in a rural community are protesting government support (through financial and infrastructure development) of a casino that they fear will bring more noise, traffic, congestion and crime than benefits from tourists? If public input is not sought in the planning and policy domain, and fair procedures are lacking for public participation in the allocation of public resources or for conflict resolution, then we must look to issues of participatory and *procedural justice* (including fair processes in legal proceedings).

Amartya Sen, an Indian economist and philosopher, grew up in Bengal and draws upon diverse thinkers globally to inform his theoretical work on human development and justice. Let us take some pointers from Sen's *The Idea of Justice* (2009) as we begin to think about the idea of justice in tourism, focusing on the idea of social justice here (the discussion continues over the next few chapters):

1. It is very important to identify the difference between various theories of justice, and understand the grounds on which judgments of justice are based.

This is a crucial point, for the grounds on which judgments of social justice are based vary depending on ethical and political perspectives being adopted. A society based on utilitarianism would see morally right actions as those that aim to maximize utility (understood broadly to include such goods as pleasure, wealth, security, and general happiness), other things being equal. But how well does it work as a general ethical principle? Seeking to maximize the general happiness of residents and visitors by approving the destruction of a large habitat to build a big entertainment facility at the expense of the cultural survival of a small ethnic group whose well-being is intricately connected with it does not appear to be just. Utilitarianism has no basis to defend this small ethnic group in this situation.

By contrast, a liberal egalitarian view of justice would seek the fair distribution of a society's income, wealth, and opportunities, and would favor programs that

32 Equity and Justice

increase welfare through redistributive schemes (e.g., redistribution of tourism tax revenues towards health and education).[2] Liberal egalitarians would approve of John Rawls's formulation of distributive justice discussed further below. They might also see synergies with tourism programs and policies that aim to enhance standards of living through equitable (fair) distribution of income, jobs, and opportunities, for example, Fair Trade Tourism and Pro-Poor Tourism. Among other principles, Fair Trade Tourism strives to ensure fair wages, operations and working conditions, equitable distribution of benefits (http://www.fairtrade.travel/Home/). Pro-Poor Tourism aims to ensure that net benefits flow to the poor. Worker exploitation in hospitality and tourism services that provide low-income jobs with little opportunity to advance is a common criticism, and in destinations where tourism has inflated land and property values, it is not uncommon to finds residents working at least two jobs in order to make ends meet because they lack affordable house or a living wage. Meanwhile, the government struggles to manage adverse "impacts" amidst a flourishing tourism industry and increasing number of tourists who derive great pleasure in visiting "paradise." This, you may agree, does not seem fair or equitable—the destination's residents bear most of the burdens of tourism whereas the benefits flow disproportionately to visitors and commercial interests.

2. Freedom and equality are two very important principles of justice.

Treating people as equal at some basic level appears to be common across different views of justice, as Sen notes—it is not a question of "why equality" but "what equality" (Sen, 2009, p. 295). For example, is the equality to do with income, wealth, and utilities, or something else (e.g., equality in terms of rights, liberties, etc.)? Similarly, liberty appears to be a critically important principle across justice perspectives but differences and nuances among them need to be teased out. Liberty in John Rawls's theory of justice as fairness has a special concern with personal freedom as well as freedom from intrusive interference by the state and others. A fully liberal perspective sees all persons as free and equal. The Universal Declaration of Human Rights (UDHR) proclaimed and adopted by the United Nations General Assembly in 1948 "articulated the rights and freedoms to which every human being is equally and inalienably entitled" which the international community has a duty to uphold and defend (United Nations, 1948):

> [The UDHR] has become a yardstick by which we measure right and wrong. It provides a foundation for a just and decent future for all, and has given people everywhere a powerful tool in the fight against oppression, impunity and affronts to human dignity (United Nations, 1948).

Given the immense reach and scope of tourism and its effects (see Chapter 1), laws, policies and guidelines that work to protect the rights and freedoms of people worldwide who are engaged with tourism or affected by it seem important to adopt. Let us take a look at one of the articles in the UDHR document. Article 13 says:

1. "Everyone has the right to freedom of movement and residence within the borders of each State.
2. Everyone has the right to leave any country, including his own, and to return to his country."

But consider, for example, the freedom of a disabled person to travel. Article 13 specifies the right and freedom to travel by everyone, but is she actually able to engage in travel? What if she has no help at the boarding gate for wheelchair assistance? Setting up just institutions and rules is very important, but justice cannot be indifferent to the lives people live, Sen argues. The freedom to choose is a significant aspect of human life, but it is also important to consider a capability approach here: "can the person actually do these things or not?" (Sen, 2009, p. 307). The freedom to choose between different kinds of lives can make a significant contribution to our well-being, but it is up to us to use the freedoms and capabilities we have. Facilitating access and mobilities for persons with disabilities is crucial if they are to exercise their rights, freedoms, and capabilities to travel.

3. The opportunity to freely choose or decide what we should do also brings with it another important aspect of freedom: "it makes us accountable for what we do" (Sen, 2009, p. 19).

A capability is "the power to do something," and the accountability that emanates from that ability (that power) is part of a capability perspective—it brings with it demands of duty, explains Sen. Thinking of this in the context of tourism then, what kind of duties might a capability approach engender? One might think here of the duty to obey the moral rules or norms set up by society, for instance, to *respect* women, ethnic minorities, and people with different sexual orientations, and treat them as equals. A visitor would be duty bound to follow the norm, and not engage in forms of tourism that promote inequality and disrespect.

Consider, for instance, the tourist traveling to an impoverished region that engages in trafficking women and children into the sex trade the visitor intends to engage with. Or the relatively well-off tourist seeking a medical transplant of organs harvested from very poor people who desperately need the money and accept a pittance for their own or their child's liver or kidney. Who would you hold accountable for the injustices you perceive in these two cases: the visitor, the parents selling their son's organ or their daughter as a sexual commodity, the government of that country for human rights violations and lack of laws to control trafficking of organs, women, and children? Reasoned judgments arrived at through scrutiny and rational argument with others are important to strive for here even though conflicts between views may remain. And when such debates are enacted in the public sphere, justice can align with democratic principles. Sen makes a strong connection between

34 Equity and Justice

the idea of the justice and the practice of democracy, where he describes democracy simply as government by discussion. He notes the valuable contribution made by German social theorist Jürgen Habermas to proper procedures for public deliberation, but perfect democratic institutions and processes are inadequate for the success of democracy, says Sen. It also requires activism on the part of politically engaged citizens to seek just outcomes through public reasoning (via interactions and reasoned engagement with information available in the public sphere). Sen sees the task of democracy as advancing justice globally, with the goal being practical action across borders. We take this up further in Chapters 4 and 6.

4. Make sure to distinguish the aim of justice (including in theories and other readings addressing justice that you may encounter in tourism studies).

As you're weighing the scales of justice, contemplate not only of the local to global scale of tourism, but also the context and aim of theoretical perspectives on justice. Take social justice theory, for instance. As Sen asks, is it focused on just institutional arrangements—identifying pure justice and perfectly just institutions? Or is the aim to reduce injustices or advance justice in society, by comparing societies, behaviors, and justice in relative terms (more just, less just), seeking criteria that identify alternatives and actions that are less unjust than others, and facilitating social realizations in the societies that emerge? John Rawls's justice as fairness (Rawls, 1971) is an ideal theory of (perfect) justice situated within a liberal social contract tradition. It is oriented towards setting up perfectly just institutions and equity and fairness in distributing society's basic goods. We take a look at his theory of justice as fairness a bit more below as it has had immense reach and influence on governments of liberal pluralist societies. By contrast, a capability approach as advanced by Amartya Sen and Martha Nussbaum is a human development approach that is concerned with the overall advantages (not functions!) a person might have. It offers the other option mentioned above—a comparative view and *practical* guidance as it seeks to reduce injustices and advance justice. Proponents argue that it fits human development goals worldwide. This is a good reason for us to look at the capability approach to see if it can offer some grounding and direction for "just" development of tourism, locally and globally.

There are other social justice theories aimed at perfect justice or undertaking comparative approaches that should be examined, too. In the limited space here, we can only touch on a couple and emphasize the need to explore other different perspectives. Karl Marx, for instance, focused not on perfect justice but on people's lives. He was especially concerned about labor exploitation and the right to the fruits of one's labor, and his work also addressed the fair distribution of wealth in society (distributive justice). At the highest phase of communist society, a just allocation of society's wealth would involve the right to receive a portion of societal goods and services that is based on individual needs. Note that for Marx, it is not an equal distribution of wealth, it does not depend on entitlement nor does it depend on the kind of work you do—it does not depend on desert, which relates to the notion of "giving someone what they deserve" (see Miller, 1991, 2017 for a more detailed discussion of desert). Hence the popular slogan you may have heard of which can be found in the *Critique of the Gotha Program* that Marx wrote in 1875 (Marx & Engels, 1970; also see https://www.marxists.org/archive/marx/works/1875/gotha/ch01.htm).

From each according to his ability, to each according to his needs!

Distributive Justice and Equity: Justice as Fairness

Justice is being approached in very different ways by various theorists. At the societal level, what social goods (income, opportunities, honors, power, etc.) and how they are being allocated (i.e., the grounds of fairness in their distribution, e.g., need, entitlement, merit, etc.) is the subject of social justice, more specifically, *distributive justice* as described here. Among modern theories of justice, an important one to be acquainted with is John Rawls's theory of justice as fairness. As the preeminent political theorist of justice in the 20th century, Rawls has also had a significant practical influence on liberal democratic societies and his formulation of *equity* in the distribution of societal goods and wealth has been seen as a good fit with the welfare state. A brief acquaintance with his theory is therefore merited here, due to its dominant influence and to think about it in relation to other justice approaches that can help to inform tourism.[3]

Rawls's ideal theory of justice as fairness focuses on just allocations and just institutions. The central idea of justice set out in his seminal work *A Theory of Justice* (Rawls, 1971) is: "All social primary goods—liberty and opportunity, income and wealth, and the bases of self-respect—are to be distributed equally unless an unequal distribution of any or all of these goods is to the advantage of the least favored" (Rawls, 1971, p. 303). In the hypothetical experiment he sets up, participants come together in a social contract as free and equal beings who would jointly arrive at principles of justice that would guide the setup of the basic structure of society and the distribution of primary goods. Moral equality is assured as they negotiate from behind a *veil of ignorance*. Rawls asks us to imagine sitting behind this veil of ignorance. In the *original position* (OP) in which these contractors gather, they have very little knowledge of their social or cultural background or their individual desires. They do have a general sense of things they might need to be able to live a good life, generally conceived. They operate from a position of self-interest in arriving at the principles and basic structure governing the distribution of primary goods. Using the notion of *reflective equilibrium*, Rawls explains that the best account of a person's sense of justice is arrived at after examining and weighing other proposed conceptions of justice. Reflective equilibrium is reached "after a person has weighed various proposed conceptions and he has either revised his judgments to accord with one of them or held fast to his initial convictions (and the corresponding conception)" (Rawls, 1971, p. 48).

36 Equity and Justice

Participants in the OP acting behind the veil of ignorance arrive at two principles of justice through the process described above (Rawls, 1971, p. 302; these principles are a modification of the ones on p. 60):

> *First principle*: Each person is to have an equal right to the most extensive total system of equal basic liberties compatible with a similar system of liberty for all.

> *Second Principle*: Social and economic inequalities are to be arranged so that they are both: (a) to the greatest benefit of the least advantaged, consistent with the just saving principle, and (b) attached to offices and positions open to all under conditions of fair equality of opportunity.

A Political Conception of Justice: Political Liberalism

Rawls subsequently revisited justice as fairness in *Political Liberalism* (Rawls, 1996). Here, he attempted to clarify how a political conception of justice addresses pluralism in a liberal democratic society. He poses again here: "What are fair terms of cooperation between free and equal citizens as fully cooperating and normal members of society over a complete life?" (Rawls, 1996, p. 181). As in his early work, participants come together behind a "veil of ignorance," with no knowledge of their social or cultural background. In order to address how a political conception of justice can be reasonably achieved amidst a pluralism of views, values and beliefs, Rawls develops a process of *overlapping consensus* whereby these contractors in the original position (OP) can hold different comprehensive doctrines and agree on a political conception of justice. The notion of overlapping consensus takes into account "all the reasonable opposing religious, philosophical, and moral doctrines likely to persist over generations and to gain a sizable body of adherents in a more or less just constitutional regime, a regime in which the criterion of justice is that political conception itself." (Rawls, 1996, p. 15).

The two principles that arise from the hypothetical negotiations as expressed in *Political Liberalism* (Rawls, 1996, Lecture 1.1, pp. 5-6) are:

(a) Each person has an equal claim to a fully adequate scheme of equal basic rights and liberties, which scheme is compatible with the same scheme for all; and in this scheme the equal basic liberties, and only those liberties, are to be guaranteed their fair value.
(b) Social and economic inequalities are to satisfy two conditions: first, they are to be attached to positions and offices open to all under conditions of fair equality of opportunity; and second, they are to be to the greatest benefit of the least advantaged members of society.

The first principle clarifies the equal basic rights and equal basic liberties that each person can lay claim to (e.g., freedom of speech, right to vote, etc.).

The second principle is similar to that in *A Theory of Justice* (Rawls, 1971). The second part of the second principle (also known as the "difference principle") is aimed at equitable distribution of society's primary goods to the worst-off, ensuring fairness to the low-income and poor, as well as other disadvantaged groups. Think here of "a rising tide lifts all boats," so only allocations that make the least well off better are acceptable (note here that it does not have to be equal distributions).[4] The first principle takes precedence over the second, and in the second, equality of opportunity has priority before the difference principle.

Scrutinizing Justice as Fairness

Despite its dominant influence as a theory of justice that defines "the appropriate division of social advantages" (Rawls, 1971), justice as fairness has come under scrutiny and criticism. One concern is that the focus on institutional structures and processes and a very limited set of basic goods in justice as fairness seems unable to relate to an individual's basic capabilities. A basic capability is "the ability to satisfy certain elementary and crucially important functionings up to certain levels" (Sen, 1992, p. 45, footnote 19). As a development theorist, Sen argues that the most important thing when evaluating well-being is to consider what people are actually able to be and do. He points out that Rawls's index of basic goods lacks natural goods (hence cannot address health directly, for instance) and is disconnected from addressing at least basic capabilities that are necessary for survival or to avoid poverty, etc., such as education, health, nutrition, shelter (Sen, 1999).

Martha Nussbaum, another development theorist, and philosopher, has worked closely with Sen on the capability approach. Her Capabilities Approach (CA) differs theoretically from Sen's approach (see Robeyn, 2016). She notes that Rawls's theory does not address disability well, among other things (Nussbaum, 2011). For example, while a disabled person may receive social goods equitably as per her social class, she faces higher medical and transportation costs, and a greater burden to live a good life due to her circumstances, not her choice (Kymlicka, 1990). Thinking about this from a tourism perspective, a similar concern might be that her ability to travel may be further restricted due to extra costs and services needed to facilitate her mobility and access.

Another concern is the rational, autonomous, and self-interested liberal person in Rawls's theory. Do people really conform to such a modern, individualistic conception, is there no room for difference, being other-regarding, being in caring relations with other people and other living things, etc.? If there is, then are the basic goods that Rawls forwards really enough? What else might a diverse, pluralistic society engaged in different ways of being and different economic practices (e.g., volunteering, barter, gift exchange, cooperative enterprises, which can occur even in western liberal societies) need in terms of basic societal goods? As noted above, Sen and Nussbaum mention the importance of considering

38 Equity and Justice

health, but think also of natural goods (ecological goods, animal welfare, etc.) that Rawls does not include.

We can also ask how well justice as fairness can attend to inequalities such as historical, institutionally entrenched racism against minority ethnic groups. Rawls's hypothetical contractors behind the "veil of ignorance" have no knowledge of their own social or cultural background, so they negotiate impartially to seek mutually advantageous principles of justice. After all, they would want to be treated fairly if they were to be citizens in the just society they are tasked to envision. They don't know their gender, ethnicity, or heritage, and have no knowledge of historical discrimination, racism, genocide, or other atrocities committed in the past. The case study of the Maya in Quintana Roo at the end of this chapter suggests, however, that it may be difficult for some groups to get fair treatment as a minority population. Like the discussion above, it alerts us to the possibility that more than distributive justice (at least the way Rawls portrays it) needs to be considered when we think of the idea of social justice.

Tourism's intricate interweaving with local and global systems, public and private spaces, raises puzzling questions in the context of Rawls's notion of distributive justice. How are "net benefits to the poor" (a common principle of pro-poor tourism) figured out? An economic calculus only? Getting equitable water rights for lower income residents and the poor in the destination is good, but it won't attend to water contamination, or the loss of vital ecological services and cost to health that may result, for instance, due to an unscrupulous industry practice of dumping toxic waste into the water system. Take another example: Should a destination marketing organization (DMO) that receives funding via hotel and motel tax distributions from a liberal government promote and sell the destination to stimulate tourism *growth*, with no systematic accounting or accountability for fair distribution of the anticipated costs and benefits (tangible and intangible)? Think of the Amsterdam example in Chapter 1 (Case 1.1), the psychological stress on residents, the loss of vibrant public spaces that residents once gathered in before they became "colonized" by hordes of tourists.

Fortunately, new comparative approaches and new conceptions of social justice are arising that offer hope for developing clearer pathways toward identifying and reducing inequalities and injustices in practice, as well as advancing new theoretical understandings of social justice and well-being. We commence exploring some of these over the next few chapters, but in order to do this, a little further thought on the idea of justice is needed. For instance, what is your normative position on justice—do you believe in universal principles such as Kant's Categorical Imperative discussed above? How well does Rawls's justice as fairness really apply to liberal *pluralistic* societies—does one size fit all the diverse groups in a society such as the USA? It would seem that much further thought needs to be given to the particular context and to intangible relationships and consequences of commodification.

Grappling with the General Versus the Particular

The 2030 Sustainable Development Agenda and the Sustainable Development Goals (see United Nations Department of Economic and Social Affairs, 2014) that replaced the Millennium Development Goals are illustrative of global aims for just, fair and equitable societies today and in the future:

> We resolve between now and 2030, to end poverty and hunger everywhere; to combat inequalities within and among countries; to build peaceful, just and inclusive societies; to protect human rights and promote gender equality and the empowerment of women and girls; and to ensure the lasting protection of the planet and its natural resources (United Nations, 2015).

There are good principles of justice in the above quote that apply generally to all societies worldwide, such as protecting human rights and promoting gender equity. These are reflected in the Tourism Bill of Rights as well as in the United Nations Global Code of Ethics for Tourism (see below). But given the complexity of the tourism system, the interrelatedness of "impacts" discussed in Chapter 1, the diverse social and cultural settings and stakeholders involved, it would be fair to ask: Won't different cultural, political, religious, ethnic perspectives around the world of travel and tourism require different considerations for justice? Are there objective, generalizable principles of justice? Or is justice relative to local norms, the moral standards of a group of people, or to some person? Rawls attempts to leave room for people to have their own comprehensive moral doctrine (e.g., their own religious views, their own moral beliefs about right to life, or gay marriage, capital punishment, etc.), while following his political conception of justice. But if you are a relativist, you might argue against there being any principles that are generalizable to all, and support positions where principles and values arise relative to the particular context, e.g., a specific cultural group's beliefs, or a local resident community's social norms.

It is really important to think through and see where you stand. Are there any conditions under which it is morally right to put a 10-year-old to work in a sweatshop that makes tourist souvenirs? If you said no, then can you be a moral relativist? There may be some norms that you might argue are objective and globally applicable, like the human rights principles in the UDHR, various rights discussed in the Tourism Bill of Rights and Tourist Code (UNWTO, 1985) and the UN Global Code of Ethics (UNWTO, 1999). Both draw upon the UDHR to assert a range of human rights, as well as rights related to work, leisure, travel, and tourism. Article 2 in the Global Code of Ethics, for example, addresses the subject: "Tourism as a vehicle for individual and collective fulfillment." Note the justice-oriented principles in Article 2.2, related to gender equality and the individual rights of the most vulnerable groups:

40 Equity and Justice

> Tourism activities should respect the equality of men and women; they should promote human rights and, more particularly, the individual rights of the most vulnerable groups, notably children, the elderly, the handicapped, ethnic minorities and indigenous peoples;

Article 2.3 specifically states that human exploitation, particularly sexual, and especially when applied to children, should be "energetically combatted with the cooperation of all the States concerned. . ." Articles 7 and 8 in the Global Code of Ethics relate to the "Right to tourism" and the "Liberty of tourist movements" respectively. They are particularly interesting to read in light of the tensions over domestic and international terrorism and their effect on travel to many popular tourism destinations (see Chapter 1).

> The prospect of direct and personal access to the discovery and enjoyment of the planet's resources constitutes a right equally open to all the world's inhabitants. . .; (excerpted from Article 8.1)

> The universal right to tourism must be regarded as the corollary of the right to rest and leisure, including reasonable limitation of working hours and periodic holidays with pay, guaranteed by Article 24 of the Universal Declaration of Human Rights and Article 7.d of the International Covenant on Economic, Social and Cultural Rights; (Article 8.2)

> Tourists and visitors should benefit, in compliance with international law and national legislation, from the liberty to move within their countries and from one State to another, in accordance with Article 13 of the Universal Declaration of Human Rights; they should have access to places of transit and stay and to tourism and cultural sites without being subject to excessive formalities or discrimination; (Article 8.1)

Such universal declarations of rights and principles are ones that appeal to common sense in the local-global context of tourism. Of course, neither the Tourism Bill of Rights nor the Global Code of Ethics has any regulatory force; the United Nations encourages states to adhere to the stipulated rights and to regulate tourism related activities.

Aside from the United Nations (UN) and the state governments, a number of other stakeholders can be identified whose tasks range from protecting or advocating for rights, calling for good practices and responsible behaviors, to playing a watchdog role to help with regulation. Some of these are discussed below. Their efforts demonstrate both the importance and challenge of asserting broad principles of justice, and the issue of addressing particular situations and conditions that may need more than the kind of social justice framework that Rawls's justice as fairness provides.

Stakeholders in Social Justice and Tourism

In addition to global organizations like the UN and local, state, and national governments, a number of nonprofit and nongovernmental organizations, industries and businesses are involved in tourism. Various civic and social service organizations, trade unions, new social movements, and tourists, too, can play a vital role in responsibility and stewardship of tourism related resources and the well-being of a destination's inhabitants (human and other living things). Visitors, for instance, can build solidarity with local residents and choose to use services that engage in responsible practices. Case 2.1 below by Johan Edelheim shows the valuable role played by Finnish trade unions in protecting labor rights and work conditions in the hospitality sector in Finland. It also illustrates the difficulty of trying to generalize and apply a set of fair labor principles to protect workers in larger and smaller operations in the hospitality industry.

Case 2.1: Worker Protection, Entrepreneurship and Loopholes: New Challenges for Finnish Trade Unions

Johan R. Edelheim

Trade unions around the world are doing good and necessary work in that they protect and represent employees in their dealings with employers. Their work should not be necessary, if all parties involved would act in ethical and just ways, but that is not always the case. Trade unions have, since the industrial revolution, developed into formidable forces in many nations, jointly putting pressure on other stakeholders to further the rights of their members. Employees in many Western countries can thank trade unions for rights and privileges that nowadays are taken for granted by many, such as standardized work hours, holiday entitlements, occupational health and safety regulations, to mention a few.

For unions to remain relevant they need to collect a substantial number of the available workforce as their members, and they need to deliver perceived benefits to these members. Benefits are easier to negotiate during times of high employment and rapid economic expansion, and many important changes have been made during times when employers have been in a weaker negotiating position, needing to accommodate their counterpart to secure smooth operations. Employers have to adjust their practices and services offered in response to changing marketplaces and therefore need leeway in their entrepreneurial efforts to be able to react in appropriate ways. One substantial change in recent years has been a growing foreign-born workforce which might not be accustomed to union membership, and might even be afraid of joining one for fear of being discriminated against by employers, and for not being re-employed to their time-restricted contracts.

Finland has traditionally had a strong workers' movement and unionization of workplaces. The first unions were established in the 1860s, and the initial central union organization in the early 1900s. National minimum salaries, social benefits, other work agreements as well as tax details have been negotiated in "Three-party negotiations" (with representatives from Workers unions, Employer organizations, and the ruling Government) since 1940. These negotiations act still today as reoccurring agreements where the three parties agree on salary raise or caps for the following two to three years, though nowadays with own negotiations for each profession. The current day PAM Service Workers Union, which hospitality workers belong to, is a combination of four field specific unions (Facilities; Trade; Special technic fields; and Hotel and Restaurant Workers) that joined forces in 2000. The union for Hotel and Restaurant Workers was founded in November 1933, a year after the alcohol prohibition (1919–1932) ended (Pohls, 2016).

Hotels and tourist destinations were developed through the 1920s–1940s in a nation-building effort. Iconic landscapes and places were elevated to national fame and importance by building hotels and infrastructure that allowed domestic travelers to enjoy their country. The provision of hospitality services, and the monopolized sale of alcohol, both instilled after the abolition of the prohibition rules, lead to strict rules about services available, with only international standard, in many cases state-owned, hotels being given rights to serve stronger alcohol in their restaurants, and wine-, or beer-serving privileges being strictly controlled and enforced. The post WWII period 1950–1970 focused on rebuilding, and the products remained rather unchanged. Employees in the industries were unionized to a high degree, and unions dictated the rules relating to compensations for working odd hours, or expectations of staff social areas to be built. All of these rules and expectations made sense in the heavily protected hospitality industry which was dominated by large employers and places of employment.

The gradual and lately accelerated pace of changes in the Finnish hospitality and tourism (H&T) industries from the 1980s towards the current day have created some large challenges for trade unions to stay relevant, and for the whole industry to evolve. Deregulation of air traffic, a successful branding of Finland as the official home of Santa Claus, good snow conditions, and growing attraction of the Aurora Borealis (the northern lights), have all lead to an unprecedented growth of tourism demand and supply, especially in the north of Finland, in the region of Lapland. This region makes up a third of Finland's landmass, but is home to just 3.7% (approximately 200,000 people) of the country's total population. As such, it offers new challenges to the development of tourism services and the role of the unions. Finnish unions are typically accustomed to addressing urban and medium to larger businesses.

There are over 900 H&T companies registered in the region—but these companies' average size is only 1.4 employees on a full-time equivalent (FTE). There are a handful of larger companies serving the region, some involved in hospitality, others in leisure and travel experiences (e.g., safaris), who employ the bulk of employees. If these large companies were deducted from the total, the actual average size of a H&T company would only be 0.7 FTE (Regional Council of Lapland, 2017).

In other words, the vast majority of H&T businesses in Lapland are one-person companies operating seasonally, drawing on family or hired rush-helpers only during peak demand, from mid-November until Easter (see Photo 2.1.1). Lots of calls are made in political circles that seasonality needs to be addressed, so that such companies could employ a larger workforce on an ongoing basis. However, the rules for employment are governed by the unions whose rules were traditionally developed for larger H&T companies. A stated principle unions have is that privileges achieved are not to be traded away, which leads to a conservatism that does not take into account a substantially changed marketplace.

PHOTO 2.1.1   Visitor preparing for a Husky Safari tour in Muonio, Lapland
Photo Credit: Sri Edelheim

Whereas nobody wants to infringe on common sense achievements, such as a healthy and safe workplace, or appropriate periods of rest between work, there is a need to look more holistically at changes in society when adjustments are proposed by small- and micro-business entrepreneurs. Being highly seasonal, and tied to the rhythm of natural changes, the current brand of Lapland is connected to the winter season. The unions' expectations of employers to hire full-time employees for all around the year

44 Equity and Justice

does not make sense, neither does their strictly enforced work hours during peak demand.

One compromise has been locally reached: Unions are nowadays allowing workers in some destinations to work more hours than the average 112.5 h per 3 weeks, which is stated elsewhere. This means that employees can work even double shifts when needed and are paid for the extra weeks after the season is over. This means that the time of employment is extended by the number of weeks and days that the worker has worked beyond the average 112.5 hours per three weeks during peak season, but the employee is free to go on holidays then. Employers do not incur over-time payments for this arrangement, and therefore do not have to employ two people to do the job during peak seasons.

Other union demands are not as flexible—such as assigned social areas for employees. Dressing rooms, lunch-break areas, and toilets make perfect sense in a city hotel, but do not make any sense for a family-owned safari company wanting to hire a husky dog-sled guide for Aurora Borealis tours in the non-light-polluted wilderness. Also, new fledgling companies avoid employing staff due to having to pay social benefits connected to full-time employment. It is in such examples that originally just and ethical rules create challenges for local entrepreneurship.

Some employers have come up with practices that bypass the rules, while still not breaking any laws directly. One entrepreneur turned a residential building into a high-quality hotel, but built a minimum of employees' social spaces, by keeping the number of employees under a specific threshold. To make up for the bulk of operational staff, a local outsourcing company hires staff into specific positions at the hotel, but writes in the job contracts that the employees can be utilized in any hospitality setting. Contractually the hotel simply buys services, and the hotel is therefore not obliged to offer their staff any benefits. The union is in this case ensuring that the agreed upon rules are upheld by the employer, i.e., the outsourcing company, but cannot protect the workers against any hotel owner's unjust behavior.

Mobilities, open borders and 'globalization' have increased the challenge of unions protecting workers. Another entrepreneur has taken outsourcing even further, by buying services from a company in Latvia, which is allowed inside the European Union. The Latvian company, following Latvian rules, pays travel and salaries, which are just a quarter of Finnish salaries (Simoska, 2017). The entrepreneur avoids hiring Finnish-born staff, and is paying attention so that no unionization takes place at the resort, by actively hiring first generation immigrants, or by buying outsourced services.

The case illustrates both the importance and challenges created by union rules aimed to protect employees from unjust employers. Compromises to existing rules as conditions change allow employers to hire staff, and give them salaries and benefits that they deserve. Too rigid rules can hold back entrepreneurship, and lead to employers wishing to be fair and ethical being outcompeted by other entrepreneurs using loopholes to bypass regulations created. It is this balance; protecting employees from abuse they could face, and allowing entrepreneurs to establish new businesses under conditions of seasonality and small firm size that Finnish trade unions will have to strive towards.

References

Pohls, M. (2016). *Viini, laulu ja taustajoukot.* Helsinki, Finland: Inokustannus. Retrieved from https://intokustannus.fi/kirja/viini-laulu-ja-taustajoukot/

Regional Council of Lapland. (2017). Tourism in Lapland. Retrieved May 10, 2018, from http://www.lappi.fi/lapinliitto/lapin-matkailu

Simoska, M. (2017). Kiistelty liikemies kaavailee Utsjoelle isoa investointia - paikalliset yrittäjät epäileväisiä: "Aivan järkyttävä tieto" Retrieved May 10, 2018, from http://www.iltalehti.fi/talous/201708312200364160_ta.shtml

Case 2.1 shows the importance of engaging stakeholders like trade unions to help with social justice and workers' rights in Finland. The rules and rights espoused by the PAM Service Workers Union that Finnish hospitality workers belong to are meant to apply to across the board to all Finnish workers in the hospitality industry. In protecting workers' rights, however, they also have to negotiate the tensions between the needs of small businesses versus larger ones and the specific location (e.g., rural versus urban), as well as other variable circumstances such as hiring needs that fluctuate with the season.

Nonprofit and nongovernmental organizations are another important stakeholder group engaged in different kinds of environmental, social, or political activism. See, for example, the role of *Tourism Concern*, a UK based non-profit organization that campaigns for ethical and fair tourism. Human rights and fair distribution of economic and social benefits are among a wide range of social justice actions it engages in, but note also the other principles mentioned in its approach to tourism development (Tourism Concern, n.d.-a). Italics are added to demonstrate the range of principles being advocated:

- *Human rights* and *self-determination* of communities must be at the core of every tourism development. This includes the *right to meaningful participation and consultation* including *free, prior, and informed consent* on whether to what extent and in what form tourism takes place.
- If tourism is developed, it needs to seek a *widespread and fair distribution of economic and social benefits* throughout the recipient communities, including *improving local prosperity, quality of life* and *social equity.* Tourism industry operators and governments must be *accountable* to the people whose land and cultures are being utilized for the benefit of tourists and tourism businesses.

46 Equity and Justice

- Strategies must *empower* people to *have a say* in the development of their communities and country.
- *Attention must be given to marginalized and vulnerable groups* such as women, children, minorities, illegal workers, and indigenous people working or affected by the tourism industry.
- Tourism should be a *positive and beneficial experience for travelers and hosts alike* in order to *act as a force for mutual understanding, empathy, and respect.*

These sound like good principles for a socially just tourism. Under its campaigns page, Tourism Concern makes it clear that tourism "can be a force for good and as a tool for international development" and it will "work with industry to improve their operations and provide advice and information to tourists, in order that they can make better and more informed decisions about their holidays—ensuring that holidays bring real benefits to destination communities" (Tourism Concern, n.d.-b). In March 2018, one of its campaigns on the above site was to seek signatures from the public globally for an online petition for London (UK) hotels to treat their staff fairly and pay a living wage. In terms of hotel workers, London is one of the most "unethical" tourist destinations; hotel "owners and managers refuse to recognize the issue of low pay and exploitation in hotels which trumpet their sustainability credentials," said the campaign website. New York, a comparable destination, pays its workers better than the £4 pounds for 37 minutes of room cleaning that London Hoteliers provide (a living wage in London is £9.15 an hour), which is "unethical" and "unacceptable" (Tourism Concern, 2018).

Social equity and rights to living wages, healthy environments, and fair distribution of societal resources have received added stimulus with the rise of new social movements, social media platforms and increasing access to the Internet worldwide. Social media like Facebook and Twitter have helped to generate activism and solidarity, sharing vital and timely information, stimulating online petitions and street demonstrations. Fair wages and ethical treatment for women in the workplace are making progress with the help of the #MeToo movement, for instance. This hashtag took off on social media in October 2017 and has helped women around the world to speak out against sexual violence and harassment, drawing on the idea of "empowerment through empathy": https://metoomvmt.org/.

Social media and the democratizing of information is of varying quality, of course, with good to dangerous consequences. But organizations are paying attention, too, observing and responding to product feedback and opinions posted on their website and on other hospitality and tourism related platforms like Trip Advisor, Yelp, etc. The instantaneous mobility of information globally via the Internet and social media can wreak rapid consequences on corporate and destination image and revenues. Consider, too, the wider consequences for environmental and social good when corporations take a proactive role in responding to social injustices. As stakeholders in tourism, they are stakeholders in wider society, and their Corporate Social Responsibility (CSR) extends not simply to the "tourism system" described in the previous chapter. What do you think of the actions of Delta Airlines (followed swiftly by United Airlines) in response to the tragic loss of lives in the Florida high school shooting in February 2018? Delta announced it would end discounts for National Rifle Association (NRA) members attending the group's annual meeting in Dallas, Texas (Josephs, 2018). Their intent was to remain "neutral" by removing any implied affiliation with the NRA, said the CEO, Ed Bastian, and he also said "our values are not for sale" when Delta's home state of Georgia withdrew a jet-fuel tax exemption in response to Delta's action (see Josephs, 2018).

Delta's CEO said they would review discounts for other "politically divisive" groups as well. Their intentions are not to demonstrate social responsibility but, rather, to seek "neutrality." It took a school shooting to do that (attempt neutrality)? Is the state of Georgia's response (withholding a jet fuel tax exemption) unfair, is it an example of distributive injustice? Airlines are a key stakeholder in tourism, and this example is a good reminder that tourism is a complex system that is thoroughly enmeshed in other systems—ecological, societal, local, regional, and global. Stakeholders are interrelated and sometimes interdependent (they are mutually dependent on each other), and include the public and private sectors, as well as civic organizations, residents, and visitors (nature, too, may be considered a stakeholder). Visitor activities occur in both public and private spaces, but do residents have clear rights to their public spaces and public/ common pool goods and services? Disproportionately high water consumption in tourism in Labuan Bajo, Indonesia, for example, not only disadvantages local residents but also creates greater hardship on local women (Cole, 2017). Rich residents and tourists in Cape Town can afford to pay more for water, but the poor who use a fraction of the water supply stand to suffer immense hardships and have little voice or influence. Tourism continued as Cape Town's water crisis intensified in early 2018 (NowThis World, 2018).

Legal rights for local residents to secure fair access and equitable use of public and common pool resources are critical, but the power and influence of local elites and other stakeholders also need to be addressed. We return to the tour guide Pablo and the Maya of Quintana Roo in the final section below to get a better sense of this among other issues and possibilities for advancing social justice in practice and in theory.

Are Distributive Justice and Basic Rights Enough?

If you live in a liberal democracy, you have many basic rights that Rawls's justice as fairness affirms, freedom and equality being among them. You can vote for new elected representatives, use your rights to free speech and freedom of association to engage in active social media to lobby for change, or get out on the street to engage in civil disobedience and protest, join a social movement, etc. You are also lucky if your government protects your rights to leisure and

48 Equity and Justice

reasonable work conditions, as well as a fair wage (a living wage), all of which contribute to your well-being. But that is if you have the capabilities to take advantage of all these opportunities, of course (recall Sen and Nussbaum's concern about this above, which we will examine further in Chapter 3). Take a look at the case study at the end of this chapter of the Maya in Quintana Roo. Distributive justice is clearly important but is equitable distribution of tourism income and revenues adequate to advance social justice for the Maya? For Pablo? What else is needed?

Recall from the beginning of this chapter that Pablo is a local resident and self-employed tour guide in Cozumel, Quintana Roo (his story is real, though his name is changed here to protect his identity). He is keen to share his island's beauty and abundance of natural and cultural treasures with visitors. Interactions between visitors and local Maya people are generally friendly, and he is grateful for whatever income he gets (and for the hurricane-safe concrete house his government helped to provide). But does he have the equivalent of a "living wage," adequate income to enable a reasonable quality of life where he can take some time for leisure and vacation, so that his children can visit their *abuelos* (grandparents) more than infrequently, perhaps even visit Mayan sites and experience "edutainment" about Mexico's rich, diverse cultural traditions at theme parks like Xcaret? What can he do about the fact that much of the tour business he seeks is tied up by larger tour operators with close ties to the powerful cruise industry? He is a lone tour guide in a highly competitive business. His gratitude for tourism in Cozumel is clear, though—life would be even harder without it.

Pablo is Maya, part of a minority Indigenous group that is still experiencing the hardships of a contentious history of colonization and conquest. Case 2.2 by Blanca Camargo at the end of this chapter discusses some of the challenges they face. Locally facilitated Mayan cultural experiences are available to visitors in Quintana Roo and the Yucatán through hard work and perseverance by the Maya people (read these two interesting articles: Dudenhoefer, 2013; Rushby, 2017). Useful to note is the role of online travel platforms like Sumak Travel, an "ethical tourism platform" which sources local operators that follow ethical principles such as listed on Sumak Travel's site (https://www.sumak-travel.org/):

> This is an ethical holidays platform with a difference, designed to help you find a trusted local operator to organize all or part of your holiday . . .You can do it in an environmentally responsible manner, respecting local cultures, with your money going on a transparent and fair trade basis towards the sustainability of local people and communities.

But Pablo is a solitary operator with very few contacts and no formal training. He spends all his available time on the promenade and by the cruise ship terminals, seeking income as a tour guide. He has little influence in the political arena to protest inequalities or argue for fair distribution of tour guide business. Neither do many Mayan workers in the Riviera Maya. In Cancun (a planned resort destination), the most vulnerable, including the poor and the working poor, are segregated spatially, economically, and culturally; they are almost invisible. Torres and Mumford (2005) provide a good look at that destination's "back stage" which you don't see if you happen to be in Cancun during your short college spring break. Or perhaps you're there on winter vacation fleeing cold northern climes? The problem is exacerbated by the power of stakeholders such as large foreign cruise operators and globally prevalent neoliberalism—which eschews government intervention, regulation and monitoring, preferring voluntary self-regulation and the free reign of markets (see Amore & Hall, 2017).

Meanwhile, how do Pablo and other Cozumelinos feel when they see brochures enthusiastically promoting their family's favorite public beaches as a honeymoon destination with images of pristine beaches devoid of local residents (though occasionally there are images of subservient worker roles)?[5] They have little control over the tourism related processes that permeate their everyday life and places of work and leisure, and on which many depend for their livelihood. For the low-income and working poor, it is a vulnerable existence. Distributive justice is important for the Maya as Case 2.2 also indicates, but more appears to be needed to advance social justice, such as building capabilities to facilitate well-being.

An additional challenge that Case 2.2 raises for social justice is how to address particularity and difference, the needs and issues of particular groups, including groups facing historical racism, stigmatization, domination, oppression or other inequalities and injustices. Getting fair treatment and procedural justice will be important for the Maya, and part of building capabilities will be to develop the skills and abilities to gain recognition and representation—these important principles will be discussed in Chapter 3 and further.

Finally, you may agree that it is important to understand the local to global, and the past and present context in which tourism development is embedded. Discrimination, racism, gender inequities and other injustices may be entrenched historically in political and social processes and institutional structures, and be affected by the actions of stakeholders from within and across borders (e.g., international tour operators, airlines, and global cruise industry). Political theorist Iris Marion Young (2011) argues against reducing social justice to distributive justice and calls for closer attention to social processes and institutional structures. We will see more of her in future chapters.

Summary and Further Considerations

Tourism is a powerful lens into understanding the practicality of what it means to live in a just and good society, to live a good life and engage in good actions as a tourist or resident, and to be treated fairly both as an individual and as a group (e.g., a religious group, an ethnic group, a transgendered group) at home and in travel. This chapter commences to explore the idea of justice, noting the

50 Equity and Justice

importance of looking at justice and ethics together, and not isolating the notion of well-being from this discussion. Future chapters will continue to explore approaches to justice toward the end of good tourism. From this chapter we can take away one iteration to build on: Good tourism is tourism that is just, fair, and equitable, and contributes to the well-being of human beings and nonhuman others. As we shall see, integral to human well-being is cultural well-being, which includes consideration for cultural heritage and relationships with land and Nature.

The chapter offers ways to think about justice as you progress through the book. Impartiality, reasoned judgment and scrutiny are needed to examine various approaches to justice, as Sen (2009) recommends, as well as with respect to one's own intuitions and values. Discussing these with others and taking the time to carefully read primary sources (original works) to become familiar with theories of justice is crucial. Exploring theories of justice as well as ethics helps to provide ways to think about various issues and challenges in tourism development and practice, and seek ways to address social justice. Inequalities, human rights, poverty alleviation, the rights of vulnerable populations and diverse groups, women and children, and much more will need to be thought about in the context of social justice and tourism in the 21st century. Neoliberal globalization and rapid technological development portend new challenges like wage and labor inequalities that require new governance forms and policy tools (e.g., worker's rights in the collaborative/sharing/gig economies).

The topic of distributive justice later in the chapter helps to lays some preliminary groundwork for future chapters to build on. Distributive justice has dominated social justice theories in the 20th century, but can Rawls's justice as fairness really address *particular* needs and different worldviews and comprehensive moral conceptions that groups and societies hold in a liberal pluralist society? It may not be able to address historic and institutionally entrenched injustices, and the rational, autonomous liberal subject may fit poorly with other ways of being and relating with the world. What room is there for emotional connection, concern, and caring relations with others? Within the local to global landscape of tourism lies *difference*, different belief systems and values of diverse groups, other worldviews not embedded in scientific discourses and the economics of market capitalism, as well as views that eschew the dominant western liberal view. Chapter 3 commences this investigation, which future chapters will build upon.

Questions for Further Reflection

1. What is the difference between equity and equality? Give examples of equitable distribution versus equal distribution of a good or resource.
2. What do the Tourism Bill of Rights, Global Code of Ethics, and the UDHR say about the rights of refugees and the mobilities of travelers?
3. What are the pros and cons of a political conception of justice such as Rawls's when we think about it in the context of tourism and public policy? For example, how can Rawls's theory of justice help to better understand the

meaning of "net benefits to the poor" in government policies supporting pro-poor tourism?

4. What injustices do the Maya of Quintana Roo experience, according to Case 2.2? What would help advance social justice for the Maya with respect to the tourism-related inequities shown in the case? (see Tourism Concern's principles listed in the chapter for some inspiration).

5. This chapter raises a warning sign about the tension between the particular and the general. What is the issue (tension) and what insights do Case 2.1 and 2.2 provide to help contemplate this issue?

Case 2.2: Mayan Cultural Tourism in Quintana Roo, Mexico

Blanca Alejandra Camargo

Introduction

My research interest in the Yucatán Peninsula in Mexico in 2007 arose while pursuing my doctoral degree at Texas A&M University. At the World Heritage Site of Chichen Itza, indigenous Maya women and children were begging rich international tourists to buy their souvenirs. The severe economic disparities between us, tourists, and local people, and the shame and sadness in these children eyes sparked my academic interest in exploring issues related to tourism and the Maya in this region. This case study builds on my dissertation research (Camargo Ortega, 2011; see also Jamal & Camargo, 2014).

Background and Setting

The state of Quintana Roo (pop 1.5 million in 2015), in the southeast coast of Mexico is home of the most important tourism destinations of Mexico. In 2016, the state received 11.1 of the 34.9 million (31.8%) international tourists that visited the country and generated 34% of total tourism revenue for Mexico (Datatur, 2018; SEDETUR 2017a). It became a tourism mecca in the 1970s, led by the controversial, state-sponsored first Integrally Planned Resort of Cancun and subsequent tourism developments such as enclavic resorts and cruise ports. Prior to that, Quintana Roo was a peripheral and inaccessible part of the Yucatan peninsula, inhabited mostly by Maya dwellers in the interior and some indigenous settlements along its coast (pop. 27,000 in the 1950s). The presence of the Maya in what is known as Quintana Roo today dates to 300 BC but many are descendants of the *Cruzoob*, Maya rebels who settled in the state after the bloody "Caste War" (1847–1901), plus others escaping Spanish control in other regions during colonial times. In Quintana Roo, they developed their own society, a mix of Spanish colonial and pre-Hispanic Maya

52 Equity and Justice

culture (Reed, 2001). In 2015, 40% of the Quintana Roo population self-described as indigenous and approximately 12% reported speaking Maya as a first language (Gobierno de Quintana Roo, 2017).

For tourism statistical purposes, the state government divides Quintana Roo into five major tourism destinations: the consolidated destinations of Cancun, the Riviera Maya (which includes Playa del Carmen and Tulum), and Cozumel, and the emerging destinations of Chetumal and Isla Mujeres (see Table 2.2.1 for key tourism statistics). Invisible in tourism statistics is the Zona Maya (which comprises the municipalities of Felipe Carrillo Puerto and Jose María Morelos), a less known rural area located in central Quintana Roo, home of ancestral Maya archeological sites and a living indigenous culture that strives to survive and maintain its traditions, language, beliefs, and ways of life. Because of its immense living and historical cultural significance, this area is widely recognized as the "center" or the "heart" of the Maya culture in Quintana Roo. Tourism in this area is incipient—operations are small scale, usually taking the form of community-based projects that offer cultural and nature tours. The Zona Maya struggles with high levels of poverty, illiteracy and lack of infrastructure. In Felipe Carrillo Puerto and Jose María Morelos, the two municipalities with the highest concentration of Maya population in the state, 71.6% and 73.2% of its inhabitants live in poverty, compared with 26.3% of Cancun, 30.3% of Playa del Carmen and Tulum, and 31.7% of Cozumel (Coneval, 2012).

TABLE 2.2.1 Key Tourism Statistics Quintana Roo 2016

Destination Area	Overnight tourist visitation	Tourism revenue (US$ million)	# of hotels	# of rooms
Riviera Maya	4,790,056	$3,071.74	411	45,217
(Playa del Carmen, Tulum)				
Cancun	4,761,482	$4,700.64	187	35,549
Cozumel	719,046	$710.57	21	3,748
Chetumal	480,384	$57.65	114	2,815
(and Mahahual)				
Isla Mujeres	435,677	$115.89	57	3,724
Zona Maya (Felipe Carrillo	n/a	n/a	21	235
Puerto and José María Morelos)				
Bacalar	n/a	n/a	47	515
Puerto Morelos	n/a	n/a	25	5,052
Lazaro Cárdenas (Holbox and	n/a	n/a	50	751
Kantanukin)				
Total Quintana Roo	**11,186,645**	**$8,602.48**	**963**	**97,606**

Adapted from SEDETUR (2017a)

Tourism Development and Marketing in Quintana Roo

Tourism is the most important economic activity in Quintana Roo, contributing to approximately 86% of the state GDP (ProMexico, 2017), 15% of all jobs in the state (INEGI, 2015), foreign investments and infrastructure development. Because of its importance, tourism development and marketing is a state priority overseen by the Secretariat of Tourism of Quintana Roo (SEDETUR). SEDETUR seeks to "conduct and establish the criteria and policies for the promotion and development of the tourist activity in the state with the participation of all pertinent government agencies and the private sector" (SEDETUR 2017b). Quintana Roo Tourism Law (2010, updated 2014) determines the objectives, priorities, roles and responsibilities, and other relevant programs and policies that support the planning, development, and programming of all tourist activity in the state under the criteria of social well-being, sustainability, competitiveness and *equitable* state and municipal development in the short, medium, and long term (Article 3, Numeral III). In regard to community tourism, the state law seeks "to foment and develop actions plans to diversify the tourist activity, where all tourism modalities will be considered as an integrated local development factor, supporting the use of the activities of the community" (Numeral XVI). In the Tourism Diversification and Development Sectorial Program (SEDETUR 2017b), the Zona Maya is seen an "alternative to complement the attractions of the northern area of Quintana Roo" (i.e., Cancun and Riviera Maya). However, in-depth research conducted on site revealed challenges and injustices related to development and marketing of tourism in the Zona Maya.

(i) Inequitable allocation of government resources for tourism promotion

Tourism revenue generated by overnight tourists gives the state a significant marketing and advertising budget to promote its destinations in international tourism markets. Until 2014, key destinations in the state, Cancun, Riviera Maya (Playa del Carmen and Tulum), Cozumel, Costa Maya, and Isla Mujeres funded their marketing and promotion activities through a lodging tax (3%). The more developed destinations raised more money and received more state funds since they have a higher number of hotel rooms and overnight tourists. Table 2.2.2 shows the marketing funds of each promotion board.

The Zona Maya did not have a formal tourism promotion board to conduct marketing and promotions activities in national or international markets. The small amount of money raised by the lodging tax (the Zona Maya had 150 hotel rooms in 2010, 235 in 2016) is collected by SEDETUR, who can channel funds directly to municipalities without a formal tourism board. The Zona Maya not only did not raise significant funds to

TABLE 2.2.2 Approved Marketing Funds for Key Destinations in Quintana Roo from 2010–2016 ($MXN)

Destination Area	2010[1]	2011[2]	2012[3]	2013[4]	2014[5]	2015[6]	2016[7]
Cancun*(Benito Juarez)	$126,021,545	$144,526,403	$148,566,360	$153,538,858	$174,000,000	$183,750,000	$192,937,500
Riviera Maya* (Playa del Carmen, Tulum)	$101,232,399	$116,099,771	$119,908,508	$133,135,593	$154,000,000	$161,700,000	$169,785,000
Cozumel*	$8,206,728	$9,411,049	$9,060,930	$7,186,549	Became part of the Rivera Maya Promotion Board and budget		
Isla Mujeres*	$2,944,767	$3,367,040	$4,030,241	$4,720,256	Became part of Cancun Promotion Board and budget$1,000,000		
Costa Maya* (Othón Blanco)	$2,437,880	$2,792,948	$2,402,951	$2,420,449	$8,000,000	$8,400,000	$8,820,000
Zona Maya** (Felipe Carrillo Puerto, José María Morelos)	$0	$3,000,000	$0	$0	$0	$0	$0

* Funds raised through 3% lodging tax

** Funds assigned by SEDETUR; does not have a formal tourism board.

1 Source: Presupuesto de Egresos del Gobierno del Estado de Quintana Roo para el Ejercicio Fiscal 2010. Retrieved January 26, 2018 from http://www.sefiplan.qroo.gob.mx/documentos/pe2010.pdf

2 Source: Presupuesto de Egresos del Gobierno del Estado de Quintana Roo para el Ejercicio Fiscal 2011. Retrieved January 26, 2018 from http://archivo.transparencia.qroo.gob.mx/SIWQROO/Transparencia/Documentos/10_12933_8.pdf

3 Source: Presupuesto de Egresos del Gobierno del Estado de Quintana Roo para el Ejercicio Fiscal 2012. Retrieved January 26, 2018 from http://archivo.transparencia.qroo.gob.mx/SIWQROO/Transparencia/Documentos/10_14292_8.pdf

4 Source: Presupuesto de Egresos del Gobierno del Estado de Quintana Roo para el Ejercicio Fiscal 2013. Retrieved January 26, 2018 from http://www.ordenjuridico.gob.mx/Documentos/Estatal/Quintana%20Roo/wo76489.pdf

5 Source: Presupuesto de Egresos del Gobierno del Estado de Quintana Roo para el Ejercicio Fiscal 2014. Retrieved January 26, 2018 from http://www.ordenjuridico.gob.mx/Documentos/Estatal/Quintana%20Roo/wo89936.pdf

6 Source: Presupuesto de Egresos del Gobierno del Estado de Quintana Roo para el Ejercicio Fiscal 2015. Retrieved January 26, 2018 from http://documentos.congresoqroo.gob.mx/leyes/fiscal/ley002/L1420141211236.pdf

7 Source: Presupuesto de Egresos del Gobierno del Estado de Quintana Roo para el Ejercicio Fiscal 2016. Retrieved January 26, 2018 from http://documentos.congresoqroo.gob.mx/leyes/fiscal/ley002/L1520161111013.pdf

promote themselves in national and international markets but did not receive sufficient state funding to support such activities. Only in 2011 were official funds approved specifically for municipalities in Zona Maya (Table 2.2.2). Starting in 2014, the number of tourism promotion boards was reduced to three (Cancun, Riviera Maya and Costa Maya). SEDETUR allocates marketing and promotion funding to each of three tourism boards independent of how much lodging tax is generated by the destinations. As Table 2.2.2 shows, the Zona Maya was entirely excluded. According to the tourism director of the Zona Maya, the only support they have received from SEDETUR in the past few years are a few tourism brochures (Pat, 2016).

Similarly, financial resources for tourism infrastructure development were found to be unevenly allocated among the different destinations. According to SEDETUR's officials interviewed during fieldwork, government funds for tourism infrastructure were assigned, first, to the consolidated destinations of Cancun and the Riviera Maya and second, to the emerging destinations of Holbox, Chetumal, Isla Mujeres and Cozumel. The Zona Maya has the least priority, according to one of its directors, as it generates little tourism revenue. Official documents on state funding for tourism development (SEDETUR (Secretariat of Tourism of Quintana Roo), 2009) also shows that in 2007, while the government invested approximately US $4.7 million in infrastructure development in sun and sea tourism destinations, it did not provide any funding for projects in the Zona Maya. In 2008, this area was only allocated 7.4% of all approved investments for tourism development in the state.

Yet, government support for tourism development and promotion is critical for the economic and cultural survival of the Maya population that inhabits the Zona Maya. Out-migration to seek jobs elsewhere is high. Cultural tourism entrepreneurs and Maya residents in Zona Maya have felt angry and abandoned by the government, who, in their view, have only looked out for the rich investors in Cancun and the Riviera Maya.

(ii) Political marginalization and institutional discrimination

SEDETUR is also responsible for the formulation, implementation and evaluation of the state's tourism policy. As articulated in Quintana Roo's Tourism Legislation, Chapter II, tourism policy, strategy and decision making can be done in consultation with an Advisory Council (Consejo Consultivo) presided over by the state governor and the members he/she appoints, the state Secretary of Tourism, and the mayors of the state municipalities. Representatives of key tourism private business (restaurants, tour operators, and transportation companies), NGOs, social and cultural grassroots groups, academia, and local residents, do not have formal representation in the Advisory Council; as stated in Article 13, they can be invited to express their opinions and concerns about tourism but are not granted voting rights. Inclusion of local residents in advisory councils is optional and there are no formal mechanisms established for consulting and/or involving local communities in tourism decision-making at the municipal or state level (Quintana Roo's Tourism Legislation, Chapter II). Unless they are in a higher government position, the Maya residents are thus effectively excluded from decision-making. The institutional arrangements deny them formal representation, voting rights, and meaningful consultation, a situation that continues to exacerbate under-development as well as lack of progress of tourism in the Zona Maya area.

It can be argued that political and socioeconomic marginalization is related to the historically entrenched cultural racism and ethnic prejudice against the Maya (see Castellanos Guerrero, 2003). Government officials and important tourism stakeholders interviewed in my study perceived the local Maya to be hospitable, hardworking, noble, honest, and respectful, but also uneducated, unqualified, and unable to participate in tourism decision-making. Maya participants shared personal stories with me related to discrimination, racism and cultural ridiculing experienced, not only throughout their childhood, but also in their current interactions with fellow Mexican nationals, in particular those from the more developed cities who arrived to Quintana Roo to work in tourism. The humiliation, ridiculing and prejudice many Mayas experienced were, according to several respondents, the reason why many families stopped teaching their children their native language and traditional cultural practices. My research indicates that discrimination is almost ubiquitous in the tourism industry in Quintana Roo. Furthermore, tourism does not provide equal work opportunities for all: Mayas are mostly employed in menial, low-paid, and physically intensive positions, while managerial positions are commonly occupied by foreigners. Labor statistics show that 50% of all employed Maya population in Quintana Roo work in low-entry positions, including domestic service (27% of all employed women) (INEGI, 2004).

Discrimination was evident not only in exclusion of local stakeholders from tourism decision-making but also in the marginalization of local culture and heritage from advertising and promotion. Numerous promotion media and images represent the places and beaches which have been used by Mayans as far back as 300 BC as devoid of local presence (see Photo 2.2.1 for sample advertising for the 2010 tourism campaign *Cozumel: Heaven on Earth*). Cultural sites and history, although important, are not what most tourists want to see, said a representative from the tourism promotion board. "If I go to Texas to talk about the Maya, they are going to laugh at me."

PHOTO 2.2.1   *Cozumel: Heaven on Earth* 2010 campaign sample ads
Source: www.visitmexico.com. Retrieved May 21, 2010

Conclusion

The state of Quintana Roo presents its tourism as being developed under the criteria of social well-being, sustainability, competitiveness and equitable development. However, the present case illustrates several issues related to justice, fairness and equity for residents of Mayan descent, who are a minority population in the state. Among these are inequitable distribution of government resources for tourism promotion and infrastructure, inequitable promotion of cultural heritage, and the exclusion of Maya stakeholders from tourism decision-making. In addition, the local Mayans perceive discrimination, disrespect and prejudice in interactions with Mexican nationals. These inequities have severely inhibited the economic and cultural well-being of the Zona Maya, the most culturally rich yet most impoverished area of Quintana Roo. Out-migration to seek jobs in tourist centers throughout the state continues. The opportunity for visitors to know that the Maya are part of a living culture and learn about their rich cultural heritage is also being lost.

References

Camargo Ortega, B. A. (2011, July 16). *Justice and Fairness in Tourism: A Grounded Theory Study of Cultural Justice in Quintana* Roo, *Mexico*. Texas A&M University, College Station, TX, U.S.A. Retrieved from https://oaktrust.library.tamu.edu/handle/1969.1/ETD-TAMU-2011-05-9102

CAPÍTULO ÚNICO DISPOSICIONES GENERALES. (2010). Quintana Roo Tourism Law.

Castellanos Guerrero, A. (2003). *Imágenes del racismo en México*. Mexico City: Universidad Autónoma Metropolitana, Unidad Iztapalapa. Retrieved from https://books.google.ca/books/about/Imágenes_del_racismo_en_México.html?id=FRuLxgleWLMC&redir_esc=y

Coneval. (2012). *Informe de pobreza y evaluación en el estado de Quintana Roo, 2012*. Retrieved from https://www.coneval.org.mx/coordinacion/entidades/Documents/Informesdepobrezayevaluación2010-2012_Documentos/Informedepobrezayevaluación2012_QuintanaRoo.pdf

Datatur. (2018). Cuenta de Viajeros Internacionales. Retrieved January 16, 2018, from http://www.datatur.sectur.gob.mx/SitePages/VisitantesInternacionales.aspx

Gobierno de Quintana Roo. (2017). Grupos Indígenas. Retrieved January 16, 2018, from http://www.qroo.gob.mx/atencion-grupos-en-situacion-de-vulnerabilidad/grupos-indigenas

INEGI. (2004). *Censos Económicos 2004. Quintana Roo: Resultados Generales*. Retrieved from www.inegi.gob.mx

INEGI. (2015). *Estadísticas a Propósito del Día Mundial del Turismo (27 De Septiembre): Datos Nacionales*. Retrieved from http://www.inegi.org.mx/saladeprensa/aproposito/2015/turismo0.pdf

Jamal, T., & Camargo, B. A. (2014). Sustainable tourism, justice and an ethic of care: toward the Just Destination. *Journal of Sustainable Tourism, 22*(1), 11–30. https://doi.org/10.1080/09669582.2013.786084

Pat, B. (2016, November 4). Exigen mayor promoción turística para la zona maya. Retrieved January 26, 2018, from https://sipse.com/novedades/turismo-zonamaya-quintanaroo-fideicomiso-promocion-turistica-229024.html

ProMexico. (2017). *Inversión y Comercio Quintana Roo*. Retrieved from http://mim.promexico.gob.mx/work/models/mim/Documentos/PDF/mim/FE_QUINTANA_ROO_vf.pdf

Reed, N. A. (2001). *The Caste War of Yucatán*. Stanford, CA, USA: Stanford University Press. Retrieved from https://www.sup.org/books/title/?id=700

SEDETUR (Secretariat of Tourism of Quintana Roo). (2009). *Turismo comunitario en el Caribe Mexicano*.

SEDETUR (Secretariat of Tourism of Quintana Roo). (2017a). *Indicadores turísticos enero-diciembre 2016*.

SEDETUR (Secretariat of Tourism of Quintana Roo). (2017b). *Programa Sectorial de Diversificación y Desarrollo del Turismo de Quintana Roo*. Retrieved from http://caribemexicano.travel/ARCHIVOS/(1) Programa Sectorial de DDT (Publicado) (Opt).pdf

Notes

1 Rawls attempted to develop a transnational (global) idea of justice in *The Law of Peoples* (Rawls, 1999). We won't discuss this here though we will think about justice beyond borders in Chapter 4 (Responsibility).
2 As Arneson (2013) explains, an egalitarian favors equality of some sort, e.g., receiving the same, being treated the same way, being treated as equals, etc. In modern societies with market economies, as he says, "an egalitarian is generally thought to be one who supports equality of income and wealth (income being a flow, wealth a stock)."
3 See Miller (2017) for an authoritative discussion on justice and Wenar (2015) on rights.
4 See also Rawls (2001), for a restatement of justice as fairness as a form of political liberalism. For a libertarian contradiction to Rawls's conception of justice, see Hayek (1976).
5 See Jamal, Camargo, Sandlin and Segrado (2010) and Camargo (2012).

References

Amore, A., & Hall, C. M. (2017). National and urban public policy in tourism. Towards the emergence of a hyperneoliberal script? *International Journal of Tourism Policy, 7*(1), 4–22. http://doi.org/10.1504/IJTP.2017.082761

Aristotle. (1999). *Nicomachean ethics*. (T. Irwin, T., Ed.) (2nd ed.). Indianapolis, IN: Hackett Pub. Co. Retrieved from https://books.google.ca/books/about/Nicomachean_Ethics_Second_Edition.html?id=-Drs3dmYWuEC&redir_esc=y

Arneson, R. (2013). Egalitarianism. In E. N. Zalta (Ed.), *The Stanford encyclopedia of philosophy*. Retrieved from https://plato.stanford.edu/archives/sum2013/entries/egalitarianism/

Burns, P., & Novelli, M. (Eds.). (2008). *Tourism development: Growth, myths, and inequalities*. Wallingford, UK: CABI.

Camargo, B. (2012). *Justice and fairness in tourism: A grounded theory study of cultural justice in Quintana Roo, Mexico. Dissertation, Texas A&M University, College Station, Texas*. Retrieved from http://ezproxy.library.uvic.ca/login?url=http://search.ebscohost.com/login.aspx?direct=true&db=psyh&AN=2012-99090-148&site=ehost-live&scope=site

Cole, S. (2017). Water worries: An intersectional feminist political ecology of tourism and water in Labuan Bajo, Indonesia. *Annals of Tourism Research, 67*, 14–24. http://doi.org/10.1016/j.annals.2017.07.018

Cole, S., & Morgan, N. (2010). Introduction: Tourism and Inequalities. In S. Cole & N. Morgan (Eds.), *Tourism and inequality: problems and prospects* (pp. 15–24). http://doi.org/10.1079/9781845936624.A

Connell, J. (2011). A new inequality? Privatisation, urban bias, migration and medical tourism. *Asia Pacific Viewpoint, 52*(3), 260–271. http://doi.org/10.1111/j.1467-8373.2011.01454.x

Crisp, R. (2017). Well-Being. In E. N. Zalta (Ed.), *The Stanford encyclopedia of philosophy* (Fall). Retrieved from https://plato.stanford.edu/archives/fall2017/entries/well-being/

Dudenhoefer, D. (2013, September 13). Dead Mayans Only, Please! Mexico Tourism Driven by Ruins, Shuns Natives. Retrieved March 18, 2018, from https://newsmaven.

60 Equity and Justice

io/indiancountrytoday/archive/dead-mayans-only-please-mexico-tourism-driven-by-ruins-shuns-natives-RrakopDhv0aEPjYABX2byw/

Fennell, D. A. (2017). *Tourism ethics* (2nd ed.). Bristol, United Kingdom: Channel View Publications. Retrieved from https://www.world-of-digitals.com/en/fennell-tourism-ethics-ebook-pdf

Gert, B., & Gert, J. (2017). The definition of morality. Retrieved July 1, 2018, from https://plato.stanford.edu/cgi-bin/encyclopedia/archinfo.cgi?entry=morality-definition&archive=fall2017

Goodwin, H. (2011). *Taking responsibility for tourism*. Woodeaton, UK: Goodfellow Publishers Limited.

Hayek, F. (1976). *Law, legislation and liberty: The mirage of social justice*. Chicago, IL: University of Chicago Press.

Higgins-Desbiolles, F. (2009). International solidarity movement: A case study in volunteer tourism for justice. *Annals of Leisure Research, 12*(3–4), 333–349. http://doi.org/10.1080/11745398.2009.9686828

Jamal, T., Camargo, B., Sandlin, J., & Segrado, R. (2010). Tourism and cultural sustainability: Towards an eco-cultural justice for place and people. *Tourism Recreation Research, 35*(3), 269–279. http://doi.org/10.1080/02508281.2010.11081643

Josephs, L. (2018, March 2). Delta CEO says, "Our values are not for sale," after Georgia lawmakers drop tax break. Retrieved March 3, 2018, from https://www.cnbc.com/2018/03/02/delta-ceo-our-values-are-not-for-sale.html

Kant, I. (1998). *The groundwork of the metaphysics of morals*. (M. Gregor, Ed.). Cambridge: Cambridge University Press.

Kymlicka, W. (1990). *Contemporary political philosophy: An introduction*. Oxford: Clarendon Press.

Lieberman, K., & Nissen, B. (2008). *Ethics in the hospitality and tourism industry* (Second). Lansing, MI: Educational Institute of the American Hotel & Lodging Association.

Lovelock, B., & Lovelock, K. (2013). *The ethics of tourism: Critical and applied perspectives*. Abingdon, Oxon: Routledge.

Marx, K., & Engels, F. (1970). *Critique of the Gotha programme. Marx/Engels selected works* (Vol. 3). Moscow: Progress Publishers.

Miller, D. (1991). Review article : Recent theories of social justice. *British Journal of Political Science, 21*(3), 371–391.

Miller, D. (2017, June 26). Justice. Retrieved from https://plato.stanford.edu/archives/fall2017/entries/justice/

Mowforth, M., & Munt, I. (2016). *Tourism and sustainability: Development, globalisation and new tourism in the Third World* (4th ed.). New York, NY: Routledge.

NowThis World. (2018, February 25). Why is Cape Town running out of water? [Video]. Retrieved June 24, 2018, from https://youtu.be/SViZEtsoHyA

Nussbaum, M. (2011). *Creating capabilities: The human development approach*. Cambridge, MA: The Belknap Press of Harvard University Press.

Rawls, J. (1971). *A theory of justice*. Cambridge: Belknap Press of Harvard University Pres.

Rawls, J. (1996). *Political liberalism*. New York: Columbia University Press.

Rawls, J. (1999). *The law of peoples: With "The Idea of Public Reason Revisited."* Cambridge, MA: Harvard University Press. Retrieved from https://www.amazon.com/Law-Peoples-Public-Revisited-1999-11-30/dp/B01A0D7JEQ

Rawls, J. (2001). *Justice as fairness: A restatement*. Cambridge, MA: The Belknap Press of Harvard University Press.

Robeyn, I. (2016). The capability approach. In *The Stanford encyclopedia of philosophy* (Winter 201). Edward N. Zalta (ed.). Retrieved from https://plato.stanford.edu/archives/win2016/entries/capability-approach/

Rushby, K. (2017, February 11). Meet the Mayans: A tour of the real Yucatán, Mexico. Retrieved from https://www.theguardian.com/travel/2017/feb/11/meet-mayans-tour-real-yucatan-mexico-kevin-rushby

Sandel, M. J. (1998). *Liberalism and the limits of justice* (Second). Cambridge: Cambridge University Press. http://doi.org/10.1017/CBO9780511810152

Sandel, M. J. (Ed.). (2007). *Justice: A reader.* Oxford: Oxford University Press.

Sandel, M. J. (2009). *Justice: What's the right thing to do?* New York: Farrar, Straus and Giroux.

Scheyvens, R. (2002). *Tourism for development: Empowering communities.* Harlow, UK: Prentice Hall. http://doi.org/10.1016/j.tourman.2005.07.013

Sen, A. (1992). *Inequality reexamined.* Cambridge, MA: Harvard University Press.

Sen, A. (1999). *Development as freedom.* Oxford: Oxford University Press.

Sen, A. (2009). *The idea of justice.* Cambridge, MA: Belknap Press.

Smith, M., & Duffy, R. (2003). *The ethics of tourism development.* New York, NY: Routledge.

Torres, R. M., & Momsen, J. D. (2005). Gringolandia: The construction of a new tourist space in Mexico. *Annals of the Association of American Geographers, 95*(2), 314–335. http://doi.org/10.1111/j.1467-8306.2005.00462.x

Tourism Concern. (n.d.-a). About. Retrieved December 1, 2017, from https://www.tourismconcern.org.uk/about/

Tourism Concern. (n.d.-b). Campaigns. Retrieved March 8, 2018, from https://www.tourismconcern.org.uk/campaigns/

Tourism Concern. (2018). London hotels to treat their staff fairly and pay a living wage. Retrieved March 8, 2018, from https://www.tourismconcern.org.uk/campaign/london-hotels-treat-staff-fairly-pay-living-wage/

United Nations. (1948). *Universal Declaration of Human Rights. Universal Declaration of Human Rights.* United Nations. Retrieved from http://www.un.org/en/udhrbook/pdf/udhr_booklet_en_web.pdf

United Nations. (2015, August 11). Transforming our world: The 2030 Agenda for Sustainable Development. Retrieved October 1, 2016, from https://sustainabledevelopment.un.org/post2015/transformingourworld

United Nations Department of Economic and Social Affairs. (2014, August 7). Sustainable development goals. Retrieved June 24, 2018, from https://sustainabledevelopment.un.org/sdgs

UNWTO. (1985). Tourism Bill of Rights and Tourist Code. Retrieved from http://www.aitr.org/wp-content/uploads/2014/04/omt_sofia1985.pdf

UNWTO. (1999, October 1). Global code of ethics for tourism: For Responsible tourism. Retrieved from http://cf.cdn.unwto.org/sites/all/files/docpdf/gcetbrochureglobalcodeen.pdf

Wenar, L. (2015). Rights. Retrieved July 1, 2018, from https://plato.stanford.edu/cgi-bin/encyclopedia/archinfo.cgi?entry=rights

Wood, R. E. (2009). Tourism and international policy: Neoliberalism and beyond. In T. Jamal & M. Robinson (Eds.), *The SAGE Handbook of Tourism Studies* (pp. 595–612). Thousand Oaks, CA: SAGE.

Young, I. M. (2011). *Justice and the politics of difference* (Paperback). Princeton, NJ: Princeton University Press.

3

DIVERSITY AND RECOGNITION

Introduction

A couple of keyboard clicks is all you will need to find the website of the United Nations Educational, Scientific and Cultural Organization (UNESCO), which is tasked with the "identification, protection and preservation of cultural and natural heritage around the world considered to be of outstanding value to humanity" (UNESCO World Heritage Centre, n.d.). A marvelous journey unfolds as you look through some of the areas and sites protected as World Heritage. As it says on the UNESCO website referenced above:

> Places as unique and diverse as the wilds of East Africa's Serengeti, the Pyramids of Egypt, the Great Barrier Reef in Australia and the Baroque cathedrals of Latin America make up our world's heritage.

Browsing through the World Heritage List and the New Inscribed Properties on it produces a dizzying sense of the ecological and cultural richness within this finite space we call Earth. It beckons visitors to travel and enjoy not just World Heritage but many other diverse landscapes and types of experiences. UNESCO also protects intangible cultural heritage related to cultural expressions and practices "inherited from our ancestors and passed on to our descendants" and its Representative List of Intangible Cultural Heritage illustrates "those intangible heritage elements that help demonstrate the diversity of this heritage and raise awareness about its importance" (UNESCO, n.d.). They range from oral traditions and rituals to ethnic food and regions, as well as social and cultural practices related to nature and the universe.

But you are already thinking: "Wait a minute, who decides what to include, why to include it, how some cultural heritages make it to UNESCO's lists, while others that seem just as special have gained no recognition?" These are political questions, political in the sense of being steeped in issues of authority, power and influence, legitimacy, and control. Case 2.2 at the end of Chapter 2 raised some similar political questions in addition to the economic challenges that a minority ethnic culture might face, especially where there is a history of contestation and violence due to economic, religious, or other differences. The Maya in that case struggled with lack of recognition, fair treatment, and voice in representing their interests. They also suffered from inequitable distribution of tourism income and opportunities. As noted in Chapter 2, Rawls's justice as fairness has dominated the discourse of justice in liberal pluralistic societies, but with an emphasis on distributive justice. Yet, in matters of social justice, is closer attention not needed to issues of diversity, voice, and participation in social and political processes? Redistribution is needed, but so is *recognition* and *inclusiveness* of diverse groups plus minority and historically oppressed populations who may be subject to disrespect, discrimination, marginalization, and exclusion (politically and socially).

Newer perspectives on justice since Rawls show there is much more to do, including a closer examination of the particular, local, and everyday context in which diverse groups and touristic practices interact. Chapter 3 commences with an exploration of diversity in the context of tourism. As used here, diversity with respect to social groups (e.g., diverse groups) refers to groups differentiated along dimensions like gender, sexual orientation, and ethnicity, and includes vulnerable populations (e.g., the elderly, children, economically disadvantaged, racial and ethnic minorities, the homeless, chronically ill, people with disabilities). There is, too, diversity of natural and cultural goods and heritage, which is of interest to tourism developers and heritage conservationists, for instance. Urban and land-use planners may think of diversity in terms of things like mixed-use neighborhoods and affordability to different groups, diversity of public and green spaces, diverse transportation options, and diverse social uses of the city. These are highly relevant to tourism too. For instance, what social justice considerations arise as tourists "join" (compete with?) residents for *use* and *access* to common pool resources like limited groundwater, and public environmental, social and cultural goods, and services like public parks and transportation, public markets and plazas, etc.?

There's a lot to cover! We will draw on various examples incorporating women, ethnic minorities and Indigenous people, with apologies to those who might have hoped to see more on other topics. For instance, in addition to political rights, issues of human rights and social rights, as well as emotional and physical abuse and safety, are very important to address in LGBT+ (lesbian, gay, bisexual, transgender, other orientations) travel. LGBT+ friendly spaces of leisure and recreation offer opportunities for psychological and physical well-being, social togetherness and solidarity, but can also be subject to discrimination, abuse and prejudice based on societal norms and political ideologies. Diverse Pride spaces like Pride parades and post-parade parties, for instance, are "extra-ordinary spaces" in which both pleasure and politics play out, challenging heteronormativity as a public and political action, seeking and gaining rights to the social space, etc. (Browne, 2007, p. 64). Guaracino

64 Diversity and Recognition

and Salvato (2017) discuss homophobia and transphobia, harassment, violence and threats even in gay-popular destinations.[1]

So, bring along rational scrutiny and the critical lens discussed in Chapter 2, but combine it with a *charitable* gaze, an openness to seeing the world differently, not just from our own social norms and cultural background, values, and beliefs. We cannot separate ourselves from these, but we can be sensitive to our own ethnocentric perspectives (*ethnocentrism* is a worry in tourism impacts textbooks—do look it up if you're not familiar with it). The first part of the chapter continues the discussion on building capabilities that was commenced in Chapter 2. It then goes on to examine *recognition* and *difference*, introducing a couple of theoretical approaches to social justice. In addition to the various stories that weave through Chapter 3 is a case contributed by Blanca Camargo on the Palenquera women of Colombia, plus a case study by Jeff Wahl on diverse commemorations at Little Bighorn Battlefield, USA.

Reclaiming the Local: Building Capabilities

If you've flown into Hawai'i on a sunny day, the image of a string of emerald green dots nestling in a vast sea reflecting crisp blue skies may spring to mind as you read this. Memories come flooding back (good and not so good sometimes), connecting you in a flash to the places you visited there. This is part of the magic of travel and tourism—it makes the world a smaller place as many things in everyday life back home can suddenly make you pause to recall something from that recent or long-ago trip. For Hawai'i, you may recall those golden sands and surfing/snorkeling fun, that informative tour of sacred sites and their spiritual meanings to the islanders, watching the sunrise on Mount Haleakala, visiting the Iolani Palace, participating in one of many traditional cultural events, or sampling Native Hawaiian foods like *poi* (cooked, mashed, taro root). You may even recall the little sign on one of the lava fields that says, "It's bad luck to take lava rock away with you." Or the other rather ominous sign that said to beware of volcanic activity! Layered together with those fascinating lava formations and green canopies is a rich, dark, and complex history.

After massive depopulation through various diseases after Captain Cooke and his crew arrived in 1798, followed by loss of political and socioeconomic independence, shattering of Indigenous worldviews and cultural traditions, Hawai'i is now experiencing a cultural revival which commenced in the late 1960s (Salzman & Halloran, 2004). There is much healing to do, addressing cultural trauma and extensive physical health disorders as well as social fragmentation with the collapse of traditional religion, ancient Polynesian beliefs and customs, etc. (Salzman & Halloran, 2004). A trip in 2004 to gather information on a sustainable tourism initiative Hawai'i had just undertaken led me to a sobering realization. Many local workers were carrying two to three jobs just to make ends meet. Cost of living and rising land prices made affordability a severe issue without a living wage. So why not engage more with community-based tourism to help provide direct economic benefits, involving local residents directly in sharing stories and experiences related to food, cultural traditions and customs, etc.? A crucial consideration, as I learned

Diversity and Recognition **65**

then, is that residents and local people *have to be ready physically and emotionally to extend hospitality*. This can sometimes be a slow and lengthy process till the community is strong and resilient, and able to gain or retain control over its natural and cultural goods (see Apo, 2004).

Emotionally ready? I had given little thought to this until then, but you can see the wisdom in Mr. Apo's words (he was the Director of the Native Hawaiian Authority then). Like the historical colonization they had undergone, Native Hawaiians have had to "react" to the relentless assimilationist pressures of modern mass tourism, driven exogenously (from outside Hawai'i), changing land-use values, appropriating and commodifying their natural and cultural heritage, enveloping all within the dominant discourse of late modernity's market capitalism. It was a textbook example of *neocolonialism* through tourism. Britton's (1982) analysis of the political economy of tourism fits well here (do read it). Fortunately, an active cultural renaissance is offering opportunities for community-oriented tourism to be developed on their terms, endogenously (from within). Mr. Apo wrote out and shared his vision of what this meant. Community Tourism, he said, means *empowering communities to tell their own stories*:

> Community Tourism **is a *process* not a product**. It is a process whose planning must be inclusive of, understood by, and embraced by the general population of the place in which it occurs. It is for the most part small scale tourism whose planning and execution is driven by a genuine desire of a community willing to share itself, its history, traditions, and customs with strangers, as a means by which to support economic growth.
>
> Community Tourism initiatives are travel related offerings created and operated by local, traditional, or indigenous populations to enhance their quality of life, protect and restore their environmental and cultural assets and engage visitors on terms defined by the area's inhabitants. . . . It is a process that must yield a fair exchange of value between the host and the hosted, preserves the community's sense of place, and brings dignity and pride to the host.
>
> Community Tourism invites far more intimacy in the relationship between host and guest than is normally afforded by other tourism business models. **It generally features far more authentic and genuine activity for the guest, because it is activity that exists for its own sake and is not constructed specifically to entertain a stranger**. It is a community sharing its real culture by the people who practice it.
>
> Community Tourism **is a more sustainable business model**. Current models often result in creating more problems for a community than they solve, and can be particularly damaging to the culture, traditions and customs of the destination and its sense of place. [It] is about maintaining a direct connection between the host population and the visitor and minimizing the

66 Diversity and Recognition

> reliance on gate keeper systems of sales and marketing strategies that eventually separate the host from the hosted.
>
> It is about preserving the sense of place of a community by making the place, not the visitor, the center of care and attention, recognizing this as the best way to honor the visitor. . . .By making caring for the place the priority, you also preserve the customs, traditions, landscapes and history of the people who live there. What better way to welcome and honor a stranger than to present the community at its very best.
>
> Community Tourism is **a community celebrating its own greatness and inviting strangers to join the celebration**. . . . It is about honoring the past and connecting it to the future in a dynamic evolution of the living culture of the local population—celebrating where they came from, defining who they are in the present, and crafting new dreams that extend an unbroken persona of themselves into the future through their children. In the end, Community Tourism is about preserving the dignity of a people willing to open their hearts to strangers from other places (Apo, 2004).[2]

Examples Mr. Apo provided of engaging with this in Community Tourism included "walking tours, home and farm stays, storefront museums, recreational offerings, craft cooperatives, nature and wildlife treks, cultural performances, dining experiences, lectures on local culture and history, healing and health services, storytelling, etc." More than merely an economic development strategy, it can "promote cultural diversity and an understanding of tolerance, and generate more revenues for local businesses" (Apo, 2004). The Community Tourism Mr. Apo sketched out above in the Hawaiian experience seeks "fair exchange of value," and offers "activity that exists for its own sake," not products created for the sole purpose of generating money. There is a rich sense of *intrinsic value* in his approach, for the offerings are not oriented instrumentally to be merely commodities for sale.

Note, too, in the above, Mr. Apo's references to "dignity and pride" of the host, "care" and "caring" for place, "willing to open their hearts to strangers," and "welcome and honor a stranger." Compare his approach to some other community-based tourism (CBT) approaches and the cornucopia of principles and definitions related to CBT.[3] You may see terms like "capacity building," "local control," and "empowerment," but how well are the emotional resonance, care and concern that fill Mr. Apo's description represented? The endogenous approach he advocates puts *care* for place and people first. "What better way to welcome and honor a stranger. . .preserving the dignity of a people willing to open their hearts and minds to strangers. . .," said Mr. Apo above. However, he explained patiently, the community has to be ready *physically* and *emotionally* to extend hospitality. Without thoughtful attention to the historical and social-political context of the Kānaka Maoli (Native Hawaiians), it might be easy to miss the significance of his statement. Can *just hospitality* be extended without such emotional and physical readiness?

Williams and Gonzales (2017) question whether there is such a thing as *just hospitality* in a context of ongoing occupation and indigenous struggle for decolonization and de-occupation. Drawing upon French philosopher Jacques Derrida, they argue that sovereignty must limit hospitality—a just hospitality preserves the rights of hosts (Derrida, 2000). They also point out that Pacific genealogies of hospitality draw extensively on notions of reciprocity and situate the authority of hosts over their place. Mr. Apo's vision of Community Tourism seems to resonate with these views, and it is also situated in relations of care and concern about people and place. Thinking back to Chapter 2's discussion of social justice and the self-interested, autonomous subject of Rawls's justice as fairness (Rawls, 1971, 1996), his view of caring and concernful relationships does not seem to fit well with Rawls's liberal subject. And while distributive justice is certainly important, Mr. Apo's perspectives offer an opportunity to look at a richer picture of social justice. We start below with *building capabilities* and then go on to explore *recognition* and *difference* in relation to diversity and tourism.

The Capabilities Approach

Development theorists Amartya Sen and Martha Nussbaum forward a valuable people-centered "Human Development" approach, also referred to as "Capability Approach" or "Capabilities Approach." There are some differences in the way each of them approaches it, and we focus on here on Nussbaum's Capabilities Approach (she uses this term) which offers useful insights for small community-oriented tourism and larger destinations. She provides an ethical and evaluative approach to public policy and social justice, and addresses some important aspects that are missing in Rawls's influential theory of justice as fairness and relevant for tourism. Nussbaum (2006) criticizes Rawls's theory for not being able to address: (i) impairment and disability, (ii) global justice (Rawls's approach applies at the state level of a liberal society), and (iii) species membership (animals are excluded by Rawls). She retains liberal ideas of equal persons, equal respect, and the principle of reciprocity (but not the principle of mutual advantage present in Rawls's theory). Like Rawls, she develops a political conception of justice based on political liberalism. Her approach complements Rawls's approach, she states, but rather than the distribution of income and opportunities, the Capabilities Approach focuses on the individual's ability "to do and be":

> It holds that the key question to ask, when comparing societies and assessing them for their basic decency or justice, is: "What is each person able to do and be?" In other words, the approach takes each person as an end asking not just about the total or average well-being but about the opportunities available to each person (Nussbaum, 2011, p. 18).

Nussbaum develops her theory in *Women and Human Development: The Capabilities Approach* (2000) and *Frontiers of Justice* (2006). In addition, *Creating Capabilities: The*

68 Diversity and Recognition

Human Development Approach (2011) offers an accessible discussion. Capabilities, she says, answer the question of what each person is able to do and be. Capabilities are not the same as functionings, however. Capability means "opportunity to select" (Nussbaum, 2011, p. 25). For instance, the ability to vote is a capability, but voting is a functioning, i.e., it is an outcome of the capability. To promote capabilities is to promote areas of freedom, which is not the same as making people function in a particular way. Capabilities have value "in and of themselves, as spheres of freedom and choice"; people make their life choices by choosing from the set of capabilities apportioned to them, hence: "Options are freedoms, and freedom has intrinsic value" (Nussbaum, 2011, p. 25). The political goal of all human beings in a nation should be the same, she says, which is to get above a certain threshold level of combined capability, with substantial freedom to choose and act.[4] But what is the minimal threshold of capability necessary for a decent life that a "minimally just society" might be willing to facilitate? The Capabilities Approach asks:

> [A]mong the many things that human beings might develop the capacity to do, which ones are the really valuable ones, which are the ones that a minimally just society will endeavor to nurture and support? (Nussbaum, 2011, p. 28)

Respect and human dignity are central to answering this question. The basic idea is that "some living conditions deliver to people a life that is worthy of the human dignity that they possess, and others do not ... A focus on dignity is quite different, for example, from a focus on satisfaction" (Nussbaum, 2011, p. 30). Moral values of *equal dignity* and *equal respect for people's dignity* guide the concept of *well-being* in her approach as a "dignified and minimally flourishing life" enabled by a set of ten Central Capabilities:

> What does a life worthy of human dignity require? At a bare minimum, an ample threshold level of ten Central Capabilities is requires. Given a widely shared understanding of the task of government (namely, that government has the job of making people able to pursue a dignified and minimally flourishing life), it follows that a decent political undertaking must secure to all citizens at least a threshold level of these ten Central Capabilities... (Nussbaum, 2011, pp. 32–33).

Nussbaum argues for ten Central Capabilities that are important for the idea of a life that accords with human dignity, i.e., so that life is not so impoverished as to not be worthy of dignity as a human being (Nussbaum, 2006). These are: 1. Life; 2. Bodily health; 3. Bodily Integrity; 4. Senses, imagination and thought; 5. Emotions; 6. Practical reason; 7. Affiliation; 8. Other species; 9. Play; 10. Control over one's environment (Nussbaum, 2011, pp. 33–34). Let us look at a few aspects here (it would be good to read all ten Central Capabilities in your own time). As she explains in *Creating Capabilities* (2011), the Central Capability listed as "Emotions" includes having attachments to people and things, to love, to grieve, to experience longing, gratitude, etc. "Not having one's emotional development blighted by fear and anxiety" is important too, which means supporting forms of human association that are important to the development of this capability (2011, p. 34). By "Other species," she means "[b]eing able to live with concern for and in relation to animals, plants, and the world of nature" (2011, p. 34). The capability related to "Control over one's environment," includes political aspects like having the right to political participation and material dimensions, e.g., having the right to seek employment on a mutual basis with others (2011, p. 34). This approach accords with compassion and benevolence, as well as care and respect (for animals as well as human beings for it recognizes their dignity too). By "Play" she means: "Being able to laugh, to play, to be able to enjoy recreational activities" (2011, p. 35). The list can be applied globally, not just to a liberal society, she says, and can be implemented at the local level to take account of local particularities (additional capabilities can be added there as needed). While all ten capabilities are essential rights and all "citizens" are due a threshold amount of all these to choose to pursue, they may be apportioned differently in different social systems.[5] Individuals can tailor the set of universal capabilities to their own lives.

Martha Nussbaum thus offers an ethical and a political approach to building capabilities that can be applied locally and globally. There is room for a Rawlsian "overlapping consensus" between the comprehensive moral conceptions people may hold and the core moral and social entitlements in the Capabilities Approach (recall the Chapter 2 discussion on Rawls). The list of capabilities can be used to evaluate human rights abuses, inequality, and other injustices (including toward animals/other sentient beings). And it can be tailored to specific, particular needs and situations worldwide that comport with its principles. However, it is only a partial conception of justice; it cannot address how inequalities might be treated above the minimum threshold level, nor can it evaluate the procedural justice of the process (Nussbaum, 2006, 2011). Nonetheless, it offers an evaluative standard for policy oriented to poverty alleviation and improving livelihoods and well-being in areas where minimum threshold levels of well-being have not been achieved.

As such, the Capabilities Approach is relevant to consider for all tourism destinations, not just for approaches like Pro-Poor Tourism. The ten Central Capabilities include "Emotions" which could be particularly helpful for addressing aspects like cultural trauma and post-traumatic stress in postcolonial places. If you believe that one important task of government (at least a liberal one) is "raising all citizens above the threshold on all ten capabilities" (Nussbaum, 2011, p. 109), then it would seem an argument can be made that public revenues from hotel and motel taxes and other tourism related sources in a destination should be equitably apportioned to provide *all* "citizens" a threshold level of capabilities (rather than a disproportionate amount going toward marketing

70 Diversity and Recognition

and promotion).[6] Of course, fair or equitable distribution of benefits can quickly become an issue if influential stakeholders at the destination demand a far greater proportion of its redistribution for reasons other than building capabilities, e.g., for public infrastructure to support new luxury attractions, etc. A brief look at Responsible Tourism is interesting to undertake in light of the above discussion.

Building Capabilities Through Responsible Tourism?

> Accepting that, in the words of the Global Code of Ethics, an attitude of tolerance and respect for the diversity of religious, philosophical and moral beliefs, are both the foundation and the consequence of responsible tourism (ICRT [International Conference on Responsible Tourism in Destinations], 2002).

The *South African Guidelines for Responsible Tourism* were presented at the International Conference on Responsible Tourism in Destinations (ICRTD) in Cape Town, South Africa, just prior to the World Summit on Sustainable Development in Johannesburg in 2002. This Cape Town Conference was facilitated by the Responsible Tourism Partnership and Western Cape Tourism. Conference delegates examined and field-tested the guidelines that had been developed through a national consultative process. The resulting Cape Town Declaration on Responsible Tourism presented guidelines to shape sustainable tourism in South Africa. It acknowledged that different destinations would have different priorities, so while the principles had potential to be applied elsewhere, locally situated policies and guidelines would need to be tailored from them with the help of collaborative, multi-stakeholder processes. Generally, Responsible Tourism embraces the following characteristics (ICRT [International Conference on Responsible Tourism in Destinations], 2002):

- minimises negative economic, environmental, and social impacts;
- generates greater economic benefits for local people and enhances the well-being of host communities, improves working conditions and access to the industry;
- involves local people in decisions that affect their lives and life chances;
- makes positive contributions to the conservation of natural and cultural heritage, to the maintenance of the world's diversity;
- provides more enjoyable experiences for tourists through more meaningful connections with local people, and a greater understanding of local cultural, social, and environmental issues;
- provides access for physically challenged people;
- and is culturally sensitive, engenders respect between tourists and hosts, and builds local pride and confidence.

The declaration called on countries, destinations, multilateral agencies and enterprises to develop similar practical guidelines, and to "encourage planning authorities, tourism businesses, tourists and local communities—to take responsibility for achieving sustainability, and to create better places for people to live in and people to visit" (ICRT, 2002). Reading through the Cape Town Declaration, its goals and guidelines on the Responsible Tourism Partnership's website (see website in ICRT (2002) in the References section), you will notice synergies with Mr. Apo's Community Tourism vision and with Martha Nussbaum's Capabilities Approach. All three of these approaches address the well-being of those who live and work in the places visited by tourists. As Mr. Apo expressed so well, residents and local people *have to be ready physically and emotionally to extend hospitality.* The Capabilities Approach offers an evaluative framework for a minimum threshold level of individual well-being facilitated by the ten Central Capabilities. At the very least, these capabilities have to be assured in order to commence a conversation about the prudence and necessity of developing or diversifying into tourism and how to do this responsibly, with care and thoughtfulness to the historical and social context.

Nussbaum's Capabilities Approach also addresses well-being with respect to non-human others, which needs closer attention in responsible tourism and in tourism studies overall (see Fennell, 2012, 2014). Central Capability 8 is: "Being able to live with concern for and in relation to animals, plants, and the world of nature" (Nussbaum, 2011, p. 34). There are many social and cultural issues to be addressed here, including intangible relationships that may easily be missed (intangible in the sense of invisible and not measurable, hence of less interest to those wanting quantifiable impacts). They include social as well as cultural relationships like spiritual relationships and traditional relationships that are woven intricately with land, nature, and the biophysical world. What issues arise when relationships of concern and care are broken, both with respect to affiliations with each other, and with nonhuman others? How do minority, historically oppressed, diverse cultural groups and communities of color obtain recognition and resources to develop capabilities, protect and conserve goods and relationships that are important to their well-being, and *when ready* (think of Mr. Apo's principle of readiness), engage in tourism development for mutual well-being of the "hosts," "guests," and the social-ecological systems that sustain them? The next section looks at social justice with respect to personal and political *recognition*, including recognition of *difference*.

Recognition and Difference

Martha Nussbaum's Capabilities Approach offers an alternative view to social justice for the allocation and distribution of societal goods, but it is partial as noted above. Feminist philosophers as well as other political theorists and philosophers, have forwarded various perspectives on justice that offer rich insights and can

72 Diversity and Recognition

further our understandings of the role of tourism in enabling or helping to redress various injustices. Let us look specifically at two approaches that relate to diverse groups and individuals: Justice as recognition and the recognition of difference. To commence, journey to Colombia with Blanca Camargo and see how the Afro-Colombian people in Case 3.1 are faring. What issues do the Palenquera women face in Case 3.1? Are they seen as equals in Colombian society? Are they being treated with *respect*? Why are they not deemed worthy of *equal dignity* and *recognition* for who they are? What role does tourism play here? A critique of *ethnocentrism* would be fair to raise, i.e., tourists and service providers are viewing or judging other groups and cultures from their own beliefs, norms, and values, leading them to perceive the other as morally inferior. But more is at stake here than simply an attitude of moral superiority.

Case 3.1: Palenqueras in Colombia: A Case of Cultural Injustice in Tourism

Blanca Alejandra Camargo

Introduction

After severe security problems caused by drug trafficking, political upheaval, and guerrillas and paramilitary presence in vast areas of the country, international tourism in Colombia is flourishing. From about 622,000 international tourists per year in the late 90s, visitation increased annually since 2006, reaching 3.2 million international tourists in 2017 (CITUR, 2018). Cartagena, located on the northern Caribbean coast, is one of the main destinations for these tourists, who are attracted by its rich colonial history and architecture, and flourishing Caribbean culture. In 1984 the historic center of Cartagena was declared World Intangible Heritage by UNESCO as "an eminent example of the military architecture of the 16th, 17th, and 18th centuries, the most extensive of the New World and one of the most complete" (UNESCO World Heritage Centre, n.d.). Cartagena was also one of the most important ports during colonial times in the Americas where thousands of slaves who arrived from Africa were traded. Slaves who escaped from the port founded small communities or *palenques* in remote areas where they developed their own economic, social and cultural structures. Of all the palenques in Latin America, only San Basilio de Palenque (henceforth referred as Palenque), located approximately 40 miles from Cartagena survives to this day. Thanks to its intangible socio-cultural heritage that has been preserved since colonial times (see Camargo & Lawo-Sukam, 2015) and its historic significance, Palenque was declared a UNESCO Masterpiece of the Oral and Intangible Heritage of Humanity in 2005. However, poverty and marginalization has forced almost half of the Palenqueros to migrate to Cartagena and Barranquilla, another important city in the Caribbean coast of Colombia. Palenquera women, known as Palenqueras, became maids or sold corn buns on the streets. Recently, the Palenqueras have become part of the touristic landscape of Cartagena (see Photo 3.1.1).

PHOTO 3.1.1 Palenquera selling fruits to tourists
Credit: Blanca Camargo

Palenqueras in Cartagena: Two Realities

Palenqueras have become a tourist icon in Cartagena and abroad. They can be seen wearing colorful dresses and selling fruits and traditional sweets in almost every corner of the walled city. Eroticized and exoticized representations of them are sold in souvenir stores throughout the city (Photo 3.1.2); and their image is used in tourism brochures, websites, and blogs (Photo 3.1.3). But behind the smiles of these happy looking women hides another reality. Despite their World Heritage designation, Palenque (pop. 3,762 in 2007) is one of the most isolated, marginalized and impoverished communities in the state: 76.7% of its residents lives below the poverty line; 50.4% do not have access to water and sewage services, and 50% of household heads are illiterate, among other indicators (PNUD, 2007). The town also lacks political autonomy and is considered a subdivision of the bigger town of Mahates. Rodriguez Morales (2010) called attention to the statistical invisibility of Afro-Colombian populations as a form of structural racism that hinders the recognition of their rights and ability to influence public policies to improve their well-being.

74 Diversity and Recognition

PHOTO 3.1.2　Palenquera figurines sold in souvenir shops in Cartagena
　　　　　　Credit: Blanca Camargo

PHOTO 3.1.3　Palenquera in the 2017 national tourism campaign "Colombia
　　　　　　the Land of Sabrosura"
　　　　　　Credit: Colombia Travel website, accessed May 30, 2018

　　Poverty and armed conflict in the 1990s caused mass migration of Palenqueros to other cities where they have suffered discrimination, racism, and cultural ridiculing from fellow Colombians, in particular the white elites (Hidalgo Arango & Pérez Caballero, 2016). Their cultural manifestations, recognized as World Intangible Heritage since 2005, were seen as backward and uncivilized (Restrep & Pérez, 2005, p. 205). It resulted in parents discouraging their children from speaking the Palenquero language and engaging in traditional activities. The UNESCO declaration has brought attention to the community; initiatives to preserve their culture and improve their socio-economic well-being, among them ethnic tourism, were initiated but they have yet to bring tangible benefits.

Cultural Inequities in Tourism Marketing

While Cartagena and its tourism stakeholders benefit from the Palenqueras, the women have received very little in return. Their income, which fluctuates with the tourist season, depends on the sales of fruits and sweets and the tips they get from tourists after posing for a picture. They receive no economic compensation from the use of highly essentialized, stereotypic images of them or their culture in various touristic media; several Palenqueras mentioned during informal on-site conversations how often people tell them they saw pictures of them in brochures, magazines, posters and other media, pictures they did not consent to be used or distribute for any purpose. They also lack government sponsored health care and social security, as they are part of the informal economy of Cartagena. Furthermore, conflict has arisen because women from other Afro-Colombian groups posing as Palenqueras are taking their place in key tourist locations of Cartagena (Diaz, 2008).

While the commodification and promotion of Palenquera women and their images to international visitors is highly visible, the existence of the Palenque as an Afro-Colombian ethnic group is almost invisible in the tourism scene of Cartagena. There is little promotion of Palenque as a tourist destination in local, state or national tourism campaigns. Palenque does not appear in the maps, tourism brochures, or tourism information centers in the city for tourists interested in visiting the village. All the development promises from the government are yet to be seen, and the community is exhausted from being seen as a source of information for anthropologists, NGOs, and other national and international culture stakeholders (Camargo & Lawo-Sukam, 2015).

Concluding Remarks

Palenqueros are strong, resilient, and their spirit and identity have helped them survive to this day. Aware of the interest they generate among national and international tourists, and tired of being treated like a tourist commodity, they do exert agency to increase their benefit from tourism and protect their cultural heritage. Palenqueras resist economic and cultural inequality by

76 Diversity and Recognition

charging tourists hefty prices for the fruit they sell, refusing to answer questions about themselves or their culture, or requesting tips from tourists for pictures (Photo 3.1.4). They have also founded an association to protect their rights and cultural identity. In the village, they have mobilized to develop ethnic tourism *on their own terms*, with many growing pains but also positive benefits for the community and its culture (see Obezo Casseres, 2013 for more).

PHOTO 3.1.4   A Palenquera fruit stand displaying the message "to take a picture with us collaborate by purchasing a fruit or leaving a tip" (translated for clarity)
Credit: Blanca Camargo

References

Camargo, B. A., & Lawo-Sukam, A. (2015). San Basilio de Palenque (re)visited: African heritage, tourism, and development in Colombia. *Afro-Hispanic Review, 34*(1), 25–45.

CITUR (Centro de Información Turística). (2018). Estadísticas Nacionales. Retrieved March 30, 2018, from http://citur.linktic.com/estadisticas/ver/index/19#menu

Diaz, J. C. (2008). Palenqueras falsas aprovechan ahora la fama de las originales. Retrieved April 11, 2018, from http://www.eltiempo.com/archivo/documento/MAM-3103959

Hidalgo Arango, S. L., & Pérez Caballero, A. J. (2016). Rescate de saberes ancestrales: la revitalización de la lengua palenquera por la comunidad de San Basilio de Palenque. *Aguaita*, (28/29), 67–76.

Obezo Casseres, K. G. (2013). *Turismo, patrimonio y etnicidad: Dinámicas del turismo étnico cultural en San Basilio de Palenque*. Universidad Tecnológica de Bolivar, Cartagena, Columbia.

PNUD (Programa de Naciones Unidas para el Desarrollo). (2007). *San Basilio del Palenque: Frente a los Objetivos de Desarrollo del Milenio*. Retrieved from https://www.cepal.org/MDG/noticias/paginas/6/44336/Palenque_final.pdf

Restrep, E., & Pérez, J. N. (2005). San Basilio de Palenque: caracterizaciones y riesgos del patrimonio intangible. *Janwa Pana: Revista Del Programa de Antropología de La Universidad Del Magdalena*, (4), 58–69.

Rodríguez Morales, M. M. (2010). The statistical invisibility of black, Afro-Colombian and Palenque-rooted populations in Colombia. *Trabajo Social*, (12), 89–99.

UNESCO World Heritage Centre. (n.d.). Port, fortresses and group of monuments, Cartagena. Retrieved March 30, 2018, from http://whc.unesco.org/en/list/285/

(Mis)Recognition Through Tourism

Lest we forget due to all this serious talk about justice and ethics, pause for a moment and think of the many good things have happened during your travels elsewhere. Was your grandmother happy to see you after so many weeks or months (years?) had elapsed since your last visit? Did you decide to become a biologist after diving in Belize or wandering meadows and fields not far away? Perhaps you are recalling that small community you visited in a rural region that made you so nostalgic because small mom and pop businesses greeted you cheerily with the same hospitality you were accustomed to in your childhood—everyone knew everyone in the little town you grew up in! Many environmental, economic, social and cultural benefits are possible through travel and tourism,

78 Diversity and Recognition

ranging widely from cross-cultural learning, peace and solidarity, to *sustainable livelihoods* and environmental conservation (see Mbaiwa & Stronza, 2010; Scheyvens, 2002). Consider, too, opportunities for empowerment of diverse groups, women, and vulnerable populations. As an example, Ateljevic and Doorne (2003) studied practices related to traditionally produced tie-dye fabrics for tourist consumption by groups of local Bai women working for the Zhoucheng village factory cooperative in the Dali area of Yunnan Province, China. This activity facilitated cultural heritage conservation, as well as social engagement, economic reward and opportunity for the women to participate in "broader and more active interpersonal and community relations, beyond the extended family household" (Ateljevic & Doorne, 2003, p. 130). Poverty alleviation and women's empowerment are evident in Tucker and Boonabana's (2012) study of gender relations and community run tourism initiatives by the Bakiga people in Mukono parish, Kanungu District, in southwestern Uganda. Married women employed in various tourism enterprises had to negotiate permission and approval from their husbands, and deal with related issues of trust and suspicion as they ventured out of the household space and interacted with visitors. Attitudes changed as income-generating benefits arrived, however, and the women began to receive recognition and appreciation:

> [B]ecause local men are beginning to appreciate women's development efforts, some men and parents are beginning to relax their negative attitudes towards their wives and daughters working in tourism. Women are being seen to significantly improve not only their own personal situation but also that of their household, and even that of their neighbors through the provision and sharing of basic household items, such as salt, soap and sugar. One woman commented, "Most families here are surviving on the power of women. Actually, that's why we thank tourism so much." (Tucker & Boonabaana, 2012, p. 448)

Tucker and Boonabaana's research shows the importance of a more nuanced study of groups and gendered relationships, including between the men and women above, within groups (families) and overall in the community. Examples such as the above are a reminder of the central role of dignity and respect in the Capabilities Approach discussed earlier, where securing a threshold level of ten Central Capabilities helps to enable a life worthy of the human dignity that people possess (Nussbaum, 2006, 2011). Among the ten Central Capabilities, the seventh one is Affiliation, which includes:

(A) Being able to live with and towards others; to recognize and show concern for other human beings, to engage in various forms of social interaction; to be able to imagine the situation of another...

(B) Having the social basis of self-respect and non-humiliation; being able to be treated as a dignified being whose worth is equal to that of others. This entails provisions of nondiscrimination on the basis of race, sex, sexual orientation, ethnicity, caste, religion, national origin (Nussbaum, 2011, p. 34).

Tourism seems to be empowering the Bakiga women in the Mukono parish study economically and in their social relationships within the family and community. But are the Afro-Colombian Palenqueras in Case 3.1 being treated with equal dignity, respect, and recognition of equal worth? They are a small, vulnerable population group with a high level of poverty and social inequalities. Historically entrenched discrimination plays out in social processes (e.g. in everyday interactions between the Palenqueros people and the Colombian elites) and in institutional structures (notice various examples of this in Case 3.1). Tourism's role is not insignificant here. The Palenqueras receive little in terms of redistribution of the income generated by the commodification and sale of their cultural representations by others, including in tourism related media. Stereotyped and fetishized, they exist as a colorful, exotic symbol in the tourist imaginary—almost *invisible* as a social group in Colombian society and generally disrespected by fellow Colombians (Camargo & Lawo-Sukam, 2015). While they attempt to actively resist domination and exploitation, their efforts for self-determination, legitimation and inclusion in tourism mirror similar struggles overall in their social world (at the societal level). Let us delve into this doubly thorny challenge by posing two questions:

1. Is *fair distribution* of tourism-related income and opportunities, and *fair compensation* (see Whyte, 2010) for the use of their cultural images sufficient?
2. What else is needed to overcome subordination and subservience to tourism interests, and the fetishizing and commodification of their cultural images and cultural goods?

Commodity fetishism, as Mowforth and Munt (2016, p. 66) explain this Marxist term, is:

> a concept that embodies the way in which commodities hide the social relations of those that have contributed to the production of that commodity (be it a good or bad experience) from the consumer (such as the tourist). In a nutshell, tourists are generally unaware of the conditions of life experienced by the waiters, cooks, tour guides and so on, the people who service their holidays and the other people who form part of their tourist gaze.

So an important task might be to reveal the social relations that contribute to producing the commodities, commodified relationships and injustices, and seek strategies for fair compensation, fair trade, and fair treatment. Good tourism enabled through fair trade tourism, social enterprise, homestays, experiential

80   Diversity and Recognition

marketing (carefully!) and other approaches that aim to facilitate equity and fairness would also seek ways in which relationships between tourists and "hosts" can be humanized, equalized in respect and dignity, and treated with care and concern. *Visibility* and *recognition* of diverse cultural groups in the touristic space could help to generate resources for capacity building and cultural protection through *redistribution* of tourism related revenues and income (see further below). It could also help to advance political recognition, e.g., self-determination, participation in public decision making, procedural justice, as well as social recognition—equal respect by fellow citizens and tourists and inclusiveness at a societal level, such as in community gatherings, recreational events, public celebrations, local festivals, etc.

However, the very same places and spaces that holds so much potential for justice and good practices in tourism are also subject to pitfalls of abuse and injustice. The "tourism system" is highly dynamic, interrelated with other systems locally to globally, and embedded in historical processes that continue to shape its form and structure in the present day. Case 2.2 in Chapter 2 and Case 3.1 above show how injustices such as misrecognition and maldistribution (to use Nancy Fraser's terms, see further below) are related to the *context* and *history* of the destination. Deconstructing the relationship between tourism, capitalism, and colonialism as well as imperialism is critical to understanding historically and institutionally entrenched oppression and domination of minority ethnic and Indigenous populations in tourism destinations. Modern mass tourism flourished and expanded from the European metropole centers, playing a complex role in the global expansion of political and economic power through colonialism and imperialism (political and also cultural imperialism—think of Pablo's comments in regard to his children). Directly or indirectly, tourism related processes have played a significant role in the economic exploitation and appropriation of foreign land and resources, and in facilitating a dominant discourse of market capitalism worldwide that depends on growing markets and mass consumption (Mowforth & Munt, 2016). The examples below look at some of these relationships and processes, and related issues of social justice. As you can guess, now is a good time to put on that critical and charitable hat, being open to possibilities of seeing the landscape of travel and tourism just a little bit differently.

Justice as Recognition

A tour guide at Chichen Itzá (Mayan World Heritage Site) once mentioned that a good number of visitors seemed unaware that the Maya are a living culture. His wistful expression echoed a similar sentiment heard in the quiet words of an Indigenous woman at the Tjapukai Aboriginal Cultural Park, Cairns, Australia. She wished visitors to their cultural site understood that the Djabugay people continued to live on. She didn't want visitors to feel bad after exiting the film room that showed some of their "dark" history, nor did she seek apologies for being taken away as a child and put in a mission school. But it *was* important that

Diversity and Recognition **81**

they understood that the Djabugay are alive today. For her, *recognition* (being acknowledged as a living cultural group, as Djabugay) mattered. At this successful cultural center, tourists can interact directly with its Traditional Owners. The cultural center's website mentions that the site is wheelchair and pram friendly, their performers demonstrate their culture with "immense pride," and the center's revenues benefit the local Indigenous community:

> Tjapukai is the largest Indigenous employer of any tourism enterprise in Australia with more than two-thirds of the team Indigenous. Tjapukai works in consultation with Traditional Owners and has injected in excess of $35 million into the local Indigenous community through wages, royalties, and the commissioning and purchasing of authentic art and artifacts (Tjapukai Aboriginal Cultural Park, n.d.).

A young Australian woman during a tour at a different Indigenous site, the Dreamtime Cultural Center in Rockhampton, Australia, mentioned she was taking the tour because her high school history said little about the Aboriginal people of her country. She wanted to learn more. Tourism can potentially contribute to cultural conservation and civic education at such cultural centers, offering visibility and recognition to groups that may be suffering discrimination, racism, dispossession, marginalization, or other forms of social and political exclusion. Direct involvement and control over the cultural experiences and knowledge being shared by the cultural group is crucial here, to prevent exploitation and inappropriate use of cultural symbols and goods. Face-to-face interaction with the Indigenous owners also opens different possibilities for healing and reconciliation through dialogue and learning, quite aside from formal mechanisms of restorative justice like Truth and Reconciliation Commissions. For instance, Strange and Kempa (2003) point to the reconciliatory and nation-building purpose of Robben Island, South Africa, where Nelson Mandela and many other anti-apartheid political prisoners had been incarcerated. Commemorated as a museum and inscribed as a UNESCO World Heritage Site in 1999, the site symbolized civil peace and values of the nation building enterprise that was under way, including struggle, hope, resistance and reconciliation in the fledgling democracy (Strange & Kempa, 2003).

But tourism can also contribute to continuing or possibly exacerbating injustices. The case of the Palenquera and the example below of Indigenous women workers in the hop fields around Puget Sound, Washington, USA, indicate a complex relationship between institutionally entrenched racism, colonialism, and the distribution of environmental and social goods as well as tourism goods in society. Redressing these historically engrained injustices and inequalities can involve seeking various mechanisms (e.g., laws prohibiting discrimination and racism, repatriation of Indigenous goods, reparations, restorative justice) and social justice approaches for *recognition* and *inclusion* in political and social processes, such as Nancy Fraser and Iris Marion Young, among others, forward (Fraser, 2010;

82 Diversity and Recognition

Young, 2011). Let us journey back to a moment in history, late 19th century in the hop fields of northwestern USA, to get a sense of these issues and then discuss justice as *recognition* a bit further.

> In the late nineteenth century, thousands of Indigenous women journeyed hundreds of miles annually along the Pacific Northwest coast and converged around Puget Sound. They came to pick hops in the fields of farmers who occupied lands in western Washington.... These women were also independent vendors and craft workers. On their way to and from the harvest, they sold baskets and mats, beadwork and carvings, clams, game, and skins and pelts. A tourist boom grew up around the Puget Sound hop harvest... (Raibmon, 2006, p. 23).

These Indigenous hop pickers were primarily women. Crowded in temporary hop camps, their living conditions suffered, with sanitation issues plus epidemic diseases exerting a high mortality rate on the children and infants they brought along. As Paige Raibmon explains, nineteenth-century observers and labor historians failed to recognize them as workers or wage earners; in the colonial binary of "traditional" (culture) and "modern" (worker), they were put into the former and the term "Indian worker" was an oxymoron (Raibmon, 2006).

> Much like British Columbia, its neighbor to the north, late-nineteenth-century and early-twentieth-century Washington was in the throes of the most colonial of processes: the appropriation of land and resources and the dispossession of Indigenous peoples. This was nothing new. Settler societies relied upon turning Indigenous properties into capital through alienating Indigenous people from the means of production.... To be sure, Indigenous people often entered the wage economy for their own reasons and of their own volition. At the same time, however, it is undeniable that colonial usurpation of hereditary lands and resources steadily narrowed the range of Indigenous economic choices (Raibmon, 2006).

Settler colonialism as a strategy of imperialism or colonialism facilitated the ability of the colonizing's state's own people to take up residence on land being occupied or used by native populations (who, of course had their own relationships with the land, not western notions of property ownership). Depicting them as inferior provided easy justification for dislocating and exploiting them. As settler appropriation of Indigenous land and resources advanced in the Pacific northwest, income from selling finely hand-crafted needlework, beadwork, baskets and blankets ("curios" was the dismissive touristic label) on the city sidewalks on the way home was a welcome supplement to meager hop picking wages (Raibmon, 2006). Among the tourists who arrived in throngs during the hop season to satisfy their curiosity about the rapidly declining Indigenous populations, were middle-class white women tourists who purchased the "curios" to adorn their living rooms and took Kodak photographs. These were seen as markers of taste and privilege, symbolizing a bourgeois identity affiliated with a dominant modern nation (Raibmon, 2006). By contrast, the Indigenous women were a spectacle to gaze upon and "consume" in different ways; their cultural identity was constituted by tourists, writers, photographers, advertisers, and other media as needed for bourgeois self-expression and continued justification for industrial capital development and appropriation of Indigenous lands, resources, and labor:

> Writers characterized Indian women as "stolid," "stoic," "sluggish," and nearly inanimate "ornaments," barely capable of displaying human emotion or attending to the "papoose" in the crooks of their arms...In denying the existence of these women's emotional lives, accounts situated them in opposition to the emotionality of so-called real women, like those who tastefully consumed the products that they produced (Raibmon, 2006).

The story of the women hop-pickers and how they are constituted under the settler colonial gaze is illuminating, revealing complex relationships between capital, land, colonialism, and tourism. Tourism in this late nineteenth century context operated through micro-practices of *everyday life* through relationships and activities of daily life, labor, and touristic encounters on the city streets. But its effects continued even at home, e.g., through the cultural accouterments and souvenirs displayed by the women tourists. This insight is valuable even today with respect to the critique of tourism as *neocolonialism* (think of modern mass tourism's power, control, and exploitation of a destination's economic and social-cultural wealth, particularly on poorer countries through international tourism).[7] A study of tourism even today needs to be watchful of such "everyday colonialism" (Raibmon, 2006), operating through the intersections and interstices of tourism in everyday life of work and leisure.[8] As discussed in the next section, issues of cultural identity and *cultural survival* arise in the context of diverse groups and vulnerable populations that have been subject to colonization (sometimes multiple layers of it), and who exist today in neocolonized touristic places and spaces.

The Politics of Recognition

The personal *is* political, as feminist theorists have pointed out, and there is so much to be learned from them with respect to gender, sexuality, ethnicity, discourse and power, etc. Alas, with limited space we will only touch lightly on some issues and discuss social justice in relation to *recognition* and *difference*. It will hopefully stimulate you to explore the rich, interdisciplinary literature available to inform tourism studies. So, a question (pop quiz?) to start:

> How do cultural media and entertainment venues (e.g., film, televisions, music festivals, etc.) contribute to recognition or misrecognition of cultural groups?

84 Diversity and Recognition

Here are a couple of "hints" to help contemplate the above question:

i. Beyoncé performed at the 2018 Coachella music festival in Indio, California, on April 14 to adoring, screaming fans: "Coachella, thank you for allowing me to be the first black woman to headline," Beyoncé said, before singing "Run the World (Girls)" (Chavez, 2018).
ii. Think also about how pop culture shapes racial and ethnic representations. The documentary film *The Problem with Apu* (2017) argues that Apu Nahasapeemapetilon (representing an Indian convenience store owner) in *The Simpsons* is a caricature, stereotyping South Asians in a way that increased their vulnerability to racial discrimination, to being mocked, bullied, marginalized, etc.[9] Remember that the viewers of the popular animated television series *The Simpsons* are not simply residents—they are tourists or visitors wherever they travel on holiday, and their cultural understandings, beliefs and values travel with them too.

Critical theorist Nancy Fraser contributes to social and political theory as well as feminist theory. She offers some valuable guidance to help bridge the discussion started in Chapter 2 on distributive justice to the social and cultural issues being raised in Chapter 3. She presents a *political* approach to social justice that encompasses both distributive justice and the politics of recognition. It is not one or the other; in fact it would be a mistake to separate economic and social-cultural domains, for instance, address class politics and class-based economic maldistribution of societal goods as separate from identity politics that include struggles over gender, sexuality, ethnicity and "race" (Fraser, 2010; see also Fraser & Honneth, 2003). Both are distinctive perspectives on social justice and should be assessed jointly. Seen this way, distributive justice issues would include socioeconomic injustices within the economic structures of society (e.g., labor exploitation and deprivation of adequate material standards of living, employment practices related to gender and sexual orientation, etc.). Solutions to these could seek the *redistribution* of societal goods *and* necessary socio-economic transformations or reforms to address gender and racial-ethnic injustices (Fraser, 2003, 2010).

The possibility of social change is engendered by a *status model of recognition* that operates at the institutional level (which includes social institutions). "To view recognition as a matter of justice is to treat it as an issue of *social status*" (Fraser, 2003, p. 29). When institutionalized patterns of cultural value "constitute participants as peers, capable of engaging on par with each other in social life, then we can speak of *reciprocal recognition* and *social equality*" (p. 29). But when institutionalized norms and cultural values render some citizens as less than full partners in social interaction (e.g., as inferior, excluded, invisible), we should speak of *misrecognition* and *status subordination*, she says. The normative core of her approach is *parity of participation* where, as can be discerned above, "justice requires social arrangements that permit all (adult) members of society to interact with one another as peers" (Fraser, 2003, p. 36). Misrecognition and recognition arise when institutions structure interactions according to cultural norms that impede or facilitate *parity of participation* respectively.

Parity of participation encompasses both redistribution and recognition, the one is not reducible to the other. It is important to note the relationship between economy and culture here, which is clearly spelled out in her notion of *perspectival dualism*: "redistribution and recognition do not correspond to two substantive social domains, economy and culture. Rather, they constitute two analytical perspectives that can be assumed with respect to any domain" (Fraser, 2003, p. 63). One might examine, for instance, how redistributive policies related to hotel and motel tax income could address injustices related to the social status of gay and lesbian employees in the hospitality sector (e.g., being seen as less than peers in the social context). Her later work builds on this "bivalent" approach by adding a political dimension related to participation in the social and public sphere that results in a "trivalent" theory of social justice involving redistribution, recognition *and* representation in a globalizing world (Fraser, 2010). We will look at justice beyond borders in later chapters.

The politics of recognition as discussed by Nancy Fraser can be used to address cultural injustices related to *misrecognition* within a diverse range of movements (e.g., cultural feminism, black cultural nationalism, gay identity politics, queer politics, etc.). Cultural injustices are "presumed to be rooted in social patterns of representation, interpretation, and communication" and remedies would be oriented toward cultural or symbolic change, such as by recognizing cultural diversity, or "transforming wholesale societal patterns of representation, interpretation, and communication in ways that would change everyone's social identity" (Fraser, 2003, p. 13). Case 3.3 at the end of this chapter is a case study by Jeff Wahl on contestation and conflict over commemoration of the Battle of the Little Bighorn in 1876, known in the popular imagination as "Custer's Last Stand." Issues of recognition in this case may be helpful to contemplate in light of both Nancy Fraser's approach to social justice above and Iris Marion Young's perspective below.

Recognition of Difference

Especially important for justice is careful exploration of diversity and *difference* as they play out in social processes and institutional structures. Iris Marion Young, another proponent of justice as recognition, has her own criticisms of the dominant distributive paradigm in liberal welfare economies. For instance, a distributive conception of justice does not bring under scrutiny the institutional structures and social processes and relations in which misrecognition, maldistribution and other injustices may be embedded (Young, 2011). Like Nancy Fraser, her approach is political and institutional. But she situates justice within two important categories: oppression and domination. Injustice should be understood in terms of these two social conditions, which she believes holds for any social context worldwide, and for the relationship among nations or states. As described in *Justice and the Politics of Difference* (Young, 2011 originally published in 1990):

86 Diversity and Recognition

1. *Domination* refers to "the institutional constraint on self-determination" (p. 37) and is defined as a "lack of participation in determining one's actions and the conditions of one's actions" (p. 258).
2. Oppression is the "institutional constraint on self-development" (p. 37). She identifies "five faces of oppression" and points out they should be examined contextually rather than in isolation of social structures and processes, for example, in terms of *structural and systematic oppression*. The five faces of oppression described by Young (2011) are:

   - *Exploitation* (e.g., gender and labor exploitation);
   - *Marginalization* (e.g., as related to material deprivation by not being able to secure a job due to being elderly, a racial minority, or having a disability or a different sexual orientation);
   - *Powerlessness* (best described negatively, as she says: "the powerless lack the authority, status, and sense of self that professionals tend to have..." (p. 57));
   - *Cultural imperialism* (this "involves the universalization of a dominant group's experience and culture, and its establishment as the norm" (p. 59));
   - *Violence* (including physical violence, harassment, intimidation, etc. Important here is systematic violence embedded in social and institutional structures in a way "which makes them possible and even acceptable" in the social context surrounding them (p. 61)).

Can you identify any of the above faces of oppression in the example of the Indigenous women hop pickers discussed earlier? Under the face of *cultural* imperialism, says Iris Marion Young, subjected groups are paradoxically both marked out by *stereotype* and rendered invisible at the same time as being marked as different, e.g., deviant, inferior, etc. They are often vulnerable to discrimination, symbolic violence, and physical violence. Disempowered and marginalized, their ability to speak out or participate effectively in the public sphere, or in other social institutions that are relevant to their well-being is severely curtailed. The injustice of cultural imperialism is that "the oppressed group's own experience and interpretation of social life finds little expression that touches the dominant culture, while that same culture imposes on the oppressed group its experience and interpretation of social life" (Young, 2011, p. 60).

Both Nancy Fraser and Iris Marion Young are highly concerned about the recognition of group-specific *difference* and concerned with social and democratic representation of diverse groups. As we see further in Chapter 6, Iris Marion Young also discusses the importance of democratic participation in public and social institutes, and argues that democratic cultural pluralism requires a dual system of rights: a general system of rights plus group conscious policies and rights (specific to the cultural group), which can help enable social equality (Young, 2011, p. 174). Social equality as she means it does not refer to the distribution of social goods, though she is clear that distributions are a necessary aspect for social equality. Rather, social equality "refers primarily to the full participation and inclusion of everyone in a society's major institutions, and the socially supported substantive opportunity for all to develop and exercise their capacities and realize their choices" (Young, 2011, p. 173). Importantly, she also pays particular attention to difference within groups, not just between groups. Groups are *heterogeneous*, its members may have multiple group affiliations, their identities are partly constituted by these affiliations and relations, but each group member should be seen as an individual and *heterogeneous* too (Young, 2011, p. 48).

It would be a sad mistake to see a cultural group as homogenous and undifferentiated, or to simply extend "tolerance" to diverse ethnic groups in a multicultural society or destination. Individuals must be respected and valued for their own humanity. Their worldviews and experiences, their places and everyday lives matter, their quality of life and well-being matter, as much as ours do to each of us. Read Case 3.2 below with thoughtful attention to the discussion above on recognition and difference, keeping in mind the *politics* of recognition and difference.

Case 3.2: "A Teardrop on the Cheek of Time" in Agra, India

Tazim Jamal

How does one describe the Taj Mahal? Serene and breathtaking, it is a "teardrop on the cheek of time," a phrase attributed to the Noble Laureate and Indian poet and novelist, Rabindranath Tagore (1861–1942). It is from his poem on the Mughal emperor Shah Jahan, in *One Hundred and One Poems* (Tagore, 1966). This white marble mausoleum was built between 1631 and 1648, commissioned by the Mogul Emperor, Shah Jahan, as a timeless remembrance and eulogy of love for his wife Mumtaz Mahal. Her tomb lies within and he, too, is buried there. It was inscribed on the World Heritage List by UNESCO in 1983 ("Taj Mahal—UNESCO World Heritage Centre"). When visitors travel to the Taj Mahal, how do they experience it? Take a look at reviews posted by visitors on Trip Advisor: https://www.tripadvisor.ca/Attraction_Review-g297683-d317329-Reviews-Taj_Mahal-Agra_Agra_District_Uttar_Pradesh.html. Accessed June 25, 2018).

The young couple you see in Photo 3.2.1, were international visitors who had already visited the Taj a couple of times. The photo was taken in January 2005, when they took family members (parents/in-laws) to see this symbol of perfection and love.

88 Diversity and Recognition

PHOTO 3.2.1 A family of four international visitors at the Taj Mahal
Photo credit: Sheeraz Lakhani

Unlike the previous trips where they were students or struggling young professionals, this was a luxurious train trip of the Golden Triangle, so named due to the triangular shape marked by the three highly visited cities of New Delhi, Jaipur and Agra, where the Taj Mahal is located. Crisp linen sheets in the carriages for overnight rest, a cornucopia of food and sightseeing, helped by tour guides on the train and at every destination they visited. A wheelchair was always ready at every stop for one of the elderly couple. They were all born and raised in East Africa, specifically, present day Tanzania and Uganda. Their ancestors had left India around the start of the 20th century, most likely due to a famine in Gujerat and Kutch (now part of the state of Gujerat today). They scattered through India, Burma/Myanmar, some followed the trade winds across the Indian Ocean to see safety and livelihoods in East Africa, where the British who ruled India then, too, had established colonies in Kenya and Uganda (and eventually Tanganyika, now called Tanzania). This young couple finally ended up in Texas, after emigrating to Canada via several years in England for college education and career training. Their journeys out of Africa were also to gain livelihood and safe shelter. They were part of a diasporic ethnic group, but not roots seeking tourists, really. India was one of many countries they traveled too, visiting family and relatives, but also keen to experience their cultural heritage. The Taj called to them, not simply as a must-see Wonder of the World, but also for its Muslim architecture and history. These travelers were Muslim, among an ethnic group converted from Hinduism to Islam in the 19th century.

It was a strange experience to be among a sea of "brown" people who generally looked like them (though ethnic differences were evident), and who shared many similar food traditions (the East African cuisine had incorporated African and British influences, along with uniquely East African vegetables and legumes, etc.). They experienced no discrimination or racism in India, though it had been a common accompaniment through every "homeland" since leaving India over a century ago. In rural Texas, the couple owned and ran several motels in various communities plus a 24-hour restaurant for almost 30 years. They were subjected to name-calling at their restaurant: "sand-n*****" (the racially charged N-word) and "camel jockey," and experienced deep-seated discrimination throughout their business dealings. There was no escape, neither "home" nor "homeland" to return to, so they made Texas their home. In rural Canada where they had emigrated from to Texas, "Paki" was a common derogatory name that members of their ethnic group encountered. But they were not from Pakistan, a good number of them had not visited Pakistan, or even India, for that matter. They identify as "Ismailis," more specifically, they are "Shia Imami Nizari Ismailis."

But, for a little while, the pain of psychic and physical dislocation was forgotten as they looked upon the eternal "teardrop" that Tagore described so lyrically. They loved the architecture and the sublime beauty of the Taj, observed where precious gems had been stolen off the mausoleum's walls, learned from their guide how little is known about many thousands of laborers and craftspeople engaged to build it. But the poverty they saw on the car journey from the train stop at Agra to the Taj shocked them, and those memories trouble their images and experiences of the Taj even today. They felt even more shocked to learn subsequently through stories from family, and various readings, that Muslims and Muslim cultural heritage have increasingly become targets of hostility, violence and severe discrimination in various parts of India. The Taj has already been struggling with physical deterioration from acid rain and other environmental damage, and its Moghul architecture and heritage has not been immune to social and political conflict either (Patel, 2016). News media reported in October 2017, that the Taj Mahal had been removed from Uttar Pradesh's tourism booklet *Apaar Sambhavnaen* (Limitless Possibilities) (Kumar, 2017; Naqvi, 2017). The Uttar Pradesh government hastily responded to clarify that the Taj was part of "our proud heritage" when BJP MLA Sangeet Som called the Taj Mahal "a blot on Indian culture" ("Amid Taj Mahal Controversy, Prime Minister Narendra Modi Says Can't Move Ahead Without Pride in Heritage," 2017).

90 Diversity and Recognition

References

Amid Taj Mahal controversy, Prime Minister Narendra Modi says can't move ahead without pride in heritage. (2017, October 17). Retrieved April 4, 2018, from https://www.news18.com/news/india/amid-taj-mahal-controversy-prime-minister-narendra-modi-says-cant-move-ahead-without-pride-in-heritage-1548987.html

Kumar, K. (2017, October 17). The BJP's attack on the "Muslim" Taj Mahal is part of a wider project. Retrieved April 4, 2018, from https://thewire.in/history/taj-mahal-bjp

Naqvi, S. (2017, October 8). Good news: The Taj will not be demolished. Retrieved April 4, 2018, from http://www.tribuneindia.com/news/sunday-special/columns/good-news-the-taj-will-not-be-demolished/478820.html

Patel, H. (2016, August 1). The slow decay of the Taj Mahal. Retrieved April 4, 2018, from https://thediplomat.com/2016/08/the-slow-decay-of-the-taj-mahal/

Tagore, R. (1966). *One hundred and one: Poems*. Asia Publishing House. Retrieved from https://books.google.com/books?id=Pf2fjwEACAAJ

Taj Mahal—UNESCO World Heritage Centre. (June). Retrieved April 12, 2018, from https://whc.unesco.org/en/list/252

Summary and Further Considerations

This chapter continues the discussion of social justice commenced in Chapter 2, but the focus here is on diversity and disadvantaged groups. It moves from Mr. Apo's vision of "Community Tourism" and Hawai'i to a discussion of building capabilities, drawing on Martha Nussbaum's "Capabilities Approach." We begin to see here the value of *endogenous* development (from within rather than externally driven) and also the importance of examining historical and institutional structures, and the *particular* context in which justice and injustice plays out. Throughout the chapter, various examples show a complex role of tourism in relation to capitalism, colonialism, and imperialism.

In touristic places and destinations that have experienced imperialism and colonization historically, it is very important to understand the processes and institutional structures that have driven changes in Indigenous land relations, means of provisioning and social-cultural practices. Tourism is not free of this scrutiny, for instance, with respect to how various activities can perpetuate "cultural imperialism" and facilitate settler colonialism as well as neocolonialism, as cases and other examples in this chapter illustrate. They alert us also to how power relations play out through touristic and other practices in everyday life that can contribute to oppression, domination, misrecognition as well as stereotyping and stigmatization of diverse cultural groups.

The latter part of the chapter focuses on justice as *recognition*, with some help from Nancy Fraser's bivalent notion of justice (later to become trivalent). The recognition of *difference* is an important part of recognition justice, as we learn from Iris Marion Young. Insights include examining the historical context, social processes and institutional structures in which tourism occurs. If you agree that tourism related processes and structures are interrelated with other economic, social-political (and environmental!) processes and structures of the destination, then you may agree that injustice emanating in the latter could influence the former. "The institutional racism of ongoing legacies is not bound by a particular institution, it is infused throughout societal institutions" (Figueroa, 2003, p. 33). Moreover, *habitual racism* such as the Palenquera women experience regularly from other Colombians, particularly local elites in Case 3.1, "may signify institutional racism when we speak of practices guided by policies, laws or customs" (Figueroa, 2003, p. 33; see also Moreno Figueroa & Saldívar Tanaka, 2016). Habitual racism engrained in social processes and institutions relations is also indicated in Case 3.2.

This complex thing called "tourism" has the potential for harm but also for much good. Though a number of Indigenous people have taken historically learned skills, customs and traditions and adapted them for tourist markets, it is important to not see them as passive recipients of the tourist dollar. For instance, Bruner and Kirshenblatt-Gimblett's (1994) interesting study shows how the Maasai in Kenya "perform" (enact) their resistance to powerful stakeholders in international tourism and in their homeworld. They are active participants on tourism's stage and fulfill their own needs and objectives as they display their traditions and sell their cultural goods to visitors. Case 3.3 by Jeff Wahl at the end of the chapter offers hope for justice as *recognition* and for *redistribution* to facilitate recognition justice, aided by participatory inclusion in decision making.

Questions for Further Reflection

1. What are the most important insights that Mr. Apo's discussion of "Community Tourism" offers you? How well do other notions of community-based tourism (CBT) responsible tourism (RT), and pro-poor tourism (PPT) fit with the insights you discovered?
2. What does Martha Nussbaum "Capabilities Approach" offer to tourism development (recall she said it's applicable globally, not just in western liberal settings)? How do principles and policies related to the development of CBT, RT, and PPT address the threshold level of ten Central Capabilities in her approach?
3. Consider Rawls's approach (justice as fairness, see Chapter 2) and Nussbaum's Capabilities Approach. Is it fair to compare them as theories of social justice? What are the similarities and differences between the two approaches?

92 Diversity and Recognition

4. What similarities and differences do you see between the case of the Palenqueras and the example of the Indigenous women hop pickers in the Puget Sound? What is the role of tourism in each case?

5. How can tourism help: (a) in facilitating justice as recognition? And (b) in enabling recognition of difference? What examples does the chapter provide of such ("just") roles for tourism?

Case 3.3: Commemoration and Contestation: The Little Bighorn Battlefield National Monument, USA

Jeff Wahl

Introduction

Heritage commemoration is an important social and cultural practice that represents different aspects of the past through the erection of statues, monuments, interpretative plaques, etc. The public commemoration of events of national or international historical significance plays an important role in society that serves many benefits, including being sites for gathering, enabling collective memory, remembrance, and civic education. However, sites of public commemoration are not "neutral" spaces, rather, they should be seen, like all heritage sites, as cultural and political spaces. For instance, they can be used by dominant cultural groups to champion their perspectives of the past while minimizing or completely excluding others, such as more vulnerable and historically oppressed groups, including women, racial minorities, and LGBTQ communities (Foote, 2003; Loewen, 2010). As Dwyer (2004, pp. 425–426) notes, "From their inception, monuments are designed and planned, with all of the narrative choices and biases this entails, by those who have the time, resources and, most importantly, the state mandate to define the past." This imbalance has stratified the "winners" and "losers" of heritage commemoration, whose respective perspectives may then be over-emphasized and underrepresented. Fortunately, sites of public heritage commemoration also present an opportunity for underrepresented stakeholders to contest the dominant meanings and values being presented and shift the discourse towards greater inclusiveness in representing diverse cultural groups and their histories (Hanna, 2017).

The case presented below is part of an ongoing study commenced in 2015 at the Little Bighorn Battlefield National Monument (Wahl, 2015). It illustrates how traditionally excluded stakeholders successfully contested longstanding inequities in the representation of their history and heritage at the Little Bighorn Battlefield National Monument, and have now become more fairly included in commemorative practices (see www.nps.gov/libi/index.htm. Accessed May 16, 2018). Site visits involving semi-structured interviews, informal conversations, and observations with different stakeholders including tourists, amateur historians, re-enactors, Native Americans, and National Park Service (NPS) employees were conducted in 2015, 2016, and 2017.

History and Context

The Battle of the Little Bighorn was fought in 1876 in what is now Montana. At this historic event, soldiers of the 7th U.S. Cavalry, government-contracted civilians and scouts from the Crow and Arikara tribes faced off against a force of Native Americans comprised of members of the Sioux, Cheyenne and Arapaho tribes. The Battle of the Little Bighorn (also referred to as "the Battle" below) was a decisive victory for the Sioux, Cheyenne and Arapaho, who were fighting to maintain their traditional ways of life and homelands against the encroachment of Anglo-American settlers and confinement to government reservations. On June 25, 1876, General George Custer, a renowned military hero in America at the time, led a force of over 600 soldiers into battle against an estimated 2000–3000 Native American warriors (Donovan, 2008). Custer was defeated and killed along with over 210 of his soldiers; Native American casualty estimates ranged between 20–300 warriors (Hardorff, 1999). Since its occurrence, the Battle has been celebrated as a watershed event in American history, with Hollywood films, artwork, literature and other forms of cultural media enshrining iconic figures like Custer, Sitting Bull, and Crazy Horse in the public imagination. While the epic event popularized as "Custer's Last Stand" has long been celebrated by society (Elliott, 2007) less attention has been paid to Native American roles in the Battle, or its cultural importance as the apex of Indigenous tribes' resistance against nearly 400 years of conflict and tribal dispossession in America (National Park Service, 2015).

The United States government began to officially commemorate the Battle of the Little Bighorn (1876) soon after the event: designating and protecting a portion of the historic Battlefield as the Custer Battlefield National Monument (1879), erecting individual headstones for each of the military personnel who died in the Battle in the approximate locations of where they fell (1876–1890), and installing a granite obelisk inscribed with each the names of each of the military personnel who had died (1881) (Buchholtz, 2012). Today, the site of the Battle of the Little Bighorn is a national monument managed by the U.S. National Park Service (NPS) that attracts approximately 300,000 annual tourists (National Park Service, 2017). Commemoration is exhibited through monuments, gravestones and interpretative talks that strive to represent both sides of the historic conflict, providing visitors "a spiritual landscape, a learning place where multiple points of view can be expressed and explored respectfully" (National Park Service, 2015, p. 9). However, equitable cultural heritage representation has not always been a feature of this space.

For approximately 100 years, those charged with officially commemorating the site of the Battle, first the U.S. War Department (1879–1940) followed by the NPS (1940–present), emphasized the American military perspective at the expense of the Sioux, Cheyenne, Arapaho, Crow and Arikara tribes. During this period, Battlefield managers "viewed the Indians largely as faceless people without historical investment in the struggle... even though the short-term aftermath had proved cataclysmic to their traditional existence" (Greene, 2008, p. 226). Ethnocentric attitudes reflected dominant beliefs that Native Americans would assimilate into the dominant white American culture, embracing its heroes (Buchholtz, 2012). It did not prevent Native American stakeholders from commemorating their own perspectives, as discussed below.

Commemoration Through Contestation

Wanting to be fairly included and to educate the public about their perspectives of the Battle, members of Native American tribes soon began to contest early government commemorations with their own perspectives. One way this occurred was through the practices each side used to commemorate those who had died during the Battle. In the days following the Battle, fallen soldiers were buried by the military where they were discovered, and permanent white marble gravestones were subsequently installed in the years following (Buchholtz, 2012). Unlike the military, the Native Americans carried their dead away from the Battlefield to be laid to rest in accordance with their own cultural practices. While early managers of the Battlefield may have had little interest in commemorating individual Native American casualties (Greene, 2008), it did not mean that the tribes did not independently commemorate the sites where warriors died in the Battle. Tribal members kept oral records of these locations and in the years following the Battle, they returned to the places where their ancestors had died to mark them with small stone cairns (Stands In Timber, Liberty, & Utley, 1998). John Stands in Timber, a historian of the Cheyenne, commented on what he felt was a need to commemorate the Cheyenne losses, and his own efforts to erect mnemonic objects to the fallen Cheyenne before their locations were lost to the passage of time (my annotations in parenthesis below):

> They [the NPS] should mark more places on the battlefield, from the Indian side. They [Cheyenne participants] told me some of the stories over and over for many years, and remembered where things happened. I have marked many of the places myself with stones, but it's getting harder for me to find them now. I have tried to show other people the places so they would not be forgotten, and tell them what happened there (Stands In Timber et al., 1998, p. 207).

The first formal commemoration of Native American casualty by the NPS came in 1956 when, following multiple requests by the family members of a Cheyenne warrior who died in the Battle, a gravestone was erected in his honor (Buchholtz, 2012). Native American stakeholders continued to pressure the NPS for individual grave commemorations into the 1990s, when the NPS began working to improve their relationship with tribal stakeholders and present a more holistic representation of the Battle. This relationship-building effort included diligent historical research undertaken with cooperation between NPS historians and tribal members to assist with the placement of official Native American gravestones (Reece, 2008). In 1999, 123 years after the Battle, the very first gravestones to commemorate fallen Native Americans were installed on the Battlefield, and others have been added since, aided by ongoing NPS research (Reece, 2008). Each gravestone is red granite and features the name of fallen Native Americans in their own language, an English translation and a brief inscription; for example, "O'Xasehe, Cut Belly, a Cheyenne warrior died here on June 25, 1876 while defending the Cheyenne way of life." Finally, over a century after the Battle, Native American casualties are being officially recognized and commemorated in a fair and respectful manner.

A second form of Native American contestation occurred during the 1970s–1980s. During this period, the American Indian Movement (AIM), emboldened by the Civil Rights Movement and growing social activism across America, staged several demonstrations on the Battlefield site. These protests were aimed at asserting their rights to equitable representation of their role in the Battle and pushing for increased recognition for their tribes (Buchholtz, 2012). During a demonstration at the site in 1988, members of AIM installed a plaque honoring the "Indian Patriots" who fought in the Battle near the longstanding cavalry obelisk (Greene, 2008, p. 228). Although the plaque was removed by the NPS after two months, this symbolic protest helped influence NPS site managers to commit to the construction of a permanent Native American monument (Greene, 2008).

Finally, in December of 1991, President George H.W. Bush signed an act into law that renamed the Custer Battlefield National Monument to the Little Bighorn Battlefield National Monument, and authorized the creation of a permanent memorial for Native American participants (National Park Service, 2012). In order to ensure fair representation of the tribal stakeholders, an eleven-person planning committee was formed including representatives of the tribes who had taken part in the Battle, artists and historians (National Park Service, 2012). The NPS also opened the planning committee meetings to the public with the hope of encouraging additional Native American participation in the planning process (Greene, 2008). The planning committee focused their design efforts on intercultural reconciliation and chose the theme "Peace through Unity" (Buchholtz, 2012). The memorial as it can be seen today at Little Bighorn Battlefield National Monument contains individual panels that acknowledge each of the different tribes that participated in the Battle—including those who were employed as scouts for the cavalry. It also features traditional pictograph artwork depicting the Battle, along with quotes from Native American participants, and a list of known Native American casualties (Greene, 2008). The Native American memorial was installed near the existing cavalry obelisk (Photos 3.3.1 and 3.3.2), and was formally dedicated on June 25, 2003, during the 127th anniversary of the Battle.

PHOTO 3.3.1 Native American Memorial at Little Bighorn Battlefield National Monument, erected in 2003 (National Park Service, n.d.)

Source: https://www.nps.gov/media/photo/view.htm?id=6DF6EA36-1DD8-B71B-0BABE7BA009D46E0. Accessed: May 18, 2018

PHOTO 3.3.2 Cavalry obelisk at Little Bighorn Battlefield National Monument, erected in 1881 (National Park Service, n.d.)

Source: https://www.nps.gov/media/photo/view.htm?id=6EEA08A1-1DD8-B71B-0B74BF8B2333CFC2. Accessed: May 18, 2018

Towards Commemorative Justice

From the first official designation of the Custer Battlefield National Monument in 1879 to the unveiling of the Native American monument in 2003, the history of commemorations of the Little Bighorn Battlefield has changed considerably. As of 2008, in addition to the Native American monument, 17 individual gravestones have been placed to honor fallen members of the Sioux, Cheyenne, Crow and Arikara tribes (Reece, 2008). Though Native American visitation statistics are unavailable, the Friends of the Little Bighorn report that since the placement of Native American gravestones began in 1999 that Native American Indian visitation had increased; and had increased again following the 2003 memorial dedication (Reece, 2008). The Little Bighorn Battlefield National Monument now stands as example of how "commemorative justice" was served as traditionally excluded stakeholders contested commemorative inequalities and achieved participation and voice in reshaping the representations of an epic period in American history. Today, the Battlefield serves as a protected cultural heritage site that represents the perspectives of diverse stakeholder groups and interests more equitably, and restores the symbolism and meaningfulness of the site to the tribal people involved.

References

Buchholtz, D. (2012). *The Battle of the Greasy Grass/Little Bighorn: Custer's last stand in memory, history, and popular culture.* New York, NY: Routledge.

Donovan, J. (2008). *A terrible glory: Custer and the Little Bighorn.* New York, NY, U.S.A.

Dwyer, O. J. (2004). Symbolic accretion and commemoration. *Social & Cultural Geography, 5*(3), 419–435. https://doi.org/10.1080/1464936042000252804

Elliott, M. A. (2007). *Custerology: The enduring legacy of the Indian Wars and George Armstrong Custer.* Chicago, IL: University of Chicago Press.

Foote, K. E. (2003). *Shadowed ground: America's landscapes of violence and tragedy* (Revised and Updated). Austin, TX: University of Texas Press.

Greene, J. A. (2008). *Stricken field: The Little Bighorn battlefield since 1876.* Norman, OK, U.S.A.: University of Oklahoma.

Hanna, J. (2017). Charlottesville: A monumental week after the violence. Retrieved May 11, 2018, from https://www.cnn.com/2017/08/18/us/char lottesville-week-in-review/index.html

Hardorff, R. G. (1999). *Hokahey! A good day to die!: The Indian casualties of the Custer fight.* Lincoln, NE: University of Nebraska Press. Retrieved from https://books.google.com/books/about/Hokahey_A_Good_Day_to_Die.html?id=xj9oFICvaRYC

Loewen, J. W. (2010). *Lies across America: What American historic sites get wrong.* New York, NY, U.S.A.: The New Press.

National Park Service. (2012). Indian memorial design competition: Little Bighorn Battlefield National Monument. Retrieved from https://www.nps.gov/libi/indian-memorial-design-competition.htm

National Park Service. (2015). *Foundational document: Little Bighorn Battlefield National Monument Montana.*

National Park Service. (2017). Park statistics: Little Bighorn Battlefield National Monument. Retrieved from https://www.nps.gov/libi/learn/management/statistics.htm

Reece, B. (2008). History of the Warrior Markers: Little Bighorn Battlefield National Monument. Retrieved May 11, 2018, from http://www.friendslittlebighorn.com/warriormarkershistory.htm

Stands In Timber, J., Liberty, M., & Utley, R. M. (1998). *Cheyenne Memories.* New Haven: Yale University Press.

Wahl, J. (2015). *Where else would you find blacktop trails to a 130-some year old ravine: Negotiated authenticity at the Little Bighorn Battlefield National Monument* (Unpublished master's thesis). Vancouver Island University, Nanaimo, BC, Canada.

Notes

1 See Chapter 1 in their book and Chapter 5 too, on opportunities and challenges for LGBT+tourism in various destinations, plus Chapter 6 for advocacy organizations.

2 Excerpted portions from Apo, P. (2004). Bold formatting as in the original source. A fuller description is provided in Jamal and Dredge (2014).

3 See Dangi and Jamal (2016) and also Jamal, Camargo and Wilson (2013). Both these are freely available as open access articles on the Sustainability journal's website.

4 Sen's approach takes freedom as an overall good, and is oriented to comparative quality of life assessment, where each nation selects specific capabilities that its constitutional structure would protect. See Sen (1999), Nussbaum (2006, pp. 11–15) and also Nussbaum (2011, pp. 69–76 plus Appendix B) for a short discussion of their differences, which are not addressed here.

5 Citizens being the core example she uses, but is not meant to exclude others such as resident aliens. Consider here the influx of migrants seeking safety, basic sustenance, and a life of dignity beyond impoverishment and extreme hardship.

6 See previous note about the use of "citizens." Not to be forgotten are the needs of animals, including the millions of animals used for human enjoyment in the tourism industry (Fennell, 2014).

7 The critique of tourism as *neocolonialism* draws an analogy between modern mass tourism (particularly in the form of international tourism) and colonialism, i.e., tourism as a colonizing endeavor. See, for example, Chapter 3 on "Power and Tourism" in Mowforth and Munt (2016). See also Britton (1982), Akama (2004).

8 For interest, note the symbolic roles of the foods and drinks consume by travelers and tourists voyaging to and from colonial homelands in the past. If you ever wondered why "India Pale Ale" beer is labeled as such, take a look at Raibmon (2006) and also note the interpellation of past and present! Also, see Foster and Clark (2018) for a Marxist lens on the expropriation of land (nature) through mercantilism and the expansion of industrial capitalism.

9 See this official documentary trailer on the film: https://www.youtube.com/watch?v=zGzvEqBvkP8. See also the interview with the standup comic Hari Kondabolu, who made the documentary film (Nevins, 2017).

References

Akama, J. S. (2004). Neocolonialism, dependency and external control of Africa's tourism industry: A case study of wildlife safari tourism in Kenya. In C. M. Hall & H. Tucker (Eds.), *Tourism and postcolonialism* (pp. 140–152). London, UK: Routledge.

Apo, P. (2004). Community tourism: Empowering communities to tell their own stories. Hawaiian Hospitality Institute, a branch of The Native Hawaiian Hospitality Association, 1244 N. School Street, Honolulu, HI 96817 – www.NaHHA.com – Peter Apo, Director, copyright 2004.

Ateljevic, I., & Doorne, S. (2003). Culture, economy and tourism commodities: Social relations of production and consumption. *Tourist Studies*, *3*(2), 123–141. https://doi.org/10.1177/1468797603041629

Britton, S. (1982). The political economy of tourism in the Third World. *Annals of Tourism Research*, *9*, 331–358.

Browne, K. (2007). A party with politics? (Re)making LGBTQ pride spaces in Dublin and Brighton. *Social and Cultural Geography*, *8*(1), 63–87. https://doi.org/10.1080/14649360701251817

Bruner, E. M., & Kirshenblatt-Gimblett, B. (1994). Maasai on the lawn: Tourist realism in East Africa. *Cultural Anthropology*, *9*(4), 435–470.

Camargo, B. A., & Lawo-Sukam, A. (2015). San Basilio de Palenque (re)visited: African heritage, tourism, and development in Colombia. *Afro-Hispanic Review*, *34*(1), 25–45.

Chavez, N. (2018, April 16). Beyoncé makes history with Coachella performance. Retrieved April 18, 2018, from https://www.cnn.com/2018/04/15/entertainment/beyonce-coachella-performance/index.html

Dangi, T. B., & Jamal, T. (2016). An integrated approach to "sustainable community-based tourism." *Sustainability*, *8*(5). https://doi.org/10.3390/su8050475

Derrida, J. (2000). *Of hospitality* (trans. R.). Stanford: Stanford University Press.

Fennell, D. A. (2012). *Tourism and animal ethics*. New York: Routledge.

Fennell, D. A. (2014). Exploring the boundaries of a new moral order for tourism's global code of ethics: An opinion piece on the position of animals in the tourism industry. *Journal of Sustainable Tourism*, *22*(7), 983–996. https://doi.org/10.1080/09669582.2014.918137

Figueroa, R. M. (2003). Bivalent environmental justice and the culture of poverty. *Rutgers University Journal of Law and Urban Policy*, *1*(1), 27–42.

Foster, J. B., & Clark, B. (2018). The expropriation of nature. *Monthly Review*, *69*(10). Retrieved from https://monthlyreview.org/2018/03/01/the-expropriation-of-nature/

Fraser, N. (2003). Social justice in the age of identity politics: Redistribution, recognition, and participation. In N. Fraser & A. Honneth (Eds.), *Redistribution or recognition? A political-philosophical exchange* (pp. 7–109). London and New York: Verso.

Fraser, N. (2010). *Scales of justice: Reimagining political space in a globalizing world*. New York, NY: Columbia University Press. Retrieved from http://www.jstor.org/stable/10.7312/fras14680

Fraser, N., & Honneth, A. (2003). *Redistribution or recognition? A political-philosophical exchange*. London and New York: Verso.

Guaracino, J., & Salvato, E. (2017). *Handbook of LGBT tourism and hospitality: A guide for business practice*. New York: Harrington Park Press.

ICRT (International Conference on Responsible Tourism in Destinations). (2002). Cape Town declaration on responsible tourism. Retrieved April 4, 2018, from http://responsibletourismpartnership.org/cape-town-declaration-on-responsible-tourism/

Jamal, T., Camargo, B., & Wilson, E. (2013). Critical omissions and new directions for sustainable tourism: A situated macro–micro approach. *Sustainability*, *5*(11), 4594–4613. https://doi.org/10.3390/su5114594

Jamal, T., & Dredge, D. (2014). Tourism and community development issues. In R. Sharpley & D. Telfer (Eds.), *Tourism and development* (pp. 178–204). Clevedon, UK: Channel View Publications. Retrieved from http://www.academia.edu/download/35627333/Tourism_and_Community_Development_Issues.pdf

Mbaiwa, J. E., & Stronza, A. L. (2010). The effects of tourism development on rural livelihoods in the Okavango Delta, Botswana. *Journal of Sustainable Tourism*, *18*(5), 635–656. https://doi.org/10.1080/09669581003653500

Moreno Figueroa, M. G., & Saldívar Tanaka, E. (2016). "We are not racists, we are Mexicans": Privilege, nationalism and post-race ideology in Mexico. *Critical Sociology*, *42*(4–5), 515–533. https://doi.org/10.1177/0896920515591296

Mowforth, M., & Munt, I. (2016). *Tourism and sustainability: Development, globalisation and new tourism in the Third World* (4th ed.). New York, NY: Routledge.

Nevins, J. (2017, November 15). "Apu was a tool for kids to go after you": Why The Simpsons remains problematic. Retrieved April 18, 2018, from https://www.theguardian.com/tv-and-radio/2017/nov/15/problem-with-apu-simpsons-hari-konabolu-documentary

Nussbaum, M. (2000). *Women and human development: The capabilities approach*. Cambridge: Cambridge University Press.

Nussbaum, M. (2006). *Frontiers of justice*. Cambridge, MA: The Belknap Press of Harvard University Press.

Nussbaum, M. (2011). *Creating capabilities: The human development approach*. Cambridge, MA: The Belknap Press of Harvard University Press.

Raibmon, P. (2006). The practice of everyday colonialism: Indigenous women at work in the hop fields and tourist industry of Puget Sound. *Labor: Studies in Working-Class History of the Americas*, *3*(3), 23–56. https://doi.org/10.1215/15476715-2006-004

Rawls, J. (1971). *A theory of justice*. Cambridge: Belknap Press of Harvard University Pres.

Rawls, J. (1996). *Political liberalism*. New York: Columbia University Press.

Salzman, M. B., & Halloran, M. (2004). Cutural trauma and recovery: Culture, meaning, self-esteem and the re-construction of the cultural worldview. In *Handbook of experimental existential psychology* (pp. 231–246).

Scheyvens, R. (2002). *Tourism for development: Empowering communities*. Harlow, UK: Prentice Hall. https://doi.org/10.1016/j.tourman.2005.07.013

Sen, A. (1999). *Development as freedom*. Oxford: Oxford University Press.

Strange, C., & Kempa, M. (2003). Shades of dark tourism. *Annals of Tourism Research*, *30*(2), 386–405. https://doi.org/10.1016/S0160-7383(02)00102-0

Tjapukai Aboriginal Cultural Park. (n.d.). About Tjapukai. Retrieved April 18, 2018, from http://www.tjapukai.com.au/about-tjapukai

Tucker, H., & Boonabaana, B. (2012). A critical analysis of tourism, gender and poverty reduction. *Journal of Sustainable Tourism*, *20*(3), 437–455. https://doi.org/10.1080/09669582.2011.622769

UNESCO. (n.d.). Intangible heritage. Retrieved November 1, 2017, from http://www.unesco.org/new/en/dhaka/culture/intangible-heritage

UNESCO World Heritage Centre. (n.d.). World heritage. Retrieved November 1, 2017, from https://whc.unesco.org/en/about/

Whyte, K. P. (2010). An environmental justice framework for indigenous tourism. *Environmental Philosophy*, 7(2), 75–92.

Williams, L. K., & Gonzalez, V. V. (2017). Indigeneity, sovereignty, sustainability and cultural tourism: hosts and hostages at 'Iolani Palace, Hawai'i. *Journal of Sustainable Tourism*, 25(5), 668–683. https://doi.org/10.1080/09669582.2016.1226850

Young, I. M. (2011). *Justice and the politics of difference* (Paperback). Princeton, NJ: Princeton University Press.

4

RESPONSIBILITY AND CARE

Introduction

Responsibility. What a heavy word! It would be no surprise if your brows are already furrowing, wondering what this chapter will cover, or what it ought to cover. Common topics in tourism textbooks, like "corporate social responsibility" and "green" certifications for tourism operators, hotels, and destinations would be fair game. Responsible tourism aimed toward environmental and social good, poverty alleviation and community well-being, may also come to mind, e.g., ecotourism, volunteer tourism, philanthropic tourism, etc. Then there are pressing global environmental issues like climate change and biodiversity loss. So, where to start?

Tourism's immense reach and scope, from the local to the global, raises important questions about our own roles and responsibilities in this "local-global" domain, in addition to those of other stakeholders. Home and the world are inextricably linked after journeying elsewhere. Many activities bring memories flooding back, like watching a National Geographic film on a national park that you loved hiking in, or visiting an ethnic restaurant in the neighborhood to seek out the tastes and smells of fragrant spices and foods discovered on a recent trip. Even reading a book or poem about a place one has visited brings it alive in a different way. The world seems a smaller place, and "home" now has a different sense of belonging in it. Being able to freely travel and experience diverse places, environments and cultures raises interesting possibilities about a different relationship to the world—a form of *cosmopolitanism* that evolves with every journey where one negotiates differences between being grounded somewhere and traveling elsewhere. Beyond taking care of the local and environments within borders that call on civic duties, it raises questions about responsibility toward places beyond borders. Notions of *global citizenship* and *global justice* arise here. These sound like heavy terms to unravel, but they are fascinating passengers on long journeys through the landscape of travel and tourism. They will be among the topics this chapter explores.

Chapter 4 builds directly on the previous chapters to examine responsibility to others and to places and spaces of visitation beyond and within borders. It is a huge subject and many topics are necessarily excluded (it is already a long chapter!), but Chapter 5 will continue to add to the picture emerging here. While we start with the global, the local continually weaves in and out, it is where concrete actions can be undertaken. The next section starts with a destination that offers fun, memorable, unforgettable experiences: The Great Barrier Reef. Other examples follow along with several cases from contributors around the world: Carolina Manrique on design and conservation in the post-disaster context in Japan, Linda Enoh discusses diasporic places and spaces of healing and belonging, Dianne Dredge and Eóin Meehan examine social enterprise in the urban Copenhagen context, while Emily Höckert forwards a radical responsibility to "the other" in her Nicaragua case study. The plan here is to engage with these in the spirit of debate and reflection, tease out some important themes (and a few principles), and hopefully stimulate new ideas toward responsibility for justice *and* care in touristic spaces. The concept of care that starts to emerge here builds on Chapter 3 and points to a rich understanding of care: *care for others* as well as *care about* the places and spaces in which tourism plays out.

Global Travel, Global Responsibility

Did you know that the world's coral reefs support 25% of all marine life, and that the livelihoods of around 500 million people depend on coral reefs for coastal protection, food and tourism income (Ocean Health Index, n.d.)? From a tourism perspective, about 70 million tourist trip equivalents are supported by the world's coral reefs annually and the reefs represent approximately US$36 billion a year in economic value globally, creating employment and revenue in over 100 countries and territories (Spalding et al., 2017). The Great Barrier Reef (GBR), an amazing ecosystem that stretches over a length of 2,300 kilometers off the east coast of Australia, is protected by UNESCO as a World Heritage Area. It contributes over AU$5.6 billion dollars to the Australian economy, generates over 70,000 jobs, and "is the sea country home for the first Australians—more than 70 Traditional Owner groups—whose connections to the marine environment date back more than 60,000 years" (Great Barrier Marine Park Authority, 2018).

Even if you have visited the GBR, check out the website of the Great Barrier Reef Marine Park Authority (GBRMPA), watch the video on the reef and read some fascinating facts and programs being undertaken: http://www.gbrmpa.gov. au/about-the-reef. This is your "virtual" trip to the reef and you have plenty of time, it's a long-haul flight unless you live in the south Pacific! Among numerous environmental threats to coral reefs globally are warming sea temperatures and ocean acidification. Many reef ecosystems around the world have experienced back-to-back bleaching events in 2016 and 2017, and parts of the GBR have

104 Responsibility and Care

sustained significant damage from the recent bleaching events and a "record-breaking marine heatwave" that impacted coral assemblages in 2016 (see Hughes et al., 2018, p. 492). In addition to various sustainability plans and programs managed by GBRMPA, the Australian government announced on April 29, 2018, that it has pledged over 500 million Australian dollars (US$379 million) toward conserving the Great Barrier Reef (George & Westcott, 2018).

Visitors to the GBR even prior to these recent stressors had raised concerns about the health and conservation of this vast ecological system. It is listed by UNESCO as a global heritage of "outstanding universal value" (see UNESCO World Heritage Centre, n.d.). Large complex ecosystems like the Great Barrier Reef prod us into wakefulness. How much responsibility do "we" (visitors, residents, government, service provider, etc.) bear for addressing the severe environmental threats it is facing? What difference does it make to live close to the reef, versus someone who lives on the other side of the world, who has never visited the reef, nor desires to do so? What does it mean to be "socially responsible" as the Australian reef visitor below mentions?

> It was a _memorable experience_ and a _newfound appreciation_ for the need to preserve it and be _socially responsible. (Australian resident visitor)_

> I'm concerned that there is _too little action taken by state and federal government_ to protect the reef and would hate to see the situation of "too little too late." I'm completely in favor of preserving the reef and marine life, but _not clear what I as an individual can do._ (Visitor from USA)

The above quote and all the reef quotes and related visitor insights information in this section are based on an online survey of visitors who went to various locations in the Great Barrier Reef in 2013–2014, primarily with reef tour operators based in Cairns (see Jamal & Smith, 2017). Of the 92 people who provided information on country of origin, 61% were from Australia (with the majority being from Queensland, followed by New South Wales and Victoria), 21% were from the United States, 8% from the U.K. and the rest from elsewhere. See what these visitors below said, also before the severe back-to-back bleaching events noted above occurred:

> I really _learned a lot_ while I was on my last trip and have over years of undertaking ecotourist marine adventures. _Tourist activities such as swimming with the minke whales have really heightened my understanding of issues of marine conservation and I share these with others, write letters, vote appropriately and keep myself informed about them._ Certainly key issues such as the impact of farming, mining, shipping, over-fishing, global _warming and tourism on the Great Barrier Reef are extremely important to me and I will continue to fight for these things including making informed decisions at the upcoming election._ I want to know that the twenty years or so of activities I have been enjoying the GBR so far are things I can share with my nieces and nephews when they get older. (Resident of Brisbane, Queensland, Australia)

> Visitors trust that the company they are taking a tour with, and the government and other responsible bodies are managing the impacts appropriately and a suitable level. After all, we are in a "developed" country... At the moment I cannot see a way to tell the difference between the operators... People want to enjoy their trip to the reef, but should they be picking up sea cucumbers, or trying to stroke the fish, swimming behind turtles, or kicking the coral? (U.K. visitor)

Reef visitors who participated in the online survey conducted expressed a strong desire to learn more about the *actions various groups are taking* to minimize negative environmental impacts to the reef overall. This figure was over 80% when it pertained to learning about what reef operators and the tourism industry are doing. They also ranked the national and state governments as *most responsible* for addressing environmental threats to the GBR, followed by the tourism industry and local coastal communities. Nonprofit groups were viewed as being least responsible for dealing with environmental threats to the GBR relative to the entities above. Interestingly, many respondents felt that they themselves had to assume some level of responsibility for addressing environmental threats to the reef; a third felt somewhat responsible to assist and over half felt strongly responsible (ranging from feeling mostly responsible to completely responsible).

Of course, to recognize one's own role and responsibility entails *being informed about the destination and one's own effects on it.* Many visitors in the exploratory survey above expressed wanting more information about the reef as well as the environmental threats it faced. In the open-ended comments invited from survey participants, several reef visitors mentioned the need for greater reef regulation and conservation actions by the Australian government, as well as impact management and education of tourists by reef tour operators. Reef operators seemed quite concerned about damaging the "destination image" of the GBR by talking about threats to the reef like global warming and climate change. After all, news spreads quickly via the Internet, especially now with a growing number of social media tools joining Facebook (Twitter, Instagram, etc.). Moreover, raising visitors' awareness about environmental impacts while they are on hard-earned vacations appears counter-productive to ensuring they have a fun time and spend money. Talking about the carbon emissions of long-haul flights or what visitors can do to help seems a risky proposition? It might make them feel guilty or like they are being blamed for harm that may have befallen the people or place, even if it occurred before their arrival (e.g., in the past), or if they are not directly responsible for it! Really?

"Cosmopolitan" Tourist–Resident Responsibility

Well, there is good news! Visitors need not feel guilt or blame, nor feel paralyzed or disinclined to act or to go on a holiday. There is much they can do, like seeking responsible forms of transportation, "green" accommodations and tour operators (the reef operators used by the survey participants above are ecotourism certified), restaurants that serve local foods, recycle, and minimize waste and carbon emissions, etc. It is not difficult to avoid buying plastic bottles and plastic shopping bags when reusable, recyclable ones are available. Long-haul travelers might even purchase carbon offsets and be thoughtful about less visible consequences of their visit, like the amount of water tourist hotels use and what chemicals get washed into the ocean from various skin products (use eco-friendly, reef-safe sunscreen!). To protect marine ecosystems, legislation banning the sale of sunscreen containing oxybenzone and octinoxate (without a prescription) was passed in Hawai'i in July 2018, and will take effect on January 1, 2021 (Senate Bill 2571: Relating to Water Pollution, 2018).

Raising visitors' awareness of the environmental threats and their own role in it can play an important role in facilitating good actions, and it can be done without scaring them off. Disney specializes in *edutainment*, after all, and visitor education is a key principle of ecotourism.[1] Dawson et al.'s (2010) study of polar tourism to the Arctic showed that many tourists keen on this "last chance tourism" adventure could not connect the dots between their own long-haul travel to the Arctic, and the melting snowcaps, deteriorating habitats, and impacts on polar bears. What responsible actions might have ensued had they been better informed? It could be argued that international tourists ought to do to more when they visit destinations like the Arctic and the Great Barrier Reef that are being affected by climate change. The need for greater visitor responsibility becomes even more compelling as neoliberal governance dominates and global regulatory mechanisms of international tourism seem to be lacking (see, for example, Mosedale, 2016). Large-scale, structurally embedded injustices like human trafficking for sexual exploitation and issues like climate change and climate injustice that transcend borders are simply beyond the ability and responsibility of any single government to manage. Such wide-ranging, systemically embedded issues require a different frame of thinking and acting in a globalized world.

One way is shifting one's worldview from being a citizen within a country to envisioning home and the world holistically, living and acting like the world is "home" and being concerned about moral, political and cultural aspects of being a global citizen. Some call this being a cosmopolitan. Traveling (e.g., as cultural tourists) is perceived to broaden and enrichen such cosmopolitanism. You could be a *rooted cosmopolitan* (Appiah, 1997, 2006), grounded in your own particular cultural/national values, but celebrating the cultural diversity experienced in travels elsewhere. In fact, following Appiah (2006), you could be a rooted, *ethical cosmopolitan*, exercising good virtues and moral principles wherever you travel. Being an ethical cosmopolitan tourist is a good start, but is it enough?

A common objection that arises here is that time and resources are limited; shouldn't more urgent responsibilities, such as taking care of family, take priority over taking care of others, other people, other places? Well, is it an "either/or" scenario, e.g., it's *either* my family *or* helping conserve the reef, or can it be "both/and" as in how to attend to *both* the good of family *and* the good of the destination?

Just take the family along for an enriching volunteer tourism experience, exercising respect and care (see Case 4.4 at the end of this chapter)! It looks simple so far to be a global citizen in travel and tourism: make ethical travel choices, get involved in conservation, community development and poverty alleviation projects, etc. Is that enough or do some kinds of injustices demand more?

Structural Injustices Within and Across Borders

Alas, more is at stake when it comes to *structural injustices*. Structural injustices "are harms that come to people as a result of structural processes in which many people participate. These participants may well be aware that their actions contribute to the processes that produce the outcomes, but for many it is not possible to trace the specific causal relation between their particular actions and some particular part of the outcome" (Young, 2003, p. 7). It is very difficult to assign moral responsibility for injustices that are widespread and beyond our control, such as the exploitation of workers in sweatshops and poorly regulated Free Trade Zones, some of whose products end up being consumed by unsuspecting tourists.[2] Or for socially and institutionally embedded racism against ethnic minorities and religious groups, or historical injustices and dispossession from traditional lands due to imperialism or colonialism, or even culturally engrained oppression against women in patriarchal societies. Such injustices seem so complex and overwhelming that it is easy to turn away and say there isn't a problem, or that "it's clearly not my problem."

It is unfortunately not so easy and conscience may prick the traveler despite all efforts to focus on the holiday. There may be a sense of a larger injustice, for instance, if the visitor recognizes the impacts of air travel on global warming and its effects on vulnerable populations and the poor worldwide. Or if numerous incidences of gender discrimination and racial violence in the urban destination one inhabits are evident in everyday life and constantly in the news. Young (2004, p. 378) says we may judge that structural injustices exist when "at least some of the normal and accepted background conditions of action are not morally acceptable." Responses arise when moral conscience awakens. Viral social media "witnessing" now enables social movements and protests to form quickly around recurring egregious incidents in everyday life that for many years have lain hidden and unproven. Let us a look at an instance of social media witnessing that is driving good action and change on difficult structural issues, offering hope to tackle large structural issues that appear so daunting that avoidance is an instinctual response. The example below relates to an urban hospitality space that is familiar to many in USA and other destinations where Starbucks is established.

Responsibility for that Latte

A video of the arrests of two black men who asked to use the bathroom at a Starbucks in Philadelphia on April 12, 2018, went viral after it was posted by a

108 Responsibility and Care

customer who witnessed the incident. Protests arose nationwide. Starbucks CEO Kevin Johnson acted rapidly and announced that on May 29, 2018, all Starbucks across the country would be closed for staff to undergo racial bias education. As he said (Whitten, 2018):

> While this is not limited to Starbucks, we're committed to being a part of the solution. Closing our stores for racial bias training is just one step in a journey that requires dedication from every level of our company and partnerships in our local communities.

Michelle Saahene, a customer at Starbucks at that time said that as a black woman, she was "slightly nervous when the police officers entered the coffee shop," but after the two men were arrested and led away, she experienced solidarity and care from "multiple white women" (McCausland, 2018) (underline for emphasis):

> Saahene, meanwhile, said she was overwhelmed by the support she received from the multiple white women who stood with her and then walked out of the Starbucks with her. They helped bring attention to the injustice of the situation, she said. "That's so important because <u>for us to be successful we need those in the majority to take a stand</u>," Saahene said. "We as minorities have been crying for help have been pushing for social justice, but it's not going to get better until we have the majority standing up for us."

Across the border, in Canada, Starbucks Canada's president, Michael Conway, announced a similar closure of all Starbucks in Canada on June 11, 2018, for its partners to "participate in a training session designed to address implicit bias, promote conscious inclusion, and ensure everyone inside a Starbucks store feels safe and welcome" (Floody, 2018). These moves are a step in the right direction, but much more is needed to address structurally engrained injustices like systemic racism and stigmatization of African Americans (and other people of color facing similar institutionally engrained discrimination). Structural injustices are embedded in societal norms, symbols, habits and practices of everyday life, and systematically reproduced in social, economic and cultural institutions (Young, 2011). It requires examining political, economic and social structures and processes, looking at the whole of society, rather than just focusing on the basic structure of justice that Rawls uses (see Young's 2011 critique of Rawls on this). Lee Mun Wah, Chinese American film director and diversity trainer said:

> what happened at Starbucks is really symptomatic of a much larger and historical "problem" facing this country, ever since its inception…When Serena and Venus Williams first came onto the tennis scene, a radio broadcaster said, "Look at those two…who would want to date those two apes?" Even former President Obama and his family has often been depicted as monkeys and apes in blogs and throughout the internet. Unless we are

willing to acknowledge that these depictions of blacks have seeped into the very psyche of our culture and institutions, affecting how we see and experience black children and adults, we will continue to be "dismayed" and "shocked," but still ignorant and unwilling... As James Baldwin wrote: "Not everything that is faced can be changed. But nothing can be changed until it is faced." (Lee, 2018)

Customers showed solidarity with Michelle Saahene above and public protest on social media (along with accompanying news media) arose quickly in response to the posted video. "Corporate social responsibility" at Starbucks responded quickly. It will take more than one implicit bias training workshop, but it's a gesture of hospitality from this global hospitality stakeholder and an acknowledgement of a deeply rooted problem. The question still remains: How do we respond to structural injustices that are institutionalized and entrenched within a society, or dispersed across borders?

Political Responsibility for Justice

> Being responsible in relation to structural injustice means that one has an obligation to join with others who share that responsibility in order to transform the structural processes to make their outcomes less unjust (Young, 2011, p. 96).

Iris Marion Young was a political philosopher and feminist theorist. She argued that rather than a *backward-looking approach* seeking to individualize wrongs and assign blame and punishment for offenders (retributive justice), a more forward-looking political approach is needed to tackle ongoing structural injustices. The liability or punitive model (the backward-looking model) relates to legal and moral responsibility:

> To say that an agent is responsible means that they are blameworthy for an act or its outcome. The conditions for holding an agent morally responsible are similar to that of legal responsibility: we must be able to show that they are causally connected to the harm in question and that they acted voluntarily and with sufficient knowledge of the consequences (Young, 2013, pp. 97–98).

A *forward-looking approach*, rather than trying to assign blame and punishment (though looking backward is not to be ignored entirely), tries to understand the structural conditions and history of social processes and practices, the outcomes being produced, how our actions contribute to identified injustice(s) and then assuming responsibility for changing the processes to reduce or avoid injustice.

The incident at Starbucks above relates to systemic racism stretching back several hundred years in the US (see Case 4.2 further below). A backward-looking model

110 Responsibility and Care

is ineffective to address this. A forward-looking approach is needed where all who contribute to processes that continue these injustices need to work to change them. That includes Starbucks customers. In the words of Michelle Saahene, the Starbucks customer above, the majority have to stand up for the minority. They have to join together with others to help change this situation. Starbucks' CEO Kevin Johnson has even greater responsibility. Actually, both the US and Canadian CEOs seem to recognize this, looking at their words and actions. The scope and density of social and economic ties help to determine responsibility for justice, for "the greater the connections, the more principles of justice apply" and responsibilities for global justice, just like within cities or institutions, similarly "fall more heavily on those whose actions more profoundly affect the conditions of the actions of others" (Young, 2000, p. 250).

An example of structural injustice that Young discussed is the case of sweatshops located internationally. Their owners and managers are legally and morally responsible in the sense of liability. But even if one can identify such institutional responsibility, the lack of transnational regulatory institutions inhibits collective action for change. Furthermore, when it comes to large-scale social structures and processes in which many people (publics, consumers) participate but none are primarily or solely responsible for the cause of the injustice, it is difficult to reason about individual responsibility, and much easier to deny or avoid it! Referring to structural processes that condition the lives of distant others, such as in sweatshops, Young (2004, pp. 376–377) said of consumers of apparel and clothing that may have originated in such places:

> While they probably have not intended that the social processes in which they participate and from which they benefit have harmful consequences to others, and they should not be blamed or found guilty for these consequences, they are responsible under a different conception.

How many T-shirts produced under pitiful wages and working conditions have been bought as souvenirs by unsuspecting visitors in countless souvenir shops around the world? What is their (and our) global responsibility toward justice in this instance?

A Social Connection Model

Iris Marion Young provides a *social connection model* that applies to structural injustices within as well as across borders. It is primarily a *forward-looking approach* as described above. Buying clothing made in a sweatshop, or even participating in a society that permits the sale and distribution of garments produced by sweatshop labor far away, creates a forward-looking responsibility to understand the social and economic relations that connect us to the distant places of production and the people who work in those factories, and to act to transform the processes producing the ongoing injustices identified (Young, 2006, 2013). Responsibility in the model is a *shared responsibility*: "all those who contribute by their actions to the structural processes that produce injustice share responsibility for those harms," for it is a responsibility "I *personally* bear but I do not bear it alone" (Young, 2013, p. 109). We must then *join in relations* with others (including those who are oppressed, like the sweatshop workers) to engage in collective action, i.e., assume *political responsibility*. By politics or the political, Young means something broader than government. She uses these terms in reference to

> the activity in which people organize collectively to regulate or transform some aspect of their shared social conditions, along with the communicative activities in which they try to persuade one another to join such collective action or decide what direction they wish to take it (Young, 2004, p. 377).[3]

Political responsibility is based on questioning and evaluating the structural background conditions through explicit reflection and deliberation, followed by political action.

Following Iris Marion Young, if tourists contribute to structural or global injustices, even simply by being part of a network or structure that connects them to the source of injustice, then they *are* responsible to do something about it. It requires understanding the social systems and processes related to the observed injustices and where they fit into it, and engaging in political responsibility to change these to reduce or eliminate unjust outcomes, Young argued. Humanitarian acts based on human dignity and respect for persons are important, but political action is essential to deal with structural injustices.[4] Refraining from taking a packaged tour whose revenues might support an oppressive government that violates human rights is a good action, but it is insufficient to address structural injustices. One can, for instance, join a political action group, or a social movement that lobbies for government sanctions against a popular tourism destination where human rights violations are an issue (see, for example, the tourism-related boycotts placed on Burma/Myanmar in Chapter 1).

It is also important for victims to take some responsibility to challenge and change the structures producing the injustice they suffer, so finding ways to support their efforts is an important task. As Young explains (the underlining is for your attention here):

> We share responsibility to fashion organized means of changing how the processes work so they will issue in less injustice...The form of responsibility, then, is political in these senses that acting on my responsibilities involves joining with others in a public discourse where we try to persuade one another about courses of collective action that will contribute to ameliorating the problem... In the case of labor exploitation, the workers themselves ought to resist if they can by means of their own collective organization. Without the support of others taking responsibility for

112 Responsibility and Care

working conditions in ways that support them, however, they are less likely to succeed (Young, 2004, pp. 380–381).

Reasoning Through to Action: Some Helpful Parameters

In *Responsibility For Justice* (2013), which was published posthumously after her untimely death, Iris Marion Young offers a succinct discussion of the features of the *social connections model* introduced above: (i) It is *not isolating* (does not focus on identifying and assigning blame to particular agents; (ii) It enables *judging background conditions* (examining the situation of structural injustice also helps ascertain one's own role in it); (iii) It is *more forward looking than backward looking*; (iv) It involves *shared responsibility* which (v) can be *discharged only through collective action*. While Iris Marion Young's approach has been critically evaluated and some limitations have been identified,[5] it offers a useful way to start thinking about *our* responsibility for structural injustices in a complex tourism system that is intertwined with other local-global systems (note the discussion in Chapter 1 on this). The political responsibility of public, private, and nongovernmental organizations identified by the Great Barrier Reef study participants seem to fit this model and so does the personal responsibility many reef participants felt to conserve the reef. Over half the reef visitors in the Great Barrier Reef survey felt *strongly responsible* to act!

Similarly, to follow up on the sweatshop example raised above, visitors do need to think about ethical sourcing while buying things (e.g., sun-protective clothing) on holiday, but they also bear *some* responsibility to get involved in political action to redress labor injustice they discover to be related to their purchases. It's a lot to consider and the burden of responsibilities seems onerous, whether on holiday or back home after. The tourist elsewhere is a resident *somewhere* and can exercise responsibility in everyday life after returning home. You could argue additionally that responsibility also awaits the resident of a tourism destination to address tourism-related structural injustices that affects the destination and its inhabitants (human and nonhuman others), regardless of any travels. Iris Marion Young offers some guidance to better understand how to allocate precious time and resources toward responsibility for justice. Think through the opportunities and capacities presented by the institutional or social positions we hold in the structures producing unjust outcomes, she suggests. She offers four parameters to help reason through action in relation to structural injustice (Young, 2006, 2013):

1. *Power.* Where individuals or organizations lack resources, time, and energy to respond to all the structural injustices they may be connected to, they should pick the process (or processes) where they can exert the most power and influence. For instance, major transnational apparel retailers like Benetton and Gap, have the size, reach and relative influence to change working conditions in the sweatshops, while individuals or organizations with

relatively less power but some ability to pressure important stakeholders to act, can exercise their political responsibility by exercising pressure on such larger ones to act on unjust outcomes (see, too, Young, 2004).

2. *Privilege*: There are privileged persons in most situations of structural injustice, but they may hold little power as individuals in institutional positions. North American college students or European office workers who buy shirts made in sweatshops (her example) may have little power, but do have privilege relative to sweatshop workers. They have more resources and ability to adapt to consequences of their actions without suffering serious deprivation, compared to the struggling sweatshop workers (who could really benefit from support to help their own efforts to institute change).

3. *Interest*: The interests of agents and victims may coincide sometimes with respect to promoting justice. There are too many issues, institutions and people involved to take on every injustice, so pick one that aligns one's own interests with those of agents suffering the injustice. Young (2004) points out that it may help, too, to identify and prioritizes issues to work on where particular *connections* can be traced between the distant entity or distant persons and the social group or institution the agent is positioned in (e.g., one's workplace, church, city).

4. *Collective Ability*: Shared responsibility has to be exercised through collective action, but coordinating new structures or reorganizing existing ones can be highly challenging. Collective ability may be enhanced by drawing on the resources of entities that are already organized and have many members (e.g., church groups, unions, universities) and using them in new ways to address the structural injustice (e.g., campus campaigns politicizing the university's apparel purchasing decisions, calling attention to sweatshop related injustices, and working with civil organizations to facilitate change).

Using Young's social connection model and four parameters above helps to identify some of the responsibilities tourists have with respect to the destinations they visit. Let's say Jenna, a young African American professional in a large media firm in the USA, discovers after she returns home from a packaged reef tour led by an international tour operator that the retail shop (affiliated with a popular chain across the USA) where she had purchased several souvenir T-shirts gets all its apparel from sweatshops located in the region she had visited. She also learns the following. These sweatshops are located in a low-lying coastal town that is vulnerable to sea level rise. Many residents are impoverished as their small fishing boats are returning with fewer and fewer fish to sell in the local market. The small fringing coral reef on the horizon has undergone extensive bleaching events over the past few years. Jenna knows climate change is affecting ecosystems including coral reefs and human populations dependent on them in destinations worldwide. She is a kind and caring person, and quite upset about the source of her souvenir T-shirts. She feels a sense of responsibility, but she also feels helpless about what to do.

114 Responsibility and Care

What guidance would you give Jenna to help her figure out how to proceed? Justice across borders is clearly a challenging topic. A closer look at the some of the local-global spaces in which tourism plays out may offer some ideas before you respond to Jenna.

Transnational Solidarity and Local–Global Action

You may recall what we discussed in Chapter 2 about ideal theory. Iris Marion Young's approach to justice both across and within borders is a non-ideal approach. It is grounded in practice, in the voices and experiences of people's struggles for freedom from oppression, for recognition of their cultural difference, and for self-determination and inclusiveness in social and political processes. As shown above, she is advocating *political responsibility* to deal with structural inequalities. Collective action is required to help resolve structural injustices. Important players in public communication and advocacy for political change both within and across borders include civil society organizations like local and national level non-governmental organizations (NGOs), and social movements that are targeting fair trade, anti-human trafficking, gender rights, etc.[6] Ethical consumer movements, for instance, lobby for government action, engage in media and other campaigns to inform the public of connections between the products they consume and unjust sources and outlets, organize solidarity boycotts of products and outlets, etc.

Certainly, the globalization of free market capitalism and the proliferation of global issues and concerns lie beyond the ability of any one state to govern and resolve them. Global organizations like the United Nations World Tourism Organization (UNWTO) play an active role in promoting and sharing knowledge and information on sustainable tourism. The UNWTO compiled a Global Code of Ethics to guide responsible and sustainable tourism (UNWTO, 1999), but this institution lacks regulatory force and has been criticized for catering to neoliberal interests (see, for example, Smith & Duffy, 2003). Fortunately, social action and resistance have mobilized worldwide over the past few decades, giving rise to "transnational solidarity and social justice among geographically dispersed civil society organizations, non-government organizations and disempowered indigenous groups, with the intention of constructing more just and egalitarian social orders" (Bianchi & Stephenson, 2014, p. 63). New social movements, organized protests and grassroots resistance in civil society are arising. Well-cited examples of advocacy networks and organizations in tourism include Tourism Concern (discussed in Chapter 2), The Ecumenical Coalition on Tourism (ECOT), which had its origins in the Ecumenical Coalition on Third World Tourism (ECWT) based in Thailand, and the NGO called Equations in India (see http://www.equitabletourism.org/). Global Exchange, founded in 1988, is an international human rights organization that offers "reality tours" and campaigns for sustainability and justice with a vision of a "people-centered globalization" (Global Exchange, 2016).

Not to be forgotten are private sector organizations like Patagonia, which is involved in environmental action and activism and offers "sustainable" clothing for sale to its customers (Patagonia, n.d.). As you can see, Jenna has much to think about and a range of actions she can engage in (remember Jenna at the end of the previous section?). She could engage in political activism at home, e.g., get involved in a local or global civil society organization or a social movement lobbying for fair trade policies on imported apparel. She could participate in *justice tourism* initiatives abroad, e.g., acting on climate change policies, or advocating for living wages. Or both, if she has the resources and the will to do that!

Jenna the "Justice Tourist"?

Jenna awaits guidance on how she can she fulfill her *shared responsibility* as per Iris Marion Young's "social connections model." At the moment, she is contemplating taking a Pro-Poor Tourism or a Volunteer Tourism trip to the sweatshop region where rural community residents are struggling to develop sustainable livelihoods. While there, she would like to get involved with local women interested in starting a cooperative as she believes it could contribute to women's empowerment. You could say Jenna would be a *virtuous tourist*. However, she does not appear to be thinking about taking *political responsibility* which is integral for redressing structural injustice as per Young's social connections model.

So many possibilities await Jenna for exercising political responsibility if she wished. She could join an anti-sweatshop movement and/or a global climate justice movement to address the two structural injustices she has identified. She could try to involve her workplace (organization and colleagues) to raise public awareness and organize a boycott of the retail chain domestically. Or she could become a politically active *justice tourist*. Regina Scheyvens introduced the term *justice tourism* (Scheyvens, 2002) as an ethical and equitable approach that encompasses social change through political activism by organizations (e.g., NGOs, reality tour operators) as well as by "tourists of conscience" (Scheyvens, 2011, pp. 107–108). She incorporates principles of alternative tourism that "seeks to achieve mutual understanding, solidarity and equality among participants" as Holden (1984, p. 15) put it. Freya Higgins-Desbiolles (2008, pp. 347, 354) applies Scheyvens' notion of justice tourism toward contesting inequities due to "capitalist globalization" and provides examples of justice tourism along a solidarity continuum involving varying depths of solidarity: responsible tourism, pro-poor tourism, fair trade in tourism, volunteer tourism, reality tours and transnational solidarity activism.

Seeds of Hope

While academics mull over responsibilities for global justice and policy makers play chess with powerful transnational interests, *shared responsibilities* as identified above still call upon all who are connected to tourism to evaluate their role (see the four helpful parameters provided by Young above) and take up responsibility

116 Responsibility and Care

to act on structural injustices. It is vitally important to not underestimate the scale and scope of this phenomenon, and the immensely influential role of the tourism "industry" and all who participate in it. The tourist is a metaphor for the social world (Dann, 2002). The way tourism is structured and how it plays out in various social-ecological systems is a powerful lens into societal norms and values, human-environmental relationships, economic processes, and political agendas. Within the various places and spaces in which tourists, hosts, services providers and other related institutions and organizations interact lie insights into not only inequities and injustices, but also possibilities and potential for addressing harms and facilitating well-being.

Case 4.1 below is your first test of this. It calls you to adopt an interdisciplinary (transdisciplinary?) lens and patiently explore heritage conservation and visitor experience in relation to post-disaster recovery. Observe the physical and psychological engagement with destination, how the site of visitation communicates the event, how design and other strategies orient the visitor toward remembrance and emotional resilience, nurturing local activism and gathering in *solidarity* not only locally on site but also transnationally! Note the symbolic role of the Phoenix tree as its seeds are planted during different ceremonies and events around the world. The seeds represent hope, continuity (sustainability?), solidarity, and remembrance. Furthermore, *both local and global participants are called to remember a traumatic event and engage in the shared responsibility of ensuring it doesn't happen again.*

Take a short break now and travel "virtually" with Carolina Manrique to Japan in Case 4.1 below. Walk besides her and see how she sees these sites (she was a heritage conservation graduate student then), and bring to it your own *critical, charitable* gaze. See how the Hiroshima Peace Memorial and Park (HPMP) is "performed," i.e., how it is presented and being experienced by various participants. Consider joining the petition against nuclear proliferation (notice it gathers international and domestic signatures), and don't forget to ring the Peace Bell! Perhaps someday you may be in a place where you can plant a seed of hope from the Phoenix tree, metaphorically or really!

Case 4.1: Japan: Resilience through Conservation and Tourism

Carolina Manrique

Funded by a graduate student scholarship from the Department of Architecture at Texas A&M University, I traveled to Japan in spring 2013 to understand how heritage sites affected by disasters had recovered. I chose Japan due to recent catastrophic events (e.g., Tohoku earthquake in 2011) and its historical variety of natural and anthropogenic disasters. I was particularly interested in learning how heritage conservation contributes to community disaster resilience. The notion of resilience was appearing in architecture more and more due to recent catastrophic events (2011). It was actively being used in diverse disciplines such as disaster management, as a conceptual shift from a previous approach on vulnerability (aimed towards identifying weaknesses that needed to be strengthen in socio-ecological systems) towards an approach of community disaster resilience—addressing strengths and proactive capacities for recovery in communities (Mayunga, 2009).

My trip occurred during the initial stages of my PhD in Architecture (heritage conservation). I felt my pursuit was aligned to the purpose of heritage conservation as "passing on to later generations architectural ideas and forms that represent meaningful expressions of, and contributions to, cultural history" (Levine, 2008). But what did this mean? I was challenged by claims that "preservationists care about *buildings, not history*" (Milligan, 2007). To Milligan, any relevant history referred to the history of the built environment rather than the histories of events and people or larger cultural processes. Key insights from my trip, however, seemed to *go far and deep into culture and socio-ecological landscape*, though I felt that I was missing much due to the language barrier (I don't speak Japanese). Well-organized interpretive tools in each location helped a great deal. Most of the information provided was translated into English, and provided in both text and graphic form. Displays were in diverse formats (physical models of diverse scales, photographs, paintings, artifacts, graphs, maps, etc.), allowing for going through the exhibits at a personal and silent pace. In 28 days I visited Tokyo (Kantō Earthquake Memorial Museum; Memorial Victims Tokyo Air Raids), Sendai (Mediatheque exhibit Center for Remembering 3.11—the Tohoku Earthquake in 2011; War Reconstruction Memorial Hall; Kyogamine Cemetery), Nagoya, Ise (Naikū and Gekū Shrines), Hiroshima (Peace Memorial and Park), Miyajima (Itsukushima Shinto Shrine), Osaka, Kobe (The Great Hanshin-Awaji Earthquake Memorial), Koyasan (Mount Koya-temple settlement), Kyoto, Nara and Ibaraki.

The majority of visitors in every site I visited were Japanese. It sometimes felt as if I was intruding in a *sacred pilgrimage* through their ancient heritage. This feeling was reinforced by the ceremonial way in which multiple layers were exposed by tying physical, natural, sensorial, emotional, spiritual and social dimensions throughout history, networks, and generations. An example of this multilayered approach is through the ceremonial routine of reconstructing and relocating the shrine buildings at Naikū and Gekū every 20 years. This process simultaneously preserves technological knowledge (traditional construction techniques) and cultural traditions. Cyclic renewal was also undertaken, involving the transference of both tangible (materials to build) and intangible (construction knowledge, sacredness of remains from shrines, religious rituals) aspects of heritage through historical donation of logs from these shrines to rebuild areas damaged in recent natural disasters (Edahiro, 2004).

The multilayered approach was also evident in one of the most intense sites experienced during my journey: The Hiroshima Peace Memorial (Genbaku

Dome; A-Bomb Dome) and the Hiroshima Peace Memorial Park (The City of Hiroshima, 2018) (United Nations, 2018) (see Photos 4.1.1 and 4.1.2).

An axis connects the Hiroshima Peace Memorial Museum and the remains of the skeletal dome and building structure of the A-Bomb Memorial. The dome was my main reference point in walking through the different sections of the park. It is the first structure before and after crossing the bridges over the Motoyasu River. It forms the background for contemporary ceremonies (religious and non-religious), as well as protests such as one I saw promoting peace and abolishment of nuclear weapons. It is the focal point framed by the cenotaph, like it was a way to enshrine its corpse as a living memory. It appears and disappears through the grown trees where normal life activities in the park unfold (e.g., picnics, band practices, citizens walking their dogs). It appears framed, one last time, through the façade windows in the last section of the museum's itinerary, where activism is reinforced through the request for voluntary signatures against nuclear weapons.

Each of the moments where the A-bomb structure is framed seemed to aim towards *different ways of breaking any indifference or detachment with the events it is linked to*. If the reflection of the structure in the river on a clear night seemed to present the ruin as an unreal ghost, then its presence in daylight after a thorough, very detailed and graphical walk-through (factual records; testimonies) in the museum would remind me of the events tied to its reality. If physical reality and the meaning of a building ruin did not

PHOTO 4.1.1 View of the Peace Memorial Park and the A-bomb Dome from the Museum
Photo credit: Carolina Manrique, 2013

PHOTO 4.1.2
Hiroshima Peace Memorial (Genbaku Dome; A-Bomb Dome)
Photo credit: Carolina Manrique, 2013

provoke a reaction, then the voice of a child in the song that I heard at the Phoenix tree transplanted close to the museum did. The Phoenix trees (Chinese Parasol Trees) survived after being exposed to the radiation of the atomic bomb and were transplanted to their current location in the Hiroshima Peace Memorial Park in May of 1973. Their seeds have been given to people in Japan and other countries in order to guarantee its continuity; "offspring of these trees are thriving around the world" (Hiroshima Peace Memorial Museum, 2001). Then there was the Peace Bell that activated a present, in-the-moment experience. Visitors were instructed to "step forward, and toll this bell for peace" (fragment of text from plaque by the bell from September 20, 1964; also see Hiroshima Peace Memorial Museum, 2018).

Just as important were reminders of how this site connects to current generations of Japanese, such as through music enacted at the site, and the activism of high school children towards abolishing nuclear proliferation (Photos 4.1.3 and 4.1.4). I felt I had learned that heritage conservation in the context of major historical disasters and the disaster recovery had to ensure that the "community's emotional links with place are resilient" (Spennemann, 2007). These occur in culturally related ways within socio-ecological systems, connecting people to the past in a way that facilitates social well-being, healing and gathering people in solidarity and peace through multi-layered approaches such as described above. After this trip, I felt overwhelmed with the responsibility of being a heritage conservationist. I had learned that an integrated approach between conservation and tourism was needed to understand the complex interactions between tangible and intangible aspects of heritage sites.

PHOTO 4.1.3 Band playing in the Hiroshima Peace Memorial Park.
May 25, 2013
Photo credit: Carolina Manrique 2013

PHOTO 4.1.4 High school girls collecting signatures to abolish nuclear weapons with the A-Bomb Memorial as background. The banner states that "the signatures collected will be handed to the United Nations." May 25, 2013
Photo credit: Carolina Manrique 2013

120 Responsibility and Care

References

Edahiro, J. (2004, October). *Rebuilding every 20 years renders sanctuaries eternal – The Sengu Ceremony at Jingu Shrine in Ise*. Retrieved from JFS - Japan for Sustainability: https://www.japanfs.org/en/news/archives/news_id027786.html

Hiroshima Peace Memorial Museum. (2001). *24 Phoenix Trees (China Parasol Trees) exposed to the A-bomb*. Retrieved from Hiroshima Peace Memorial Museum: http://www.pcf.city.hiroshima.jp/virtual/VirtualMuseum_e/tour_e/ireihi/tour_24_e.html

Hiroshima Peace Memorial Museum. (2018, March 24). *Peace Bell*. Retrieved from Hiroshima Peace Memorial Museum: http://www.pcf.city.hiroshima.jp/virtual/VirtualMuseum_e/tour_e/ireihi/tour_08_e.html

Levine, N. (2008). Building the unbuilt: Authenticity and the archive. *Journal of the Society of Architectural Historians, 67*(1) 14–17.

Mayunga, J. S. (2009). *Measuring the measure: A multi-dimensional scale model to measure community disaster resilience in the U.S. Gulf Coast region*. College Station: Texas A&M University.

Milligan, M. J. (2007). Buildings as history: The place of collective memory in the study of historic preservation. *Symbolic Interaction, 30*(1),105–123.

Spennemann, D. H. (2007). The importance of heritage preservation in natural disaster situations. *International Journal of Risk Assessment and Management*, 993–1001.

The City of Hiroshima. (2018, March 24). *World cultural heritage sites "A-Bomb Dome" & "Hiroshima Peace Memorial Park"*. Retrieved from The City of Hiroshima: http://www.city.hiroshima.lg.jp/english/

United Nations. (2018, March 24). *Hiroshima Peace Memorial (Genbaku Dome)*. Retrieved from UNESCO World Heritage Centre: https://whc.unesco.org/en/list/775/

Restorative Spaces of Healing and Belonging

Justice seems to be on the move, leaving us with the challenging task of attending to responsibilities for justices at the local level with its own very specific particularities, as well as more "universal" global inequalities and injustices that transcend borders. The rest of this chapter continues to grapple with this thorny issue, guided by the voices and research of additional case contributors. Herein lies a treasure trove of insights! A few guidelines may be helpful as you navigate through the different worlds they present:

- As with the above case, each of the cases below invites you to look at tourism and hospitality *differently*. Substitute yourself into *being* one of various participants in each case—feel what it might like to be in the position of the local resident, disaster, or atrocity survivor.

- Contemplate the potential and possibilities of different mechanisms, processes and activities discussed in the cases to facilitate benefits like healing and empowerment, or solidarity and caring, or safety and belonging. Note how responsibilities toward justice for various groups are being taken up, though sometimes failing (e.g., Case 4.4). Keep up your critical, charitable gaze!
- Like the case above, each of the cases below offer unique insights, but they share some common themes. Can you identify these? A few aspects are highlighted below to provide some signposts to the gems of hope and inspiration to be gathered. So, practice "slow tourism" (virtually, at least), dwell and linger within each case, keeping the local and the global in mind with respect to responsibility and good "citizenship."

Sites of Recognition and Restoration

All the cases relate to vulnerable populations and groups in different contexts. What are some of the practices that facilitate solidarity and healing over generations of survivors and descendants in the above case? Historic sites like the African Burial Ground National Monument (abbreviated as ABG below) in New York City and Elmina Castle in Ghana ("Elmina Castle," n.d.) discussed by Linda Enoh in Case 4.2 below represent sacred spaces to which secular pilgrimages are undertaken by many roots-seeking, diasporic visitors. Some find moments of peace and identity through connecting to ancestors and paying homage at the site (do you see any problem in calling them "dark tourism" sites?). They are sites of emotional healing and existential meaning for many diasporic groups whose enslaved ancestors were dispersed far and wide during the trans-Atlantic slave trade. Here, diasporic visitors can build solidarity and collective memory, pay homage to lost ancestors, seek roots and identity, and find temporary refuge and respite.

Such sites also play an important role in raising pride and self-esteem, facilitating *psychological recognition*. Like Nancy Fraser, philosopher Axel Honneth argues that *recognition* is an element of justice, but unlike Nancy Fraser's political conception of justice as recognition (see Chapter 3), he focuses on the psychological dimension of recognition (see Honneth, 1995, 2001; for a different perspective, see Taylor, 1994). Positive interactions with others, and the approval of others, are important for our sense of dignity, self-worth, and integrity—it is more than simply being tolerated, say Honneth. By contrast, Nancy Fraser argues for a status model of recognition where, rather than focusing on an individual or group's specific identity, justice as recognition aims to ensure that groups have "standing as full partners in social interaction, able to participate as peers with others in social life" (Fraser in Dahl, Stoltz, & Willig, 2004, p. 376; see Fraser, 2010). For Fraser, by definition, justice pertains to social structures and institutional frameworks; rather than focusing on the goodness or badness of a society, a

122 Responsibility and Care

theory of justice should allow us to evaluate social arrangements from one very important angle, she says:

> How fair or unfair are the terms of interaction that are institutionalized in the society? Does the society's structural–institutional framework, which sets the ground rules for social interaction, permit all to participate as peers in social interaction? Or does it institutionalize patterns of advantage and disadvantage that systematically prevent some people from participating on terms of parity? Do the society's institutionalized patterns of cultural value create status hierarchies, which impede parity of participation? Does its economic structure create class stratification, which also forecloses the possibility of parity? (Fraser in Dahl et al., 2004, p. 378; see Fraser, 2010)

Nancy Fraser and Axel Honneth differ significantly in how they conceptualize recognition and its role in relation to redistribution. For more on this, check out their debates in Fraser and Honneth (2003). It would seem that the history and heritage of cultural heritage sites need to be designed, developed, represented, and shared with attention to all aspects of *recognition*: psychological, social, economic, and political. Tourism can play a valuable role here to help legitimize the group, making it socially "visible" to the public and facilitating opportunities for dialogue and interaction that can contribute to psychological recognition. Of course, site design and development require care and thoughtfulness to the psychological needs of the cultural groups, e.g., cultural trauma stemming from colonialism and post-traumatic stress disorder resulting from wars and traumatic events—atrocities like holocausts, slavery, atomic bombing of Hiroshima and Nagasaki, as well as natural disasters.

Political and power relationships also require careful identification and mediation. As the slogan in feminism goes, "the personal is political." See, for example, the two different stories presented at Magnolia Plantation in Case 4.2 by Linda Enoh below. African American visitors to plantations sites in the southern US have expressed concern about "whitewashing" or sanitizing of their history and heritage. Without fair *representation* and *direct participation* in the development, conservation, marketing and management of their cultural heritage, the histories and stories of minority, oppressed or colonized groups risk being marginalized or framed according to the interests of the "winners," i.e., by the dominant groups in power. Moreover, participation and *voice in decision making* opens avenues for fair interpretation of their rich cultural traditions and significant social and political accomplishments and successes. There are many missing stories to fill in. Sharing success stories of scientific and technological contributions by African American women and men can help dispel stereotypes and gender biases, contributing to forward-looking efforts to address structurally engrained racial injustices. As an example, read the story of Gladys May on BBC online (Butterly, 2018). Constructive narratives and voices in growing women's movements like the Me Too Movement (#MeToo) are rising to gain recognition and oppose

Responsibility and Care **123**

labor inequalities, sexual abuse, and patriarchal oppression worldwide. Emerging historical and archeological evidence, such as of the participation of enslaved Blacks in the American Civil War, for instance, needs to be shared with citizens and visitors—their presence and contributions toward democracy and freedom have primarily been suppressed in historical accounts and public awareness (see Thoms, 2008).

Case 4.2: Roots-Seeking and Belonging in the African Diaspora

Linda Lelo Enoh

Like many graduate students, my dissertation journey into slavery tourism was not a straight line. The more I learned about heritage tourism, the more I dug into it, from roots tourism to dark tourism and finally to slavery tourism. I'm still amazed by how my research work has transformed my own approach to slavery, from being ashamed every time slavery was mentioned at school or on television, to feeling such pride once I took ownership of the history of slavery and acknowledged it as a part of my personal heritage. The case below draws from the qualitative research I conducted on site at the African Burial Ground National Monument in New York City in 2008 and 2010.

More than 45% of the enslaved Africans transported to the "New World" during the Trans-Atlantic Slave Trade came from the region called West Central Africa and St. Helena (which includes today's Republic of the Congo, the Democratic Republic of the Congo, and Angola). Only 3.6% of those who survived the Middle-Passage ended up in the North American mainland (the first enslaved Africans were brought by Dutch traders to the British colony of Jamestown, Virginia in 1619) (Eltis & Richardson, 2002).

Since the 1950s, many African American descendants have been attracted to the African continent and to Ghana in particular, in search of their cultural heritage and roots. The expression "Roots Tourism" applies to such diasporic populations that seek connection, identity and meaning by traveling to their country of origin. Finley (2004, p. 114) describes roots-seeking tourists to Africa as people who "seek a return to an ancestral homeland often made visible by the idea or racial memory of Africa as a place of familial origin in the transatlantic slave trade."

Visiting cultural events and festivals like the Oshun festival in Nigeria and slavery-related sites like to the popular UNESCO World Heritage Site of Elmina Castle in Ghana offers to many a sense of connection and cultural identifica-tion. With that said, the African continent, commonly referred to as "the motherland," represents a place of pride, a place of beginning and harmony (Bruner, 1996, p. 290). Most African American visitors to Elmina Castle in Ghana book their trip with travel agencies that cater to black tourists and

124 Responsibility and Care

participate in activities that are exclusively tailored to Black visitors, including walking the "Through the Door of No Return—The Return" which reenacts the capture of African slaves and the return of their descendants to Africa (Bruner, 1996). The fact that visitors can walk through the same doors, dungeons, and other areas in the castle that their ancestors once walked through centuries ago makes the experience quite powerful for African Americans. For many, participating in these activities (reenactments, libations, prayers, songs, dances, and so on) enables them to feel more connected to each other and to the land of their ancestors (Bruner, 1996).

On the American side of the Atlantic, and particularly in southern states like Louisiana, former plantations and other enslavement related sites offer an opportunity to examine a dark period in US history. For black visitors, it is a chance to learn more about how their enslaved ancestors lived and ultimately overcame such terrible conditions. Magnolia Plantation in the Cane River area of Louisiana is the perfect illustration of the duality in visitors' experiences. One side of the plantation, owned and operated by the descendant of the plantation owner, focuses on the privately owned main house, its family history and architecture, and presents a relatively whitewashed picture of the opulent lives of plantation owners, with enslaved Africans portrayed as "servants" at the house (Dann & Seaton, 2001. See also http://www.magno liaplantation.com/house.html. Accessed April 29, 2018). The side of Magnolia Plantation that is operated by the U.S. National Park Service attempts to provide a more comprehensive and fairer story of the experience of the enslaved men, women and children who worked and lived on the property (see https://www.nps.gov/cari/learn/historyculture/magnolia-plantation-his tory.htm and http://www.magnoliaplantation.com/slaverytofreedom.html. Accessed April 29, 2018). Plantation history is slowly being revised to offer a fairer interpretation of this terrible period of US history, see for example, the description of the experience offered at McLeod Plantation Historic Site, in Charleston, South Carolina: https://ccprc.com/1447/McLeod-Plantation-His toric-Site (accessed April 29, 2018).

The African Burial Ground National Monument (U.S. National Park Service, USA)

Contrary to popular belief, slavery in America didn't just concentrate in the South, and African presence in the United States has a much longer history than simply the image of southern cotton plantations and lynchings that commonly come to mind. The unearthing of a 17th-century cemetery during the construction of a federal building in lower Manhattan (New York City) revealed that an estimated 15,000 free and enslaved Africans were buried there.

The African Burial Ground National Monument (ABG henceforth) which commemorates and protects this site was born from a strong grassroots movement that led to its Presidential Proclamation as a United States

National Monument in 2006 (see: https://www.nps.gov/afbg. Accessed May 9, 2018). Before the plans for the design of a memorial were finally approved in April 2005, the U.S. General Services Administration (GSA) and the National Park Service (NPS) engaged the community through listening sessions, public meetings, visitor experience workshops, and a research roundtable (National Park Service, 2009). Though slavery-related sites like former plantations have tended to be poorly visited by African Americans in the past,[1] the ABG receives mostly Black visitors, including African American high school and college students from New York City. As do African American visitors at other sites with enslavement history, they pay particular attention to how black history, or slavery, is represented. An "honest" representation that shows the valuable contributions made by Africans and a richer picture of their cultural traditions and practices was appreciated by visitors participating in my study. For instance:

> "I'm always very mindful of how people talk about slavery. […] Because I'm black and because I know the people working were slaves. And the white people benefited from it and a lot of times it's a white person doing the talking [at historical sites], unable to acknowledge the fact that they benefited from that. And so by saying servants, that dismisses the cost that we paid and that they benefited from. […] Even though it may be difficult for them, but it needs to be honest, be truthful. Lance: Black male in his 40s (all first names used are pseudonyms)

> […] the more I understand the critical role that the Africans played in the life of the colony, the less patience I have with versions of history that leave that out. Natasha: Black female in her 60s

Several participants in this study stated that they go to the ABG on a regular basis to communicate with their African ancestors, and to "pray" and remember, as more than one participant put it (see Photo 4.2.1 which depicts the burial of an enslaved adult and an infant). Through these communications, these visitors claim they receive solace and even answers to questions. Also, a good number of the participants described their first visit to the new visitor center as highly emotional, as Erika describes:

> And that's why now, the film, I just saw the film […] that they produced. I cried the whole time. Because going from having nothing […] And just orating the story, which is also part of our tradition […] to having drawings, to having events and commemorations and dramatizations, to having this film. It's awesome. Erika: Black female in her 30s

PHOTO 4.2.1   The burial scene is a central space of gathering at the African Burial Ground National Monument visitor center
Photo credit: Linda Lelo Enoh (July 2010)

Managers of African American heritage sites like Magnolia Plantation and the ABG should be aware that these are sites of great significance for African Americans and Black people in general because they represent places for possible reconnection to a lost past and enable the possibility of forging a collective memory. Indeed, the depiction of the other side of slavery that presents enslaved Africans as human beings with rich cultural roots, strength, resilience, and an incontestable sense of resistance and spirit, as supported by historical evidence, is proven to be critical to social and cultural well-being. The development and management of slavery heritage sites require the recognition and inclusion of all key stakeholders related to the conservation, development and management of the site and/or objects from the site. Inclusion of all key stakeholders (particularly the African American (Black) community) from the start of the planning process should favor collaboration and reduce conflict (see Lelo, 2012 for more).

Note

1 See Buzinde (2007) on Hampton Plantation in South Carolina, Lawton & Weaver (2008) in relation to Congaree National Park in South Carolina, and Butler, Carter, & Dwyer's (2008) study of Laura Creole Plantation in Louisiana.

References

Bruner, E. M. (1996). Tourism in Ghana: The representation of slavery and the return of the Black diaspora. *American Anthropologist, 98*(2), 290–304. https://doi.org/10.1525/aa.1996.98.2.02a00060

Butler, D. L., Carter, P. L., & Dwyer, O. J. (2008). Imagining plantations: Slavery, dominant narratives, and the foreign born. *Southeastern Geographer, 48*(3), 288–302. https://doi.org/10.1353/sgo.0.0026

Buzinde, C. N. (2007). Representational politics of plantation heritage tourism: The contemporary plantation as a social imaginary. In C. McCarthy, A. S. Durham, L. C. Engel, & A. A. Filmer (Eds.), *Globalizing cultural studies: Ethnographic interventions in theory, method, and policy* (2nd ed., p. 541). Peter Lang Inc., International Academic Publishers.

Dann, G. M. S., & Seaton, A. V. (Eds.). (2001). *Slavery, contested heritage, and thanatourism.* New York, NY: Routledge. https://doi.org/10.4324/9780203062586

Eltis, D., & Richardson, D. (2002). The achievements of the "numbers game." In D. Northrup (Ed.), *The Atlantic slave trade* (2nd ed., pp. 95–100). Boston, MA: Houghton Mifflin Company.

Finley, C. (2004). Authenticating dungeons, whitewashing castles: The former sites of the slave trade on the Ghanaian coast. In *Architecture and tourism: Perception, performance and place* (pp. 109–128). London, UK: Berg.

Lawton, L. J., & Weaver, D. B. (2008). Factors associated with non-visitation by area to Congaree National Park, South Carolina. *Journal of Park and Recreation Administration, 26*(4), 66–82.

Lelo, L. (2012). *Victims Or Victors?: Exploring America's slavery roots.* Doctoral Dissertation, Texas A&M University, College Station, Texas.

National Park Service. (2009). General Management Plan Newsletter 2—Fall 2009.

Care and attention to site design, representation, and interpretation, offer possibilities for *forward looking* reconciliation and respect (not simply tolerance), enabling new opportunities for learning and appreciation. Sites like the African Burial Ground in Case 4.2 demonstrate potential for *restorative practices* that facilitate learning, cross-cultural communication and reconciliation, such as through events celebrating art, music, and food traditions, as well as hosting community discussions and rehabilitation programs. They offer synergistic opportunities to help advance *restorative justice*, an alternative justice approach that seeks to repair harm from criminal behavior and build peace through cooperative processes involving key stakeholders (Gavrielides, 2007).

Small community museums like the Brazos Valley African American Museum in Bryan, Texas, similarly offer restorative spaces for healing the past and building new relationships of care and solidarity. This museum arose through grassroots

128 Responsibility and Care

efforts and strives toward inclusiveness, reaching out to community members through various social and cultural events. Among its displays are the stories of local African American residents and businesses that have contributed to community cohesion and social good ("Brazos Valley African American Museum," n.d.). Like other small community museums and heritage sites, it has struggled over the years to obtain adequate resources for staffing, developing interpretive exhibits, marketing, etc. and collaborative initiatives are crucial for its well-being. See, too, the Indigenous stories, rights and responsibilities represented at the Canadian Museum of Human Rights (Canadian Museum for Human Rights, n.d.). Indigenous *control, self-determination* and *ownership* are important issues in Indigenous cultural sites. In all cultural heritage spaces, a key principle is *direct participation in decision making by those who stand to be most impacted* by the design, development, conservation, management, and marketing of their cultural heritage (e.g., sites like HPMP, ABG, and the museums noted above).

Care and Empowerment

Important issues of *redistribution* also arise in relation to the above. How can minority groups subject to socially and institutionally embedded discrimination received fair distribution (or redistribution as Nancy Fraser put it) of public resources toward conserving or developing their cultural heritage? Social and political *recognition* is crucial for securing resources and support to develop and sustain not only cultural heritage sites, but also intangible cultural heritage, cultural events and spaces that are important to solidarity, identity, recognition, and safety of diverse groups. The Peace Park at the Hiroshima Peace Memorial in Case 4.1 is a place of social gathering as well as political activism and solidarity. Other examples include, for instance, support for Gay Pride parades and *safe* places of hospitality, solidarity and gathering for LGBT+ visitors; inclusiveness and access to neighborhood parks for leisure and recreation for minority groups; funding of community museums, social and cultural events that enable learning, recognition and solidarity building for marginalized and stigmatized groups.

Fair trade organizations, micro-credit NGOs and social enterprises are also actively engaged in social responsibility, enabling opportunities for disadvantaged groups and vulnerable populations to gain living wages, recognition, and inclusion in society. Case 4.3 on Street Voices is an innovative case offered by Dianne Dredge and researcher Eóin Meehan. Located in Copenhagen, Street Voices is a social enterprise that works toward capacity building and rehabilitating vulnerable groups (many of whom have experienced substance addiction, homelessness, and prostitution), as well as combating social prejudices against this marginalized segment of Danish society. It provides training to become street guides and offers collaborative opportunities to participate directly in the development and delivery of walking tours. As in the above case, psychological and social *recognition* is enabled as well as *empowerment*. Guides learn skills, develop a sense of self-worth and gain confidence as they interact with visitors.

Visitors gain unique perspectives on city life and of different areas in the city, and develop respect and appreciation for the responsibility and care that the guides extend to their guests.

Case 4.3: Street Voices, Copenhagen, Denmark

Dianne Dredge and Eóin Meehan

The prevailing rhetoric argues that tourism can simultaneously deliver social, environmental and economic value while also improving quality of life and well-being. Under late modern capitalism however, tourism has predominantly been framed as an economic activity where growth and profit are emphasized. There is little evidence that tourism has delivered large scale socio-cultural benefits, with evidence tending to be extrapolated from case studies and individual projects and not necessarily generalizable. Moreover, responsibility for delivering well-being, quality of life, community empowerment and other benefits of tourism has been positioned "out there," attributed to no one in particular, and bestowed like magic from trickle-down economics (Dredge, 2017a). It is little wonder that marginalized groups, especially in heavily touristed locations, are asking how they, too, can tap into, and benefit from, the flows of visitors and capital that glide in and out of the touristed landscapes they inhabit.

In response to late modern capitalism, a moral, caring turn is taking hold, and within this tourism social entrepreneurship is a small but growing movement (Sheldon, Pollock, & Daniele, 2017) (Sheldon & Daniele, 2017). Social entrepreneurship is a particular type of entrepreneurial activity where social objectives, not profit, provide the core focus of the business model (Mair & Marti Lanuza, 2009). Tourism social entrepreneurship pushes the opportunity for meaningful action well beyond what "Corporate Social Responsibility" (CSR) offers, with three noteworthy features. First, tourism social entrepreneurship marks an ethical shift in the way we define responsibility. It calls us to care *about* things less and to care *for* others more. In doing so, social entrepreneurship challenges universal principles about how we should act and behave, and instead, argues for a relational form of care ethics, wherein caring and responsibility are framed as reciprocal, and deeply embedded in our personal commitments to others (Gilligan, 1982). Furthermore, the intimacy of caring creates bonds that foster relational ecologies, characterized by empathy, trust and equity. Second, tourism social entrepreneurship incorporates social benefit as a central mission of the business and, in doing so, invites us to appreciate other kinds of value produced by tourism beyond economic benefit. Third, by leveraging relational ecologies, tourism social enterprise seeks to scale social benefits beyond the individual social enterprise, and in doing so empower a social movement that cares for and takes responsibility for others (Dredge, 2017b).

Street Voices (Gadens Stemmer) is a Copenhagen-based registered social enterprise that provides walking tours of the city's neighborhood. The guides are from vulnerable and disadvantaged backgrounds, having experienced substance addiction, homelessness and prostitution. In the process of being trained as street guides, participants develop a sense of independence and self-worth, and they also develop a range of professional and personal skills that help them enter and operate within the formal structures of society. On the tour, they share their stories of living on the streets and existing at the margins of society where the social welfare system does not reach. In the process of delivering their stories, the guides are empowered as survivors and they build awareness, empathy, and understanding with tour participants about the challenges that they have previously faced, or currently confront (see Photo 4.3.1). As a social enterprise, the main objective of Street Voices is to encourage and support guides' re-entry into mainstream economic and social participation through, for example, employment, paying taxes, and participating in planning meetings and product development. Street Voices also seeks to combat a range of prejudices prevalent in society about less fortunate and marginalized members of society that late modern capitalism has perpetuated. These prejudices include ideas that homelessness, drug addiction and prostitution are lifestyle choices people make, and that marginalized people are less valuable members of society, cannot be rehabilitated, and will remain a drain on society over their lifetimes. Street Voices turns these prejudices around. However, the social enterprise is not without challenges.

Street Voices is a social business that seeks to pay its own way. Profits from the walking tours are reinvested into the development of the street tours and in supporting the guides, and it does not use charitable, philanthropic or government funds to help balance its budget. This means that the organization not only needs to make a profit, but in order to scale up its social impact, it also needs to grow its business. The main market for the tours offered by Street Voices are school groups, and in the summer, when the streets of Copenhagen are crowded with tourists, the schools are on vacation and guides have little work. The social enterprise has found it difficult to tap into the right tourist markets. It rejects the label "poverty tourism"; it does not want to encourage voyeurism; and the organization remains skeptical that tapping into mass tourism will bring tourists with an appropriate mindset. Street Voices has also experienced some challenges with established marketing channels, with the DMO not keen to promote tours that offer a shadowy perspective on Copenhagen.

Tapping into and developing appropriate products that address seasonality issues, etc., are ongoing challenges for the organization. Street Voices now offers tours on the city's canals. These offer visitors an alternative

PHOTO 4.3.1 Students and faculty members of Tourism Studies from Aalborg University Copenhagen being led by our guide from Street Voices through Halmtorvet in the Vesterbro district of Copenhagen. The building directly ahead hosts "Venligbohus," a volunteer organization for welcoming those with refugee backgrounds into the community. The building to the right is used as a communal space in the daytime for vulnerable individuals to cook and rest
Photo Credit: Eóin Meehan

perspective on the city's idyllic waterfronts, architecture, and historical monuments while accessing a larger visitor base and a more central position in the tourism offer. Street Voices further extends its activities to matters of environmental concern through a recycling initiative at the Roskilde Festival. Drinks containers (cans, glass bottles, plastic containers) under a recycling deposit scheme are collected with proceeds reinvested in the social enterprise. Street Voices arranges free entry for guides and other volunteers who, throughout the week-long festivities, devote time to gathering recyclables. This initiative demonstrates the organization's interest in extending their income stream in support of their core mission which states "All people should have the opportunity to develop and interact with the rest of society."

Street Voices clearly demonstrates an ethic of care towards its guides, where responsibility is enacted through the nurturing of direct, tangible and caring relationships. The relational dimensions of this caring mean that responsibility is not "out there," the responsibility of no one in particular, and delivered, as if my magic, from trickle-down economics. Instead, it is performed in the daily practices and relationships between people who care, including guides and managers. The manager demonstrates care in everyday work, firstly, by providing employment pathways for vulnerable individuals to re-enter society, and secondly, by fostering guides' skills and confidence. For example, guides give tours in languages other than Danish, including German and English, and in this process, have been empowered and built confidence in language and communication skills. They have organized themselves into a collective to engage with management about pay and other conditions, and have established their own communication channels through which they care for and support each other. Street Voices also positions the guides as carers as they shepherd visitors off the beaten track through winding urban arteries. They take responsibility for their guests, avoiding alleys and doorways that might harbor disagreeable or vulnerable locals, and are careful not to make a spectacle of less fortunate street dwellers. They offer explanations of the hard realities faced by disadvantaged members of society and a social welfare system that is admired globally, yet not without problems. This care work and the responsibility given to the guides also empowers them, it builds confidence and trust, which they take with them into their daily lives and relationships.

References

Dredge, D. (2017a). Responsibility and care in the collaborative economy. In D. Dredge & S. Gyimóthy (Eds.), *Collaborative economy and tourism: Perspectives, politics, policies and prospects* (pp. 41–57). Springer, Cham. https://doi.org/10.1007/978-3-319-51799-5_4

Dredge, D. (2017b). Social entrepreneurship and tourism. In P. J. Sheldon & R. Daniele, (Eds.), *Social entrepreneurship and tourism: Philosophy and practice* (pp. 35–55). Cham: Springer International Publishing. https://doi.org/10.1007/978-3-319-46518-0

Gilligan, C. (1982). *In a different voice: Psychological theory and women's development.* Cambridge, MA: Harvard University Press.

Mair, J., & Marti Lanuza, I. (2009). Entrepreneurship in and around Institutional Voids: A case study from Bangladesh. *Journal of Business Venturing, 24*(5), 419–435. https://doi.org/10.1016/j.jbusvent.2008.04.006

Sheldon, P. J., Pollock, A., & Daniele, R. (2017). Social entrepreneurship and tourism: Setting the stage. In P. J. Sheldon & R. Daniele (Eds.), *Social entrepreneurship and tourism: Philosophy and practice* (pp. 1–18). Springer, Cham. https://doi.org/10.1007/978-3-319-46518-0_1

Social enterprise and other models of social entrepreneurship offer alternative modes of provisioning and strengthening the local than instrumental market-based approaches. Profit in Street Voices is socially motivated, it aims to reduce inequalities among vulnerable and disadvantaged residents, and facilitate their well-being and reintegration into social life through *relations of care*. The case illustrates many social justice and ethical principles discussed previously, e.g., building capabilities, respect (for others and for human rights), solidarity, recognition, inclusiveness, and participation of marginalized and vulnerable groups in civic society. Socially just economies eschew neoliberal market capitalism premised on unlimited growth, consumption, and maximizing of corporate profit to the benefit a few. Instead, they encourage local forms of exchange and fair trade, and aim to reduce inequalities through practices based on social justice and relations of care and concern (see also Peredo & McLean, 2006, 2013).

Summary and Further Considerations

This chapter raises questions related to our personal and shared responsibility not just in the world of travel and tourism, but when we return home. Responsibility doesn't stop in the destination, especially not in a globalized world of climate change and neoliberal globalization. Questions of *global citizenship* and local-global responsibility arise for the tourist, who is also a resident or citizen somewhere. In matters of structural injustices within and across borders, *shared responsibility* and *political responsibilities* arise that are important to address in a *forward-looking* approach such as Young's social connection model offers (Young, 2006, 2013). Her approach offers a way to understand our roles and responsibilities with respect to structurally embedded injustices, how to think about it, which ones to engage in, and the kind of actions needed.

Various cases reveal responsibilities such as: (i) facilitating restorative practices that enable forward-looking ways to reconcile different groups involved in structural injustices; (ii) creating safe spaces to heal from cultural trauma and loss, and to gather in solidarity and care; (iii) developing, protecting and sharing cultural heritage of racially oppressed or marginalized groups; (iv) enabling inclusiveness, respect and *recognition* (political, social and psychological); (v) ensuring *representation* and participation of those who stand to be most impacted by the development, conservation, management and marketing of their own culture and heritage. They also point to the importance of *redistribution* and *self-determination* for cultural groups to identify the stories and practices they wish to share and to be fully involved in the process. Many of these priorities may require *building capabilities* for effective participation and inclusion.

The various examples also speak to an ethic of care that complements responsibility for justice. It is an ethic of *care for* the other and *care about* places and spaces. For example: Caring for vulnerable groups (including post-disaster and diasporic populations, and their homes and cultural heritage); care that strengthens the local, creates just economies and creates designs and development

134 Responsibility and Care

that facilitate psychological as well as social and political recognition; caring about place and the impacts of global issues like climate change on ecosystems and people. Case 4.4 on Nicaragua below by Emily Höckert reveals a number of problems to which insights from this chapter and previous chapters can be applied. She alerts us to another form of hospitality, a *radical* responsibility for "the other." It is a challenging one to embrace, but the question of responsibility by visitors to those who have suffered the consequences of imperialism and colonialism is worth contemplating in regard to this case.

Questions for Further Reflection

1. Pretend you were on that trip with Jenna and share her concerns and worries (you, too, are now informed about the situation). Based on the social connections model and parameters provided by Iris Marion Young, which structural injustice would you pick to get involved in? How would you undertake the task, if you do choose to get involved? If you don't feel you have a responsibility to be involved, explain why.
2. Do Starbucks customers in the US and Canada bear any responsibility in relation to the Philadelphia issue mentioned in the chapter? Draw on Young's social connection model to discuss your response.
3. What is the relationship between justice and an ethic of care?
4. Revisit the guidelines on Responsible Tourism presented at the Cape Town Declaration on Responsible Tourism, noted in Chapter 3 (Responsible Tourism Partnership, n.d.). What synergies do you see between Street Voices and the Responsible Tourism guidelines? What additional principles does Street Voices offer for Responsible Tourism?
5. Imagine you are one of the visitors ("guests") mentioned in the case below. What is your responsibility in this case? How would you exercise it?

Case 4.4: Responsible Tourism Development in San Ramón, Nicaragua

Emily Höckert

The idea of community participation has played an important role in the search for responsibility, sustainability, and social justice in tourism development. By involving local residents, the hope is to focus on the well-being of those being visited, instead of primarily on tourism promotion and growth. Participatory tourism projects are often led by a vision of a small-scale tourism development that brings complementary income and new employment opportunities to economically marginalized communities. During the last few decades, community-based tourism has been posed as an alternative way of developing tourism, by enhancing local communities' possibilities to plan, run, control and reap benefits from tourism activities (e.g., Scheyvens, 2002; Tosun, 2000). However, critique and skepticism about these goals and aspirations have grown steadily. Critics have pointed out that the tourism initiatives tend to be motivated by outside interests and make local communities dependent on external actors (e.g., Zapata, Hall, Lindo, & Vanderschaeghe, 2011). Many scholars and practitioners have argued that the idea of local participation is misleading as rural communities often lack needed skills, knowledge and material conditions needed for tourism development (Goodwin, Santilli, & Armstrong, 2014; Tosun, 2000).

This case study of San Ramón discusses some possibilities and challenges of community-based tourism, focusing on the notion of responsibility to others. Research for the case is based on a longitudinal ethnographic study (2007–2013) on tourism development in the coffee cultivating communities of Nicaragua. The purpose of the study is not to describe how members of rural communities "do" participation, but to explore host–guest relations in what appear to be responsible, participatory tourism encounters. Among other insights, this research project taught me that responsibility requires a readiness to interrupt one's own ways of thinking and helping (Höckert, 2018).

Rapid Growth of Tourism in Nicaragua

Nicaragua is a good example of a Central American country that has recently been seeking and seeing exponential growth in international tourism. Back in the 1980s, most foreign visitors to Nicaragua were US soldiers, volunteer workers on coffee plantations and representatives from development aid organizations. Growing interest in the volcanoes, pristine beaches and colonial towns in the country has raised tourism to one of the most important sources of foreign income, alongside coffee beans. Today, there are more than 1.5 million international tourists crossing Nicaragua's borders every year (INTUR, 2016).

Foreign investors and tourism entrepreneurs have been attracted not only by the colonial history and beautiful nature, but also by extremely low costs of labor, very attractive tax incentives and privatization of the Pacific coastline. Amidst an invasion of luxury resorts and residential tourism on the country's Pacific coast, it has become highly uncertain who is actually reaping the benefits from the boom in the tourism sector. Although tourism's potential contribution to development and poverty reduction has been the fundamental justification for Nicaraguan government to encourage tourism growth, the benefits from tourism initiatives have not spread equally around the country. Many tourism activities have led to a wide range of negative impacts, such as, sky-high land prices, land tenure conflicts, increased poverty, sexual exploitation of children and adolescents, water scarcity and

136 Responsibility and Care

environmental bulldozing. Attempts to increase the welfare of some have negatively affected the welfare of others, and have exacerbated the inequalities between the rich and poor (Gascón & Cañada, 2007; Hunt, 2011).

In response to emerging demands for fairer tourism, the Nicaraguan tourism ministry (INTUR), international aid agencies and non-governmental organizations have adopted rural tourism as a model aimed towards creating more sustainable forms of development. Nicaragua's National rural tourism strategy is supported by the law on Sustainable Rural Tourism (Law 835); both emphasize the importance of developing tourism that is based on active participation and local community control, and fair distribution of benefits (INTUR, 2009). The efforts of making tourism more democratic and equitable have led to heightened focus on previously excluded groups in development such as women, children, indigenous groups and Afro-descendants. This has led to a situation where many of Nicaragua's rural tourism initiatives have been founded as social projects, supported by a considerable influx of funds from the Nicaraguan government and development aid agencies such as USAID, Lux Development, and Swiss Development Agency COSUDE.

Tourism in the Coffee Trails of San Ramón

Four communities within the municipality of San Ramón located in the northern coffee highlands are among the pioneers of community-based rural tourism in Nicaragua. These communities had been receiving visitors already during the Sandinista revolution and international solidarity movements in the 1980s. During that time, thousands of left-leaning volunteers from the United States and Western Europe visited Nicaragua on organized study tours and coffee brigades, along with individual volunteers. These early guests picked coffee alongside local farmers and were interested in learning from the collective spirit of the Nicaraguan socialist revolution and the newly founded coffee cooperatives. More organized tourism development in the form of community-based tourism and agro-ecotourism began around 2003, after a severe crisis in global coffee prices (see http://www.tourism.ucasanramon.com/. Accessed April 7, 2018). The rural tourism program described here was spearheaded by the Central Association of Northern Coffee Cooperatives (CECOCAFEN) and the local coffee cooperative union UCA San Ramón. The initiative was supported by international non-governmental organizations (INGOs), like the United Nations Development Programme (UNDP), that offered financial and technical help (Photo 4.1.1). In addition to providing supplementary income and new contacts with coffee consumers, it was hoped that the project would contribute to gender equality by creating new job opportunities for women (e.g., offering homestays), and also for young people to act as guides (Photo 4.2.2).

Responsibility and Care **137**

PHOTO 4.4.1 Representatives of UNDP visiting one of the tourism communities in San Ramón in October 2008
Photo Credit: Emily Höckert

PHOTO 4.4.2 Bienvenidos. Welcome sign in front of a home offering accommodation
Photo Credit: Emily Höckert

The four communities also received voluntary help from other visitors who arrived with interest in helping the locals. They included Nicaraguan and foreign tourism practitioners, tour operators, researchers and students, and will be referred to below as "guests" (distinct from leisure tourists). Local hosts who committed to the rural tourism program were offered different forms of hospitality related training. They seemed grateful to the cooperative unions and INGOs who had invited them to such training and capacity-building sessions. Consultants offered training and courses that helped participants to gain more confidence in their skills for being "good hosts." This was particularly heartening to Doña Hilda, who told me that after her first child was born almost twenty years ago, she had lost her right to be a member in the local cooperative:

> Earlier I could not be part of almost anything. But when the coffee price went down my husband came and asked if I would like to start to work as a lodger for the tourists. I said "Yes!" It meant that I was able to go to official meetings and workshops and training sessions with the other women. Before that I had never been able to do so. I have also been able to visit other communities when there have been these workshops.

In fact, many of the women experienced that membership in the tourism project and availability of microloans for tourism development brought them more alternatives, flexibility and mobility (see also Scheyvens, 2002). The village landscapes were also enriched with painted boards that said "bienvenidos" ("welcome") to visitors and pointed to houses offering tourist accommodation (see Photo 4.4.2 above). Other signs showed how to get to the waterfall, the old gold mine and the scenic lookouts. The boards also provided information to help identify different trees and explained which coffee plants were organic. Posters paid tribute to generous donations from INTUR and different aid organizations. Perhaps the largest project was the construction of huts for guests. The local hosts were persuaded to take microcredit loans with relatively high interest rates, in order to build the huts, which were not locally designed and required imported, expensive building materials. Many of the locals found it problematic that they were not able to use local resources, and were concerned about how they could pay back these loans. While the number of leisure tourists increased during the first years of the program, visitation dropped drastically quite soon after the huts were built. Reasons for the decline were attributed to various factors, ranging from the global financial crisis of 2008 to challenges of cooperating and creating new contacts with external tour operators. The host families ended up paying back the tourism development loans they had taken (and the interest on them) with their coffee beans.

Feeling weary of waiting for tourists who were no longer coming, the local communities began to show resistance towards new development interventions and research projects proposed by some of the visiting groups. Although leisure tourist numbers had declined, representatives of many bilateral aid organizations and NGOs, volunteers, students and researchers were still frequent visitors. Many arrived with good intentions to help the locals to participate in tourism in the "right" way and to improve their learning of hospitality and tourism development. Doña Hilda, who had earlier welcomed the tourism project with open arms, gave an example of tourism consultants' visits with the following words:

> This consultant came from the capital city. She looked at the rooms and said that we could not receive visitors in rooms like these. So she wanted to make changes in the place. She said we should have curtains, raise the ceilings and so on. We thought that we do not want to do this. It is too risky to take new loans for tourism development.

Several local hosts subsequently decided that the "helpful" guests like these were no longer welcome to their homes and home community. That is, the local hosts became so tired of some of the helpers that they began to say "no" to those who arrived with good intentions to help. Simultaneously, some of the representatives of the Nicaraguan tourism ministry INTUR and international donors were expressing disappointment with rural communities that were, in their view, missing the right attitudes to work with tourism.

How Did Good Intentions Turn into Mutual Frustration?

It merits mentioning that there are obviously participatory projects where the local communities have managed to reap a wide range of positive impacts from tourism development. However, the case of San Ramón offers important lessons about the difficulties of spearheading community development through tourism. Why have these supposedly joint collaborations between locals and external volunteers and groups, developing local services and home-based accommodation for income to benefit locals, etc., caused so much frustration among both hosts and guests? One explanation lies in the ways in which the well-intended guests who visited San Ramón tended to trivialize or romanticize the historical, social and material experiences of the people living in host communities. For instance, many of the guests failed to understand how overwhelming these loans were to families living under the poverty line. There were also researchers and volunteers who wanted to help, but used the local tourism services for free. These guests took it for granted that rural communities would receive them and their help unconditionally.

140 Responsibility and Care

Another common error lay in preset agendas of participation and pre-set assumptions of what tourism "is." Guests traveled with ready-made plans and a strong desire to support the local hosts, but forgot to ask what kind of support and guidance their hosts actually needed. Hence, despite—or actually because of—strong emancipatory intentions to help the local communities, these well-intended visitors end up dominating the dialogues and spheres of participation. Despite these challenges, however, community participation—being, knowing and doing together—can contribute toward local capacity building and democracy through direct engagement and residents taking charge of their own development. Direct resident participation and control over the kind of visitor experience they wish to provide can enable a more genuine form of hospitality to emerge. The form of tourism being engaged in San Ramón offers valuable insights into the idea of responsibility in tourism and how external control might be averted. Among other things, responsibility involves caring for the wellbeing of the "other." French philosopher Emmanuel Levinas's work on ethics and responsibility offers an alternative way of understanding what has been happening in San Ramón and why these kinds of supposedly responsible actions and encounters might lead to disappointments among hosts and guests.

Emmanuel Levinas and Responsibility for the Other

In an important work, *Totality and Infinity*, Levinas (1969) suggests that the Western intellectual tendency to treat responsibility as a project of an individual and spontaneous subject should be resisted by thinking of ethics as openness towards "the other." For Levinas, ethics are not situated in the self, but in the intersubjective relation with the other person and it involves a strong sense of hospitality, an obligation to be there for that person, and to take responsibility for her or his well-being. This obligation to welcome the other "calls in question the naïve right of my powers, my glorious spontaneity as a living being" (Levinas, 1969, p. 85). He eschews oppressive dichotomies between self and other, subject and object, and emphasizes a *relational* mode of being with the other.

Reading Levinas' thinking on phenomenology as openness to other, helps to recognize how tourism development encounters include not only epistemological conflicts (conflicting ways of knowing), but equally the potential for conflictive ontological encounters (different ways of being). To put it differently, there are not only different ways of knowing, but also being with the "other," and "multiple others." Some of these ways of experiencing are more categorizing and aggressive than others (Rae, 2017). However, it seems like the ongoing debates on community participation in tourism, have paid only limited attention to understanding the different foundations of the social, and different ways of being responsible to another (or to others, which Levinas says involves considerations of justice, i.e., when there's a third person or more) (see also Grimwood, Yudina, Muldoon, & Qiu, 2015). Too little attention has also been paid to the notions of hospitality and care for the other in community-based tourism. In line with Levinas' notions, this study argues that participation in community-based tourism cannot be based on totalizing conditions and rules that are meant to dominate the other. Instead, the conditions of participating become constantly negotiated in intersubjective relations between self and the other that involve a very strong responsibility and caring for the other. By contrast, the case study from San Ramón showed a great deal of inequality between hosts and guests. The guests were primarily behaving as "experts"—asymmetrical power relations were evident in the way knowledge was being communicated (one-way, rather than mutually engaging and inviting local and traditional knowledge and culturally sensitive dialogue).

In line with Levinasian ethics, being responsible is always relational. Being responsible requires continuous negotiation between self and the other, and readiness to interrupt one's pre-assumptions about what kind of help the other needs and hopes for. Being responsible requires readiness to interrupt one's own ways of being, knowing and doing. To engage with the "other" one encounters in the context of tourism *makes us fully responsible for the well-being and care of the other* (following Levinas). The case of San Ramón reveals how hospitality went astray and that responsibility involves, among other things, at least (i) being equitable not just in relation to profits and income, but also in terms of power relationships, sharing knowledge and inviting reciprocity in knowledge sharing, (ii) engaging in dialogue and extending care for the other in the encounter, and (iii) being willing to assume responsibility for the well-being of the other (Levinas calls for assuming full responsibility).

References

Gascón, J., & Cañada, E. (2007). El turismo y sus mitos. Managua, Nicaragua: Fundación Luciernaga.

Goodwin, H., Santilli, R., & Armstrong, R. (2014). *Community-based tourism in the developing world: Delivering the goods?* (H. Goodwin & X. Font, Eds.), *Progress in Responsible Tourism* (Vol. 3). Goodfellow Publishers Limited.

Grimwood, B. S. R., Yudina, O., Muldoon, M., & Qiu, J. (2015). Responsibility in tourism: A discursive analysis. *Annals of Tourism Research*, *50*, 22–38. https://doi.org/10.1016/j.annals.2014.10.006

Höckert, E. (2018). *Negotiating hospitality, ethics of tourism development in the Nicaraguan highlands*. London, UK. https://doi.org/978-1138551497

Hunt, C. (2011). Passport to development? Local perceptions of the outcomes of post-socialist tourism policy and growth in Nicaragua. *Tourism Planning & Development*, *8*(3), 265–279. https://doi.org/10.1080/21568316.2011.591155

142 Responsibility and Care

> INTUR. (2009). *Definición de la Política y Estrategias para el Turismo Rural Sostenible de Nicaragua*. Managua, Nicaragua: Instituto Nicaragüense de Turismo.
>
> INTUR. (2016). *Comportamiento de las Estadísticas de Turismo*. Managua, Nicaragua: Instituto Nicaragüense de Turismo.
>
> Levinas, E. (1969). *Totality and infinity: An essay on exteriority*. (A. Alphonso Lingis, Trans.). Pittsburgh, PA, U.S.A.: Duquesne University Press.
>
> Rae, G. (2017). The politics of justice: Levinas, violence, and the ethical–political relation. *Contemporary Political Theory*, *17*(1), 49–68. https://doi.org/10.1057/s41296-017-0141-z
>
> Scheyvens, R. (2002). *Tourism for development: Empowering communities*. Harlow, UK: Prentice Hall. https://doi.org/10.1016/j.tourman.2005.07.013
>
> Tosun, C. (2000). Limits to community participation in the tourism development process in developing countries. *Tourism Management*, *21*(6), 613–633. https://doi.org/10.1016/s0261-5177(00)00009-1
>
> Zapata, M. J., Hall, C. M., Lindo, P., & Vanderschaeghe, M. (2011). Can community-based tourism contribute to development and poverty alleviation? Lessons from Nicaragua. *Current Issues in Tourism*, *14*(8), 725–749. https://doi.org/10.1080/13683500.2011.559200

Notes

1 See what the International Ecotourism Society says about this under its "Principles of Ecotourism": http://www.ecotourism.org/what-is-ecotourism.
2 See www.lifeanddebt.org. The documentary film *Life and Debt* (2001) briefly describes the poor wages and work conditions in the Free Trade Zone in Jamaica, and Jamaica's struggle with structural adjustment policies and crushing debt repayment programs to the IMF, World Bank, and other international lenders. A postcolonial writer's voiceover highlights mass tourism effects on the island (she is Jamaica Kincaid).
3 Young (2004, p. 377) mentions that she follows Hannah Arendt in calling it political responsibility, despite her "disagreement with Arendt on the question of whether the ground of this form of responsibility lies in being members of the same nation-state."
4 As Young (2006, p. 103) explains: "There are some moral obligations that human beings have to one another as human; these are cosmopolitan obligations or obligations to respect human rights." However: "While the basic moral respect owed to all persons grounds the cosmopolitan obligations that Immanuel Kant calls hospitality..., obligations of justice require more and are based on more than common humanity" (Young, 2006: 104). See also Chapter 1 in Miller (1999).
5 See, for instance, various contributors in Ferguson and Nagel (eds.) (2009), including Chapter 11 by Martha Nussbaum and Chapter 16 by Carol Gould.
6 Norma (2016) discusses the global "justice for comfort women" movement based in Korea, which spread to Japan, USA, and other countries in Southeast Asia. See page 34 in Norma (2016) plus Soh (1996) for a brief discussion on *kisaeng* sex tourism as a form of neo-jungshindae (form of sex tourism in Korea today that is linked to "comfort women" in colonial Korea). Panko and George (2012) highlight some anti-Child Sex Tourism movements.

References

Appiah, K. A. (1997). Cosmopolitan patriots. *Critical Inquiry*, *23*(3), 617–639. https://doi.org/10.1086/448846

Appiah, K. A. (2006). *Cosmopolitanism: Ethics in a world of strangers*. New York: Princeton University Press.

Bianchi, R. B., & Stephenson, M. L. (2014). *Tourism and citizenship: Rights, freedoms and responsibilities in the global order*. New York: Routledge.

Brazos Valley African American Museum. (n.d.). Retrieved May 15, 2018, from http://www.bvaam.org/

Butterly, A. (2018, May 20). 100 women: Gladys West – the "hidden figure" of GPS. Retrieved May 20, 2018, from http://www.bbc.com/news/world-43812053

Canadian Museum for Human Rights. (n.d.). Indigenous perspectives. Retrieved May 15, 2018, from https://humanrights.ca/exhibit/indigenous-perspectives

Dahl, H. M., Stoltz, P., & Willig, R. (2004). Recognition, redistribution and representation in capitalist global society: An interview with Nancy Fraser. *Acta Sociologica*, *47*(4), 374–382. https://doi.org/10.1177/0001699304048671

Dann, G. M. S. (Ed.). (2002). *The tourist as a metaphor of the social world*. Wallingford: CABI. https://doi.org/10.1079/9780851996066.0000

Dawson, J., Stewart, E. J., Lemelin, H., & Scott, D. (2010). The carbon cost of polar bear viewing tourism in Churchill, Canada. *Journal of Sustainable Tourism*, *18*(3), 319–336. https://doi.org/10.1080/09669580903215147

Elmina Castle. (n.d.). Retrieved April 30, 2018, from http://elminacastle.info/

Ferguson, A., & Mechthild, N. (Eds.). (2009). *Dancing with Iris: The philosophy of Iris Marion Young*. Oxford: Oxford University Press.

Floody, C. (2018, May 4). Starbucks Canada to close stores for sensitivity training following the arrest of two Black men at a U. Retrieved from https://www.thestar.com/news/gta/2018/05/04/starbucks-canada-to-close-stores-for-sensitivity-training-following-the-arrest-of-two-black-men-at-a-us-location.html

Fraser, N. (2010). *Scales of justice: Reimagining political space in a globalizing world*. New York, NY: Columbia University Press. Retrieved from http://www.jstor.org/stable/10.7312/fras14680

Fraser, N., & Honneth, A. (2003). *Redistribution or recognition? A political-philosophical exchange*. London and New York: Verso.

Gavrielides, T. (2007). *Restorative justice theory and practice: Addressing the discrepancy Helsinki 2007*. Helsinki, Finland: European Institute for Crime Prevention and Control, affiliated with the United Nations (HEUNI). Retrieved from http://www.heuni.fi/material/attachments/heuni/reports/6KkomcSdr/Hakapainoon2.pdf

George, S., & Westcott, B. (2018). Australia to invest millions in Great Barrier Reef restoration and protection. Retrieved April 30, 2018, from https://www.cnn.com/2018/04/30/asia/australia-great-barrier-reef-protection-intl/index.html

Global Exchange. (2016). Reality tours. Retrieved April 30, 2018, from https://globalexchange.org/realitytours/

Great Barrier Marine Park Authority. (2018). Reef facts. Retrieved June 27, 2018, from http://www.gbrmpa.gov.au/about-the-reef/reef-facts

Higgins-Desbiolles, F. (2008). Justice tourism and alternative globalisation. *Journal of Sustainable Tourism*, *16*(3), 345–364. https://doi.org/10.1080/09669580802154132

Holden, P. (Ed.). (1984). Alternative tourism: Report of the workshop on alternative tourism with a focus on Asia, Chiang Mai, Thailand, April 26–May 8, 1984. Bangkok Thailand: Ecumenical Coalition on Third World Tourism. Retrieved from http://www.

144 Responsibility and Care

worldcat.org/title/alternative-tourism-report-of-the-workshop-on-alternative-tourism-with-a-focus-on-asia-chiang-mai-thailand-april-26-may-8-1984/oclc/16095468

Honneth, A. (1995). *The struggle for recognition: The moral grammar of social conflicts*. Cambridge, MA: MIT Press.

Honneth, A. (2001). Recognition or redistribution? Changing perspectives on the moral order of society. *Theory, Culture & Society, 18*(2–3), 43–55. https://doi.org/10.4135/9781446215272.n24

Hughes, T. P., Kerry, J. T., Baird, A. H., Connolly, S. R., Dietzel, A., Eakin, C. M., . . . Torda, G. (2018). Global warming transforms coral reef assemblages. *Nature, 556*(7702), 492–496. https://doi.org/10.1038/s41586-018-0041-2

Jamal, T., & Smith, B. (2017). Tourism pedagogy and visitor responsibilities in destinations of local-global significance: Climate change and social-political action. *Sustainability (Switzerland), 9*(6). https://doi.org/10.3390/su9061082

Lee, M. W. (2018). The "problem" with Starbucks is really more about "our problem." Retrieved from http://www.stirfryseminars.com/pdfs/newsletter.pdf

McCausland, P. (2018). Protests follow outrage after two black men arrested at Philly Starbucks. Retrieved May 15, 2018, from https://www.nbcnews.com/news/us-news/protests-follow-outrage-after-two-black-men-arrested-philly-starbucks-n866141

Miller, D. (1999). *Principles of social justice*. Cambridge, MA: Harvard University Press.

Mosedale, J. (Ed.). (2016). *Neoliberalism and the political economy of tourism*. Abingdon, Oxon and New York: Routledge.

Norma, C. (2016). *The Japanese comfort women and sexual slavery during the China and Pacific Wars*. London and New York: Bloomsbury Publishing Plc.

Ocean Health Index. (n.d.). Coral reefs. Retrieved April 18, 2018, from http://www.oceanhealthindex.org/methodology/components/coral-reefs-area

Panko, T. R., & George, B. P. (2012). Child sex tourism: exploring the issues. *Criminal Justice Studies, 25*(1), 67–81. https://doi.org/10.1080/1478601X.2012.657904

Patagonia. (n.d.). Company history. Retrieved April 30, 2018, from http://www.patagonia.com/company-history.html

Peredo, A. M., & McLean, M. (2006). Social entrepreneurship: A critical review of the concept. *Journal of World Business, 41*(1), 56–65. https://doi.org/10.1016/j.jwb.2005.10.007

Peredo, A. M., & McLean, M. (2013). Indigenous development and the cultural captivity of entrepreneurship. *Business and Society, 52*(4), 592–620. https://doi.org/10.1177/0007650309356201

Responsible Tourism Partnership. (n.d.). Responsible tourism partnership – Creating partnerships for change. Retrieved April 30, 2018, from http://responsibletourismpartnership.org/

Scheyvens, R. (2002). *Tourism for development: Empowering communities*. Harlow, UK: Prentice Hall. https://doi.org/10.1016/j.tourman.2005.07.013

Scheyvens, R. (2011). *Tourism and poverty*. New York, NY: Routledge.

Senate Bill 2571: Relating to water pollution (2018). Honolulu, Hawai'i: The Senate, Twenty-Ninth Legislature, 2018, State of Hawaii. Retrieved from https://www.capitol.hawaii.gov/measure_indiv.aspx?billtype=SB&billnumber=2571&year=2018

Smith, M., & Duffy, R. (2003). *The ethics of tourism development*. New York, NY: Routledge.

Soh, C. S. (1996). The Korean "comfort women": Movement for redress. *Asian Survey, 36*(12), 1226–1240. https://doi.org/10.1525/as.1996.36.12.01p01922

Spalding, M., Burke, L., Wood, S. A., Ashpole, J., Hutchison, J., & zu Ermgassen, P. (2017). Mapping the global value and distribution of coral reef tourism. *Marine Policy, 82* (May), 104–113. https://doi.org/10.1016/j.marpol.2017.05.014

Taylor, P. (1994). *Multiculturalism*. (A. Gutman, Ed.). Princeton, NJ: Princeton University Press.

Thoms, A. V. (2008). Obscured in the midst of the Civil War: Enslaved African Americans at Camp Ford. *Journal of History and Culture, 1*(1), 25–49.

UNESCO World Heritage Centre. (n.d.). Great Barrier Reef. Retrieved April 30, 2018, from https://whc.unesco.org/en/list/154

UNWTO. (1999, October 1). Global code of ethics for tourism: For responsible tourism. Retrieved from http://cf.cdn.unwto.org/sites/all/files/docpdf/gcetbrochureglobalcodeen.pdf

Whitten, S. (2018). Starbucks to close all company-owned stores on the afternoon of May 29 for racial-bias education day. Retrieved May 15, 2018, from https://www.cnbc.com/2018/04/17/starbucks-to-close-all-stores-on-may-29-for-racial-bias-education-day.html

Young, I. M. (2000). *Inclusion and democracy*. New York: Oxford University Press.

Young, I. M. (2003). *Political responsibilty and structural injustice. Lindley Lectures; 41*. University of Kansas, Department of Philosophy. Retrieved from https://kuscholarworks.ku.edu/handle/1808/12416

Young, I. M. (2004). Responsibility and global labor justice. *The Journal of Political Philosophy, 12*(4), 365–388. https://doi.org/10.1007/978-90-481-3037-5_5

Young, I. M. (2006). Responsibility and global justice: A social connection model. *Social Philosophy and Policy, 23*(1), 102–130. https://doi.org/10.1017/S0265052506060043

Young, I. M. (2011). *Justice and the politics of difference* (Paperback). Princeton, NJ: Princeton University Press.

Young, I. M. (2013). *Responsibility for justice*. New York, NY: Oxford University Press.

5

SUSTAINABILITY AND CONSERVATION

Introduction

Another Earth Day just went by (April 22, 2018). Earth Day Network (EDN), a global environmental organization that leads Earth Day, has picked *End Plastic Pollution* as its 2018 theme. A World Economic Forum report calls for a *New Plastics Economy* and states that research estimates reveal the presence of over 150 million tonnes of plastics in the ocean today (plastic packaging is the major share of this), and if concerted action is not undertaken, "the ocean is expected to contain 1 tonne of plastic for every 3 tonnes of fish by 2025, and by 2050, more plastics than fish (by weight)" (World Economic Forum, 2016, p. 7). EDN's efforts to facilitate global action to address plastic pollution and regulation for disposal of plastics include working with various organizations, universities, schoolteachers, students, and citizens worldwide to End Plastic Pollution by:[1]

- Educating and mobilizing citizens across the globe to demand action from governments and corporations to control and diminish plastic pollution.
- Informing and activating citizens to take personal responsibility for the plastic pollution that each one of us generates by choosing to reduce, refuse, reuse, recycle and remove plastics.

EON's mission of environmental democracy evokes questions about our *shared responsibility* and *political responsibility* to address a structural injustice as per Iris Marion Young's social connection model in Chapter 4. Plastic pollution associated with systemically engrained industrial, commercial, and social processes is a growing threat to human health and is affecting ecosystems, species, and habitats worldwide. Evaluating the background and context of plastic pollution, it could be argued that a structural injustice is involved to which a forward-looking approach should be applied (following Young's model). Dealing with plastics pollution is one of many issues on the global sustainability agenda, along with climate change, poverty alleviation, sustainable development and environmental conservation, environmental justice and social justice issues. "Sustainable development" is a problematic notion, however. The concept of "development" itself has been thoroughly criticized as an externally imposed western paradigm of modernization, rather than a culturally sensitive approach to address inequalities and needs (e.g., by building capabilities suited to the individual, group, and local community, as discussed in previous chapters). The rise of mass tourism in modernity is based on the modernization paradigm and draws upon modernist ideas of "progress" aided by science, technological and rational interventions. The paradigm corresponds well with western economic models of "growth" that require mass consumption to feed expansion of capital markets (Telfer, 2009). Postdevelopment approaches have sought to displace these dominant discourses in favor of local, culturally situated understandings, norms and values (e.g., Escobar, 1995, 2000; Esteva, 2018).

One goal of this chapter, therefore, is to explore what a culturally sensitive view of tourism, development, and sustainability entails. A parallel goal is to examine this in relation to environmental, social and cultural justice, and the well-being of human and non-human others (animals, other living things).[2] The case contributors to this chapter present a kaleidoscope of ecological, social, and cultural topics to which insights gathered from previous chapters can be applied. Taken together, they show the importance of approaching this domain holistically. It means not divorcing the environment (nature, physical environment) as if it is something separate from human beings. The view, rather, is seeing human beings as embodied and embedded in relationships with their physical, social, and sacred/spiritual world. It requires considering not just tangible, but also intangible aspects and relationships (e.g., human-environmental relationships, traditional knowledge and practices related to land and Nature). Social processes and institutional structures are examined in a historical context, incorporating the past into the present and future of "sustainable tourism development."

A picture of *pluralistic* justice has been emerging over the previous chapters that Chapter 5 will continue to explore, focusing here on issues related to sustainability in the complex local-global tourism system. Case contributors offer diverse insights to help this endeavor. They address air travel and climate justice (Noel Healy and Tony Weis), planning for sea level rise (Dawn Jourdan), ecotourism and the Galápagos (John Friebele), sustainable tourism research (Bernard Lane), a community museum in Beijing (Mingqian Liu), and heritage conservation and Alcatraz Island in USA (Carolina Manrique). By the end of the chapter, it hopefully becomes clearer that pluralistic justice as it applies to individuals, groups and communities in society is a flexible approach. It can also accommodate a dual system of rights to better address the tension of *particular* justice versus the *general* societal context of justice and universal rights.

148 Sustainability and Conservation

Sustainable Development and Tourism

Numerous global initiatives have followed the Brundtland Commission's landmark report *Our Common Future* (UNWCED, 1987), which launched a worldwide call to action, particularly by businesses and governments, to adopt a long-term vision of sustainable development. Development should be sustainable, i.e., it should strive to "balance" the needs of economy and the environment in a way that ensures *inter-generational equity* and *intra-generational equity*. In this widely cited United Nations (UN) report, sustainable development refers to:

> *Development* that meets the needs of the present without compromising the ability of future generations to meet their own needs (UNWCED, 1987, p. 43).

Criticisms of this being a western, neoliberal paradigm are important to read. See, for example, Peterson (1997) on the rhetoric of sustainable development, in addition to previously mentioned critics like Smith and Duffy (2003). Some valuable guidelines can be gathered from the UN's efforts, but it helps to be cognizant of the criticisms in order to apply them responsibly. The Brundtland Commission was concerned about long-term sustainability, conservation, and *equity* in the use of environmental resources, and inequalities between the "North" and the "South," such as the unequal distribution of costs and benefits of development and immense disparities in poverty levels. Countries in the southern hemisphere disproportionately bear the burdens of industrialization and modernization that have benefitted the Global North (aka "the West"). Wide-scale ecological destruction, habitat fragmentation and biodiversity loss have resulted, while extractive industries and growth-driven, fossil-fuel economies continue to exacerbate climate change. Reparations and proactive measures include adaptation and mitigation strategies. The sustainable development goals (SDGs) that replaced the Millennium Development Goals target a wide range of environmental, economic, and social justice priorities, including poverty alleviation, reducing income inequalities, and tackling climate change that is affecting ecological systems and vulnerable populations in the North and South. See these SDGs and how vulnerable communities are engaging in climate action (Goal 13) at http://www.undp.org/content/undp/en/home/sustainable-development-goals.html.

The UNWTO "Tourism for Development Discussion Paper" produced in relation to the International Year of Sustainable Tourism for Development in 2017 reflects the SDGs well (UNWTO, 2017). It identifies five central pillars for sustainable development to which tourism can contribute significantly: 1) Sustainable economic growth; 2) Social inclusiveness, employment and poverty reduction; 3) Resource efficiency, environmental protection and climate change; 4) Cultural values, diversity and heritage; 5) Mutual understanding, peace and security (UNWTO, 2017). The report addresses visitors as well as hosts—their needs, rights and roles must be considered too. The principle of inclusivity and sharing tourism's benefits widely without discrimination is described there as follows:

Inclusivity—affecting destination economies and recipient communities— should also be applied as a principle to tourists. In 2005, the UNWTO included "visitor fulfillment" as one of its twelve aims of sustainable tourism, stating that "the great recreational and educational benefits brought by tourism should be made as widely available as possible without discrimination" (UNWTO, 2017, p. 24).

The discussion paper also identifies climate change among key priority areas for action. Destinations worldwide are responding to climate change, and sea level rise threatens numerous coastal communities, destinations, and historic locations. Air travel is a significant contributor of CO_2 emissions from a tourism perspective, but its role is a little more complicated than it first appears and merits a closer look.

Air Travel and Climate Justice

It is a world of mobilities, as Chapter 1 describes. Travelers are on the move, within and across borders. International tourism is growing with little sign of abating. International arrivals grew by 7% in 2017 to 1,322 million visitors, and is expected to increase by 4%-5% in 2018 (UNWTO, 2018). Case 5.1 below by Noel Healy and Tony Weis discusses inequities related to air travel and climate change that affect vulnerable populations globally and raise the issue of *climate justice*. Climate refugees are among the flows of human migrations displaced by war, conflict, and other challenges like climate change. About 65.6 million people were forcibly displaced worldwide at the end of 2016 and their situation is poignantly described by internationally renowned artist and film director Ai Weiwei in his 2017 epic film journey *Human Flow*. Check out the official film trailer online (do a Google search), but listen to this news interview with him here: https://youtu.be/B0XruFxbpg0 (KQED News, 2017). Note the discussion of travel across borders plus the name of the tourist destination hosting an exhibit of his artwork (Alcatraz Island is the site of Case 5.6 at the end of Chapter 5):

Case 5.1: Climate Justice and the Challenge to Global Tourism

Noel Healy and Tony Weis

Climate Justice: An Essential but Underappreciated Context for Tourism

As the former Secretary-General of the United Nations put it, climate change is nothing less than "an existential threat" to human civilization (Ki-moon, 2014). It is also, we suggest, something that profoundly challenges the way that global tourism is understood. There is an overwhelming scientific consensus that annual greenhouse gas (GHG) emissions must be urgently and drastically reduced if there is any hope of reducing the concentrations of GHGs in the atmosphere to a level that might stave off "runaway" warming scenarios and catastrophic levels of change (Anderson & Bows, 2010; IPCC, 2014). The most pressing mitigation challenge is to reduce carbon dioxide (CO_2) emissions, which are the greatest factor in warming.

The regressive character of climate change is well-established. Wealthy individuals and societies have by far the greatest relative responsibility for climate change, in large measure because they consume CO_2-emitting fossil fuels far above world averages. For instance, the wealthiest 10% of humanity produces roughly half of all GHG emissions, while the poorest half of humanity produces a mere 10% of all GHG emissions (Gore, 2015) (see Figure 5.1.1). This means that populations with the least responsibility and the least resources to respond to climate change face many of its most immediate threats, such as sea level rise, intensifying tropical storms, declining freshwater availability, and worsening heat stress, aridity, and drought, which have already begun to produce desperate migration, or "climate refugees" (Goodman, 2009; IPCC, 2014; Klein, 2014; Parenti, 2011).

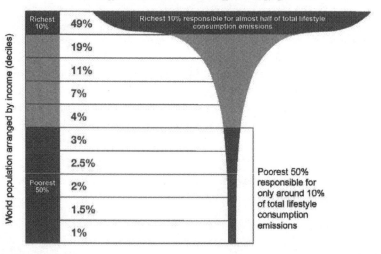

FIGURE 5.1.1 Global income deciles and associated lifestyle consumption emissions (Gore 2015). Available at: https://www.oxfam.org/sites/www.oxfam.org/files/file_attachments/mb-extreme-carbon-inequality-021215-en.pdf (retrieved on May 7, 2018)

The combination of highly unequal GHG emissions and highly unequal vulnerability to climate change is at the heart of climate justice. Climate justice builds upon the concerns of scholars and activists working in the fields of environmental racism and environmental justice, who stressed that the burden of degradation and hazards tends to be disproportionately skewed by race and class towards racialized minorities and low-income communities (Goodman, 2009; Roberts & Parks, 2007). Climate justice is now "embedded within the United Nations Framework Convention on Climate Change (UNFCCC) through the principle of 'common but differentiated responsibilities'" (Fisher, 2015, p. 74), which essentially means that wealthy countries and individuals need to make the biggest emissions reductions and the biggest contributions to finance adaptation to those changes that cannot be avoided (Hansen et al., 2013; Klein, 2014; Okereke, 2010).

Rising Air Travel as a Climate Justice Problem

International tourism is an essential part of the story of climate justice because it is a major contributor of CO_2 emissions while being dominated by citizens of high- and middle-income countries; in short, it directly relates to the uneven responsibility for climate change (McManners, 2012; Monbiot, 2006). In 2017, there were nearly 1.3 billion international tourism arrivals (WTTC, 2017), which is a major factor in the soaring scale of global air travel. From 1950 to 2012, the number of people flying increased *95-fold*, from 31 million to nearly 3 billion, and the average flight distance roughly doubled (from 903 to 1,827 km.) (Worldwatch Institute, 2013). The fossil fuel burned in rising air travel is a significant source of CO_2 emissions. At an aggregate level, air travel accounts for roughly 4% of all annual emissions, and on an individual level, the CO_2 emissions from one transoceanic flight are comparable to the amount of CO_2 emissions an average citizen from a high-income country generates in a year (McManners, 2012; Monbiot, 2006; Tyres, 2017). Lenzen et al. (2018) show that the majority of the CO_2 emissions from tourism specifically are produced by citizens of high-income countries, calculating that global tourism generated 8% of all global GHG emissions during 2009 to 2013. Their study expanded previous estimates by taking an entire supply chain approach to calculate tourism's global CO_2 emissions, going beyond air travel (which accounts for 20% of tourism emissions; 0.9 GtCO2e)[1] and factoring in the total consumption of goods and services (Lenzen et al., 2018).

International tourism is projected to continue growing quickly (WTTC, 2017) and is a primary factor in the expectation that air travel will double from 2015 to 2035 alone (to more than 7 billion passengers) (IATA, 2017). While there have been various efforts to make tourism "greener" or "more sustainable," the most pivotal environmental priority remains largely unheeded:

152 Sustainability and Conservation

the rising CO_2 emissions from air travel and other GHG emissions from tourism consumption, which must be understood in relation to the clear need for mitigation and the perilous impacts the world's poor are already facing (Lenzen et al., 2018; McManners, 2012; Monbiot, 2006; Tyres, 2017). In short, the emissions associated with international tourism are magnifying global inequalities by exacerbating the climate change-related threats to vulnerable populations worldwide.

Struggles for climate justice need to problematize the continuing growth of international tourist arrivals, which affluent populations tend to regard as a basic entitlement. More leisure needs to be oriented closer to home. Government transport policies such as the expansion of airports (e.g., Heathrow's UK third runway proposal in London) fly directly counter to the goals set in the UNFCCC Paris Agreement. Limiting dangerous climate change means questioning the perpetual growth of tourism developments and the entitlements of tourists themselves, who typically slide under the radar of accountability and responsibility. Attention to the inequality of tourism consumption also resonates with growing calls for energy justice, which seek to embed principles of fairness and social equity into energy transitions and policy decisions (Healy & Barry, 2017; Jenkins, McCauley, Heffron, Stephan, & Rehner, 2016). Monbiot (2006) presents one way to think through the climate and energy justice implications in concrete terms, calling for hard caps on total emissions on a world scale (an elemental scientific imperative) together with mechanisms for emissions rationing (an elemental principle if there is to be any equity to mitigation), which would make travelling long distances for tourism a lot more expensive than it is.

Note

1 GtCO2e is an abbreviation for gigatonnes of equivalent carbon.

References

Anderson, K., & Bows, A. (2010). Beyond "dangerous" climate change: Emission scenarios for a new world. *Philosophical Transactions of the Royal Society A: Mathematical, Physical and Engineering Sciences, 369*(1934), 20–44. https://doi.org/10.1098/rsta.2010.0290

Fisher, S. (2015). The emerging geographies of climate justice. *The Geographical Journal, 181*(1), 73–82. https://doi.org/10.1111/geoj.12078

Goodman, J. (2009). From global justice to climate justice? Justice ecologism in an era of global warming. *New Political Science, 31*(4), 499–514. https://doi.org/10.1080/07393140903322570

Gore, T. (2015, December 15). Extreme carbon inequality: Why the Paris climate deal must put the poorest, lowest emitting and most vulnerable people first. *Oxfam Media Briefing*. Oxfam. Retrieved from https://www.

oxfam.org/sites/www.oxfam.org/files/file_attachments/mb-extreme-carbon-inequality-021215-en.pdf

Hansen, J., Kharecha, P., Sato, M., Masson-Delmotte, V., Ackerman, F., Beerling, D. J., ... Zachos, J. C. (2013). Assessing "dangerous climate change": Required reduction of carbon emissions to protect young people, future generations and nature. *PLoS ONE, 8*(12), e81648. https://doi.org/10.1371/journal.pone.0081648

Healy, N., & Barry, J. (2017). Politicizing energy justice and energy system transitions: Fossil fuel divestment and a "just transition." *Energy Policy, 108*, 451–459. https://doi.org/10.1016/j.enpol.2017.06.014

IATA. (2017). 2036 forecast reveals air passengers will nearly double to 7.8 billion. Press Release No. 55. Retrieved May 15, 2018, from https://www.iata.org/pressroom/pr/Pages/2017-10-24-01.aspx

IPCC. (2014). *Climate change 2014: Synthesis report.* (R. K. Pachauri & L. Meyer, Eds.). Geneva, Switzerland: IPCC. Retrieved from http://www.pnas.org/cgi/doi/10.1073/pnas.1116437108

Jenkins, K., McCauley, D., Heffron, R., Stephan, H., & Rehner, R. (2016). Energy justice: A conceptual review. *Energy Research & Social Science, 11*, 174–182. https://doi.org/10.1016/j.erss.2015.10.004

Ki-moon, B. (2014, April 11). Remarks at press encounter with World Bank President Jim Yong Kim and IMF Managing Director Christine Lagarde. Speech presented in Washington, D.C. Retrieved May 15, 2018, from https://www.un.org/sg/en/content/sg/speeches/2014-04-11/remarks-press-encounter-world-bank-president-jim-yong-kim-and-imf

Klein, N. (2014). *This changes everything: Capitalism vs. the climate.* New York, NY: Simon & Schuster.

Lenzen, M., Sun, Y.-Y., Faturay, F., Ting, Y.-P., Geschke, A., & Malik, A. (2018). The carbon footprint of global tourism. *Nature Climate Change, 8*(6), 522–528. https://doi.org/10.1038/s41558-018-0141-x

McManners, P. (2012). *Fly and be damned: What now for aviation and climate change?* London, UK: Zed Books.

Monbiot, G. (2006). *Heat: How to stop the planet from burning.* New York, NY: Penguin.

Okereke, C. (2010). Climate justice and the international regime. *Wiley Interdisciplinary Reviews: Climate Change, 1*(3), 462–474. https://doi.org/10.1002/wcc.52

Parenti, C. (2011). *Tropic of chaos: Climate change and the new geography of violence.* New York, NY: Nation Books.

Roberts, J. T., & Parks, B. C. (2007). *A climate of injustice: Global inequality, North-South politics, and climate policy.* Cambridge, MA: MIT Press.

Tyres, R. (2017, January 11). It's time to wake up to the devastating impact flying has on the environment. Retrieved May 15, 2018, from http://theconversation.com/its-time-to-wake-up-to-the-devastating-impact-flying-has-on-the-environment-70953

154 Sustainability and Conservation

> Worldwatch Institute. (2013). *Vital signs: The trends that are shaping our future. Volume 20.* Washington, DC: Worldwatch Institute. Retrieved from http://www.worldwatch.org/vitalsigns2013
>
> WTTC. (2017). *Travel & tourism: Economic impact 2017. World Travel & Tourism Council.* World Travel & Tourism Council (WTTC). Retrieved from https://www.wttc.org/-/media/files/reports/economic-impact-research/regions-2017/world2017.pdf

Case 5.1 offers a way to think about the relationships between CO_2 emissions of international air travel and the related threats of climate change to vulnerable populations worldwide. The disproportionate burden placed on them compared to their contribution to global warming (and ecological destruction!) raises questions about the role of tourism, the continued discourse of "growth" and the implicit assumption of the right to travel as a basic entitlement of the affluent, not the poor or less fortunate. Bianchi and Stephenson (2014) examine some of these inequalities in travel, wealth, resource use, and the impacts that the Global North transfers to the poor and most vulnerable populations in the Global South. They conduct a critical assessment of the political economy of travel and migrations in tourism, examining price, commodity capitalism, and the taken-for-grant rights to travel that are embedded in liberal and neoliberal ideologies. Like Case 5.1 above, they call attention to the unexamined structural inequalities that are embedded in social processes and institutional structures in travel and tourism development and practice. Note again the relevance of Iris Marion Young's approach to structural injustices discussed in Chapter 4. It raises questions about the rights, duties and responsibilities of travelers and tourists being catered to by a global travel and tourism industry that is driven primarily by consumerism and capital market expansion, as Becken (2017) discusses.

What role do the airlines play in this, as a major stakeholder? Many offer carbon offsets and undertake recycling and waste reduction, but more rapid action is needed. Fuel and structural efficiencies have barely improved since the 1940s, said Ian Poll, Emeritus Professor of aeronautic engineering, adding: "After 70 years the environmental impact per kilometer is about back to where it was when we introduced the jet engine" (King, 2016). Discourse analysis by Peeters and Gössling (2008, p. 198) of statements made by the aviation industry on environmental performance and stability indicated that the aviation organizations sought to "create an understanding of the necessity of unrestricted growth of aviation..." and tended to show themselves in a good light, which may explain the "apparent lack of public awareness on aviation impacts." Their study indicates the aviation industry is another big player in a globalized neoliberal paradigm oriented to growth, consumption, deregulation, or self-regulation otherwise, e.g., implementing voluntary "green" certifications rather than mandated sustainability programs (Mowforth & Munt, 2016).

Sustainability and Conservation **155**

The 21st century ushers in a global imperative for decarbonization and an ethical responsibility to attend to the effects of climate change on vulnerable populations and ecosystems worldwide. While the US signaled its intent of stepping back from the Paris Climate Accord in June 2017, new actions by states, groups and other stakeholders have arisen to fill the vacuum.[3] For instance, in a precedent setting move in 2015, a group of US youth brought a lawsuit against the federal government, related to their concerns about climate change and resource exploitation. But, do youth have standing? Case 6.1 in Chapter 6 alerts us to the voice of this important stakeholder group. Case 5.2 below by Dawn Jourdan shows diverse stakeholders involved collaboratively in adaptation planning for sea level rise in the Matanzas Basin and neighboring communities on the northeast Florida coast (USA). The project included community citizens, schools, teachers, university students and faculty, officials, and scientific experts. As the final report stated: "Sea level rise in Northeast Florida is projected to be between 1.5 and 5 feet by 2100, and for all the scenarios, proactive adaptation planning is critical" (Frank, Volk, & Jourdan, 2015, p. 18). Following Case 5.2, we head into the southern hemisphere to visit Indigenous heritage and explore *relational* approaches to environmental justice and sustainability.

Case 5.2: Sea Level Rise Planning Initiative, Matanzas Basin, Florida

Dawn Jourdan

Communities across the world are grappling with the rapid effects of climate change and the ways in which these changes threaten the sustainability of the built and natural environment. Policymakers have begun to realize the importance of engaging community members in these difficult conversations to ensure that decisions that are made are sustainable and supported across communities. In many places, local governments are looking for ways to engage citizens in discussions about the future of land development and conservation practices in low lying areas that are or will be inundated by sea level rise. At the heart of all of these calls to participation is the underlying value of intergenerational equity, the notion that living beings have an obligation to pass on the Earth in the condition they received it. While not specifically built on this concept, the Planning for Sea Level Rise in the Matanzas Basin in Northeast Florida near historic St. Augustine exemplifies this principle ("Planning for Sea Level Rise in the Matanzas Basin," n.d.).

Dr. Kathryn Frank, Associate Professor of Urban Planning at the University of Florida, and Dr. Michael Shirley, the Director of the Guana Tolomato Matanzas National Estuarine Research Reserve (GTM NERR) received a multi-year grant from NOAA to understand and craft an adaptation plan to address

156 Sustainability and Conservation

the impacts of sea level rise in the study area to help inform land development and conservation decisions. The plan was commissioned by the GTM NERR to inform its land acquisition activities, as well as to provide planning support to the local governments situated in the study area. Dr. Frank and her interdisciplinary team of researchers employed a wide variety of innovative participatory tools to engage local stakeholders living and working within the study area, including the formation of a local steering committee to advise the team throughout the course of the project. Initially, the steering committee was organized to provide guidance on how best to communicate the topic of sea level rise to the local communities. Researchers felt this guidance was essential given the controversial nature of sea level rise. The steering committee was comprised of local public officials, business owners, utilities employees, environmentalists, and natural resource employees.

From the beginning of the project, the steering committee served as a vetting committee, advising the team on its research and communications approach. At the first couple meetings, the research team shared the communication materials and technical analyses generated for delivery at the first public workshops. The steering committee recommended a more local-based approach, downscaling data and images to the represented communities. Ultimately, the steering committee helped the research team develop the project's message. They stressed that the information must not be presented in a manner that was alarmist. The steering committee helped shape a message that evoked a responsibility from community members to steward the built and natural environment for future generations. At the request of the group, a videographer was made available to record the individual pleas of the steering committee members to the public to understand the importance of this exercise and a call for participation in the workshops to follow. This video recording is available for view at: https://youtu.be/TqSMiKEGX38. Accessed: June 3, 2018.

The steering committee continually reminded researchers of the importance of building a sustainable process that would generate long-term interest from community members. Garnering interest for participation in planned activities ended up being more of a challenge than expected. The steering committee became more activist-oriented over time, speaking with the media and recruiting local residents to participate in the multiple public workshops hosted by the research team at three stages throughout this process. The steering committee members became ambassadors for the project, helping coordinate sea level rise planning initiatives at the regional, county, and community levels. The final public workshop was delivered by the members of the steering committee, rather than the members of the research team. Working in pairs, the steering committee members prepared for and delivered two poster sessions for local residents as the final product of this series of workshops. At this event, the steering committee members gave short presentations on the numerous issues and adaptive strategies explored throughout the process. The goal of this transfer of leadership was done, in part, to ensure that this effort would live beyond the grant and be led by an empowered group of local stakeholders who would continue to share the knowledge that had been co-generated by the steering committee and the research team. As a result of this effort and the commitment of the steering committee members to ensuring long-term stewardship for this area, most of the local governments in the region have begun to include adaptation strategies in their short and long-range planning activities. Given the initial political resistance to planning for sea level rise in the area, the fact that plans are now being made is a testament to the power of a few committed stakeholders in coming together to shape the future development practices for an entire region (Frank, Volk, & Jourdan, 2015).

References

Frank, K., Volk, M., & Jourdan, D. (2015). *Planning for sea level rise in the Matanzas Basin: Opportunities for adaptation.* Gainesville, Florida. Retrieved from https://planningmatanzas.files.wordpress.com/2012/06/planning-for-sea-level-rise-in-the-matanzas-basin1.pdf

Planning for sea level rise in the Matanzas Basin. (n.d.). Retrieved May 23, 2018, from https://planningmatanzas.org/

Environmental Heritage and Environmental Justice

> At present, a sign at the base of Uluru, also known as Ayers Rock, politely requests that visitors refrain from climbing. "We, the traditional Anangu owners, have this to say," the sign reads. "Uluru is sacred in our culture, a place of great knowledge. Under our traditional law, climbing is not permitted. This is our home. Please don't climb." (Katz, 2017)

Uluru-Kata Tjuta National Park in Northern Territory, Australia, is Aboriginal land. It is jointly managed by its Traditional Owners, the Anangu, and Parks Australia since 1985, when ownership was returned by the Australian government to the Anangu, its Traditional Owners. A majority of the members of the Uluru-Kata Tjuta Board of Management must be Indigenous persons nominated by the traditional Aboriginal owners of land in the park. On November 1, 2017, the board members of Uluru-Kata Tjuta voted unanimously to ban the popular tourist activity of climbing Uluru by October 26, 2019 (Katz, 2017). For years the Traditional Owners, the Anangu people, had requested that visitors respect their wishes and their sacred land, and refrain from climbing the rock, but to avail.

158 Sustainability and Conservation

As the brief video on the official park site shows, the Aboriginal traditional owners of Uluru and Kata Tjuta care for land with their traditional knowledge, cultural traditions and relationships between people, plants, animals, land, and country. These are based on a foundation of *Tjukurpa*. *Tjukurpa* refers to the creation period when Uluru and Kata Tjuta were created by their creation ancestors; see https://parksaus tralia.gov.au/uluru/people-place/culture.html. The Traditional Owners extend hospitality to tourists who wish to learn from their stories about their way of life, culture, and ancestral land. Respect and care toward the land is a reciprocal relationship for visitors to engage in while visiting this sacred place (see under "Stories" on the above website). The park is listed on Australia's National Heritage List among other places of outstanding natural, historic, and Indigenous significance to the country. It is also a UNESCO designated World Heritage Site.

> We would like all visitors and people with an interest in this place to learn about this land from those who have its knowledge. We would like you to respect this knowledge, behave in a proper way, enjoy your visit, and return safely to your homes and families to share the knowledge you have gained (Uluru–Kata Tjuta Board of Management, 2010, p. i).

The Anangu's success to date has been achieved through decades of struggle and legal action for land reform. In the Northern Territory, sacred sites are now protected on all forms of land tenure including freehold. Complementing the Land Rights Act is the Northern Territory Aboriginal Sacred Sites Act of 1989 which explicitly protects the Indigenous peoples' sacred lands. This complementary legislation is "administered by the Northern Territory and confers specific functions on the Aboriginal Areas Protection Authority that include the registration of sacred sites, enforcement and approvals for access or proposed works" (see https://www.austrade.gov.au/land-tenure/Native-title/sacred-and-heritage-sites). As explained on the above website, a sacred site refers to "a site that is sacred to Aboriginal or Torres Strait Islander people or is otherwise of significance according to Aboriginal and Torres Strait Islander tradition."

Uluru's example above illustrates that human-environmental relationships and the social-political context cannot be examined in isolation, as separate from each other. Social-ecological systems, processes and relationships simply do not operate independently of economic, cultural, and political spheres. Values, interests, norms and beliefs constitute and influence relationships and practices across these spheres. They need to be viewed as interrelated and interconnected in order to better identify and address issues of justice, sustainability, and well-being. Many Indigenous groups worldwide continue to struggle for land rights, self-determination, and equality. Take, for instance, Botswana's Indigenous Peoples which includes the larger San group, also known as Basarwa. The Basarwa (pop. around 62,500 in 2015) suffer dispossession, exploitation and other injustices, as Cultural Survival (2017) describes: "Indigenous Peoples, especially those living in the Central Kalahari Game Reserve, contend with discrimination and harassment, as well as a hunting ban that infringes upon their livelihoods. Indigenous women suffer discrimination and physical and sexual violence." Even though a crucial High Court ruling on December 13, 2006, gave the Basarwa the right to return home to the Central Kalahari Game Reserve and deemed hunting bans against the Basarwa unlawful, inequalities continue:

> In January of 2014, President Khama declared that the hunting ban would now cover all of Botswana, effectively criminalizing hunting to feed a family. However, wealthy tourists and trophy hunters can still hunt within Botswana for a steep price. Banning hunting in order to feed families, but allowing the wealthy to hunt for trophies, illustrates the deeply rooted racist beliefs (Cultural Survival, 2017).

Environmental racism, loss of sovereignty, dispossession and dislocation from communal and ancestral lands, disruption of cultural relationships with land and nature, commodification and appropriation of environmental goods, are among some environmental justice issues being faced locally and globally by many minority ethnic populations.[4] Tourism is not an innocent bystander in the examples above, nor in several cases in previous chapters that raise issues of Indigenous self-determination, empowerment and control. It is not surprising, then, that Williams and Gonzalez (2017) question the notion of a *just hospitality* that preserves the rights of the hosts and nurtures reciprocity in the context of Indigenous dispossession and colonialism (see also the discussion in Chapter 3). Their study focuses on Hawai'i and they are quite skeptical of the ability of tourism to help build Native Hawaiian sovereignty or offer paths to restorative justice. For this, sustainability and tourism would require a radical reframing of how tourism was and still is implicated in colonial structures in Hawai'i, Williams and Gonzalez (2017) argue. Instead of being a predominantly eco-cultural concept, the notion of sustainability in their study is a sociopolitical one tied to Indigenous sovereignty, they say. The discussion of environmental justice in the next section reflects how diverse forms of justice are arising in the search for being and belonging in sustainable relations to human and non-human others, in the context of tourism. It shows a *pluralistic* approach to environmental justice.

Environmental Justice

> Environmental justice is the fair treatment and meaningful involvement of all people regardless of race, color, national origin, or income, with respect to the development, implementation, and enforcement of environmental laws, regulations, and policies (United States Environmental Protection Agency (EPA), 2018).

Environmental justice in the United States arose in the context of environmental health and the inequitable effects of toxic waste on minority groups, the low

160 Sustainability and Conservation

income and the poor, with increasing evidence of environmental racism and discrimination against communities of color (e.g., Perlin, Setzer, Creason, & Sexton, 1995). The relationship between environmental toxins and health came into wide public consciousness in the US with the publication of Rachel Carson's *Silent Spring* in 1962 (Carson, 1962). It provided detailed documentation and a powerful narrative of the impacts of pesticides on ecosystems and human health. With this, she also called for greater public involvement in holding the government accountable for what it permitted businesses to put into the biosphere. *Silent Spring* inspired the environmental movement in the US

On April 22 each year, Earth Day marks the anniversary of the beginning of the modern environmental movement in 1970. The definition of environmental justice by the US Environmental Protection Agency (EPA) above reflects the importance of giving voice to vulnerable groups who receive inequitable distributions of environmental harms to their health and environment (hence to their well-being).

Environmental justice issues related to tourism are wide-ranging. Commonly cited problems include issues of use and access to environmental goods, as well as harm to environmental and human health, e.g., by dumping of sewage and waste by hotels that damage ecological systems and endanger human health.[5] Cole's (2017) political ecology study of water use and inequalities related to tourism in Labuan Bajo, Indonesia, points to the need for water rights and a gendered lens to examine inequitable distribution and use of scarce water in tourism destinations. Tucker and Akama (2009) discuss resistance to eco-imperialist practices related to parks and protected areas in postcolonial Kenya. Pazzullo (2007) presents a form of advocacy tourism that involves tours to toxic sites in the US, enabling tour participants to *witness* environmental injustices first hand, interact with community members, and discover ways to help correct the harms. She links this collaborative, educational tour opportunity to a call for democratic action to address toxic waste related harms to environments and inhabitants.

Additionally, as earlier examples and the previous chapter show, loss of environmental heritage, ancestral lands, and human-environmental/other cultural relationships are critical considerations. In the Uluru example above, rights to the land, recognition, self-determination, and procedural justice, show a *pluralistic justice* is being enacted. Political *recognition* and status (in addition to redistribution) are necessary to be able to influence desired changes and just outcomes through *representation* and voice in the process (see Fraser, 2010). A number of scholars and researchers appear to support a pluralistic approach in the context of environmental justice, for instance:

1. Kyle Whyte, who studies climate and environmental justice and Indigenous environmental studies, identifies *compensation justice, participative justice, recognition justice*, and *direct participation* as appropriate norms of environmental justice for environmental tourism practices in Indigenous tourism (Whyte, 2010, 2011). "'Fair compensation' requires that environmental tourism

practices generate fair exchanges of goods, bads, and risks; 'participative justice' requires that all agents who stand to benefit or be harmed have the opportunity to give their informed consent" (Whyte, 2010, p. 77). He raises the challenge of relating the situational particularity and specificity of tribal justice with "universal" justice system of the state and of external interests like that of tourism. Self-determination and inclusion in decision making are vital in negotiating this complex justice-to-the-particular/justice-to-the-general relationship. Important here are the norms of "direct participation and cultural recognition," which he condenses under the norm of "direct participation," in other words, "participation that meaningfully represents and considers everyone's social circumstances and cultural terms" (Whyte, 2010, p. 80). His view of environmental justice in the context of environmental heritage is pluralistic, incorporating the different principles noted above (see also Fennell, 2015; Higgins-Desbiolles, 2008).

2. David Schlosberg, who has written extensively on environmental politics and environmental justice observes that Rawls and other notions of distributive justice that focus on what is to be distributed (goods, rights, etc.), and what principles govern distributions (e.g., need, desert, entitlement), have been the dominant discourse in justice theory over the past three decades (Schlosberg, 2007). He, too, calls for a pluralistic approach to environmental justice that includes *distributive justice, recognition, building capabilities*, and *procedural justice* as well as *participatory processes*. Distributive justice is necessary to help build capabilities and skills to participate effectively in deliberative democracy and procedural justice. *Procedural justice* refers to fair and equitable processes of a state, he says. Recognition, including recognition of difference, and inclusion in democratic and participatory processes are necessary to obtain and to challenge (re)distributions.

> Democratic and participatory decision-making procedures are then both an element of, and condition for, social justice (Young, 1990); they simultaneously challenge institutional exclusion, a social culture of misrecognition, and current distribution patterns" (Schlosberg, 2007, p. 26).

David Schlosberg is not proffering a rigid framework for environmental justice. It is a flexible approach where different parameters are drawn upon to address environment justice in keeping with the situation. He also calls for a pluralistic approach to *ecological justice*, again drawing on approaches to justice like equity, capabilities, recognition, and participation. While environmental justice deals with risks within human communities, ecological justice focuses on justice related to nonhuman parts of the natural world, including individual living things as well as species and ecosystems. Ecological justice is not discussed here, but see Schlosberg (2007) for his perspective and also Holden (2018) on the rights of nature in tourism. There is a paucity of studies on animal ethics in tourism studies and animal welfare is omitted in the UN's Global Code of Ethics (Fennell, 2014).

162 Sustainability and Conservation

With environmental justice discourses expanding globally and tackling topics likes climate change, climate justice, and related food and energy concerns, Schlosberg (2013, p. 38) argues that environmental justice has entered a new realm "where environment and nature are understood to create the conditions for social justice." For this, new ways of thinking and new understandings are needed, as the next section discusses.

Pluralistic Justice for the Pluriverse

> More than ever, it is imperative to go forward, but how? How to make sustainability less illusory and more tangible? Some current narratives of transition give us some clues; they involve radical proposals for moving towards a pluriverse. We can also apply novel ideas of design to think about a transition to a truly sustainable planet (Escobar, 2011, p. 137).

Arturo Escobar, a critic of "development" and an active voice in postdevelopment discourses, advocates shifting modernity's hegemonic (dominant) western ontology toward other worldviews—a "pluriverse of socio-natural configurations" that can "become a tool for reimagining and reconstructing sustainable worlds" (Escobar, 2016, p. 25). The modernization paradigm that has prevailed in international development is based on (western) modernity's vision of "progress" advanced by the application of science and technology. Measures of success in modernity have been based on *economic growth* and Gross National Product (GNP), corresponding with market capitalism and mass consumerism. Colonialism and imperial expansions through settler colonialism, etc., served to spread modernist values and capital markets expanded into distant lands. Tourism played an important role that continued in the postcolonial. Mass tourism "development" built on the systems and processes laid down during colonialism, entrenching *neocolonialism* in postcolonial destinations like Kenya (see Akama, 2004). International development programs also reinforced the modernization paradigm and furthered neocolonialism and dependency on external western markets for knowledge, "experts" and tourists. Postcolonial critics like Vandana Shiva (2018) argue that in the guise of alleviating poverty, international "development" has achieved little more than reasserting economic, social and cultural imperialism, and moral and cultural superiority.

Pursuant to stringent critiques of "development," postdevelopment perspectives like that of Gustavo Esteva strive to find ways to nurture a new commons and a post-economy rooted in social life and practices that enable social flourishing. Rather than growth and profit-focused global markets that create economic gain at the expense of common people and their habitats, a post-economic vision re-embeds economic activities in the social fabric, regenerating and nourishing relationships with land and culture (Esteva, 2018). Arturo Escobar discusses alternative perspectives, social movements and struggles in the present day that are characterized by *relational ontologies*, rich in non-instrumental, interdependent relationships with the natural and physical world, and the living beings that inhabit it. In contrast to the "subject-object," "us versus them" dualisms of a modernist ontology which "presumes the existence of One World—a universe," it is a "profound relationality of all life" that characterizes the "pluriverse" of alternative worldviews (Escobar, 2011, p. 139):

> Relational ontologies are those that eschew the divisions between nature and culture, individual and community, and between us and them that are central to the modern ontology. Some of the today's struggles could be seen as reflecting the defense and activation of relational communities and worldview (including some of those in the Arab World?), and as such they could be read as ontological struggles; they refer to a different way of imagining life, to an other mode of existence. They point towards the pluriverse... "a world where many worlds fit."

The struggles for *difference* in being and relating seen in various movements and struggles like that of the Zapatista show that these Indigenous ontologies are also *political ontologies*, Escobar explains, embracing a politics of relationality in a pluriverse that resists the One World view in favor of non-patriarchal, non-liberal or post-liberal, non-capitalist centered approaches. He describes, for instance, the holistic vision of *Buen Vivir* (BV), a non-dualist Indigenous worldview in South America (underlining is to draw your attention to the relational worldview and values of well-being embraced by *Buen Vivir*):

> The idea of alternatives to development has become more concrete in South America in recent years with the notions of <u>Buen Vivir (good living, or collective wellbeing according to culturally-appropriate ways) and the rights of Nature</u>. Defined as a <u>holistic view of social life that no longer gives overriding centrality to the economy</u>, Buen Vivir ... grew out of indigenous struggles as they articulated with social change agendas by peasants, Afro-descendants, environmentalists, students, women, and youth. Echoing indigenous ontologies, the <u>BV implies a different philosophy of life which enables the subordination of economic objectives to the criteria of ecology, human dignity, and social justice</u> (Escobar, 2016, pp. 25–26).

Degrowth and nature's rights are "fellow travelers" in these diverse endeavors toward social justice and well-being. "Together, BV and the Rights of Nature have reopened the crucial debate on how do Latin Americans want to go on living. The rights of nature movement is thus at the same time a movement for the right to exist differently, to construct worlds and knowledges otherwise" (Escobar, 2016, p. 26). Escobar discusses collaborative, place-based design that celebrates difference and a communal being and belonging with nature and the Earth in *Designs for the Pluriverse* (2018).

164 Sustainability and Conservation

Similar environmental justice and social movements are emerging in South America and elsewhere. For example, Tapia et al. (2018) discuss *endogenous* ecotourism development in the Fakcha Llakta community in Ecuador, centered on the relational worldview of the Kichwa Otavalenos peoples, and incorporating Indigenous knowledge (see also Warnholz and Barkin (2018) re. *ethnodevelopment*). Environmental stewardship, ethnic empowerment, self-determination, and inclusion were some important principles in plan development and implementation. As the authors stated, *direct participation* of community members in executing the management plan helped to increase ownership, conservation and responsibility for the area and its cultural-historic elements. Ethnic empowerment and an ethnically centered decision-making process "contributed to a status change of the ethnic minorities in a region where they had been *socially excluded, ethnically discriminated and highly exploited*" (Tapia et al., 2018, p. 109) (italics by the authors). Recognition of ethnic difference and inclusivity in the development and planning process described by these authors helped toward redressing misrecognition and misrepresentation of ethnic minority participants, among other issues.

A Pluriverse for Tourism?

Now is a good moment to pause and contemplate alternative approaches for "sustainable tourism development" which struggles with mass tourism and a modernization paradigm that thrives on growth without limits. Some argue it is a fruitless battle and striving to incorporate sustainability-oriented actions within current neoliberal globalized markets may generate more useful outcomes. Sharpley (2009), among others, advocates approaching tourism as a capitalist endeavor (of which mass tourism is a part) and focusing tourism development within parameters of environmental sustainability, managing externalities and adverse consequences related to social-cultural "impacts" on the destination. Alternative forms of tourism like *ecotourism* have arisen in the context of environmental conservation and stewardship, favoring small scale, low-impact tourism operations, and direct contribution to conserving the natural area being visited. There is hope yet to foster a different relationship with the nonhuman world, bridging the human-nature divide instilled through modernity, and facilitating alternative social-cultural and political ontologies and designs for the "pluriverse" of tourism in the Global North and the Global South.

John Friebele discusses ecotourism and the responsibilities of ecotourism operators in the Galápagos Islands in Case 5.3 below. They are a UNESCO designated World Heritage. Approach this reading from a relational perspective, i.e., envision an interrelated ecological-social-cultural-political picture in which human being are thoroughly enmeshed in relations with human and non-human others. Then contemplate after reading the case:

- What is lost when the rich biodiversity and cultural history of places like the Galápagos are damaged or destroyed?

(Hint: think about loss to civilization, present and future, of an iconic place that stimulated a historical and scientific revolution in understanding evolution by natural selection–Darwin's theory. Of course, the issue of ecological justice to other living things should not be forgotten, in addition).

- How would you conceptualize a relational ontology in ecotourism? Is Aldo Leopold's vision of humans as part of ecosystems helpful in this regard? See his poetic worldview and the land ethic he sketches out in *A Sand County Almanac* (1949).[6]

Case 5.3: Ecotourism in the Galápagos Islands

John Dirck Friebele

As The International Ecotourism Society (TIES) defined it: Ecotourism is "responsible travel to natural areas that conserves the environment, sustains the well-being of the local people, and involves interpretation and education" (The International Ecotourism Society, 2015). Ecotourism operators offer services oriented to nature conservation and resource protection, environmental interpretation and education, and localized economic benefits (Powell & Ham, 2008). Such responsible tourism forms are especially important to destinations like the Galápagos Islands, which struggles to manage the impacts of a burgeoning tourism industry on the island's fragile ecology and a growing resident population base attracted by tourism jobs and opportunities.

PHOTO 5.3.1 Galápagos Islands (Ecuador). Francesco Bandarin. © UNESCO
Source: Available at whc.unesco.org/en/documents/107413.
Creative Commons licence: https://creativecommons.org/licenses/by-sa/3.0/igo/legalcode

PHOTO 5.3.2 Galápagos Islands (Ecuador), May 18, 2007. Tui De Roy © OUR PLACE The World Heritage Collection
Source: Available at https://whc.unesco.org/en/documents/124779.
Creative Commons license: https://creativecommons.org/licenses/by-sa/3.0/igo/legalcode

166 Sustainability and Conservation

The Galápagos archipelago is located in the Pacific Ocean about 1,000 km west of Ecuador. Its geographical position cultivated an environment with one of the highest rates of endemism on earth (Galápagos Conservancy, n.d.), with unique species including the giant Galápagos tortoise, marine iguanas, the flightless cormorant, the Galápagos penguin, and Darwin's finches (see Photos 5.3.1 and 5.3.2 above). Ecuador established the Galápagos National Park in 1959 and designated the Galápagos Marine Reserve in 1998, protecting 97% of the islands' land area and waters within 40 nautical miles, respectively. In 1978, recognizing its outstanding universal value, UNESCO designated the Galápagos Islands a World Heritage Site (see: https://whc.unesco.org/en/list/1. Accessed June 2, 2018). Since its discovery by Fray Tomás de Berlanga, Bishop of Panama, in 1535, a unique socioecological system has developed, beginning with extractive exploitation by whalers, fur sealers, and fishermen, which nearly decimated the marine populations each sought (Galápagos Conservancy, n.d.). The islands were a haven for Charles Darwin's studies and his theory of natural selection, leading to international scientific interest and growing popularity of Galápagos as an ecotourism destination.

"Ecotourism" to the Islands

Since the 1970s, ecotourism has exerted strong demands for goods and services from the islands. 241,800 visitors arrived in 2017, with 77% arriving through Baltra and 23% to San Cristobal airports (Parque Nacional Galápagos, 2018). Subsequent migration from mainland Ecuador has resulted in 30,000 residents (UNESCO World Heritage Centre, n.d.) who are linked either directly or indirectly with the tourism industry, as it accounts for 80% of the local economy (Pizzitutti et al., 2017). The International Galápagos Tour Operators Association (IGTOA) represents member companies committed to responsible tourism and supporting conservation (see: https://www.igtoa.org/. Accessed June 2, 2018).

According to Quiroga et. al (2011), 81.3% of tourists indicate viewing wildlife as the activity dictating visits to the Galápagos, followed by photography (60.52%), with "tortoises, sea turtles, marine iguana, penguin, blue-footed booby, sea lion, and land iguanas" specified as the key species of importance by more than 50% of respondents (Quiroga et al., 2011, p. 90). However, Quiroga et al. (2011) also notes a shift toward more generic tourism with 53% of tourists visiting the Galápagos as part of a broader itinerary, which includes visiting for adventure sports, family or friends, and general nature enjoyment.

The Galápagos has struggled to manage visitor impacts to the environment, which include introduction of invasive species, increasing waste materials, contamination and pollution of waters from cruise ships, draining water supplies, degrading natural sites, and expanding development in urban areas (IGTOA, n.d.). Additionally, flight arrivals to Baltra and San Cristobal islands exacerbate anthropogenic climate change. Galápagos evolved under unique climatic conditions and environmental impacts due to tourism growth greatly affects its ecological resilience (Trueman, Hannah, & D'Ozouville, 2011). Gunderson and Holling (2002) define ecological resilience as the ability of an ecosystem to absorb or withstand a disturbance without transition to an alternative state, while maintaining structure and function.

Concerned about various threats including unbridled tourism and resident population growth, illegal fishing, governance issues, and invasive species, UNESCO assigned the Galápagos Islands to the List of World Heritage in Danger in 2007 (UNESCO World Heritage Centre, n.d.). Local and national government efforts to increase conservation measures and control invasive species led to subsequent removal from the List in 2010. However, in 2016, UNESCO again expressed concern about tourism growth (UNESCO, 2016). Subsequent assessment noted significant progress, but also stated the need to resolve previously mentioned issues (UNESCO World Heritage Centre, n. d.). The Galápagos National Park Directorate has attempted to promote ecotourism by introducing management practices, for example setting carrying capacity limits for sites, controlling tour routes to mitigate damage, introducing visitor fees to fund conservation efforts, requiring local guides to lead groups, educating visitors and locals, and establishing development zones for urban areas (Galápagos Conservancy, n.d.).

Ecotourism Operators

As tourist numbers continue to increase in the Galápagos Islands, ecologically sustainable tourism, both with respect to ecotourism operations and visitors, must remain a key focus. Smith et. al (2010) found 80% of ecotourism operators at the Galápagos focus on educational opportunities, three-fourths provide environmental policies and hire local employees, and two-thirds contributed financially to local conservation organizations. However, some greenwashing is occurring, and only 47% purchase carbon offsets or engage in carbon neutral policies (Self, Self, & Bell-Haynes, 2010).

Ecotourism operators should prioritize long-term sustainability of the Galápagos Islands over short-term economic benefits by providing opportunities for tourists to become environmentally educated, and actively foster attitudes and intentions toward conservation through interpretive tours and practices that directly reflect ecotourism principles. There is some evidence that Galápagos ecotourism operators can successfully increase tourists' knowledge, as well as conservation attitudes and intentions, through targeted interpretation strategies. For instance, Powell and Ham (2008) found that communication strategies delivering interpretation during ecotourism experiences increase knowledge and understanding of conservation issues and positively enhance philanthropic inclination, attitudes, and environmental behavioral intentions. Utilizing this strategy, Lindblad Expeditions raised $4.5

million for the Galápagos Conservation Fund in philanthropic contributions in its first decade (Ham, 2011; see its active global stewardship program on: https://www.expeditions.com/why-us/global-stewardship/Galapagos/. Accessed June 2, 2018).

References

Galápagos Conservancy. (n.d.). Welcome to Galapagos conservancy—preserve, protect, restore. Retrieved from https://www.galapagos.org/

Gunderson, L. H., & Holling, C. S. (2002). *Panarchy: Understanding transformations in human and natural systems*. Island Press. Retrieved from https://books.google.co.uk/books?id=DHcjtSM5TogC

Ham, S. (2011). The ask—Or is it the offer? In M. Honey (Ed.), *Travelers' philanthropy handbook* (pp. 141–149). Washington, DC: Center for Responsible Travel (CREST).

International Galápagos Tour Operators Association (IGTOA). (n.d.). International Galápagos Tour Operators Association. (n.d.). Retrieved from https://www.igtoa.org/. Retrieved from https://www.igtoa.org/

Parque Nacional Galápagos. (2018). *Informe anual de Visitantes a las áreas protegidas de Galápagos del año 2017*. Galápagos, Ecuador. Retrieved from http://www.galapagos.gob.ec/wp-content/uploads/downloads/2018/02/informe_visitantes_anual_2017.pdf

Pizzitutti, F., Walsh, S. J., Rindfuss, R. R., Gunter, R., Quiroga, D., Tippett, R., & Mena, C. F. (2017). Scenario planning for tourism management: A participatory and system dynamics model applied to the Galapagos Islands of Ecuador. *Journal of Sustainable Tourism, 25*(8), 1117–1137. https://doi.org/10.1080/09669582.2016.1257011

Powell, R. B., & Ham, S. H. (2008). Can ecotourism interpretation really lead to pro-conservation knowledge, attitudes and behaviour? Evidence from the Galapagos Islands. *Journal of Sustainable Tourism, 16*(4), 467–489. https://doi.org/10.2167/jost797.0

Quiroga, D., Mena, C., Karrer, B. K., Suzuki, H., Guevara, A., & Murillo, J. C. (2011). Dealing with climate change in the Galápagos: Adaptability of the tourism and fishing sectors. In I. Larrea & G. Di Carlo (Eds.), *Climate change vulnerability assessment of the Galápagos Islands* (pp. 81–108). WWF and Conservation International, USA.

Self, R. M., Self, D. R., & Bell-Haynes, J. (2010). Marketing tourism in the Galapagos Islands: Ecotourism or greenwashing? *International Business & Economics Research Journal (IBER), 9*(6), 111–125. https://doi.org/10.19030/iber.v9i6.590

The International Ecotourism Society. (2015, January 7). TIES Announces Ecotourism Principles Revision [Press Release]. Retrieved from http://www.ecotourism.org/news/ties-announces-ecotourism-principles-revision

Trueman, M., Hannah, L., & D'Ozouville, N. (2011). Terrestrial ecosystems in Galápagos: Potential responses to climate change. In I. Larrea & G. Di Carlo (Eds.), *Climate change vulnerability assessment of the Galápagos Islands* (pp. 29–46). WWF and Conservation International, USA.

UNESCO, W. H. C. (2016). *Report of the decisions adopted during the 40th session of the World Heritage Committee. Unesco.* Retrieved from https://whc.unesco.org/archive/2016/whc16-40com-19-en.pdf

UNESCO World Heritage Centre. (n.d.). Galápagos Islands. Retrieved from https://whc.unesco.org/en/list/1

Sustainable Tourism

> Sustainable tourism development meets the needs of present tourists and host regions while protecting and enhancing opportunity for the future. It is envisaged as leading to management of all resources in such a way that economic, social, and aesthetic needs can be fulfilled while maintaining cultural integrity, essential ecological processes, biological diversity, and life support systems (United Nations World Tourism Organization (UNWTO), 1995, p. 30).

Drawing on the paradigm of sustainable development forwarded by the United Nations (UN) World Commission on Environment and Development (UNWCED, 1987), "sustainable tourism development" as forwarded by the United Nations World Tourism Organization (UNWTO) above stresses inter- and intra-generational equity in the use and distribution of tourism-related resources. It proffers a managerialist discourse that attempts to balance human needs with cultural, social, and ecological resilience and conservation for current and future generations. Poverty alleviation and "development" initiatives facilitated by global organizations like the UN, International Monetary Fund and World Bank have provoked critiques of underdevelopment, dependency, domination and exploitation (see Britton, 1982; Holden, 2013; Sharpley and Telfer, 2014).

While critical tourism scholars worry about these, many issues and concerns have yet to be concretely addressed in tourism studies. What is lost in terms of cultural meanings and human-environmental relationships when for example, elephants, are valued in dollar terms for photo tourism and ecotourism, toward the good of conservation? What actions ought to follow awareness of such *commodification*? How, then, is the study of justice and ethics progressing in sustainable tourism studies? Take a look at Case 5.4 below by Bernard Lane, who co-founded *The Journal of Sustainable Tourism* together with Bill Bramwell.

Case 5.4: Is Sustainable Tourism Really the Key to More Ethical Forms of Tourism?

Bernard Lane

Tourism was once seen as a "win-win" activity. It claimed to provide tourists with enjoyment, host communities with work and income, and the owners of transport, accommodation and attractions, travel agents and tour operators, with profits. Discussions of tourism's ethics or lack of fairness and justice, and about its environmental, social, cultural and economic impacts, were rare. Until the mid-1980s, tourism was a conscience free activity: discussions about ethical issues were met by denial, or a shrug of the shoulders.

Sustainable tourism was a new approach to tourism development and management. It found faults in tourism's conscience free status and, from the 1990s onwards it has slowly moved to suggest practical solutions. It was largely created by academics, thinkers rather than doers (Lane, 2017, 2018). Is sustainable tourism now the key to more ethical forms of tourism? It is one of *many* keys. It has, however, already been quietly responsible for giving tourists, tourism businesses and tourism associations and lobby groups, a conscience.

This piece reflects two standpoints: that of the founder and, for 25 years, co-editor of the *Journal of Sustainable Tourism* (JOST), and that of the same person as practitioner, advising governments and businesses about sustainable tourism.

In JOST's opening paper (Bramwell & Lane, 1993), neither the word "justice" nor "ethics" appears in it, though equity does. The word "fairness" does occur, but refers to fairness between generations and nations, rather than fairness between participants in the tourism system. Gradually, however, ideas about justice and ethics entered the sustainable tourism dialogue. Two strong proponents of fairness led the way. David Fennell (2006) published *Tourism Ethics* (2nd edition 2017). Freya Higgins-Desbiolles (2008) published in JOST on "justice tourism." The discussions have moved further. They are part of many papers that are critical of the lack of ethics and justice in tourism, but often now go on to suggest ways forward. Two examples illustrate this. Linda Boukhris (2017) laments the injustice in the lack of recognition given to black people's rich heritage in Paris, but goes on to describe and evaluate the effective "Black Paris project." Carr, Ruhanen and Whitford (2016) discuss justice issues facing Indigenous peoples and sustainable tourism's answers, the opening paper in a major JOST Special Issue on that subject.

Sustainable tourism is, however, complex, and demanding to implement. It suffers from greenwash (unsupported claims) and greenhush (a fear of claiming to be ethical or sustainable, that might frighten away market share—see Delmas & Burbano, 2011; Font, Elgammal, & Lamond, 2017). At national and local governance levels, a more ethical approach as part of sustainable tourism policies is often created by smooth flowing Corporate Social Responsibility (CSR) statements. Major private sector enterprises use similar tools: smaller enterprises use fair trade products, buy organic food and linen, or local products. All these approaches can be criticized as being just tokens: all are, however, steps along the difficult sustainable tourism implementation road.

As a consultant on sustainable tourism to many businesses and local, regional and national governments, it is clear that most clients seek sustainability by reducing consumption rather than making ethical change. Hotels are classic examples. Bohdanowicz et al. (2011), reviews Hilton's Hotels in Europe environmental program. Like many companies they save materials, reduce emissions, train staff, but rarely develop an ethics-based policy, or openly discuss justice and tourism. Many clients fear that ethics lead towards religious questions or perhaps left-wing political thinking. One learns as a consultant to proceed carefully, and to build trust (Higuchi & Yamanaka, 2017).

Probe these questions more deeply, and three related aspects of the tourism world emerge. The market—tourists themselves—fear behavioral change and reject guilt about aspects of their holidays. Surveys show that tourists can cloak their ethical thinking in denial (Kroesen, 2013). The marketing manager of one of Europe's largest tour operators once explained to me that tourists will always be selfish on holiday: it is their annual escape from responsibility. Secondly, tourism tends to be not specifically governed, except in protected areas. Protected areas are, however, dominated by landscape, biodiversity, and architectural conservation, rather than the ethics or justice of tourism (see Shultis & Heffner, 2016). And there is the press and media, potentially able to encourage behavioral change. The newspaper world is compromised by its pressing need for advertising revenue from tourism providers. The TV world likes good visuals, and escapism, entertainment rather than encounters. Social media? So far, who knows!

Are there examples of good practice? There are many, but these tend to be isolated. To encourage change, we require a new input from sustainable tourism's parents—the academic community. But the current neoliberal world does not easily value those who question the status quo. To make progress, academic researchers need to become campaigners for change. They also need to understand ethical issues and injustices, not just public opinion questionnaires. Above all, they need to work with tourism providers, the market, and with governance agencies to encourage and help them to create a fairer, more ethical and sustainable tourism. That means taking a leadership role, encouraging all sides to risk change through informed and critical thought. And that, as the renowned and pragmatic Canadian economist J.K. Galbraith (1908–2006) often said, involves painful processes. Surviving exposure to public and political criticism is not taught in graduate schools. It can be much more demanding than referee's reports on journal papers. But it can be stimulating, even exciting and, in the long term,

172 Sustainability and Conservation

worthwhile. The world is slowly moving in the right direction. The ITB Berlin, the world's largest annual tourism trade fair, made social responsibility the main theme of its TO DO! Awards in 2018 (https://www.itb-berlin.com/en/Press/PressReleases/News_52611.html?referrer=/en/Press/PressReleases/#news-en-52611).

References

Bohdanowicz, P., Zientara, P., & Novotna, E. (2011). International hotel chains and environmental protection: An analysis of Hilton's We Care! programme (Europe, 2006–2008). *Journal of Sustainable Tourism, 19*(7), 797–816. https://doi.org/10.1080/09669582.2010.549566

Boukhris, L. (2017). The Black Paris project: The production and reception of a counter-hegemonic tourism narrative in postcolonial Paris. *Journal of Sustainable Tourism, 25*(5), 684–702. https://doi.org/10.1080/09669582.2017.1291651

Bramwell, B., & Lane, B. (1993). Sustainable tourism: An evolving global approach. *Journal of Sustainable Tourism, 1*(1), 1–5. https://doi.org/10.1080/09669589309514792

Carr, A., Ruhanen, L., & Whitford, M. (2016). Indigenous peoples and tourism: The challenges and opportunities for sustainable tourism. *Journal of Sustainable Tourism, 24*(8–9), 1067–1079. https://doi.org/10.1080/09669582.2016.1206112

Delmas, M. A., & Burbano, V. C. (2011). The drivers of greenwashing. *California Management Review, 54*(1), 64–87. https://doi.org/10.1525/cmr.2011.54.1.64

Fennell, D. A. (2006). *Tourism ethics*. Tonawanda, NY: Channel View Publications. Retrieved from https://books.google.com/books?id=NIXiK8v2rsEC&printsec=frontcover#v=onepage&q&f=false

Fennell, D. A. (2017). *Tourism ethics* (2nd ed.). Bristol, United Kingdom: Channel View Publications. Retrieved from https://www.world-of-digitals.com/en/fennell-tourism-ethics-ebook-pdf

Font, X., Elgammal, I., & Lamond, I. (2017). Greenhushing: The deliberate under communicating of sustainability practices by tourism businesses. *Journal of Sustainable Tourism, 25*(7), 1007–1023. https://doi.org/10.1080/09669582.2016.1158829

Higgins-Desbiolles, F. (2008). Justice tourism and alternative globalisation. *Journal of Sustainable Tourism, 16*(3), 345–364. https://doi.org/10.1080/09669580802154132

Higuchi, Y., & Yamanaka, Y. (2017). Knowledge sharing between academic researchers and tourism practitioners: A Japanese study of the practical value of embeddedness, trust and co-creation. *Journal of Sustainable Tourism, 25*(10), 1456–1473. https://doi.org/10.1080/09669582.2017.1288733

Kroesen, M. (2013). Exploring people's viewpoints on air travel and climate change: Understanding inconsistencies. *Journal of Sustainable Tourism, 21*(2), 271–290. https://doi.org/10.1080/09669582.2012.692686

Lane, B. (2017). Sustainable tourism: Its evolution and its future. *Cuadernos Económicos de Ice, (93)*, 9–28.

Lane, B. (2018). Will sustainable tourism research be sustainable in the future? An opinion piece. *Tourism Management Perspectives, 25*, 161–164. https://doi.org/10.1016/j.tmp.2017.12.001

Shultis, J., & Heffner, S. (2016). Hegemonic and emerging concepts of conservation: A critical examination of barriers to incorporating Indigenous perspectives in protected area conservation policies and practice. *Journal of Sustainable Tourism, 24*(8–9), 1227–1242. https://doi.org/10.1080/09669582.2016.1158827

Resilience: Bringing the Cultural to the Social-Ecological

Case 5.4 on sustainable tourism above expresses the need for change and intervention, and understanding ethical issues and injustices related to tourism. This section looks at some ways to advance these aims, seeking new ways to approach (i) the notion of resilience, and (ii) conservation of the built environment (broadening the notion of "sustainable development" beyond ecological conservation). In the Rio+20 "Future We Want" Outcome Document that was delivered to more than 100 heads of state and governments in 2012, Point 1.4 within the section on "Our Common Vision" illustrates the need for *change* and new approaches. It talks about sustainable consumption and production, inclusive and equitable economic growth (still a growth-oriented discourse!), reducing inequalities, enabling "integrated" and sustainable managements" of ecosystems and natural resources, environmental conservation, and *resilience*:

> We recognize that poverty eradication, changing unsustainable and promoting sustainable patterns of consumption and production, and protecting and managing the natural resource base of economic and social development are the overarching objectives of and essential requirements for sustainable development. We also reaffirm the need to achieve sustainable development by promoting sustained, inclusive and equitable economic growth, creating greater opportunities for all, reducing inequalities, raising basic standards of living, fostering equitable social development and inclusion, and promoting integrated and sustainable management of natural resources and ecosystems that supports, inter alia, economic, social and human development while facilitating ecosystem conservation, regeneration and restoration and resilience in the face of new and emerging challenges.[7]

Note the emphasis on "ecosystem conservation" in the above. The UNWCED (1987) notion of sustainable development and the subsequent UNWTO (1994) framing of sustainable tourism focused on "the environment" from a similarly

174 Sustainability and Conservation

biophysical and ecosystems view. Conservation in these earlier UN discourses was seen primarily in terms of *ecological* conservation. Very little was said about cultural relationships and social practices related to land and nature. Historic preservation/ heritage conservation emerged over time with its own silo of academics and practitioners, and "community" in the sense of geographically bound places of human residence eventually entered the discourse of sustainable tourism (see Hardy, Beeton, & Pearson, 2002).

Growing awareness of human impacts on natural and physical environments (and on climate change!) has helped to shift the view to seeing these as complex social-ecological systems undergoing rapid technological and physical changes. Unprecedented human-induced changes on global climate and the environment have ushered a period being referred to as the *Anthropocene*. Travel and tourism are significant contributors through anthropogenic emissions of greenhouse gases affecting climate change, resource intensive use (energy, water, land use, etc.), and compounding pressures on biodiversity and species loss, habitat fragmentation and ecosystem health (impacts on water and air quality, etc.). As Case 5.1 on air travel and climate justice indicates, the *vulnerability* and *adaptability* of social-ecological systems to climate and other environment changes are of increasing concern. Among various approaches, researchers have been exploring these with respect to *resilience* in relation to long-term sustainability. How resilient are ecosystems, societies, individuals, and destinations to the rapidly changing global environment, and to natural as well as human-induced crises and disasters?

Hall et al. (2018) provide a comprehensive overview of resilience in the context of tourism (including individual, organization and destination resilience), and discuss the importance of micro, meso, and macro integration to address the scale of tourism and its interrelated effects. In addition to ecological resilience, the notion of social resilience has been gaining popularity, especially as "sustainable development" continues to baffle conceptualization and implementation. Tyrell and Johnson (2008, p. 16) attempt to inform sustainable tourism policy by applying a notion of dynamic resilience, which is "the ability of social, economic or ecological systems to recover from tourism-induced stress." They use a more quantitative approach to identify thresholds, stability and change related to tourism and (i) ecological-environmental resilience, (ii) economic-fiscal resilience, and (iii) social-cultural resilience. While they note the complexity of tourism-related effects on social-cultural resilience, this dimension remains poorly conceptualized.[8] For instance, how are vulnerable populations, intangible heritage and cultural practices (rituals, traditions, music, and story-telling, etc.) being addressed in resiliency planning, adaptation planning, and ecological as well as cultural/heritage conservation (even during post-disaster recovery), and what role does tourism play here? What new designs are needed for destination and communal resilience in relation to tourism and the pluriverse, drawing on Escobar's (2018) notions of relationality and non-dualist ontologies?

In addition to ecological resilience and social resilience, *cultural resilience* may be a useful notion to investigate, especially in light of the challenges of climate

Sustainability and Conservation **175**

change, climate injustice and continuing structural injustices in the postcolonial context. Consider, for instance, ancestral, interdependent relationships between the Inuit, land, and nature in the North. When their ecological environment is depleted (damaged, fragmented), when colonial and postcolonial practices force them to settle and eat store bought food, appropriate their labor, breaks their cultural relationships to the land and ecology, it constitutes a source of domination and oppression (see Bonesteel, 2006; Young, 2011). Given that cultures are dynamic and situated in specific contexts and history, is the notion of cultural resilience helpful to address cultural survival and cultural well-being of ethnic, religious, gendered, and other diverse cultural groups in relation to tourism? Uluru illustrates the challenge of situating *particular* justice versus a *general* ethic of justice: justice for the particular cultural group(s) and traditional practices in a specific destination versus justice for all within the state. There are, too, the "rights" of the visiting public (domestic and international visitors) to consider. Can a *pluralistic* approach to justice address these multiple tensions and facilitate cultural resilience?

Case 5.6 of Alcatraz and cultural resilience by Carolina Manrique at the end of this chapter offers a thought-provoking perspective on a pluralistic approach to justice. Case 2.2 by Blanca Camargo in Chapter 2 and Case 3.3 by Jeff Wahl in Chapter 3 offer several insights for cultural justice. Like these cases, Case 5.5 of a community museum in Beijing by Minqian Liu below illustrates the sociopolitical context of culture and heritage. Planning is political, and so is conservation (ecological as well as cultural and heritage conservation). The interests and actions of all the key stakeholders (not just the government) need to be taken into account. What is being conserved? By whom? To what end? How can the past be brought to inform the present and the future with respect to sustainability and the well-being of human (and nonhuman!) others?

Case 5.5: Diversity and Inclusiveness in Community Museums: Shijia Hutong Museum, Beijing, China

Mingqian Liu

Community museums play essential roles in heritage conservation and public education in the local society. They contribute to the making of local identity, tying themselves to the culture of daily life in a neighborhood, and oftentimes growing out of local visions and needs (Sutter, Sperlich, Worts, Rivard, & Teather, 2016). Community museums can foster civil education and awareness of both local history and the need for cultural conservation, by bringing alive local stories and unique characteristics of the neighborhood. Area residents are generally important collaborators of the curatorial team, as community museums encourage public involvement in planning and decision making

176 Sustainability and Conservation

(Long, 2013). However, who gets voice among its community stakeholders, what aspects to display, and how diverse and inclusive the overall narrative is, are continuous challenges.

This case shows how Shijia Hutong Museum, a community-based institution in an inner-city historic residential neighborhood in Beijing, China, strives to conserve and communicate local arts and architecture related to vernacular forms of Hutong housing in the area, and manage the diversity of narratives and interests surrounding them. Historic neighborhoods are an important cultural resource for a city's overall image and tourism development. Protecting these through land-use planning and highlighting their value to the visiting public can help to reduce the adverse impacts of modernization and growth, such as through gentrification that can significantly alter the urban fabric of inner-city neighborhoods (Wang, 1997). From a political perspective, residents can use local institutions like community museums to publicize their concerns and attract media attention in order to slow down demolition and relocation caused by urban renewal. However, local governments can also use such institutions as conservation initiatives to establish positive images and legitimacy of urban policies (Shao, 2013). This is of particular importance in contemporary China, where museums are assigned the function of shaping the image of the nation and its past (Varutti, 2014). In Beijing, a capital city of more than twenty million residents, narratives of population migration, integration, and recognition of diverse population groups play into the political impacts of community museums (Naguib, 2013).

Shijia Hutong Museum (Photo 5.5.1), opened in 2013 as an integral part of the Shijia Hutong historic cultural district conservation scheme in Beijing, China. It illustrates many positive roles a community museum can play in contemporary society, as well as some challenges of representing contested urban history and the diversity in today's residents. It is located in a residential neighborhood in the city center, Shijia Hutong community, which is the home of numerous *hutongs* (narrow alleyways) and *siheyuans* (courtyard houses). These are traditional urban and vernacular housing styles in northern China, especially in Beijing. The urban fabric of this area has remained largely unchanged for more the eight centuries. Despite being a testimonial to the Chinese capital city's rich vernacular architectural traditions, hutong neighborhoods have faced severe challenges of urban renewal and gentrification in the past few decades. The establishment of this community museum was a result of joint efforts by the local government, preservation professionals, residents, as well as private foundations. Three important issues related to heritage conservation and tourism at Shijia Hutong Museum are identified and discussed below. These are based on my ongoing research at the museum site since 2016, using literature review, stakeholder analysis, participant observation, as well as information interviews.

PHOTO 5.5.1 Shijia Hutong Museum front entrance
Photo credit: Mingqian Liu

Exhibitions at Shijia Hutong Museum tend to showcase the bright side of urban history and ignore many episodes and challenges related to urban development in the 20th century. The museum shows well that the neighborhood is of significant cultural and historical value (see Photo 5.5.2, for example). It also discusses conservation efforts in this neighborhood in the past decade, focusing on how public-private partnerships contributed to the founding of the museum. However, the eras of intense urban renewal, heavy industrial development, as well as real estate encroachment, both after the

178 Sustainability and Conservation

PHOTO 5.5.2 Model of alleyways and courtyard houses in Shijia Hutong neighborhood
Photo credit: Mingqian Liu

establishment of the People's Republic of China in 1949 and after the Reform and Opening-Up Policy in 1978, are hardly evident in the exhibition narratives. Those were eras when governmental policies and real estate development played largely destructive roles in heritage conservation. The motivations behind these episodes are complex political, ideological, or economic concerns, but important to understanding the history of heritage conservation in Beijing in general, and hutong history in particular. Incorporating the effects of rapid modernization and growth could offer a fairer or more balanced view of neighborhood history.

Another important issue revolves around the question of who gets visibility and representation at the community museum in term of the rich cultural heritage in the neighborhood. Shijia Hutong neighborhood used to be, and remains today, a community of many famous intellectuals, politicians, artists, and educators in Chinese society. Nowadays, the demographic composition of hutong neighborhoods in Beijing's inner-city is constantly changing, as a result of population migration and rapid globalization. Representation of residents' cultural identities at Shijia Hutong Museum are not quite so diverse and inclusive of these changes. Images and stories presented at the museum do not reflect the diversity of the current population, raising the questions of possible selective representation of certain groups and certain eras. A heavy emphasis is placed on the golden era of the Republic of China between the

1910s and 1940s, when many famous residents of Shijia Hutong stood at the front line of Chinese cultural and social transformation (see Photo 5.5.3). However, who contributed to local development after the founding of the People's Republic? Who joined the community after the Reform and Opening-Up era? What roles did these later groups of residents play in the social changes of Shijia Hutong in the second part of the 20th century? These

PHOTO 5.5.3 Famous residents of Shijia Hutong during the Republic of China era
Photo credit: Mingqian Liu

questions remained untouched in the museum's narratives. Yet, more inclusive representation of the dynamic and diverse cultures of different population groups across different time periods may be helpful to demonstrate social change over time.

A final aspect is the role Shijia Hutong Museum can play in heritage conservation and civic education. Besides hutong history and conservation scheme documented and displayed in the museum, there is great potential for ongoing public education efforts. The museum curators hold significant power in shaping the future trajectories of the roles this museum could play in the neighborhood. Education programs and public events that have happened here, including community meetings, public lectures, school programs, and events related to Beijing International Design Week, could be possible topics to include in the museum's interpretive revolving exhibits in the future. Many of these events had aimed to promote civil awareness of heritage conservation and the urgent needs for public engagement in conservation efforts. Great attention at the museum to ongoing social changes in the neighborhood and how hutongs are changing through modernization and tourism (see Wang, 1997), as well as recent cultural changes and achievements in the area that Shijia Hutong Museum is situated in, could play a valuable role in public education and awareness raising (not just about the distant past but also current events happening in the community, their potential impacts, and their significances). Community museums, after all, are *community* oriented, unlike national and state museums which can be argued to have a different mandate.

References

Long, S. (2013). Practicing civic engagement: Making your museum into a community living room. *Journal of Museum Education, 38*(2), 141–153. https://doi.org/10.1179/1059865013z.00000000016

Naguib, S.-A. (2013). Collecting moments of life. Museums and the intangible heritage of migration. *Museum International, 65*(1–4), 77–86. https://doi.org/10.1111/muse.12035

Shao, Q. (2013). *Shanghai gone: Domicide and defiance in a Chinese megacity.* Lanham, MD: Rowman & Littlefield.

Sutter, G., Sperlich, T., Worts, D., Rivard, R., & Teather, L. (2016). Fostering cultures of sustainability through community-engaged museums: The history and re-emergence of ecomuseums in Canada and the USA. *Sustainability, 8*(12), 1310. https://doi.org/10.3390/su8121310

Varutti, M. (2014). *Museums in China: The politics of representation after Mao by Marzia Varutti. Suffolk: Boydell, 2014. 203 pp.* Rochester, NY: Boydell & Brewer.

Wang, N. (1997). Vernacular house as an attraction: Illustration from hutong tourism in Beijing. *Tourism Management, 18*(8), 573–580. https://doi.org/10.1016/s0261-5177(97)00079-4

Sustainability and Conservation **181**

Summary and Further Considerations

Tourism studies is a young field, and the journey toward conceptualizing justice and ethics in this area is just beginning. Equity and distributive justice as conceived in Rawls's notion of justice as fairness has been surpassed by other perspectives on social justice and sustainability. Schlosberg (2007) and Whyte (2010, 2011) lend support for a pluralistic approach to environmental justice. Additionally, postdevelopment critiques and the urgency of sustainability issues in the Anthropocene call for new ways of being and relating with each other, with economy, society, nature, and the Earth (and things within it). The Anangu of Uluru have reappropriated rights lost through colonization and externally driven (exogenous) development, displacing monetary policies for ecological, social, and cultural well-being, environmental stewardship, and care for land. Their ontological relationship with land and nature, like that of various Indigenous Peoples in the Global South, are among multiple ontologies that constitute a "pluriverse" of ways of being and belonging, radically different from a universalizing modernist, neoliberal worldview. These are political ontologies too, involving social movements and ethno-territorial struggles (Escobar, 2011, 2016, 2018).

Making space for the pluriverse, other ways of relating in social-ecological systems, other priorities than growth and a materialist existence, other economies and ways of provisioning, offers new hope, new avenues and new designs for environmental stewardship and conservation actions (both ecological and cultural) in the Global North and the Global South. It could be argued that greater attention to *cultural justice* and *cultural resilience* is needed, especially with respect to diverse groups and vulnerable populations who stand to be most impacted by climate change and other sustainability challenges in the 21st century. Here, direct participation and voice in decision making is crucial for negotiating the tensions between situated, *particular* justice suited to culturally specific worldviews, and notions of justice oriented to the general and the universal.

A *pluralistic* approach to justice in is emerging here. It is not a rigid framework, one size does not fit all! More than one approach to justice may be needed, depending on context and circumstance, with thoughtful attention to the tension between the *general* and the *particular*, and the importance of caring *for* others and caring *about* place and *relationships* with human and non-human others. A pluralistic approach to justice in tourism is flexible and situated. It can accommodate universal norms (e.g., human rights, respect for others, intrinsic value of living things) and general rights that complement specific, place-based justice principles and approaches, plus an ethic of care that is deeply *relational*. It recognizes and nurtures intangible human-environmental and cultural relationships. A pluralistic approach is also *integrated*, attentive to the sociopolitical context and scale in which environmental and cultural sustainability and well-being are being negotiated and instantiated in the local-global domain.

Many issues are regrettably not covered here that await attention, e.g., *ecological justice*, rights to the commons and other planetary resources, degrowth, etc.

182 Sustainability and Conservation

Exploring a pluralistic, integrated, *and* relational approach to justice hopefully offers new directions for future research, for responsible, sustainable practices, and for just, caring, and enriching experiences for visitors and their hosts.

Questions for Further Reflection

1. What do you think of the UN notions of "sustainable development" and "sustainable tourism development"? Would you prefer to use resilience or resiliency (consider these to be synonyms) to address changes being experienced in tourism destinations in the Anthropocene?
2. What new relationships are postdevelopment scholars recommending in relation to sustainability? How could these and notions of the "pluriverse" inform the case of Nicaragua at the end of Chapter 4?
3. What suggestions would you forward for fairer, more just practices in travel and tourism? More specifically, how would you address critiques of tourism "growth" and the right to travel?

Case 5.6: Cultural Resilience, Heritage Conservation and Tourism: Alcatraz Island, California

Carolina Manrique

The conservation of heritage sites is a highly complex area that raises many challenges, but also important opportunities related to justice and fairness to the site, to those related to its cultural heritage, and to future generations. Climate change, economic crises, wars, and terrorism are major concerns in the 21st century. The destruction or mismanagement of heritage sites has effects on an extended network of interests (e.g., tourism, economic development of communities; sustainability; cultural groups related to the site). Responsibility goes beyond addressing technical issues in the material fabric of heritage sites—conservationists have to pay attention to the values represented by the site to its stakeholders in deciding what to preserve and how. Hence, consequences extend through diverse scales of natural, physical, social, economic and cultural environments. This case study explores some of these interactions under the notion of *resilience*, specifically, *cultural resilience*. Resilience has been studied in many disciplinary areas but is defined simply here as *the capacity of a system to address challenges of diverse sorts* (Manrique Hoyos, 2015; see this and—Manrique, Jamal, & Warden, 2016 for various disciplinary approaches to resilience). Applying this to heritage conservation, Manrique et al. (2016) argue for closer consideration of intangible and tangible dimensions of cultural heritage, and propose thinking of this in terms of *cultural resilience*.

Cultural resilience in the context of heritage conservation includes considering not only tangible aspects of cultural heritage (quantitative items such as physical decay of building materials, erosion, economic costs, etc.) but also intangible aspects (qualitative aspects such as values, meaning, cultural significance, etc.) and key stakeholders involved. A key principle of cultural resilience calls for *equitable* participation and involvement in decision making by *diverse* stakeholders, especially those who are directly related to the cultural heritage of the site and stand to be most impacted by conservation decisions must be involved in heritage conservation decisions. A related principle here is *active* involvement of the *diverse* stakeholder in (i) planning and decision making related to conservation and use, as well as (ii) in developing educational and interpretive programs and exhibits, etc. It is not enough to simply listen to the voices of those who are directly related to the cultural heritage and stand to be most impacted by site related decisions. If it is a minority or oppressed group whose heritage is at issue, they must be empowered to have a role in decision making, ensuring fair or equitable distribution of benefits and costs, plus careful consideration of both intangible and tangible aspects related to culture and heritage.

An *integrated approach* to planning and decision making in heritage conservation and tourism related to the site is another key principle. Ensuring that sites are resilient to threats such as climate change, terrorism and political interests that might discriminate against the cultural group to which the site is related requires bringing scientific knowledge (e.g., conservation) together with political interests, industry interests (including tourism interests), cultural interests (ethnic groups related to the heritage site as well as cultural organizations, local and area residents, and representatives of local, state, national or international interests if the site has a related designation). McKercher and du Cros (2004), Rabady and Jamal (2006), Manrique Hoyas (2015) and others have also argued for an integrated approach to heritage conservation and tourism.

The long-term sustainability of the site depends on such shared, collaborative *responsibility* to address *cultural resilience* over time—with consideration for the past, present and future of the site's cultural heritage. The example below, Alcatraz Island in San Francisco, California (USA), illustrates the importance of the principles summarized above. Fieldwork entailing site visits, archival and bibliographical research, and participant observation was undertaken at Alcatraz Island between 2012 and 2014.

Alcatraz Island

Alcatraz Island has a diverse history of uses and its period of cultural significance between 1847 and 1973 has resulted in it being designated in the National Register of Historic Places (NRHP) and as a National Historic Landmark (NHL). These nominations illustrate Alcatraz as "the site of events that

184 Sustainability and Conservation

have had an important impact on the nation as a whole from before the Civil War through an Indian Occupation of the 1970s" (Mundus Bishop, 2010). Several Historic Preservation projects have been developed in the last decade in order to stabilize landscape elements, restore buildings, shape habitats for nesting birds, upgrade structures to building codes, etc. Sustainability efforts to reduce carbon emissions are also a priority (National Park Service, 2014).

Alcatraz Island was designated a National Park in 1972, opened to the public in 1973, and has emerged as an important heritage tourism destination with "more than 1.4 million visitors each year" (Golden Gate National Parks Conservancy, 2018). The National Park Service (NPS) offers guided tours that focus on the island's natural history, with spectacular views from and to San Francisco Bay. Interpretations include the civilian life of correctional officers, the escape attempts from the federal prison and the restored historical gardens. However, the promotion of Alcatraz Island extends beyond NPS, having been popularized in books, films and TV series. These media focus on the stories associated to the history of the island as a federal prison through "dark" topics related to former prisoners, their lives in prison and their attempts to escape. Hollywood is an extremely powerful stakeholder here (see Strange & Kempa, 2003).

However, the history of Alcatraz is more than Hollywood and the popular culture it has stimulated. It was a military fort in the 1850s, housed the West Coast's first lighthouse, and has a long Indigenous history. Bay-area native people used Alcatraz as a place for gathering food (birds' eggs; sea-life), as a punishment location for tribal members violating tribal law, and later as a hiding place "attempting to escape from the California Mission system." Indian people were also incarcerated during the military prison period (Golden Gate National Parks Conservancy, 1996; Johnson, 2015). It was also the birthplace of the Native American "Red Power" movement, sparked by tribal occupation of Alcatraz from 1969 to 1971 (Golden Gate National Parks Conservancy, 2018). Native American political activists formalized the occupation in November 1969 with ninety Indians representing an array of tribes across the continent; the movement called "Indians of All Tribes" (Golden Gate National Parks Conservancy, 1996; Johnson, 2015). Alcatraz Island's popularity helped them to gain visibility for protesting government policies (e.g., national treaties; relocation policies) (McHugh, 2007). A new layer of significance was added with the island becoming a symbol of native struggle and resistance and of "revival of Indians as real people to a generation of young Indians across the country" (Fortunate Eagle, 2002, p. x).

Conservation and related interpretation challenges illustrate the complex dynamics surrounding the diverse heritage of Alcatraz Island. One challenge relates to decisions that focus on preserving tangible remains of buildings and structures in the state in which they were left (*as found*). For example, the Warden's House served as the residence of the commandant of the military prison and the wardens of the Federal penitentiary (1934–1963). It was one of the buildings burned in a series of fires during the Native American occupation. Accounts differ as to whether the fires were accidental or intended—government and Indigenous stakeholders blamed each other (*The New York Times*, 1996; Johnson, 2015). Preservation efforts were challenged by budget restrictions but found some assistance from users such as movie companies that benefit from using of the location in its current state (*The New York Times*, 1996). Preservation actions focused on stabilizing the structure and repairing remaining portions of the building in a way that maintains its "ruin" state. Preservation efforts struggle with the continuous deterioration of the material, interpreting its complex history and its popular attraction to "dark tourism" visitors. Its decayed image fits well with Hollywood films promoting the "dark" aspects of its prison history.

A second challenge relates directly to pressures to conform to visitor expectations, resulting in transcending traditional preservation approaches that focus on material authenticity. One example of this is the rehabilitation of the Puppy Stairs which were built in the 1920s during the Military Prison period of Alcatraz (Fritz, 2011). The reinforced concrete Puppy Stairs were repaired by matching colors and textures of the existing remains that maintain a decayed-aesthetic image. This decay-state approach is a tangible change from restoring it to the history by which the site is recognized as a historic landmark towards a present state that emphasizes the layers of decay as significant (see Reed-Guy, 2011). It certainly complies with visitors' expectations for a "dark" prison-like experience.

Another example is the Restoration of the Water Tower Graffiti. Native American members of the "Indians of All Tribes" group painted a graffiti on the water tower structure on Alcatraz Island during the occupation (1969–1971) that said "Peace and Freedom. Welcome. Home of The Free Indian Land." The NPS "fully documented the graffiti work before it was painted over" as part of the rehabilitation efforts on the deteriorated and rusted tower structure in 2012 (National Park Service, 2015). Documentation by the NPS included tracing "the outlines of the original signs" and consulting with the American Indian Movement and the Indian Treaty Council (Nolte, 2013). Descendants of the occupation leader Richard Oakes and others present on the island during the Native American Occupation era, were invited up to the top of the water tower to recreate the original graffiti lettering (National Park Service, 2015).

For Alcatraz employees, the restored graffiti visible upon arrival to the island off the boat "opens your eyes to the Indian story of the island" (Nolte, 2013) reinforcing the efforts to educate most tourists who expect a prison story and are not aware of the Native American presence or the contested history of the site related to this cultural group. The NPS reports as noticing "a significant rise in the number of tourists who see the graffiti and ask questions about it" since the rehabilitation was completed (Wollan, 2012).

PHOTO 5.6.1 Puppy Stairs repaired
Photo credit: Carolina Manrique, 2013

A third challenge relates to justice through public education, interpretive projects, and participatory activities. One example is shown by some of the permanent and temporary exhibits displayed throughout the island. The "Comic Book on Restorative Justice: An Alternative to Prison" exhibit makes a comparison of the consequences of the criminal justice system vs. an alternative restorative justice (PM Press, 2014). The exhibit questions the role of Alcatraz's model of punishment and provides an active education role linking the island with initiatives in the Bay Area promoting restorative justice programs (Alcatraz Cruises LLC., 2014). Another educational effort offering recognition to Native American heritage are the multimedia project and exhibits "We Hold The Rock" (funded by the National Park Service, the LEF Foundation and the Golden Gate National Parks Conservancy), and "We Are Still Here" (funded by education and cultural centers such as the San Francisco State University College of Ethnic Studies and the Richard Oakes Multicultural Center) (information from photographs of the exhibit by Manrique, 2013). These permanent exhibits, located in the Alcatraz cellblock basement, provide an account of the Native American Occupation and explain its importance in the history of civil rights. Among those participating in this interpretive project were the Indians of All Tribes-The veterans of Alcatraz and Adam Fortunate Eagle, as well as cultural and academic organizations such as the Department of American Indian Studies (San Francisco State) and the Richard Oakes Multicultural Center.

Continued *recognition* of Indigenous presence and heritage is reflected in participatory activities such as "The Indigenous Peoples' Thanksgiving Sunrise

PHOTO 5.6.2 "@Large: Ai Weiwei on Alcatraz" exhibit guiding Art Exhibition signs throughout the island's regular tour spots. Water Tower with restored Native American Graffiti in the background
Photo credit: Carolina Manrique, 2014

Ceremony" (previously known as Un-Thanksgiving Day) also held on Alcatraz parade grounds every year since 1975 (Alcatraz Cruises LLC., 2014; Rickert, 2013). In 2017 over 1,200 people joined the Indigenous Peoples gathering organized by the International Indian Treaty Council (International Indian

188 Sustainability and Conservation

Treaty Council, 2017). The NPS provides two overnight programs to Native American youth "the night before the ceremonies which take place on Columbus Day and Thanksgiving" (National Park Service, 2013).

A final example shows the potential of sites like Alcatraz to facilitated public education and learning about human rights and freedoms. The "@Large: Ai Weiwei on Alcatraz" exhibit, September 27, 2014—April 26, 2015 (For-Site Foundation, 2014) addressed the themes of freedom of expression and human rights using Alcatraz Island as a multi-layered stage for the artist's installations in several locations. It represents voices of prisoners around the world including Ai Weiwei's own voice while he was detained in China (his passport was retained by the Chinese police in 2011 and returned in 2015) (Phillips, 2015). This exhibit attracted a different segment of visitors as expressed in the indicators reported by the For-Site Foundation: 71% increasing attendance of visitors from the region and 120% increasing attendance by San Francisco residents over the previous year (For-Site Foundation, 2015). The residents in the area are a stakeholder of Alcatraz too.

Alcatraz is a contested site of meanings, values (economic and cultural), historical interpretation and heritage conservation. It illustrates the importance of the principles outlined above related to *cultural resilience* related to the conservation of historic sites like Alcatraz. The NPS struggles to balance the needs of heritage conservation with powerful external interests (Hollywood and the tourist imaginary expecting dark prison history), and do justice to the interpretation, education and cultural heritage of the island. It includes providing voice in conservation and interpretation of Alcatraz to Native Americans whose presence here extends over to prior the arrival of Spanish and Portuguese explorers. Conservation planning and decision making must include consideration of tangible and intangible aspects (values, meaning, significance, etc.) of the cultural heritage, and an integrated approach involving key stakeholders, including those *whose history, identity and well-being are deeply interrelated with the site and all it represents.*

References

Alcatraz Cruises LLC. (2014, January 9). *Special exhibits*. Retrieved from Alcatraz Island: An Inescapable Experience: http://www.alcatrazcruises.com/website/pprog-special-exhibits.aspx

For-Site Foundation. (2014, May 12). *@Large: Ai Weiwei on Alcatraz*. Retrieved from For-Site Foundation: http://www.for-site.org/project/ai-weiwei-alcatraz/

For-Site Foundation. (2015, June 15). *@Large: Attendance, Accolades, and Impact*. Retrieved from For-Site Foundation: Art about Place: https://www.for-site.org/projects-notes/large-attendance-accolades-and-impact/

Fortunate Eagle, A. (2002). *Heart of The Rock: The Indian invasion of Alcatraz*. Norman: University of Oklahoma Press.

Fritz, S. (2011, August). *From Normandy to Alcatraz*. Retrieved from The Gardens of Alcatraz: http://alcatrazgardens.org/blog/index.php/2011/08/

Golden Gate National Parks Conservancy. (1996). *Discover Alcatraz: A tour of the Rock (self-guiding information)*. Golden Gate National Parks Conservancy.

Golden Gate National Parks Conservancy. (2018, March 31). *Alcatraz*. Retrieved from Golden Gate National Parks Conservancy: Parks for All Forever: http://www.parksconservancy.org/visit/park-sites/alcatraz.html

Golden Gate National Parks Conservancy. (2018, March 30). *Alcatraz at a glance*. Retrieved from Golden Gate National Parks Conservancy: Parks for All Forever: http://www.parksconservancy.org/visit/art/current-exhibits/alcatraz-at-a-glance.html

International Indian Treaty Council. (2017). *Event update: 2017 Annual Indigenous People's Sunrise Gatherings, Alcatraz Island, San Francisco*. Retrieved from International Indian Treaty Council: https://www.iitc.org/save-dates-2017-annual-indigenous-peoples-sunrise-gatherings-alcatraz-island/

Johnson, T., Nagel, J., & Champagne, D. (Eds.). (1997). *American Indian activism: Alcatraz to the Longest Walk*. Urbana and Chicago: University of Illinois Press.

Johnson, T. (2015, February 27). *We hold the Rock: The Alcatraz Indian occupation*. Retrieved from National Park Service: Alcatraz Island: https://www.nps.gov/alca/learn/historyculture/we-hold-the-rock.htm

Manrique Hoyos, C. (2015). *Resilience in heritage conservation and heritage tourism*. Retrieved from Doctoral dissertation, Texas A & M University: http://hdl.handle.net/1969.1/155696.

Manrique, C., Jamal, T., & Warden, R. (2016). Heritage tourism and conservation. In A. Munar, & T. Jamal, *Tourism research paradigms: Critical and emergent knowledges (Tourism Social Science Series, Volume 22)* (pp. 17–33). Emerald Group Publishing Limited.

McHugh, P. (2007). *Alcatraz: The official guide*. San Francisco: Golden Gate National Parks Conservancy.

McKercher, B., & Du Cros, H. (2004). Attributes of popular cultural attractions in Hong Kong. *Annals of Tourism Research, Vol. 31, No.2*, 393-407.

Mundus Bishop. (2010, December). *Alcatraz Island National Historic Landmark cultural landscape report*. Retrieved from National Park Service: http://www.nps.gov/goga/historyculture/alcatraz-clr.htm

National Park Service. (2013, August 5). *Indigenous Peoples Day Overnight Program*. Retrieved from Alcatraz Island: https://www.nps.gov/alca/planyourvisit/sunrise.htm

National Park Service. (2014, January 27). *Sustainability success story: Golden Gate National Recreation Area reduces carbon emissions on Alcatraz Island*. Retrieved from National Park Service: http://www.nps.gov/sustainability/parks/downloads/GPP%20Success_GOGA_Alcatraz.pdf

190 Sustainability and Conservation

National Park Service. (2015, December 3). *Rehabilitation of the Alcatraz Water Tower*. Retrieved from Alcatraz Island: https://www.nps.gov/alca/learn/historyculture/alcatraz-water-tower.htm

Nolte, C. (2013, January 14). *Alcatraz pays tribute to Indian occupation*. Retrieved from SFGATE: https://www.sfgate.com/news/article/Alcatraz-pays-tribute-to-Indian-occupation-4191169.php#photo-3996742

Phillips, T. (2015, July 22). *Ai Weiwei free to travel overseas again after China returns his passport*. Retrieved from The Guardian: https://www.theguardian.com/artanddesign/2015/jul/22/ai-weiwei-free-to-travel-overseas-again-after-china-returns-his-passport

PM Press. (2014, April). *Making sense of a senseless act: A comic about restorative justice*. Retrieved from PM Press: http://www.pmpress.org/productsheets/pm_titles/making_sense_of_a_senseless_act.pdf

Rabady, R., & Jamal, T. (2006). An integrated approach to heritage management: The case of Hearne, Texas. *Presented by T. Jamal at the Sustainable Tourism conference hosted by Wessex Institute of Technology (UK)*. Bologna, Italy.

Reed-Guy, L. (2011, July 4). *Cal State Chico students restore Alcatraz stairs*. Retrieved from SFGATE: https://m.sfgate.com/bayarea/article/Cal-State-Chico-students-restore-Alcatraz-stairs-2355720.php#photo-1877773

Rickert, L. (2013, November 27). *Hundreds of American Indians to gather on Alcatraz Island for (Un)Thanksgiving Day sunrise ceremony*. Retrieved from Native News: https://nativenewsonline.net/currents/hundreds-american-indians-gather-alcatraz-island-unthanksgiving-day-sunrise-ceremony/

Strange, C., & Kempa, M. (2003). Shades of dark tourism: Alcatraz and Robben Island. *Annals of Tourism Research*, 386–405.

The New York Times. (1996, February 18). *Alcatraz House, a timeworn landmark, cries out for help*. Retrieved from *The New York Times*: https://www.nytimes.com/1996/02/18/us/alcatraz-house-a-timeworn-landmark-cries-out-for-help.html

Wollan, M. (2012, December 24). *Antigovernment graffiti restored, courtesy of Government*. Retrieved from *The New York Times*: http://www.nytimes.com/2012/12/25/us/alcatraz-american-indian-occupation-graffiti-preserved.html?_r=0

Notes

1 https://www.earthday.org/2018/02/21/earth-day-2018-aims-end-plastic-pollution/.
2 What to include in "nonhuman others" is highly problematic. For the purpose of discussion in this book, we will be inclusive of all living things, not just categories like "animals" and "sentient beings."
3 The central goal of the Paris Agreement is to hold the increase in global average temperature to well below 2°C above pre-industrial levels. See this discussion by Todd

Sustainability and Conservation **191**

Stern, Senior Fellow, Cross-Brookings Initiative on Energy and Climate on: https://www.brookings.edu/on-the-record/the-future-of-the-paris-climate-regime/.

4 Read the news article by Fihlani (2014) where two Basarwa sisters, Boitumelo Lobelo, 25, and Goiotseone Lobelo, 21, describe life after forced relocation from their original home in the Central Kalahari Game Reserve. See also Figuero (2018; 2003) on environmental racism.

5 Lee and Jamal (2008) address environmental justice and tourism. Jamal, Camargo, Sandlin & Sagrada (2010) make an early attempt at "eco-cultural justice" in relation to tourism.

6 For a brief introduction to this work and his *land ethic*, see: https://www.aldoleopold.org/about/aldo-leopold/sand-county-almanac/.

7 http://www.earthsummit2012.org/resources/useful-resources/1157-the-future-we-want-rio20-outcome-document. CONF.216/L.1★ Rio de Janeiro, Brazil June 20–22, 2012 [Document edited June 22, 2012].

8 See, for example, Adger (2000, 2003), Hall et al. (2018), plus Jamal's (2013) discussion on disaster recovery planning, vulnerability and social equity. See also Farrell and Twining Ward (2004) on tourism as a complex adaptive system.

References

Adger, W. N. (2000). Social and ecological resilience: Are they related? *Progress in Human Geography*, *24*(3), 347–364. https://doi.org/10.1191/030913200701540465

Adger, W. N. (2003). Social capital, collective action, and adaptation to climate change. *Economic Geography*, *79*(4), 387–404.

Akama, J. S. (2004). Neocolonialism, dependency and external control of Africa's tourism industry: A case study of wildlife safari tourism in Kenya. In C. M. Hall & H. Tucker (Eds.), *Tourism and postcolonialism* (pp. 140–152). London, UK: Routledge.

Becken, S. (2017). Evidence of a low-carbon tourism paradigm? *Journal of Sustainable Tourism*, 25(6),832–850. https://doi.org/10.1080/09669582.2016.1251446

Bianchi, R. B., & Stephenson, M. L. (2014). *Tourism and citizenship: Rights, freedoms and responsibilities in the global order*. New York: Routledge.

Bonesteel, S. (2006). *Canada's relationship with Inuit: A history of policy and program development*. (E. Anderson, Ed.). Ottawa, Canada: Indian and Northern Affairs Canada. Retrieved from https://www.aadnc-aandc.gc.ca/DAM/DAM-INTER-HQ/STAGING/texte-text/inuit-book_1100100016901_eng.pdf

Britton, S. (1982). The political economy of tourism in the third world. *Annals of Tourism Research*, *9*, 331–358.

Carson, R. (1962). *Silent spring*. Boston: Houghton Mifflin.

Cole, S. (2017). Water worries: An intersectional feminist political ecology of tourism and water in Labuan Bajo, Indonesia. *Annals of Tourism Research*, *67*, 14–24. https://doi.org/10.1016/j.annals.2017.07.018

Cultural Survival. (2017). *Observations on the state of Indigenous human rights in Botswana. The 29th Session of the United Nations Human Rights Council Universal Periodic Review. January 2018*. Cambridge, MA. Retrieved from https://www.culturalsurvival.org/sites/default/files/UPRReportBotswana2017.pdf

Escobar, A. (1995). *Encountering development: The making and unmaking of the Third World*. New Jersey: Princeton University Press.

Escobar, A. (2000). Beyond the search for a paradigm? Post-development and beyond. *Development*, *43*(11), 11–14. https://doi.org/https://doi.org/10.1057/palgrave.development.1110188

Escobar, A. (2011). Sustainability: Design for the pluriverse. *Development, 54*(2), 137–140. https://doi.org/10.1057/dev.2011.28

Escobar, A. (2016). Thinking-feeling with the earth: Territorial struggles and the ontological dimension of the epistemologies of the south. *AIBR Revista de Antropologia Iberoamericana, 11*(1), 11–32. https://doi.org/10.11156/aibr.110102e

Escobar, A. (2018). *Designs for the pluriverse: Radical interdependence, autonomy, and the making of worlds.* Durham, NC: Duke University Press.

Esteva, G. (2018). Development. In W. Sachs (Ed.), *The development dictionary: A guide to knowledge as power* (2nd ed., pp. 1–23). London and New York: Zed Books.

Farrell, B. H., & Twining-Ward, L. (2004). Reconceptualizing tourism. *Annals of Tourism Research, 31*(2), 274–295. https://doi.org/10.1016/j.annals.2003.12.002

Fennell, D. A. (2014). Exploring the boundaries of a new moral order for tourism's global code of ethics: An opinion piece on the position of animals in the tourism industry. *Journal of Sustainable Tourism, 22*(7), 983–996. https://doi.org/10.1080/09669582.2014.918137

Fennell, D. A. (2015). *Ethics in tourism* (pp. 45–57). https://doi.org/10.1007/978-3-662-47470-9_3

Figuero, R. M. (2018). *Environmental justice as environmental ethics: A new introduction.* London and New York: Taylor & Francis.

Figueroa, R. M. (2003). Bivalent environmental justice and the culture of poverty. *Rutgers University Journal of Law and Urban Policy, 1*(1), 27–42.

Fihlani, P. (2014, January 7). Botswana bushmen: Modern life is destroying us. Retrieved May 15, 2018, from https://www.bbc.com/news/world-africa-24821867

Frank, K., Volk, M., & Jourdan, D. (2015). *Planning for sea level rise in the Matanzas Basin: Opportunities for adaptation.* Gainesville, Florida. Retrieved from https://planningmatanzas.files.wordpress.com/2012/06/planning-for-sea-level-rise-in-the-matanzas-basin1.pdf

Fraser, N. (2010). *Scales of justice: Reimagining political space in a globalizing world.* New York, NY: Columbia University Press. Retrieved from http://www.jstor.org/stable/10.7312/fras14680

Hall, C. M., Prayag, G., & Amore, A. (2018). *Tourism and resilience: Individual, organisational and destination perspectives.* Bristol: Channel View Publications Ltd. Retrieved from https://books.google.com/books?hl=en&id=sjQ8DwAAQBAJ&oi=fnd&pg=PT7&ots=f1GLm_Er2s&sig=bViEFRe2FLQEOuM_DkncV5K0XpY#v=onepage&q&f=false

Hardy, A., Beeton, R. J. S., & Pearson, L. (2002). Sustainable tourism: An overview of the concept and its position in relation to conceptualisations of tourism. *Journal of Sustainable Tourism, 10*(6), 475–496. https://doi.org/10.1080/09669580208667183

Higgins-Desbiolles, F. (2008). Justice tourism and alternative globalisation. *Journal of Sustainable Tourism, 16*(3), 345–364. https://doi.org/10.1080/09669580802154132

Holden, A. (2013). *Tourism, poverty and development.* London: Routledge.

Holden, A. (2018). Environmental ethics for tourism- The state of the art. *Tourism Review,* TR-03-2017-0066. https://doi.org/10.1108/TR-03-2017-0066

Jamal, T. (2013). Resiliency and uncertainty in tourism. In A. Holden & D. A. Fennell (Eds.), *The Routledge handbook of tourism and the environment* (pp. 505–520). London and New York: Routledge.

Jamal, T., Camargo, B., Sandlin, J., & Segrado, R. (2010). Tourism and cultural sustainability: Towards an eco-cultural justice for place and people. *Tourism Recreation Research, 35*(3), 269–279. https://doi.org/10.1080/02508281.2010.11081643

Katz, B. (2017). Australia will ban climbing Uluru, a sacred indigenous site, in 2019. Retrieved May 18, 2018, from https://www.smithsonianmag.com/smart-news/australia-ban-climbing-uluru-rock-sacred-indigenous-site-180967044/

King, E. (2016, October 18). British Airways: UN aviation deal won't bite till 2030s. Retrieved May 18, 2018, from http://www.climatechangenews.com/2016/10/18/brit ish-airways-un-aviation-deal-wont-bite-till-2030s/

KQED News. (2017, October 20). Ai Weiwei tackles global refugee crisis in "human flow" [Video]. Retrieved May 17, 2018, from https://youtu.be/B0XruFxbpg0

Lee, S., & Jamal, T. (2008). Environmental justice and environmental equity in tourism: missing links to sustainability. *Journal of Ecotourism*, 7 (September 2015), 44–67. https://doi.org/10.2167/joe191.0

Leopold, A. (1949). *A Sand County almanac: And sketches here and there*. Oxford, UK: Oxford University Press.

Mowforth, M., & Munt, I. (2016). *Tourism and sustainability: Development, globalisation and new tourism in the Third World* (4th ed.). New York, NY: Routledge.

Pazzullo, P. C. (2007). *Toxic tourism: Rhetorics of pollution, travel, and environmental justice*. Tuscaloosa, Alabama: The University of Alabama Press.

Peeters, P., & Gössling, S. (2008). Environmental discourses in the aviation industry: The reproduction of mobility. In P. M. Burns & M. Novelli (Eds.), *Tourism and mobilities: Local-global connections* (pp. 187–203). Wallingford: CABI International.

Perlin, S. A., Setzer, R. W., Creason, J., & Sexton, K. (1995). Distribution of industrial air emissions by income and race in the United States: An approach using the toxic release inventory. *Environmental Science and Technology*, *29*(1), 69–80.

Peterson, T. R. (1997). *Sharing the earth: The rhetoric of sustainable development*. Columbia, SC: University of South Carolina Press.

Schlosberg, D. (2007). *Defining environmental justice*. Oxford: Oxford University Press.

Schlosberg, D. (2013). Theorising environmental justice: The expanding sphere of a discourse. *Environmental Politics*, *22*(1), 37–55. https://doi.org/10.1080/09644016.2013.755387

Sharpley, R. (2009). *Tourism development and the environment: Beyond sustainability?* London: Earthscan.

SharpleyTelfer, E. (2014). *Tourism and development: Concepts and issues*. (R. Sharpley & D. Telfer, Eds.) (2nd edition). Clevedon: Channel View Publications Ltd.

Shiva, V. (2018). Resources. In W. Sachs (Ed.), *The development dictionary: A guide to knowledge as power* (pp. 228–242). London and New York: Zed Books.

Smith, M., & Duffy, R. (2003). *The ethics of tourism development*. New York, NY: Routledge.

Tapia, R. L., Trujillo, C., & de Lima, I. B. (2018). Environmental stewardship, indigenous tourism planning and the fakcha llakta community: An ethnic endogenous development model in Otavalo, Imbabura, Ecuador. In I. B. de Lima & V. T. King (Eds.), *Tourism and ethnodevelopment inclusion, empowerment and self-determination* (pp. 82–122). Abingdon: Routledge.

Telfer, D. J. (2009). Development studies and tourism. In T. Jamal & M. Robinson (Eds.), *The SAGE handbook of tourism studies* (pp. 146–165). Thousand Oaks, CA: SAGE Publications.

Tucker, H., & Akama, J. (2009). Tourism as Postcolonialism. In T. Jamal & M. Robinson (Eds.), *The SAGE handbook of tourism studies* (pp. 504–520). Thousand Oaks, CA: SAGE Publications.

Tyrrell, T. J., & Johnston, R. J. (2008). Tourism sustainability, resiliency and dynamics: Towards a more comprehensive perspective. *Tourism and Hospitality Research*, *8*(1), 14–24. https://doi.org/10.1057/thr.2008.8

Uluru–Kata Tjuta Board of Management. (2010). *Uluru-Kata Tjuta National Park: Management plan 2010–2020*. Retrieved from https://www.environment.gov.au/system/files/ resources/f7d3c167-8bd1-470a-a502-ba222067e1ac/files/management-plan.pdf

United Nations World Tourism Organization (UNWTO). (1995). *Agenda 21 for the travel and tourism industry: Towards environmentally sustainable development*. London, UK: UNWTO, WTTC and the Earth Council.

United States Environmental Protection Agency (EPA). (2018). Environmental justice. Retrieved from https://www.epa.gov/environmentaljustice

UNWCED. (1987). Our Common Future, Chapter 2: Towards Sustainable Development. In *Our common future: Report of the World Commission on environment and development* (pp. 1–16). United Nations World Commission on Environment and Development (UNWCED). Retrieved from http://www.un-documents.net/ocf-02.htm

UNWTO. (2017). *Discussion Paper on the occasion of the International Year of Sustainable Tourism for Development 2017*. Retrieved from http://www.tourism4development2017.org/wp-content/uploads/2017/05/070417_iy2017-discussion-paper.pdf

UNWTO. (2018). 2017 International tourism results: The highest in seven years. *UNWTO World Tourism Barometer, 16*(January), 1–7. https://doi.org/10.18111/wtobarometeresp. 2018.16.1.1

Warnholtz, G., & Barkin, D. (2018). Development for whom? Tourism used as a social intervention for the development of indigenous/rural communities in natural protected areas. In I. B. de Lima & V. T. King (Eds.), *Tourism and ethnodevelopment: inclusion, empowerment and self-determination* (pp. 27–43). London: Routledge.

Whyte, K. P. (2010). An environmental justice framework for indigenous tourism. *Environmental Philosophy, 7*(2), 75–92.

Whyte, K. P. (2011). The recognition dimensions of environmental justice in indian country. *Environmental Justice, 4*(4), 199–205. https://doi.org/10.1089/env.2011.0036

Williams, L. K., & Gonzalez, V. V. (2017). Indigeneity, sovereignty, sustainability and cultural tourism: Hosts and hostages at 'Iolani Palace, Hawai'i. *Journal of Sustainable Tourism, 25*(5), 668–683. https://doi.org/10.1080/09669582.2016.1226850

World Economic Forum. (2016). *The new plastics economy: Rethinking the future of plastics. World Economic Forum report*. Geneva, Switzerland. https://doi.org/10.1103/Physrevb. 74.035409

Young, I. M. (1990). *Justice and the politics of difference*. Princeton, NJ: Princeton University Press.

Young, I. M. (2011). *Justice and the politics of difference* (Paperback). Princeton, NJ: Princeton University Press.

6

DEMOCRACY AND GOVERNANCE

Introduction

> <u>A small community is a wonderful thing to live in</u> and I don't think, I still don't think that [developer X] and [developer Y] understand what they've taken from us in terms of that...you can have a small town feel, you can keep your buildings low...but <u>when you don't know everybody on [the] main street anymore</u>, you don't see that Volkswagen coming, oh that'll be Bob, you know. It loses that <u>sense of intimacy</u> that makes your community worth having...There isn't anything better than a town of 4 or 5,000 people in which everybody knows everybody. There isn't a better way to live, I don't believe, on earth...And I couldn't explain to them <u>what they've lost, what I've lost</u>. They still don't know, I mean they just don't understand. Or maybe they do and it's too late. <u>You know they've got investors, you know, you start to see every side</u>...
> (Resident-participant, 25 years in Canmore, Alberta, Canada) (Jamal, 1997, p. 145)

Located about ninety miles west of Calgary, Alberta, the picturesque town of Canmore is a gateway to the Canadian Rockies and Banff National Park (Canada's oldest national park and one of four mountain parks that constitute a World Heritage Site). Like many small mountain communities in western Canada, it was experiencing rapid growth since the 1980s. Its scenic location and ease of access to summer and winter recreational activities drew visitors and second-homes tourists from near and far. Traffic lights came to Main Street along with new amenities. Its sense of mountain place and cultural heritage changed as the proportion of long-time residents to new incomers dropped. Some residents left, either unable to afford the higher cost of living or

196 Democracy and Governance

in search of that small hometown setting they had lost. Parents watched over their children playing on dark streets when neighboring homes stayed empty due to absentee second-home owners. Today, Canmore is a vibrant, humming destination, but it is no longer what it used to be. Yes, change is inevitable in the globalized world we live in, but the question of governance and oversight of this powerful phenomenon called tourism becomes increasingly pressing with local and global mobilities of people, finance, capital, etc. (images, too!). Should residents have more voice and say in how their communities are used and enjoyed? How do they exercise their social rights to shared spaces of hospitality and leisure...as easily as tourists seem to exercise their rights to enjoy hard-earned vacations and their second-home playgrounds?

Chapter 6 approaches these questions by focusing on local-global governance and some important principle of justice related to democratic participation, inclusion and voice in policy and planning. We start in the next section with a look at global governance and global justice and then move to governance, policy, and planning within borders. Collaborative planning and democratic participation are explored, along with social rights and *difference*. The above quote shows the voice of a resident who had participated in a lengthy community-based collaboration (from mid-1994 up to June 1995) to develop a Growth Management Strategy for Canmore.[1] Some insights from long-term study of the initiative and the community will be shared as the chapter progresses. Additionally, cases provided by various contributors offer rich perspectives on ways in which tourism governance, policy and democratic participation are facilitated or inhibited. Case topics range from youth standing and tribal involvement related to conservation and sustainability (Dawn Jourdan) tourism policy in Korea (Jiyoung Choi and Songyi Kim), collaborative planning in Tel Aviv-Jaffa (Nufar Avni), plus a case involving marginalized groups through public learning destinations in Tasmania (Can-Seng Ooi and Becky Shelley).

Governance Complexities from the Local to the Global

Governance of a tourism destination is a highly complex and daunting task. It has to deal with *local to the global effects* of tourism, *multiple stakeholders*, externalities related to touristic use of public goods, resources and spaces, and diverse values and relationships that are affected by development, growth, and change over time. Rising popularity as a place of visitation often bring benefits like new amenities, jobs and income, but can also exert immense pressures on local residents and area resources, e.g., increased cost of living, living wage and affordable housing issues, habitat degradation, loss of neighborhood character and social cohesion, etc. Canmore's aesthetic charm and amenities attracts new residents, both full-time and part-time, as it gets discovered for its quality of life and leisure. According to the Biosphere Institute of the Bow Valley, a Canmore based non-profit organization:

As of the last municipal census in 2014, there were approximately 4,000 nonpermanent residents with homes in Canmore (estimated total population of approximately 18,000 people)...The need for appropriate and affordable housing remains a key community issue and is one of Council's key strategic priorities for 2016–18 (Biosphere Institute of the Bow Valley, 2017, p. 3).

Canmore's challenges are not unique. Like Amsterdam (Case 1.1, Chapter 1) and many other destinations experiencing increasing external pressures on services and facilities, it has to grapple with both tangible and intangible changes, alongside rising inequalities. Many touristic activities occur in public spaces, draw upon public goods, use public services and affect local to global commons, e.g., through carbon emissions from air travel and local facilities, visitor impacts on fragile ecosystems and historic/heritage sites, inequities in water use and allocation, etc. (see, for example, Cole, 2018). Long-term social and cultural changes that are not readily evident and difficult to "measure" tend to get ignored or under-estimated. Residents' rights to the commons, both natural and cultural (e.g., festivals, rituals and traditions celebrated by the locals in public spaces) come into tension with that of tourists as visitor numbers increase. Their *social rights* to access and enjoy their own neighborhoods and communal spaces can also be threatened by possible homogenization and gentrification. Lefebvre (1991, p. 52), for instance, discusses the *right to difference* in the urban space in which different groups (including visitors) encounter each other. He is concerned about globalization as well as local-regional pressures (e.g., capitalism flows and power relations driving rapid development and modernization), creating abstract, reductionist and instrumental space that "tends towards homogeneity, towards the elimination of existing differences or peculiarities...." Such homogenizing segregates through inclusion and exclusion of various groups, he feels, and creates passive consumers rather than an engaged public actively constructing public space and everyday life the way they want it, celebrating diversity and *difference*.

There is, too, the question of tourists' rights (of both domestic and international visitors), including the unquestioned and inequitable liberal rights and capacity of different groups and populations to freely travel worldwide (see Chapter 5). What about the governance of their carbon footprint and use of (sometimes scarce) public resources that constitute hard to capture externalities? The New Zealand government recently announced a new tax on foreign tourists (but not Australians) between NZ$25 and NZ$35 per person. Slated to commence in mid-2019 in the middle of the official "China New Zealand Year of Tourism," it could provide up to NZ$80 million in the first year to help fund conservation and tourism infrastructure. "It's only fair that they make a small contribution so that we can help provide the infrastructure they need and better protect the natural places they enjoy," said Minister for Tourism Kelvin Davis of this upcoming tax (Australian Associated Press, 2018).

198 Democracy and Governance

What a myriad of stakeholders, needs and issues to consider in this complex local-global tourism domain! Destination governance has to take an *integrated* local-global approach to address diverse stakeholders, various types of impacts and their interrelatedness through different levels and scales of governance within and across borders. All the cases you encounter in this chapter illustrate the importance of such an integrated approach to tourism development, management and governance, which also includes considering the needs of vulnerable populations in collaborative planning and policy processes.

Sustainability, Diverse Groups and Vulnerable Populations

Among key stakeholders in the tourism domain are governments, planners, attraction and service providers, civil society organizations, visitors (domestic and international) and residents. It would be a mistake to look at any of these as homogenous. A community's "residents," for instance, may be differentiated by many characteristics and demographics, like ethnicity, gender, sexual orientation, age, class, income, education, occupancy (long-term residents, migrant workers in tourism, second-home owners, etc.). Often in need of better voice and representation are vulnerable groups such as the elderly, the poor and the working poor, youth and children, people with disabilities, groups and minority populations experiencing discrimination due to sexual orientation, ethnicity, religion, age (ageism!), etc. How effectively are their rights being addressed, not just with respect to human rights and social rights, but also their rights to a sustainable future? How well do disaster planning and recovery management include the needs of vulnerable populations and the loss of their spaces of habitation, places of social gathering and cultural heritage? One of the commitments that States adopted in the Habitat Agenda at the United Nations Conference on Human Settlements (Habitat II), held in Istanbul in 1996, recognized children as a vulnerable group which should be involved in disaster planning and management:

> Ensure the participation in disaster planning and management of all interested parties, including children, in recognition of their particular vulnerability to human-made and natural disasters (The United Nations Office at Geneva (UNOG), n.d., p. 87).

Case 6.1 below on youth standing in relation to climate change and resource sustainability shows the difficult but important road ahead to enable legal rights, voice, and inclusion of this vulnerable group in decision making and governance related to conservation and sustainability. It also reminds us, yet again, that transnational governance and global justice are becoming pressing concerns to address in the tourism context too. Many social justice, conservation and sustainability issues simply do not stop at a destination's boundaries and tourism may be directly or indirectly related to them. Though

Democracy and Governance **199**

Case 6.1 says nothing about "tourism," it has implications for travel and tourism—can you identify a few?

Case 6.1: Youth Participation in Governance: Juliana v. U.S.

Dawn Jourdan

The old adage, "children should be seen, not heard," is a very telling statement about the rights of young people. In many places across the world, including the U.S., the law is seemingly paternalistic. Lawmakers, through the policies they have drafted, have sought to protect young people without much interest in hearing from them directly. This has started to change as a result of the efforts of the United Nations. For more than 20 years, the U.N. has led conversations about the rights of children to make decisions for themselves. Most of these conversations revert to discussions about capacity and the cognitive abilities of young people to make important decisions. The world's conversation about the rights of children was expanded in 1990 at the World Summit for Children's Plan for Action (UNICEF, 1990), the 1992 Rio de Janeiro Earth Summit's Rio Declaration (United Nations, 1992), and the 1996 Children's Rights and Habitat Declaration. The rights of children to participate in the decision making that affects them was a conclusion drawn as a part of the Children's Rights and Habitat Declaration (UNICEF & (Habitat), 1997).

While youth participation is becoming a more recognized activity across the world, some question the legitimacy of such activities given that law does not provide real teeth for youth to pursue their interests in through voting or legal challenges. A group of young people in Oregon hope to set precedent for such challenges in a pending legal action. In Juliana v. U.S. (*Juliana v. U.S.*, 2018), a group of young people have asserted that actions by the federal government benefiting the fossil fuel industry violate the group's rights to life, liberty, and property, as well as failing to protect public trust resources. At this point, the case has survived motions to dismiss, at both the trial and appellate court levels, in spite of aggressive efforts by the Trump administration to end the litigation based on claims that discovery requests made by the children are too burdensome. The appellate court received eight amicus briefs from a variety of scholars and legal organizations supporting the children's right to be heard. Characterizing those briefs, Phil Gregory, co-lead counsel for plaintiffs and partner with Cotchett, Pitre & McCarthy, LLP has noted:

> The unanimous support of these various groups, from the League of Women Voters, to the Sierra Club, to the Niskanen Center, shows that the Trump Administration's writ should be denied. These amicus briefs echo the need for the courts to give the youth plaintiffs access to a trial

that will protect their rights. After the devastation of Hurricane Harvey, we must take steps now to properly protect the youth of America from horrendous damage of the growing climate crisis ("QEW Supports Plaintiffs in Juliana v. U.S. Urge Dismissal of Trump's Mandamus Petition," 2017).

While the outcome in *Juliana v. U.S.* is still to come, groups concerned about climate change are leading the charge to revisit the political and legal rights of young people who are not currently able to vote politicians in or out of office. This conversation is critical as it is this same group that stands to inherit all of the challenges that adapting to climate change brings for nations across the world.

References

Juliana v. U.S., Case: 17-71692, 03/07/2018, ID: 10789188, DktEntry: 68–1, Page 1 of 17 (2018). Retrieved from https://www.ourchildrenstrust.org/court-orders-and-pleadings

QEW Supports Plaintiffs in Juliana v. U.S. Urge Dismissal of Trump's Mandamus Petition. (2017). Retrieved June 3, 2018, from https://www.quakerearthcare.org/article/qew-supports-plaintiffs-juliana-v-us-urge-dismissal-trumps-mandamus-petition

UNICEF. (1990). World declaration on the survival, protection and development of children and plan of action for implementing the world declaration on the survival, protection and development of children in the 1990s: World summit for children. In *World Summit for Children, September 29–30*. Retrieved from https://www.unicef.org/wsc/plan.htm

UNICEF, & (Habitat), U. C. for H. S. (1997). *Children's rights and habitat: Working towards child-friendly cities*. New York, NY: UNICEF. Retrieved from https://digitallibrary.un.org/record/233327?ln=en

United Nations. (1992). *United Nations Conference on Environment & Development, Rio do Janiero, Brazil, June 3 –14, 1992, Rio Declaration on Environment and Development, U.N. Doc. A/CONF.151/26 Vol. 1)*. Rio de Janiero, Brazil. Retrieved from http://www.un.org/documents/ga/conf151/aconf15126-1annex1.htm/

Other Sources Used

Dawn Jourdan, Standing on Their Own: The Parallel Rights of Young People to Participate in Planning Process and Defend Those Rights, XI:1 Sustainable Dev. Law & Pol'y 41 (Fall 2010).

https://digitallibrary.un.org/record/233327?ln=en, last accessed June 3, 2018.

Karen Malone, Children, Youth, and Sustainable Cities, 6 Loc. Env'r 5, 6–7 (2001).

The Transnational Governance Challenge

We live in a world of increasing mobilities and interdependencies. Advances in information and communication technologies (ICTs), transportation and finance have been reshaping the global landscape, enabling a globalized culture industries and robust international travel. These are beneficial in many ways, but have also exacerbated conflicts as economies and cultures collide within and across borders. Innovations and transformations being brought about by ICTs are reconstructing services and experiences in travel and tourism, raising possibilities to serve justice or to perpetuate injustices in increasingly complex physical and virtual *local-global* spaces. Good governance is no longer simply to do with exercise of power and authority by government within a state to ensure democratic rights and freedoms, responsible distribution and management of public goods and services, serve the needs and well-being of its citizens or subjects, etc. Traditional notions of the state and the public sphere are being challenged by porous borders and new governance problems (e.g., managing policy and injustices related to the new "virtual" spaces being enabled by ICTs). Global warming and climate change also transcend borders and are a critical priority on sustainability and conservation agendas in the 21st century!

Compounding the difficult task of destination development and management is the *fragmented governance domain* which is influenced by multiple stakeholders at the local, regional, national, and transnational level. The role and authority of *government* has been shifting from traditional hierarchies and markets toward governance via multi-stakeholder, collaborative "networks" and "communities" (Hall, 2012). *Voluntary schemes* for ethical practices and sustainability abound (e.g., green hotel certification programs, ecotourism certifications, Green Globe certi-fication, etc.), whereas regulatory systems are lagging under the pervasive neoli-beralizing of trade and commerce across borders (see below). So how best to address tourism governance in this intricately linked and interrelated local-global domain? Through community-based tourism (CBT) and community driven approaches for capacity building, strengthening domestic public spheres and democratic institutions within borders? Or, do you feel that new structures are needed to undertake shared responsibilities for tourism governance and justice across borders? Both? The challenges are not insignificant, as discussed below.

Global Organizations and Transnational Public Spheres?

Many supranational and multilateral organizations assist with global issues and policies related to tourism planning and development, conservation, and management (e.g., various agencies of the United Nations, like the United Nations World Tourism Organization (UNWTO), United Nations Development Programme (UNDP), United Nations Environment Programme (UNEP), and United Nations Educa-tional, Scientific and Cultural Organization (UNESCO); the World Travel and Tourism Council (WTTC), etc.). However, critiques of "sustainable tourism" and the neoliberal approaches of the UNWTO, IMF, World Bank are abundant (e.g.,

202 Democracy and Governance

Mowforth & Munt, 2016; Smith & Duffy, 2003). Structural Adjustment Programs (SAPs) enacted by the International Monetary Fund (IMF) and the World Bank continue to affect tourism destinations struggling with poverty, locking them in vicious cycles of debt and underdevelopment (see Holden, 2013). Moreover, organizations like the UNWTO do not have a regulatory mandate.

Aside from the institutions mentioned above, social movements and an active civil society are operating within and across borders. Some of these were discussed in Chapters 2 and 4 in the context of social justice. Environmental issues are also being negotiated within and across borders, with transnational environmental movements, non-governmental organizations (NGOs) and other entities taking up global conservation and related social justice issues. For instance, the NGO Nature Conservancy has over one million members and partners globally with other nonprofit organizations, Indigenous communities, businesses, governments, and multilateral institutions on key priority areas including climate change (The Nature Conservancy, 2015). On March 8, 2018, the Nature Conservancy and its partners (which include the state government of Quintana Roo, the Cancún and Puerto Morelos Hotel Owners' Association, the National Commission for Natural Protected Areas and Mexican Universities) announced an innovative trust fund and insurance policy to protect a portion of the Mesoamerican Reef along Mexico's Yucatan Peninsula. Swiss Re (a leading global insurer) and The Rockefeller Foundation provided expertise and initial funding respectively. Funds for the trust and subsequent insurance will be gathered from the tourism industry and government sources. This multistakeholder initiative is to be investigated to improve climate resilience in vulnerable communities globally (The Nature Conservancy, 2018). For more on the Mesoamerican Reef Tourism Initiative (MARTI), a sustainable tourism initiative enabled by an alliance of global, regional and local organizations, see: https://coral.org/mesoamerican-reef-tourism/.

In addition to an active civil society operating within and across borders, there are powerful transnational players with little or often insufficient regulation over their activities. Large international hotels and tour operators, airlines, marketers, and other global service providers of mass tourism have immense influence and control over the local destinations they serve. Recognizing this, sustainable tourism and responsible tourism principles call for "local control" and "community-based" initiatives for resident empowerment and capacity building. But are their current principles adequate for destination governance and management in the face of large-scale sustainability challenges, neoliberal globalization and global mobilities of goods, finance, capital, and people, as well as the rise of "virtual" collaborative economies like the sharing economy?

> We must ask: If the modern territorial state no longer possesses the administrative ability to steer "its" economy, ensure the integrity of "its" natural environment, and provide for the security and well-being of "its" citizens, then... By what means can the requisite administrative capacity be constituted and where precisely should it be lodged? If not to the sovereign

territorial state, then to what or whom should public opinion on transnational problems be addressed? (Fraser, 2010, p. 98).

Externally influenced pressures being experienced by tourism destinations and groups discussed in various cases raise similar questions: Are new forms of governance needed to address transnational problems and injustices related to tourism and, if yes, does this mean enacting one or more new transnational public spheres? Or just one coordinated, institutionalized system of global governance to enact global justice for international tourism? Considering the power issues that would surely arise in a unilateral structure like this, would a more collaborative global regulatory system involving the participation of all nation-states be more suitable? Or?

Let us first look briefly at the notion of a public sphere and then a transnational public sphere. A *public sphere* is "a space for the communicative generation of public opinion" and "a vehicle for marshaling public opinion as a political force" (Fraser, 2010, p. 76).[2] Examples of these are present in various collaborative approaches to tourism-related planning and policy within borders (see, for instance, Dredge & Jenkins, 2016; Gill, 2018; Hall, 2011). A public sphere across borders, whether it is one global public sphere or a number of transnational public spheres (TPSs) is a highly challenging proposition, however. It would entail creating new, transnational public powers, and making them "accountable to new democratic transnational circuits of public opinion" (Fraser, 2010, p. 99). Given the complexity of tourism governance discussed above, a number of TPSs rather than one may need to be envisioned, enabling the participation of various social movements, civil society organizations (including NGOs), and other publics. And, here, too, global mechanisms for democratic communication would be needed to enable citizens worldwide to make these tourism related TPSs accountable.

Another option for enacting global justice for tourism could be through some form of alliance between states. While Rawls and others have contributed to this discussion, let us look briefly to Immanuel Kant who had forwarded a distinctive new moral cosmopolitan theory that helped to guide his political cosmopolitanism. Kleingeld and Brown (2014) explain that the word "cosmopolitan" derives from the Greek word kosmopolitês ("citizen of the world"), and 18th-century cosmopolitan views like that of Kant understood cosmopolitanism to imply a positive moral ideal of a universal human community. As they describe:

> According to Kant, all rational beings are members in a single moral community. They are analogous to citizens in the political (republican) sense in that they share the characteristics of freedom, equality, and independence, and that they give themselves the law. Their common laws, however, are the laws of morality, grounded in reason (Kleingeld & Brown, 2014).

The universal moral principles that Kant (1998) developed in *The Groundwork of the Metaphysics of Morals* (originally published in 1785) helped to shape Kant's emerging

204 Democracy and Governance

moral cosmopolitanism, which served to ground the political form of cosmopolitanism he proposed. In his well-known essay *Toward Perpetual Peace* written in 1795, Kant (2006) argued that true, worldwide peace would not be possible without a *league of nations* guided by cosmopolitan law and universal hospitality.[3] A commonly cited example of a cosmopolitan vision of global political governance is the intergovernmental League of Nations (1919–1946) created after the First World War "to develop cooperation among nations and to guarantee them peace and security" (The United Nations Office at Geneva (UNOG), n.d.). It was unable to live up to its mandate for universal peace, but other forms like the European Economic Community (EEC) and the European Union (which eventually succeeded it) arose subsequently with economic and political unity in mind.

You could easily come up with a list of worries and debate the challenges of creating a global justice institution, or even one or more transnational public spheres, to govern the immense reach and scope of tourism across borders. The issue of global governance for tourism won't be resolved anytime soon, but it is important to think about. It will require, among other things, a close understanding of micro-macro relationships: how the local/regional/national interact and affect practices and policies at each level, and how transborder and global events, power relations and institutions affect activities within and across these various levels. Let us a look at another alternative below, which is to strengthen the local and foster a flourishing democratic society that can engage with governance related issues and challenges within and across borders as needed (e.g., via social movements, etc.).

Democracy and Participation Within Borders

A transnational public sphere such as mentioned above would need to involve various forms of organization and institutions working together in solidarity and interdependence for transnational justice, while enabling self-determination, inclusiveness, and democratic participation of diverse social and cultural groups. That would be quite a tension to negotiate and a challenge to enact logistically.[4] Rather than such a daunting endeavor for global assembly and global justice, another option might be to nurture an active, engaged, and *informed* civic society. Tourism can play an active role to facilitate this, e.g., through direct resident involvement in tourism development and planning, and providing visitor opportunities for good actions and experiential learning that facilitate environmental and social citizenship (within and across borders) and a "cosmopolitan" ethic of care (discussed in Chapter 4).

Understanding the history and evolution of tourism policy within the country, and how various policies and practices facilitate democracy or inhibit it at various levels of governance (local/regional/national) can prove rewarding. Micro-macro processes and relationships interact and affect practices and policies at each level, while transnational events and institutions add further complexity. Case 6.2 by Jiyoung Choi and Songyi Kim offers an opportunity to explore this through the evolving context of tourism governance and policy in South Korea. Influenced by historical and political events, changes in national governance from top-down, rational policy and planning are affecting the tourism policy domain. A growing civil society and shifts toward greater local involvement in tourism development and management are emerging over time.

Case 6.2: Democratization of Tourism Policy in Korea: Gangneung Danoje Festival

Jiyoung Choi and Songyi Kim

Until the beginning of the 20th century, Korea was governed as a dynasty with a rigid class system based on Confucianism. Following the Japanese Occupation (1909–1945) and the Korean War (1950–1953), the old political economic system collapsed and democracy began. Changes in in tourism policy followed, especially with transitions to more democratized tourism resource management. This case describes this transition and its effects on tourism policy. The example of Gangneung Danoje Festival illustrates well the gradual changes in tourism resource management and development that are occurring within the context of democratization of South Korea.

Democratization of Korean Politics and Tourism Policymaking

With the establishment of the Republic of South Korea in 1948, a democratic political system was adopted. However, it was governed by an authoritarian national government led by a series of dictators until the 1980s. The newly established administrations tried to gain legitimacy through national economic growth, and early national tourism development policies in the 1960s and 1970s were formulated to earn foreign currency through inbound tourism. The Cultural Heritage Protection Act, the national law to manage cultural resources, was enacted in 1962 to promote national unity and further ensure the legitimacy and identity of this new nation (Kim, 2016). Under this political situation, the highly centralized and autocratic national government was the most powerful decision maker in tourism policymaking.

In the 1970s and 1980s, various democratic movements emerged and civic organizations arose, stimulating a more democratized political environment from late 1980s onwards. Several new political systems to decentralize the power of a president and national government were adopted, one of which was the local autonomous system established in 1995. It requires the election of both local governor and council, and the delegation of authority from national government to local government. As a result, local governments have become key drivers for developing regional and local tourism resources. Empowered during the democratic movements, Korean non-governmental

206 Democracy and Governance

organizations (NGOs) and nonprofit organizations (NPOs) have also become significant stakeholders in diverse policy areas, encouraged by progressive administrations in 1990s and 2000s (Park, 2012). Environmental NGOs have played an advocacy role in the decision making on tourism development, and cultural NGOs began to collaborate with the government to develop and manage cultural tourism attractions such as cultural festivals.

In contrast to the previous progressive administrations, conservative administrations since 2008 limited the role of NGOs and NPOs in the policy process but implemented policies for community development in order to garner public support for their administration. Community development projects were funded by the national government and administered by local government. Although they were government-led projects, they emphasized voluntary community involvement (Tae & Park, 2010). Through increased opportunities for local businesses and residents to gather and discuss issues with local government, some of these community projects have contributed to increasing and empowering local governance for community development and revitalization (Yeo, 2017).

The Gangneung Danoje Festival

The Gangneung Danoje Festival is an annual folk festival celebrated from at least the 17th century onwards to wish for a good harvest and protection from natural disasters in Gangneung, a city of over 200,000 residents on the east coast of South Korea. Until the Japanese Occupation of the Korean peninsula in 1909, the local government and the local ruling class planned and funded the festival. They also dominated the official Confucian rituals of the festival. Nonetheless, the Gangneung Danoje Festival was a celebration of the whole community as all the residents could enjoy the festival regardless of social class. The ordinary people hosted and joined various Buddhist and Shamanistic rituals, while the lower-class merchants opened a big market during this four-week long festival. Due to the Japanese Occupation, the local authority collapsed, but a new class of local merchants who gained wealth under capitalism funded the continuation of the festival (Hwang, 2006).

It is unclear whether the festival continued throughout the Japanese Occupation and the Korean War that ended in July 1953, but it survived and continued after this turbulent era although many rituals and performances of the festival were lost by the 1960s. In 1967, the Gangneung Danoje Festival was designated as the thirteenth Important Intangible Cultural Property under the Cultural Heritage Protection Act and was managed by the then authoritarian government. The Cultural Heritage Administration (CHA) directed the restoration of this intangible heritage and the government-affiliated NPO, the Gangneung Cultural Center (GNCC), planned and hosted the restored festival. In the 1990s, under the local autonomous system, the local government of Gangneung which was responsible for local economic development and growth, actively promoted the festival as a tourism attraction. Local community organizations were encouraged to volunteer to operate program booths for visitors. The local and national government jointly worked to have Gangneung Danoje Festival proclaimed as a UNESCO Intangible Cultural Heritage in 2005 (inscribed in 2008, see https://ich.unesco.org/en/RL/gangneung-danoje-festival-00114. Accessed June 8, 2018).

The festival continued to be government-led until 2005. Policy implementation through public-private partnerships began to be encouraged in the 2000s. In 2007, the Gangneung Danoje Committee that was the festival management team within the GNCC became an independent NPO, comprised of its original members and local leaders to take charge of planning and management of the festival. At the same time, the Gangneung Danoje Preservation Association was formed as an independent NPO responsible for conserving and transmitting the rituals and folk performances of the festival. In addition, community involvement, which became a trend in Korean policy in the 2010s, also influenced the festival. Trying to restore the festival as community heritage, the Gangneung Danoje Committee successfully expanded its ceremonial street parade to include local residents from 2011 onwards. Now, the managers of the city's neighborhoods are involved in planning the street parade, enabling their residents to take part in the parade each year (Photo 6.2.1). Rituals and mask performances continue to be performed by local cultural groups (Photo 6.2.2).

PHOTO 6.2.1 Youngshin Haengcha Street Parade at the Gangneung Danoje Festival
Source: http://www.danojefestival.or.kr/contents.asp?page=284&kind=2&IDX=4491. Date accessed: June 9, 2018

PHOTO 6.2.2 A masked couple dancing at the Gwanno Mask Dance at the Gangneung Danoje Festival
Source: http://www.korea.net/AboutKorea/Culture-and-the-Arts/ UNESCO-Treasures-in-Korea. Date accessed: June 8, 2018

The case of Gangneung Danoje Festival shows how the process of democratization in South Korea is also taking place in tourism resource management and policy. As the regime of the state changed from authoritarianism to liberal democracy, the framework of tourism policy changed from centralized bureaucratic structure toward accommodating locally based, collaborative processes. This transition has enhanced the meaning of the festival as a shared asset for the local community and visitors, rather than a heritage exclusive to a specific group, or dominated by a particular political power. Increasing involvement of local residents will help further transition to inclusive, participatory governance and management of tourism and community empowerment for the maturing democracy in South Korea.

References

Hwang, R. S. (2006). The function of festival in community of modern society. *The Journal of Korean Oral Literature, 22*, 1–26. Retrieved from http://scholar.dkyobobook.co.kr/searchDetail.laf?barcode=4050025239808#

Kim, H. (2016). The culture and arts revival policy of President Park Chung-hee and the Korean modern art. *Art History Forum, 42*, 131–159. https://doi.org/10.14380/AHF.2016.42.131

Park, S. P. (2012). The development of Korean Civil Society after 1990s. *Memory and Outlook, 27*, 162–191. Retrieved from http://www.papersearch.net/thesis/article.asp?key=3126072

Tae, Y.-J., & Park, S.-H. (2010). Characteristics of Maeul-mandeulgi in Korea based on the content analysis of related local ordinances, 2000-2009. *Journal of the Architectural Institute of Korea Planning & Design, 26*(7), 175–182. Retrieved from http://journal.auric.kr/jaik_pd/ArticleDetail/RD_R/242286

> Yeo, K.-H. (2017). A Study on the local governance formation for steps of the community planning: Focused on the Jangsu Village, Seongbuk-gu. *The Korean Journal of Local Government Studies, 21*(1), 395–422. https://doi.org/10.20484/klog.21.1.16

Strengthening Local Institutions and Participatory Processes

Case 6.2 illustrates ebbs and flows of civil society and local involvement from the national to the local level (note the importance of taking an integrated approach here to evaluate tourism policy as contextualized within local-regional-national policy making). The case suggests an emergent process of increasing local level involvement and control may be occurring, but it is occurring in its own unique and specific way. Similarly, in the "western" context of liberal policy making and planning, an embodied, *situated* approach to collaborative planning and policy making, attentive to *context* and *difference* within and between groups, may yield greater benefit than a reductive focus on "interests" and consensus-based negotiation.

Take, for instance, the community-based Canmore Growth Management Strategy (GMS) process that was convened to address conflict over development and growth in Canmore, Alberta (Canadian mountain community mentioned at the beginning of the chapter). While this is an older example, extensive study of the process and its subsequent outcomes offers interesting insights into local governance and democratic participation.[5] Over 40 participants representing around 19 interest groups took part in this lengthy community-based collaboration that extended from mid-1994 to June 1, 1995 when the GMS report was finally delivered to local government. Each group strove faithfully to represent its group's interests. Some were puzzled about whether it was permissible to empathize with other perspectives or address wider community issues rather than just focusing on their own group's priorities. Others wondered how to manage the tension between striving for their own group's interests and the trade-offs it might entail, such as the "democratic" cost of restricting growth: Is it okay to shut the doors to future visitors interested in purchasing second homes, whether for investment or for recreation and enjoying mountain amenities?

Residents and other stakeholders were involved in extensive dialogue and deliberation, and they participated directly in interest-based negotiation and consensus-based decision making to develop the GMS report. It was deliberative democracy in action, and detailed ground rules were set to guide a fair process. The local government stayed at arm's length (not participants in the process) with a promise to implement the strategies proposed by the group. Local planners were present during the process only to provide technical support and act as liaison; their presence helped with ongoing continuity and implementation of the report after the collaboration ended. But it was a long and exhausting endeavor as

210 Democracy and Governance

participants tried to reconcile "interests" and forge solutions agreeable to all. Power relations and fatigue troubled the "democratic" process:

> and writing up the final document... it was supposed to be a committee, [a] word-smithing committee and I said to some of the others, we've got to get on that because otherwise it will be like the Indians and white men. You know, the white men write up the treaty and the Indians just go X and they don't know what the hell is in there. ... And then you look at the thing and you didn't think really we agreed to saying quite that but you're too exhausted to fight every clause... more and more topics got introduced and put in there and so on and most of the meat of it really got into it in the last few months. (One of the frustrated resident participants) (Jamal, 1997, p. 199)

The Canmore GMS report set a limit of 6% on growth and came up with growth management strategies, including innovative recommendations for an ongoing thresholds and monitoring program. The Biosphere Institute that eventually emerged continues to play a valuable role in implementing programs for sustainability and conservation, including resident as well as visitor education:

> The Biosphere Institute promotes sustainable communities and environmental stewardship with its outreach programs engaging youth, residents, visitors, and local businesses. The Biosphere Resource Centre engages the public with wildlife and sustainable community displays, and a library focused on the ecology of the Bow Valley ("Biosphere Institute of the Bow Valley: Ecological Integrity through Education, Research, and Outreach," 2014).

While many participants benefited from learning collaborative skills, and good outcomes were achieved, growth-related issues like affordable housing have continued. Would Canmore look different today had the long, drawn-out process not been so focused on "consensus" decision making and prolonged months of dialogue around participants' "interests"? Planning theorist Susan Fainstein (2010, 2017) argues that participative processes for deliberative democracy such as conceptualized by social theorist Jürgen Habermas, where fair processes are supposed to lead to fair outcomes, are simply not adequate to produce just outcomes.[6] Rather than trying to accommodate a wide range of interests through such dialogic processes (as the Canmore GMS process attempted), Fainstein argues the focus should be on *outcomes* and proposes justice as the primary goal for evaluating public policy. Three values define justice as the first principle for public policy evaluation in the liberal pluralist context her work is set in: equity, diversity, and democracy. In *The Just City* (2010), Fainstein explores these principles in three "western" cities governed by liberal pluralism: New York, London, and Amsterdam.[7]

Democracy and Governance **211**

Using various examples ranging from mega-events to affordable housing, Fainstein (2010, 2017) shows that tensions can arise among the three dimensions of equity, diversity and democracy. For example, encouraging a broad income range of inhabitants and expressly forbidding discrimination due to gender, ethnicity, or disability are good for a neighborhood's diversity, but it would not be fair to make residents move there against their will. Some groups may prefer to live among their own ethnic community. When conflicts arise between these three aspects, she believes that Rawlsian principles of distributive justice and equity take priority over diversity and democracy.

Drawing from Fainstein, *identifying justice principles appropriate to the social and political context* could help to guide governance and evaluate public policy resulting from collaborative processes like the Canmore GMS. A great deal of time and effort had been expended on deliberation and attempting to arriving at consensus in the GMS process, to the point of exhaustion as a number of participants expressed. Could greater focus on desired outcomes based on what they cherished about Canmore (e.g., what they valued and what they wanted their community to be) have been more helpful? Growth management to what end? Identifying justice principles to evaluate the policy implications and outcomes of the GMS report could have been useful, but note that identifying which justice principles apply to guide and evaluate resulting policy require an *integrated, relational,* and *contextual* approach. This includes a holistic view of the diverse "impacts" (tangible and intangible), understanding the historical, political, environmental, economic, and social-cultural context in which group conscious policies and *difference* are being negotiated, as well as the local, regional, state (national) and international scale and interrelationships of multiple stakeholders in tourism governance, policy, and planning!

Case 6.3 of Jaffa port's redevelopment process below by Nufar Avni offers an insightful look at the politics of difference and inclusion/exclusion as the waterfront transitions from a historic space for local livelihoods and practices into a cultural space for visitors. It raises questions, too, about the role of planners mediating power relations for fairness and inclusion in policy and planning processes, enabling not just voice and input, but also decision-making power and consideration for marginalized ethnic, gendered, and other cultural groups.[8]

Case 6.3: The Jaffa Port Redevelopment Process, Tel Aviv-Jaffa, Israel

Nufar Avni

The Jaffa port is nestled at the foot of old Jaffa—formerly a Palestinian town that was annexed to the Municipality of Tel Aviv, Israel, in 1949. It is one of the oldest ports in the world, and has served for thousands of years as an important gateway that connected Jaffa and the area to the world. The economic vitality of the port gradually diminished as more modern ports were built around it. In the late 1990s, the national government who owned the port decided to privatize it. But it had continued to serve as a fishing port and a source of livelihood for hundreds of local families, and a civic campaign was launched by fishers, residents and activists to "save the port" from privatization. In 2007, following a successful campaign, the city of Tel Aviv became the port's new owner. Inspired by a global trend of waterfront redevelopments (Shaw, 2001), the city decided to redevelop Jaffa port as a cultural district, while maintaining its historical function as a fishing port (see Photo 6.3.1).

The Jaffa port is an intricate environment in terms of heritage, identity, livelihood and culture. Jaffa has a mixed Jewish-Palestinian population, and most of the fishers are Palestinians—a national minority. While fishers often constitute a marginalized and stigmatized occupational identity globally (Nadel-Klein, 2003), in Jaffa their ethnic identity and minority status added a layer of complexity. From a different angle, injecting the port with new uses could cause controversy among the local community which values its historic role of housing fisheries. Redevelopment would have to balance conflicting needs as well as be considerate of present and future users of this space. Research worldwide has shown that in redevelopment processes, planners often prioritize economic over social (August & Walks, 2017) and ethnic considerations (Song, 2015), raising issues of access, inclusion and representation of local residents in policy making and decision making related to the redevelopment.

PHOTO 6.3.1   Fishers tend to their nets at the Jaffa port
Credit: Nufar Avni

The municipality hired an urban planning firm to plan and execute the port's renewal. The urban planner who led the process with his staff was not blind to the complexity of Jaffa and emphasized social aspects of development in addition to the economic. They launched an informal public participation process and invited local stakeholders early on—fishers, business owners, religious leaders and community members—to shape a vision for the port and voice their concerns and suggestions. Over the course of several months, their voices were heard but they were not granted formal decision-making powers. The unofficial slogan of the redevelopment process was "fixing without breaking," meaning preserving the unique ambience of the port and its mix of uses, and users, while opening it up for new audiences. The redevelopment vision specifically mentioned inclusion of diverse publics, and stated the need to repair the historical injustice of neglect and abandonment in Jaffa since 1949, as it transitioned from a lively Palestinian town into a marginalized borough of Tel Aviv.

Planning theorist Susan Fainstein (Fainstein, 2010) argues for democracy as one of the three pillars of a *Just City*. This entails a participatory planning process that represents various publics and, more importantly, ensuring that the process translates into fair outcomes. Her observation is pertinent to the Jaffa case. Despite seemingly good intentions, the democratic vision did not fully translate into action in Jaffa. Initially, the planning team opened up a dialogue with the fishers and local residents, who were suspicious of the anticipated changes. The planners built some trust with the fishers by attending to their vulnerable economic livelihood. The fishers were promised usage rights at the port, including improved facilities, unhindered access and administrative support. Local residents were also promised that the port would maintain its local, rustic atmosphere. All signage at the port was replaced from Hebrew to trilingual signs in Hebrew, Arabic and English. Physical renovations also took place, and with the exception of one warehouse that was transformed into a modern shopping center, most of the built environment remained almost intact.

Changes did take place, however, with regards to the fishers' work practices and sense of belonging. Many early promises that were made to the fishers were broken soon after the redevelopment was launched, for example, they were not granted new warehouses to replace their old ones. Their use of space for work purposes is also closely monitored by the port's administration. About a decade after the port was "saved" from privatization, the fishers feel that the port's administration has taken advantage of their presence to market the port as a "romantic" and "multicultural" attraction while their presence there is perceived as a hindrance and they do not receive the administrative support they were promised. Many local residents also feel that the port has changed from a close-knit community to an alienated space that prioritizes consumption of "outsiders" over the livelihood of locals. In other words, the participatory planning process did not lead to just outcomes from the perspective of the fishers and many local residents.

214 Democracy and Governance

The Jaffa case raises the need for institutionalized policies for collaboration and public participation. Currently, public-participation processes in Israel are encouraged but not obligatory, and Tel Aviv-Jaffa Municipality only recently published recommended guidelines for public participation in planning processes. These are usually limited to informing residents and allowing them to provide input (the lower rungs of Arnstein's (1969) ladder of citizen participation), but residents are not granted decision making powers. The Jaffa case also shows that though urban planners may understand the importance of participatory and inclusive redevelopment, it can lead to further disempowerment of vulnerable groups. A participatory process may give voice to populations that are not usually heard, but is insufficient in and of itself to result in just planning outcomes. In order for the redevelopment to be seen as truly successful in social terms, the redevelopment's vision need to be translated into action. This means, first, fulfilling the principles of equity, diversity and democracy that are articulated in the vision. Second, fishers, business owners and other stakeholders from the port's community must have voice as well as decision-making powers in the management of this delicate and extremely valuable space (see Avni, 2017).

References

Arnstein, S. R. (1969). A ladder of citizen participation. *Journal of the American Institute of Planners, 35*(4), 216–224.

August, M., & Walks, A. (2017). Urban redevelopment. In D. Richardson, N. Castree, M. Goodchild, & A. Kobayashi (Eds.), *International Encyclopedia of Geography: People, the earth, environment and technology* (pp. 1–11). John Wiley & Sons.

Avni, N. (2017). 'So long, and thanks for all the fish?' Examining the built and cultural heritage of the Jaffa port redevelopment. *International Journal of Heritage Studies, 23*(8), 679–694. https://doi.org/10.1080/13527258.2017.1317647

Fainstein, S. S. (2010). *The just city.* Ithaca, NY: Cornell University Press.

Nadel-Klein, J. (2003). *Fishing for heritage: Modernity and loss along the Scottish coast.* Oxford, New York: Berg.

Shaw, B. (2001). History at the water's edge. In R. Marshall (Ed.), *Waterfronts in post industrial cities* (pp. 160–172). London; New York: Spon Press London.

Song, L. K. (2015). Race, transformative planning, and the just city. *Planning Theory, 14*(2), 152–173.

Empowering Democratic Participation and Difference

Susan Fainstein makes a strong argument for a pluralistic justice approach to public policy evaluation in liberal pluralist settings, based on equity, democracy, and diversity. Case 6.3 also suggests that collaborative planning and resident involvement requires adopting a historical and cultural lens that addresses *recognition* (including political recognition as per Nancy Fraser's status model of recognition (see Chapter 3), as well as *difference* and *heterogeneity* between (and within) groups, as Iris Marion Young said. As should be clear by now, justice is not simply a matter of fair distribution of government revenues (including from tourism), though distribution (or redistribution to use Nancy Fraser's term) is very important. Iris Marion Young criticizes the dominance of the Rawlsian distributive paradigm that runs through contemporary theoretical discussions of justice.[9] The problem, she says, is "the tendency to conceive social justice and distribution as co-extensive concepts" for it "defines social justice as the morally proper distribution of social benefits and burdens among society's members" (Young, 2011, p. 16). While wealth, income, liberties, and opportunities are important primary goods, she points out that distributive definitions of justice often include non-material social goods such as power, rights, and self-respect. Take the example of one nonmaterial good, rights, for instance. It is not useful to conceive of rights as possessions, she says. They refer to "doing more than having, to social relationships that enable or constrain action," and are better seen as "institutionally defined rules specifying what people can do in relation to one another" (Young, 2011, p. 25).

Talking of distributing social goods like power, opportunities and respect is similarly problematic, Young argues, for these are not distributed to people apart from society, but in the *context of their identities and capacities, and their relationship to other social groups*. Your social rights as a resident to enjoy your city's amenities, or Canmore's residents to enjoy their mountain community, may conflict with others (e.g., the rights of the homeless, migrant workers, and tourists to enjoy the same public spaces). Negotiating such rights requires *democratic rights* to participate in joint dialogue and discussion about them. Of course, as Rockhill (2017) observes with respect to the United States, there can be in-groups and out-groups in the democracy—not all citizens possess equal democratic rights, though it may appear so on the surface. Redressing structural inequalities related to democratic participation and inclusiveness could require a range of approaches such as building capabilities and skills to enable effective participation by disempowered groups to contest misrecognition and possibly maldistribution, too, due to misrepresentation and exclusion.

Cultural Pluralism rather than Liberal Pluralism?

Young's approach to justice is clearly pluralistic. For democratic learning and participation to occur, the basic needs of the people have to be met, they cannot pursue lives of satisfactory work, social participation, and opportunities for expression in social and political processes otherwise (Young, 2011). People must have the right and opportunity to freely participate in public discussion and processes related to the institutions to which they contribute, or which affect their actions directly—not just government institutions but "all institutions of

216 Democracy and Governance

collective life, including for example, production and service enterprises, universities, and voluntary organizations" (Young, 2011, p. 91). *Freedom from oppression and domination* facilitates conditions for self-determination, recognition from others of one's individual and group identity, and paves the way for democratic participation and decision making:

> Democracy is both an element and a condition of social justice. If justice is defined negatively as the elimination of structures of domination, then justice implies democratic decision making. Democracy is a condition of freedom in the sense of self-determination... If all people are of equal moral worth, and no one by nature has greater capacity for freedom or moral sense, then people ought to decide collectively for themselves the goals and rules that will guide their action" (Young, 2011, p. 91).

The social contract tradition indicated above provides the main argument for democracy on the grounds of self-determination, which is a vital condition for social justice. Young argues, too, that delegating to government officials does not work as impartiality (an important liberal value) is impossible, so justice necessitates democratic processes for public participation. The goals of social justice from Young's perspective are social equality, voice and transformative action, challenging xenophobia, racism, and other entrenched injustices, creating positive group identity and embracing a *cultural pluralist* ideal. It requires at the very least: (i) Examining *institutional structures and social processes* that produce the distributions, not the distributions themselves, (ii) Identifying and addressing structural injustices related to domination and oppression (including exploitation), (iii) *Recognition of difference* between and within groups and (iv) enabling conditions for democratic participation and decision making. The importance of democratic participation and expression are evident in the ways she defines justice as:

> the institutional conditions that make it possible for all to learn and use satisfying skills in socially recognized settings, to participate in decision making and to express their feelings, experience, and perspective on social life in contexts where others can listen (Young, 2011, p. 91).

But, you may say, that's a really tall order! Yes, indeed. Policy, planning and destination management are highly complex domains with many stakeholders, including public, private, and civil sector organizations, plus diverse community groups. Tourists are also stakeholders (let's not forget, too, that tourists are residents somewhere and some may even be second-home owners, i.e., tourist-residents, within or across borders!). There is a "pluriverse" of worldviews, beliefs, values, interests, and perceptions to accommodate. Group conscious strategies (as Young put it) are needed to facilitate dialogue, cross-cultural understanding and learning, plus inclusiveness and attention to *difference*,

Democracy and Governance **217**

bringing diverse stakeholders and their knowledge to the table (e.g., traditional, local, scientific, technical, and business knowledge).

Case 6.4 by Dawn Jourdan below on tribal participation in water resource management offers an example using a participatory game to engage players (participants) in seeing how water is valued and approached from different perspectives, to be sensitive to difference among groups and to dialogue from a more informed point of view—from the viewpoint of the "other" rather than from one's own only.

Case 6.4: Indigenous Planning and Game Changing Perspective: Water Resource Planning in the Chickasaw Nation, Ardmore, Oklahoma, USA

Dawn Jourdan

Indigenous populations in North America and abroad are particularly vulnerable to impacts of climate change on the people and resources. Tribal leaders have become particularly concerned about how environmental changes such as prolonged droughts and increased temperatures, for example, will affect plants and animals that are vital to the celebration of indigenous culture. The Chickasaw Nation, headquartered in Ada, Oklahoma, is proactively working to understand and plan for changes in climate. The tribal leadership identified threats to water resources as one of the most significant issues affecting the tribe. Governor Annoatubby commissioned a task force to develop a water plan. This planning process included an invitation to provide input to a wide variety of citizen stakeholders.

Dr. Dawn Jourdan and Climate Scientist April Taylor worked with Chickasaw leaders in the fall of 2017 to design and implement an activity to bolster stakeholder input into the water plan. The purpose of this exercise was to give participants the opportunity to assess the viability of a spectrum of adaptation strategies. Members of the Chickasaw nation were invited to participate in this process via the posting of fliers at local gathering places as well as through a series of emails to employees of the Chickasaw Nation. More than 50 individuals responded to the call for participation. An equal number of men and women participated in one of four workshops held in two locations over a two-day period. The experience and knowledge of participants varied. Some were employed in activities directly related to the use of water, such as farming, water treatment, and recreation. Others attended as a result of general concerns over the potential long-term impacts of drought in the region. The call for participation even drew a few individuals unaffiliated with the tribe. One company, engaged in gravel mining operations, who seeks to do business with the tribe sent several employees to

218 Democracy and Governance

learn and participate. The majority of the participants were generally knowledgeable about the region and the impacts of drought on the natural and built environment. They did not, generally, have a background in water regulation. As such, Dr. Jourdan offered a general primer on the relevant science and regulatory tools discussed in detail as a part of the game that was played by participations. In order to make this topic more manageable (and fun), Dr. Jourdan crafted a role-playing game that allowed participants to explore a series of adaptation strategies while "walking in the shoes of another," i.e., agriculture, eco-tourism, health and human services, water resources, hazards management, and planning and land development.

The adaptation strategies ranged from no regulation to highly regulatory and are reproduced below:

1. Do nothing and let the market decide how water will be allocated
2. Price available water supply based on necessity of the use and availability
3. Creation of reservoirs to hold water for use by the tribes
4. Require efficient water use and conservation
5. Limit farming activities, including livestock cultivation
6. Limit the amount of future residential development that can occur within a 25-year period based on the amount of water available at the time of development
7. Prohibit the development of water-intensive land uses like slaughterhouses

Upon being seated at the table, each individual was asked to choose a stake of six game coins representing one of the stakeholder groups. The exercise was performed in three iterations.

In the first scenario, participants were asked to read a paragraph describing their assigned role. After considering this paragraph, participants were asked to place their chips on the adaptive strategies they felt would be most beneficial to their assigned sector (see Photo 6.4.1). They did not deliberate during the first placement of their chips.

Subsequently, each participant was encouraged to tell the group why and how they voted. After hearing these statements, the participants were given the opportunity to modify their votes and to explain why. This was the second scenario. In the third and final scenario, the participants were allowed to drop their chosen persona and to represent their own interests. They voted again, this time based on their own beliefs, and discussed the reasons they chose to move (or not) their game coins. This process was replicated in the course of six workshops.

This exercise brought together a diversity of concerned citizens who were interested in learning more about the impacts of climate change on drought conditions. Collectively, those who came together resoundingly supported the Nation undertaking efforts to educate and implement conservation strategies,

PHOTO 6.4.1   Role Playing Game Board
Credit: Eyakem Gulilat

and, where feasible, to capture excess rain and floodwaters. While groups seemed to appreciate the need for some regulation, the preferences shared demonstrated a real desire by the participants to incentivize more conservation minded behavior by the Nation and its residents. Participants showed interest in complementing these efforts with some degree of regulation as well as incentivizing sustainable development practices in the wake of climate change.

The information gathered is being used as a source of data to inform the tribe's water plan. This exercise was important because it gave members of the Nation and their partners the opportunity to participate in discussions regarding the impact of climate change on the regional water supply, with a focus on tribal resources. The process provided an opportunity for participants to discuss the ways in which the tribal members' personal and ancestral knowledge of land and water resources coincide with the models of climate change being generated by climate scientists. As designed, the exercise gave participants the opportunity to step into the shoes of those with different interests in the use of water resources. It allowed those who work in professions which treat water as a commodity the chance to understand and develop a new respect for the perspectives of those who herald conservation as a higher priority and vice versa. At the conclusion of the meeting, all participants took with them a heightened understanding and appreciation of the need to prioritize water usage as climate change threatens to diminish the supply of this vital resource.

220 Democracy and Governance

Difference and Particularity: A Dual System of Rights

Looking at how the Anangu in Chapter 5 exercise their particular group rights to care for ancestral land and to share traditional practices with visitors reveals another layer of complexity that speaks to the merit of cultural pluralism (rather than liberal pluralism), as Young advocates. The distributive paradigm of Rawlsian justice and equity, i.e., justice as fairness (Rawls, 1971, 1996), is grounded in liberal values such as individual autonomy, impartiality and neutrality. Its liberal individualistic perspective is atomistic in that individuals only relate to each other in comparison with the goods they possess, and it assumes a static conception of society. In *Justice and the Politics of Difference*, Iris Marion Young (2011) criticizes Rawls's approaches and calls us to approach justice in terms of human, bodily, affective terms, sensitive to *difference* between and within groups. Hers is an embodied approach—seeing the person situated in place, context, and time, in dynamic relations with other people, organizations and social processes. Conscious and unconscious behaviors within these processes can contribute to injustices that can become systematically sedimented in institutional structures over time, for example, in racism toward the Maya entrenched in policy as described in Case 2.2 in Chapter 2, or human rights violations toward women that permeate social processes and justice institutions in patriarchal societies.

The specific rights of a particular group relative to that of other groups, or versus generalized rights across society can create severe tensions and conflicts. What are the rights of a minority Muslim woman traveler in a destination with strong patriarchal roots that hegemonically reinforces a dominant religion that is not hers (see Bianchi & Stephenson, 2014)? Structural, systematic oppression against a particular group calls for group-specific rights and group-conscious policies, affirming group specificity and difference alongside general civic and participatory rights. As Young (2011) explains, group conscious policies rarely are gender neutral and the assertion of group difference provides a standpoint from which to evaluate and criticize prevailing (unfair) institutions and norms that may have become sedimented socially, politically and historically by the actions of dominant groups. Rather than a liberal pluralism, Young (2000, 2011) is advocating a democratic cultural pluralism that supports a *dual system of rights*. For example, in June, 2018, a new law compatible with Islamic law (which is based on Sharia) enables Saudi women to drive in Saudi Arabia; however, they still cannot travel outside the country without permission from their primary male guardian, e.g., a father, husband, or brother (Wright, 2017).

In the context of tourism, embracing a politics of difference means sharing social spaces in a way that embraces hospitality, difference and an ethic of care for the "other" in the host-guest encounters, respecting the social rights of residents, in addition to their economic, environmental and cultural rights, respecting the dignity of human beings at home, at work and in spaces of travel and leisure. Social spaces such as that of city life under such an embodied, situated, pluralistic view is a "being together of strangers in openness to group differences" (Young,

2011, p. 256). Note that group differences among different cultural groups are important to consider in academic research as well as in planning practice. Vorobjovas-Pinta (2018), for instance, discusses resisting "homogenized portrayals of LGBT people, in academic inquiry or other cultural spheres" and recognizing internal power relations within LGBT communities and LGBT-only spaces, as much as power relations between groups.

Summary and Further Considerations

What constitutes effective governance of a phenomenon that ranges from the local to the global, generates complex impacts and involves multiple stakeholders and industry/non-industry sectors, public and private spaces, residents, tourists, with diverse and sometimes (often?) divergent interests and values? Many destinations are grappling with tourism growth, exacerbated in some places due to domestic and trans-border investments driving up real estate values and cost of living. In Canmore, Alberta (Canada), efforts continue to supply affordable housing in the Bow Valley. The adjacent province of British Columbia initiated a foreign buyer tax on foreign home purchasers in the Greater Vancouver Regional District since 2016, in efforts to manage an affordable housing crisis in a destination popular with foreign home buyers (Government of British Columbia, 2018). It raises questions about the social rights of residents and tourists (including second-home owners), in addition to related issues of governance, democracy and sustainability. Gentrification was already displacing the poor and the homeless in the high rent downtown area of Vancouver as the city prepared to host visitors for the Whistler Olympics in 2010. Smoky, grungy cafés in the 1960s diner style, where the impoverished and unemployed residents found solace over lukewarm coffee, were being replaced by chic cafés and fusion restaurants attracting a young, upward mobile professional crowd. Where are these invisible poor now?

Destination residents stand to be highly affected by development and governance related to tourism, within and across borders. How can their issues and concerns be heard effectively, e.g., on rapid growth, global climate change issues, planning for resiliency, disaster planning and recovery, defending rights to their commons (social, cultural, and natural), and particularly the voices of disadvantaged groups and minority populations who face marginalization, oppression, racial or gender discrimination? The chapter offers a brief exploration of the challenges of tourism governance and justice across borders, and then returns within borders to addresses democracy and inclusion in tourism policy, planning, and governance in the context of sustainability and well-being. Taking justice as a principle and goal of public policy evaluation, as Fainstein (2010, 2017) suggests in urban planning, may offer a start to guide policy evaluation, but which values and approaches guide justice would needed to be determined based on the particular *context* (note there are other than liberal approaches to justice). Important to consider here are democratic participation and recognition of *difference* (Young, 2011) to ensure and

222 Democracy and Governance

defend the rights and abilities of diverse groups to participate in public policy as well as stewardship of their communal and ecological spaces.

An important need arises here for a well-informed public in tourism destinations. We can think here of the potential of tourism to facilitate local-global citizenship and empower the local through civic engagement and opportunities to involve diverse groups and vulnerable populations in learning about tourism in the community and engaging in "touristic" activities that enhance well-being. The partnerships described in the Children's University Tasmania program in Case 6.5 below offers access to leisure and recreational opportunities for less well-off children and their families, facilitating cultural knowledge, status, physical as well as psychological health (self-esteem, self-confidence) as they get to know their community, enjoy its green spaces, and participate in learning through diverse cultural opportunities (visits to museum. etc.). The program helps to empower and enable vulnerable groups to gain social rights to their city, enhancing potential for civic engagement and informed decision making related to tourism as they gain greater understanding and knowledge of local attractions and services. This case, too, points to the merit of exploring a pluralistic approach to justice and well-being in tourism governance, policy, and planning.

Questions for Reflection

1. How do you envision governance for tourism, which takes place in complex social-ecological relationships and interdependencies locally and globally?
2. Pick one case from the several in this chapter and discuss how democracy is being furthered by the actions taking place in the case.
3. Do destinations facing rapid tourism growth have the right to shut their doors to future tourists?
4. What synergies do you see between the democratic cultural pluralism that Young advocates here and the "pluriverse" discussed in the context of the Global South in Chapter 5?

Case 6.5: The Children's University Tasmania: The Transformative Power of Tourism

Can-Seng Ooi and Becky Shelley

Tasmania is currently experiencing exponential visitor growth. Tourism has become a new engine of economic development for this small Australian state, with a population of 520,000. A record 1.28 million people visited Tasmania in the 12 months to September 2017, up 8% on the previous year, total spending increased to A$2.3 billion (Tourism Tasmania, 2018). Like many emerging tourism destinations, Tasmanians are concerned with how tourism will change their island. A relatively high proportion of Tasmanians experience social exclusion. These people do not seem to benefit from tourism growth. For many of them, their daily activities are distant from the world of tourism, and they do not perceive the industry as particularly relevant for them. Instead they may experience cost of living pressures as long-term rental properties are converted into short-stay visitor accommodation. They may have difficulty accessing services during peak tourism and festival seasons. Despite creating jobs, it is clear that the benefits of tourism are not distributed evenly. There are emerging concerns that tourism may be exacerbating social inequalities (Burness, 2018; Farnsworth, 2018). This case shows how a particular program—Children's University Tasmania—redistributes benefits from tourism to the local community. The case uses data from a mixed-methods evaluation of the Children's University being led by Becky Shelley at the Peter Underwood Centre, as well as interviews the authors conducted during 2017.

This case considers children and families who live in marginalized communities in Tasmania. They may not have the resources or ability to enjoy tourism sites that are freely available, such as going to museums or visiting parks (which are among the "trickle down" effects of government redistribution of tourism income toward infrastructure, services and welfare). They may not benefit directly from the growth in tourism unless family members work in the industry. This section of the community has largely been ignored in tourism policy discussions even though policy-makers and the industry often make claims that tourism will benefit society at large. In what ways can the local tourism industry work with children and their families to build up social capital and "cultural capital" in a Bourdieusien sense so that these children will have a better foundation to succeed? Bourdieu identified three forms or "guises" of capital: economic, social and cultural. Depending on the field in which it functions social capital and cultural capital can be converted into economic capital. However, as Bourdieu and Passeron (1977) articulate in their theory of social reproduction, the different types of "capital" children and their families possess may pose a barrier to social mobility. Children experiencing the effects of socioeconomic disadvantage may not exhibit the embodied sense of cultural capital that tends to supplement or enhance achievement in the education system.

Tasmania and the Children's University

The continuing relative underperformance of Tasmania in areas such as gross state product, labor market participation, productivity levels, health and well-being outcomes, and life expectancy are referenced to make a case for prioritizing improving the state's educational outcomes (Eslake, 2016). Tasmania is home to 112,884 children and young people. Tasmanian families have higher levels of socioeconomic disadvantage than the national average (Commissioner for Children and Young People Tasmania, 2017).

Within Tasmania, and nationally, there is a high-level consensus on the centrality of education as a policy lever to achieve broader social, economic and well-being goals. This consensus contributed to the creation of the Peter Underwood Centre for Educational Attainment at the University of Tasmania, where the Children's University Tasmania is based. The Children's University Tasmania uses Australian Bureau of Statistics Socio-Economic Indexes for Areas to determine which government schools to partner with to implement the program.

The Children's University Tasmania is a member of a social franchise that is currently implemented in the United Kingdom, Australia, Malaysia and China. The Children's University identifies informal learning as a rich site to foster aspiration, parental engagement and educational success—if the social, economic and cultural barriers to participation can be reduced (Macbeath, 2013). It aims to promote social mobility by providing high quality out-of-school-hours learning activities to children aged 7–14. It targets children and young people facing socio-economic disadvantage to ensure that every child, irrespective of parental means, has access to quality extracurricular learning:

> Impact is...measured by three inter-related aspects—knowing, feeling and doing. It is concerned with questions such as...Does the Children's University experience widen children's conceptions of learning and ignite a desire to be more adventurous and self-directed? (Macbeath, 2013)

Using the narrative of travel, when a child becomes a member of the Children's University they are given a "Passport to Learning" in which they record their participation in activities at Public Learning Destinations (Figure 6.5.1). After completing 30+ hours of validated learning, their achievement is celebrated at a formal graduation ceremony, a significant cultural experience itself (Photo 6.5.1). The Children's University builds a bridge for parents and guardians to expose children to diverse cultural experiences.

Tourism

There is a significant body of literature that identifies the significance of extracurricular participation on educational outcomes, and the ways in which access and opportunity to engage in extracurricular activity is impacted by socioeconomic characteristics (Cummings et al., 2012). So, how does tourism fit into this discussion? The Children's University Tasmania has partnered with over 100 local services and attractions that serve residents and/or visitors. They include museums, historic sites, wildlife sanctuaries, regional galleries, and events such as festivals. The Children's University

Democracy and Governance **225**

FIGURE 6.5.1 Children's University Australia Passport to Learning
Image Credit: Children's University Australia

Tasmania encourages tourism services to become validated Public Learning Destinations by highlighting their potential to enrich the local community:

> Being a Learning Destination is a great way to promote your organization to the local community and to engage with young people in your service delivery. Learning Destinations can enrich communities

PHOTO 6.5.1 Children's University Tasmania graduation ceremony (December 2016, Hobart Tasmania) http://www.utas.edu.au/underwood-centre/aspiration-attainment. Retrieved April 26, 2018
Image Credit: Peter Underwood Centre, University of Tasmania

and build valuable networks that help support children and their families in their educational journey (Children's University Tasmania, 2017).

An unpublished report prepared by researchers at the Peter Underwood Centre supports the claim that families also engage in a learning journey (Eyles, Shelley, & Stratford, 2017).

> [the] family has now become involved in visiting Public Learning Destinations on weekends and holidays—they are looking through the destinations for opportunities they can follow up...Previously a lot of her weekend time was spent at home "filling" in time so the whole family have benefited and their outlook has been altered. (School Coordinator)

> The program offers/creates the opportunity for families to venture to surrounding sites they may never have gone to. This has been very evident as the parents and children have come to me with stories of their "adventure." From one child wanting to go to a particular destination, a whole family enjoys the benefits. (School Coordinator, unpublished report (Eyles et al., 2017)).

The authors conducted interviews with Children's University Tasmania employees and Public Learning Destinations in 2017. An employee of the Children's University Tasmania observed that:

it provides a structure for parents to understand how and what to engage in with kids outside of school... But I think that is important as parents struggle sometimes with knowing what to do. (Employee, Children's University Tasmania)

Early evidence suggests that the program is having a positive influence on school attendance, a sense of achievement and awareness of further learning as a pathway to a "dream" job in the future. The Children's University Tasmania also highlights an avenue for the local tourism industry to be more proactive in using their social license (Ooi & Shelley, 2018). While many of them serve visitors, they should use similar resources to serve residents. They can become Public Learning Destinations, and not just tourist attractions.

Obstacles remain. It is important to observe that the economic and cultural barriers to participation in local tourism and informal learning opportunities need further analysis. It is evident that even where people have free access to tourist attractions, there are cultural barriers to visitation. The renowned Museum of Old and New Art (MONA) is free to Tasmanian residents but that may not be sufficient to encourage visitation (Booth, O'Connor, Franklin, & Papastergiadis, 2017).

The Transformative Opportunity

The Public Learning Destinations that are part of the Children's University Tasmania are not all tourism sites. Nonetheless, the case suggests resources created for tourism can also be deployed to support broader societal goals, such as raising educational aspiration and attainment. During off-peak tourist seasons, more can be done to engage local children in extracurricular, experiential learning through tourism related services and attractions. The tourism industry has benefitted from skill development initiatives funded by government. Fostering skills in inclusive and child-friendly practices within the tourism industry could be encouraged. The beneficiaries of this approach include the child-participants, but also the industry as they build connections with a new audience, or customer base.

One Public Learning Destination notes they had done work training customer services officers. They observed:

the staff are getting a really good basis in educational principles so that when they are actually teaching or showing students...they are able to give them the information that they need in a way that has meaning to them...it means that the kids are walking away with something a little bit more than just an experience which is fantastic....We want to engage with the Children's University. For one, in terms of pure numbers, it brings us a new audience (Public Learning Destination officer).

In some instances, rich and interesting learning content at tourism attractions can also be harnessed to create online learning opportunities. This is particularly relevant for regionally dispersed communities. Tourism assets can be crafted into mobile "destinations." These can be physical, and digital, or a combination. For example, the Tasmanian Museum and Art Gallery has an outreach program. They provide a box that contains items and information that schools can use, while a museum employee connects via video-link and discusses contents of the box. The museum becomes a mobile supporter of learning. Currently, this is used to support formal learning within the curriculum. There are opportunities to develop content that supports informal learning.

While key public institutions such as museums, art galleries, and historic sites often have an explicit educational purpose and resources to support engagement strategies, the Children's University Tasmania case suggests that similar principles can be extended more broadly across the tourism sector. The narrative of travel is a tool that can stimulate the imagination and provide creative, fun and engaging ways to enhance learning about culture, history, science, natural and social environments. As such, it can support broader social and economic goals of improved educational attainment for the children and young people, as well as fostering an understanding of their place (self and community) in a globalized world.

> Learning in this environment has really helped me to explore different parts of myself, and learn to be a positive role model in my community (Children's University Tasmania member, age 11).

The Children's University Tasmania is also about the adults. The role of parents, caregivers and home environments as influential agents on levels of educational engagement and attainment is well documented. As noted above, Tasmanian families have higher levels of socio-economic disadvantage than the national average. All parents have aspirations for their children. Yet, navigating to achieve those goals can be hard, especially for socially excluded families. They may benefit from programs like the one described here to understand what experiences and events are available in their local community.

This study illustrates how tourism resources are being used for local and community development, enhancing individual, social and cultural well-being. Tourism policies often aim to bring tourism benefits to local society; this is easier said than done (Ooi, 2013). This study shows one concrete way that tourism can be made to serve the needs of local society, and support disadvantaged families and children to create and fulfill their visions for the future.

References

Booth, K., O'Connor, J., Franklin, A., & Papastergiadis, N. (2017). It's a museum, but not as we know it: Issues for local residents accessing the

Museum of Old and New Art. *Visitor Studies, 20*(1), 10–32. https://doi.org/10.1080/10645578.2017.1297121

Bourdieu, P., & Passeron, J. (1977). *Reproduction in education, culture and society*. Beverly Hills: SAGE.

Burness, G. (2018, March 15). Hobart housing crisis: Crown land release to ease shortage but no quick fix, Government warns. Retrieved from https://www.abc.net.au/news/2018-03-15/crown-land-release-to-ease-land-shortage-tas-govt-says/9550308

Children's University Tasmania. (2017). Learning destinations are places and organisations to which children can "travel" with their passport to learning. Retrieved from http://childrensuniversity.com.au/adults/learning-destinations/why-become-a-learning-destination/?cu_region=NT

Commissioner for Children and Young People Tasmania. (2017). *Health and wellbeing of Tasmania's children, young people and their families report.* Hobart, Tasmania. Retrieved from http://www.childcomm.tas.gov.au/wp-content/uploads/2017/03/Health-and-Wellbeing-of-Tasmanias-Children-Young-People-and-their-Families-Report.pdf

Cummings, C., Laing, K., Law, J., Mclaughlin, J., Papps, I., Todd, L., & Woolner, P. (2012). *Can changing aspirations and attitudes impact on educational attainment? A review of interventions*. York, UK.

Eslake, S. (2016). *Tasmania report 2016*. Hobart: Tasmanian Chamber of Commerce and Industry (TCCI).

Eyles, K., Shelley, B., & Stratford, E. (2017). *Children's University Tasmania: Preliminary evaluation (unpublished report)*. Hobart, University of Tasmania.

Farnsworth, S. (2018). Airbnb in Australia: Entire homes, commercial listings "surge" amid growing concerns. Retrieved from https://www.abc.net.au/news/2018-02-23/entire-homes-commercial-listings-have-surged-on-airbnb/9473368

Macbeath, J. (2013). *Evaluating provision, progress and quality of learning in the Children's University: 2012. Fourth Report to the CU Trust January 2013.* Retrieved from http://www.childrensuniversity.co.uk/media/13021/cu_evaluation_2012-13_full.pdf

Ooi, C.-S. (2013). Tourism policy challenges: Balancing acts, co-operative stakeholders and maintaining authenticity. In M. Smith & G. Richards (Eds.), *Routledge Handbook of Cultural Tourism* (pp. 67–74). London: Routledge.

Ooi, C.-S., & Shelley, B. (2018). *Dare to dream: Comparative lesson on building cultural capital from Children's University Tasmania and Children's University Malaysia-Asia.* Hobart.

Tourism Tasmania. (2018). *Tasmanian tourism snapshot–Year ending December 2017. Tourism Research.* Retrieved from https://www.tourismtasmania.com.au/__data/assets/pdf_file/0010/62992/2017-Q4-Tasmanian-Tourism-Snapshot-YE-December-2017.pdf

230 Democracy and Governance

Notes

1 Source of above quote and other quotes related to the Canmore Growth Management Strategy in this chapter are from Jamal (1997). Underlining in the related quotes are for emphasis. Research on resident participation in this and other community-oriented initiatives was conducted over a number of years (e.g., Jamal & Getz, 1999; Jamal & McDonald, 2011).

2 Read Habermas's (1989) analysis of the liberal public sphere within the state. Calhoun (1992) contains helpful discussions of Habermas's critical assessment of the bourgeois public sphere. Given the mobilities of capital, labor, workers, tourists, etc., Dredge and Jamal (2013, p. 575) wonder if developing a more global version of "community" than is typically understood in notions of community-based tourism endangers a more vibrant public sphere of citizen action in the homeworld. See also Crack (2008) plus Chapter 8 in Fraser (2013).

3 Kleingeld and Brown (2014) provide a helpful summary of his views (space limits discussing these here).

4 See Chapter 7 in Young (2000) for an interesting perspective on this transborder governance challenge and the notion of *relational autonomy* that is entailed—being with others in relations of solidarity and interdependence, being included in democracy with recognition of difference between and within groups, yet retaining self-determination and cultural difference.

5 For an overview of the GMS process and follow-up to it, see Jamal and McDonald (2011). For an example of a community-wide process of parents, school and youth involvement, as well as door-to-door social marketing to address climate change and resource conservation through resident involvement, see Jamal and Watt (2011).

6 Bohman and Rehg (2017) provide a comprehensive overview and analysis of Habermas's notions of the public sphere and theory of communicative action. Of course, it is important to read Habermas's own work—see Note 2 above.

7 Fainstein says her justice approach works in other liberal pluralist settings. In Fainstein (2017), she uses Singapore as an example to discuss the three justice principles she forwards (equity, diversity, democracy). Jamal and Camargo (2014) draw on ideas in *The Just City* to explore some preliminary principles of social justice in the *Just Destination*.

8 Thomas (2008) discusses *equity planning* and racial diversity. Resident participation in decision making is described in Arnstein's (1969) well-cited ladder of citizen participation, also mentioned in the Jaffa case by Nufar Avni. See also the "Critical Opinion" forwarded by Jamal and Camargo (2018).

9 Schlosberg (2007) points out that the dominant Rawlsian approach has influenced environmental justice to be couched in terms of distributive and procedural justice. He proposes a pluralistic approach to justice that include representation and participation, as noted in Chapter 5

References

Arnstein, S. R. (1969). A ladder of citizen participation. *Journal of the American Planning Association, 35*(4), 216–224.

Australian Associated Press. (2018, June 14). New Zealand to tax tourists to visit—but Australians will get in free. Retrieved June 18, 2018, from https://www.theguardian. com/world/2018/jun/15/new-zealand-tourist-tax-to-exempt-australians

Bianchi, R. B., & Stephenson, M. L. (2014). *Tourism and citizenship: Rights, freedoms and responsibilities in the global order*. New York: Routledge.

Biosphere Institute of the Bow Valley: Ecological integrity through education, research, and outreach. (2014). Retrieved June 1, 2018, from http://biosphereinstitute.org/

Biosphere Institute of the Bow Valley. (2017). Canmore community monitoring program 2016 final report. Canmore, AB. Retrieved from http://biosphereinstitute.org/wp-content/uploads/2016/01/CCMP2008.pdf

Bohman, J., & Rehg, W. (2017). Jürgen Habermas. In *The Stanford Encyclopedia of Philosophy* (Fall 2017). Edward N. Zalta (ed.). Retrieved from https://plato.stanford.edu/archives/fall2017/entries/habermas/

Calhoun, C. (Ed.). (1992). *Habermas and the public sphere*. Cambridge: MIT Press.

Cole, S. (Ed.). (2018). *Gender equality and tourism: Beyond empowerment*. Wallingford: CABI. Retrieved from https://www.cabi.org/bookshop/book/9781786394422

Crack, A. M. (2008). *Global communication and transnational public spheres*. New York: Palgrave Macmillan.

Dredge, D., & Jamal, T. (2013). Mobilities on the Gold Coast, Australia: Implications for destination governance and sustainable tourism. *Journal of Sustainable Tourism*, (June 2013), 37–41.

Dredge, D., & Jenkins, J. (Eds.). (2016). *Stories of Practice: Tourism policy and planning* (First). New York, NY: Routledge.

Fainstein, S. S. (2010). *The just city*. Ithaca, NY: Cornell University Press.

Fainstein, S. S. (2017). Urban planning and social justice. In M. Gunder, A. Madanipour, & V. Watson (Eds.), *The Routledge handbook of planning theory* (pp. 130–142). New York, NY: Routledge. Retrieved from https://www.routledge.com/guilfordpressbooks/details/9781138905016?books/details/9781138905016/

Fraser, N. (2010). *Scales of justice: Reimagining political space in a globalizing world*. New York, NY: Columbia University Press. Retrieved from http://www.jstor.org/stable/10.7312/fras14680

Fraser, N. (2013). *Fortunes of feminism*. London: Verso.

Gill, A. M. (2018). Challenges to the resilience of Whistler's journey towards sustainability. In *Tourism in Transitions* (pp. 21–38). https://doi.org/10.1007/978-3-319-64325-0

Government of British Columbia. (2018, February 20). Additional property transfer tax for foreign entities & taxable trustees. Retrieved June 19, 2018, from https://www2.gov.bc.ca/gov/content/taxes/property-taxes/property-transfer-tax/additional-property-trans fer-tax

Habermas, J., (1989). *The structural transformation of the public sphere. An inquiry into a category of bourgeois society*. T. Burger, Trans., with the assistance of F. Lawrence. Cambridge, MA: MIT Press.

Hall, C. M. (2011). A typology of governance and its implications for tourism policy analysis. *Journal of Sustainable Tourism*, *19*(4–5), 437–457. https://doi.org/10.1080/09669582.2011.570346

Hall, C. M. (2012). Governance and responsible tourism. In D. Leslie (Ed.), Responsible tourism: Concepts, theory and practice (pp. 107–118). Wallingford, UK: CABI. https://doi.org/10.1079/9781845939878.0000

Holden, A. (2013). *Tourism, poverty and development*. London: Routledge.

Jamal, T. (1997). *Multi-party consensus processes in environmentally sensitive destinations: Paradoxes of ownership and common ground* (Doctoral dissertation). The University of Calgary, Calgary, Canada.

Jamal, T., & Camargo, B. A. (2014). Sustainable tourism, justice and an ethic of care: toward the Just Destination. *Journal of Sustainable Tourism*, *22*(1), 11–30. https://doi.org/10.1080/09669582.2013.786084

Jamal, T., & Camargo, B. A. (2018). Tourism governance and policy: Whither justice? *Tourism Management Perspectives, 25*, 205–208. https://doi.org/10.1016/j.tmp.2017.11.009

Jamal, T., & Getz, D. (1999). Community roundtables for tourism-related conflicts: The dialectics of consensus and process structures. *Journal of Sustainable Tourism, 7*(3), 290–313.

Jamal, T., & McDonald, D. (2011). The short and long of collaborative planning in the mountain resort destination of Canmore, Canada. *Current Issues in Tourism, 14*(1), 1–25. https://doi.org/10.1080/13683500903545040

Jamal, T., & Watt, E. M. (2011). Climate change pedagogy and performative action: Toward community-based destination governance. *Journal of Sustainable Tourism, 19*(4–5), 571–588. https://doi.org/10.1080/09669582.2011.575227

Kant, I. (1998). *The groundwork of the metaphysics of morals.* (M. Gregor, Ed.). Cambridge: Cambridge University Press.

Kant, I. (2006). Toward perpetual peace: A philosophical sketch. In D. L. Colclasure (Trans.), *Toward perpetual peace and other writings on politics, peace, and history, with essays by J. Waldron, M.W. Doyle, and A. Wood* (pp. 67–109). New Haven, CT: Yale University Press. https://doi.org/10.4324/9781315113333

Kleingeld, P., & Brown, E. (2014). Cosmopolitanism. In E. N. Zalta (Ed.), *The Stanford Encyclopedia of Philosophy* (Fall). Retrieved from https://plato.stanford.edu/archives/fall2014/entries/cosmopolitanism/

Lefebvre, H. (1991). *The production of space.* (D. Nicholson-Smith, Trans.). Oxford: Blackwell.

Mowforth, M., & Munt, I. (2016). *Tourism and sustainability: Development, globalisation and new tourism in the Third World* (4th ed.). New York, NY: Routledge.

Rawls, J. (1971). *A theory of justice.* Cambridge: Belknap Press of Harvard University Pres.

Rawls, J. (1996). *Political liberalism.* New York: Columbia University Press.

Rockhill, G. (2017). *Counter-history of the present untimely interrogations into globalization, technology, democracy.* Durham and London: Duke University Press.

Schlosberg, D. (2007). *Defining environmental justice.* Oxford: Oxford University Press.

Smith, M., & Duffy, R. (2003). *The ethics of tourism development.* New York, NY: Routledge.

The Nature Conservancy. (2015). Our history: Milestones of The Nature Conservancy. Retrieved April 30, 2018, from https://www.nature.org/about-us/vision-mission/history/index.htm?intc=nature.tnav.about

The Nature Conservancy. (2018). The Nature Conservancy and the Government of Quintana Roo announce innovative financial mechanism for insuring and conserving coral reefs | The Nature Conservancy. Retrieved April 30, 2018, from https://www.nature.org/newsfeatures/pressreleases/the-nature-conservancy-and-the-government-of-quintana-roo-announce-innovativ.xml

The United Nations Office at Geneva (UNOG). (n.d.). The League of Nations (1919–1946). Retrieved June 1, 2018, from https://www.unog.ch/80256EDD006AC19C/(httpPages)/17C8E6BCE10E3F4F80256EF30037D733?OpenDocument

Vorobjovas-pinta, O. (2018). Gay neo-tribes : Exploration of travel behaviour and space. *Annals of Tourism Research, 72*(May), 1–10. https://doi.org/10.1016/j.annals.2018.05.008

Wright, R. (2017). Why Saudi women driving is a small step forward, not a great one. Retrieved from https://www.newyorker.com/news/news-desk/why-saudi-women-driving-is-a-small-step-forward-not-a-great-one

Young, I. M. (2000). *Inclusion and democracy.* New York: Oxford University Press.

Young, I. M. (2011). *Justice and the politics of difference* (Paperback). Princeton, NJ: Princeton University Press.

7

TOWARD GOOD AND JUST TOURISM?

Introduction

One way to think about travels in tourism is whether the journey embarked upon has changed our perspective, so that we see things differently, even (especially) the mundane things that once appeared so comfortably known and understood. Make the familiar strange, said C. Wright Mills and engage the sociological imagination, cast a critical yet charitable learning gaze, see how the things and practices of everyday life are related to larger social (and political) structures (Mills, 1959). A journey elsewhere accomplishes this in travel and upon returning home, for even activities and things in the homeworld take on new meaning after coming home. You might, for instance, kick that old plastics habit after seeing how marine life in the coastal destination you visited is being impacted by plastic waste ending up in the ocean. It was so easy to discard that plastic straw from the refreshing smoothie you bought regularly after a workout at the gym. Or you might really appreciate finding that good wine you tasted on holiday in your local wine store! Can you savor it without memories of that holiday flooding back to accompany every sip? This book's journey is almost over, and the stories, cases and glimpses of justice and ethics encountered will hopefully help make the familiar strange as much as they might have served to make some of the strange more familiar. It will have accomplished its aim if it compels each of us to seek the good of tourism, as it plays out in everyday life and travels elsewhere.

What lies ahead now for those who care about this finite planet called Earth, about the joys that come from travels elsewhere, and the travails of those who are affected by all that goes on in tourism locally and globally? This chapter first looks back at previous chapters to pick up some "souvenirs" to bring home, then stops to revisit the pluralism of justice for tourism before proceeding to reflect on the above question. Two case contributors help our search here. Case 7.1 by Emily

234 Toward Good and Just Tourism?

Höckert reflects on the crucial agenda of climate change. Case 7.2 by Bernard Lane looks at conserving and developing railway heritage for tourism. Both share in common a call to action, for they point out stories, big and little, that will not survive for future generations without individual and joint efforts, aided by justice and an ethic of care.

Reflections on *Justice and Ethics in Tourism*

In this book, we seek to understand and address forms of justice and injustice that arise through everyday practices and relationships between social life, social processes, and institutional structures at home and during travels elsewhere. They are reflected in the cases and voices of diverse contributors, as well as stories and examples like that of Pablo (Chapter 2), Peter Apo (Chapter 3), the reef visitors (Chapter 4), the Anangu of Uluru and Kata Tjuta (Chapter 5), the residents of a small mountain community in Canada (Chapter 6). They offer insights that help to understand the importance of various justice perspectives presented. In turn, they can be further informed by the theoretical approaches contained in various chapters. The first chapter, Chapter 1, introduces the landscape of tourism and sets the context for exploring justice and ethics in tourism. It presents many happenings in travel and tourism, demonstrating a complex local-global system interrelated with other systems. It then calls for a relational view to understanding "impacts" and identifying injustices in tourism. Chapter 1 also situates the approach to justice and ethics taken in this book, which is toward the end of "good tourism." The journey into issues and approaches to justice then begins. Each of Chapters 2–6 takes up this challenge by discussing some key principles: equity and justice, diversity and recognition, responsibility and care, sustainability and conservation, democracy and (good) governance. They are supported by theoretical insights, cases from contributors, plus other examples and stories.

Chapter 2 builds on Chapter 1 with a discussion of the idea of justice and how to go about studying this important subject. It then commences to look at social justice and some of the organizations involved. John Rawls's approach to justice as fairness is introduced as a dominant influence on distributive justice (his approach also addresses procedural justice). It is noted that there are other approaches to consider, e.g., non-liberal perspectives as well as human development perspectives like the capability approach that Amartya Sen and Martha Nussbaum forward. The chapter also offers some guidance to studying justice and emphasizes reading original sources of the theories and theorists concerned. Mistakes have already crept into tourism research, for example, when Rawls's theory was attributed as the theoretical influence on research that focused on organizational justice and relationships between service providers and visitors (in a leading tourism journal!).

Chapter 3 continues with a look at Martha Nussbaum's Capabilities Approach, which is oriented to human well-being but is applicable to animals, too. It raises the importance of examining social process and institutional structures from a historical context in order to address individual and collective well-being. Here, following Nancy Fraser and Iris Marion Young, justice as recognition (including the recognition of difference) is important to address in situations where diverse groups are marginalized, stigmatized, experience institutionalized racism stemming from colonization or other forms of domination and exploitation. For Nancy Fraser, justice as recognition is political. It is related to groups and *status*, not recognition at the individual or interpersonal level, of which much has been written by philosophers such as Axel Honneth and Charles Taylor. They all offer valuable guidance, not just theoretically, but also in relation to tourism practice. For instance, if you favor Axel Honneth's social psychological perspective on recognition, you might favor enabling more particular relations of care, love and "good" interactions in host-guest touristic encounters that advance self-realizations, equal respect, and equal dignity. Helpful to both individual as well as social recognition here would be strategies challenging stereotypes and ethnocentric attitudes, empowering individuals in touristic encounters psychologically and socially by building capabilities, enabling interpersonal encounters that foster cross-cultural understanding and equitable relationships. It involves recognizing the other as a moral equal with whom we share a common humanity and a planet toward which we share a common responsibility.

Chapter 4 picks up on responsibility for justice which, given the interrelatedness of tourism from the local to global, means taking an integrated, local-global perspective to viewing tourism and the role of the tourist. What are our *shared responsibilities* and *political responsibilities* (as per Iris Marion Young's social connection model) to address structural injustice in the tourism context? The tourist's responsibilities are discussed in relation to political action, local and global citizenship, and ethical behavior. Note the "connection" mentioned in Isaac and Hodge's (2011, p. 106) exploratory study of tourists visiting Palestinian sites of conflict, where a number of respondents in their survey "stated that they were now more aware of a particular situation and feel a connection or duty to resolving the conflict."[1] Among justice related issues to consider here are fair distribution of public resources toward conservation of diverse heritage and recognition of minority or marginalized groups whose cultural heritage is at risk, and who want to conserve it for future generations. Chapter 4 also introduces another dimension to consider that arose in Chapter 3: an ethic of care *for* humans and non-human living things, as well as an ethic of care *about* places and things. It complements justice to further the end of "good tourism."

Chapter 5 takes up the notion of sustainability, noting that is being applied beyond the natural environment to the physical and cultural environment as well. The paucity of research and attention to ecological justice (justice for non-human living things) in tourism is noted here. The study of cultural sustainability, cultural resilience and cultural justice are in early stages, but intangible and tangible dimensions of culture and heritage need to be considered holistically and as situated in *context*. An *integrated* and *relational* perspective helps to sees humans in relations with social-cultural, natural and physical environments and

236 Toward Good and Just Tourism?

also be sensitive to the artificial separations we enact when discussing environmental justice and cultural justice. Like other chapters, Chapter 5 illustrates the need for an interdisciplinary approach (some might argue it is transdisciplinary, or postdisciplinary but we won't debate that here) to the study of justice and ethics in tourism and its applications to practice (tourism studies itself is an "interdisciplinary" enterprise, with much written on this). Important to note here are postdevelopment activists and scholars who call attention to diverse ways of being and doing, decentering the modernist, market-driven capitalistic paradigm that has been driven worldwide through colonialism and neoliberal globalization.

As Chapters 5 and 6 indicate, different approaches to governance and democracy, policy and planning, participatory processes and empowerment, are arising to tackle significant challenges related to sustainability, neoliberal globalization, and colonial legacies (among others). Consumption-driven growth and modernist principles of "progress" are being challenged by a "pluriverse" (Escobar, 2018) of worldviews, political ontologies, human-environmental and cultural relationships, demonstrating alternative ways of provisioning and sustaining livelihoods and environments, and calling for new collaborative and place-based designs to serve the needs of justice and planet Earth. Emily Höckert's reflection on Napapiiri (the Finnish word for the Arctic Circle) in Case 7.1 reinforces the need for critical reflection and new designs for a pluriverse of human and non-human others in this era of the Anthropocene (see also Holden, 2018).

Case 7.1: Smell the Melting Arctic Ice

Emily Höckert

The Finnish Lapland has become a hot spot for international tourists who travel with hopes of getting a glimpse of Indigenous cultures, Northern Lights, or a winter-wonderland with Santa Claus and reindeers. With more than 20% annual growth in tourism, international travel in Lapland is breaking all the previous records in Finland (Visit Finland, 2018). While nature-based tourism is threatened by climate change, international tourism also contributes to the acceleration of the environmental catastrophe (see Maher et al., 2014; Scott, Hall, & Gössling, 2016). Napapiiri—the Finnish word for the Arctic Circle—is getting hotter (Photo 7.1.1).

Climate change-related issues in tourism are particularly crucial in the Arctic and northern areas. Snow cover has been vanishing since the mid-20th century, which has multiple effects on Arctic livelihoods, including tourism. It is predicted that by 2100, winters will become 5 degrees Celsius warmer, and summers around 2–3 degrees Celsius warmer, which will lead to significant decrease in frost days (Tervo-Kankare, Hall, & Saarinen, 2013). Sámi artivist Jenni Laiti, the spokesperson of Suohpanterror group which fights for human and environmental justice by combining art and activism,

PHOTO 7.1.1 The Arctic Circle is getting hotter
          Photo credit: Mostphotos

describes how the current condition is experienced only too painfully in the North. She explains the feeling of apocalypse as follows:

> When you are there by the Arctic Ocean, you feel that here the world has come to an end. You can smell the climate warming. It smells of ice and it smells fresh (Cromnow, 2016, p. 54).

238 Toward Good and Just Tourism?

In this situation, tourism researchers can no longer focus merely on the well-being of human hosts and guests (visitors). We are being confronted by the task of taking care of the Earth and nonhuman others (Gren & Huijbens, 2014). This means, in Donna Haraway's (2016) words, to "stay with the trouble" and to embrace the necessity and possibility of staying with the trouble with multiple others. I believe that while fearing for the smell of the melting ice, we need to engage in storytelling and storylistening that give voice to anxieties and concerns in both human and nonhuman communities (see also Valtonen & Kinnunen, 2017). While challenging growth-oriented, extractive mindsets, we must continue to search for environmentally and culturally sensitive ways of welcoming tourists in the Arctic.

References

Cromnow, C. (2016, November 24). Ingen marks [No man's land]. *Camino*, (45), 52–60.

Gren, M., & Huijbens, E. H. (2014). Tourism and the Anthropocene. *Scandinavian Journal of Hospitality and Tourism, 14*(1), 6–22. https://doi.org/10.1080/15022250.2014.886100

Haraway, D. J. (2016). *Staying with the trouble: Making kin in the Chthulucene.* Durham, NC: Duke University Press. Retrieved from https://www.dukeupress.edu/staying-with-the-trouble

Maher, P. T., Hans Gelter, K., Hillmer-Pegram, G. H., Hull, J., Jóhannesson, Gunnar Þór, Karlsdóttir, A., Rantala, O., & Pashkevich, A. (2014). Arctic tourism: Realities and possibilities. In L. Heininen, H. Exner-Pirot, & J. Plouffe (Eds.), *Arctic yearbook 2014* (pp. 290–306).

Scott, D., Hall, C. M., & Gössling, S. (2016). A report on the Paris climate change agreement and its implications for tourism: Why we will always have Paris. *Journal of Sustainable Tourism, 24*(7), 933–948. https://doi.org/10.1080/09669582.2016.1187623

Tervo-Kankare, K., Hall, C. M., & Saarinen, J. (2013). Christmas tourists' perceptions to climate change in Rovaniemi, Finland. *Tourism Geographies, 15*(2), 292–317. https://doi.org/10.1080/14616688.2012.726265

Valtonen, A. E., & Kinnunen, V. E. (2017). Towards living ethics. In A. E. Valtonen & V. E. Kinnunen (Eds.), *Living ethics in a more-than-human world* (pp. 1–11). Rovaniemi, Finland: University of Lapland.

Visit Finland. (2018). *Foreign overnights in Finland: 2017.* Retrieved from http://www.visitfinland.fi/wp-content/uploads/2018/04/2017-Review-Travel-in-Finland.pdf?dl

Among the new designs, new governance approaches will be needed in the neoliberal local-global landscape of the 21st century, with greater scrutiny of the role of government and on policy setting. Public policy and urban planning in the

Global North have tended to focus on means (the policy process) rather than the ends (policy outcomes), planning theorist Susan Fainstein argued. She advocated justice as a key principle to evaluate public policy, where justice is approached through the values of equity, diversity and democracy (Fainstein, 2010). Chapter 6 offers preliminary support for a pluralistic notion of justice as a key principle to evaluate public policy outcomes and collaborative planning processes. It also takes a closer look at democracy and *difference*, aided by Iris Marion Young, which leads to a perspective of democratic cultural pluralism rather than liberal pluralism (Young, 2011).

What, then, of issues that transcend borders, like climate change and other global environmental and social-cultural issues (e.g., *migrations*, roots-seeking and diasporic groups, sex tourism, medical tourism, and the rights of second-home travelers)? Mechanisms for good governance across borders are needed as much as within borders. Chapter 6 commences a short discussion on global justice and transnational public sphere(s), followed by governance within borders. Traditional roles of government in governance are being increasingly challenged in a local-global landscape of neoliberal globalization. Democratic participation is a critical endeavor and even more so in this challenging domain. Those who stand to be most impacted by tourism should be involved directly in its development, planning and management processes, and in marketing, too—they must be included in decision making (not just be heard). Offering hopeful new directions are social movements, online and on the ground, along with positive roles for information and communication technologies and active social media to facilitate information sharing, action and taking up shared responsibility. A couple of chapters offer brief glimpses of this potential.

A Pluralistic Approach to Justice, But A Situated One...

This is not a legalistic book, it does not focus on matters of law. Rather, we look at social, environmental, and cultural concerns and issues in tourism that raise questions of justice and offer a few theoretical approaches to justice to stimulate thinking and further exploration. The hope is to encourage theory building, empirical research, and to inform practice. The perspectives presented here are just a few among many that await scrutiny. Theories of justice and ethics won't give us answers, but they can help guide thinking, research, reflection, and action. The approaches to justice discussed in the previous chapters have significantly influenced 20th-century theories of justice and continue to do so, surrounded by lively debate. They include John Rawls's theory of justice, plus human development, political and feminist perspectives that provide counter-arguments to Rawls and new views, e.g., from Amartya Sen, Martha Nussbaum, Nancy Fraser, Iris Marion Young, among others. The examples and cases presented in this book offer insights that help to corroborate a pluralistic approach to justice in tourism (see below), contributing to efforts commenced by Fennell (2017), Smith and Duffy (2003), and others mentioned in previous chapters.[2]

240 Toward Good and Just Tourism?

Looking across the chapters, a *pluralistic* approach to justice to guide tourism development, management, marketing, and governance is emerging that is relational and contextualized. It is vitally important to understand justice from such a *situated* perspective, in relations with the place, its past, and its inhabitants and visitors. It is situated in relation to the historical and political context, social norms, processes, and institutional structures. Several examples in this book show, for instance, how institutionalized racism in current social processes and structures can result from historical events such as wars and colonialism (entrenching the norms and values of the "winners" in the present). For Pablo and the Maya of Quintana Roo who face historically engrained discrimination and exclusion, building capabilities to participate in tourism development (including participatory skills to engage with tourism policy and planning) may help redress maldistribution and facilitate equity, empowerment and recognition (psychological and social-political), enabling self-determination and representation in social and political processes. However, depending on the circumstances (the *particular* context), political recognition (political status) and representation may be needed to garner resources (e.g., through redistribution) to build capabilities and facilitate social well-being (e.g., by participating in and controlling tourism development). What hope did the hop pickers of the Pacific Northwest have to contest dispossession and institutionalized racism without social and political recognition, representation, and redistribution (see Chapter 3 and the cases within it)?

A pluralistic approach to justice in the context of environmental heritage (Chapter 5) might similarly include, for instance, equity, recognition, and participatory processes that ensure fair representation and voice in decision making for those who care for land and live in close ancestral relationships with it. David Schlosberg's (2007) pluralistic approach to environmental justice includes distributive justice, recognition, building capabilities, procedural justice and participatory processes. He also discusses a pluralistic approach to ecological justice that is not addressed in this book. He, too, points out that he is not presenting a rigid framework, but rather one that is adapted to the situation and context. This is a crucial consideration in this book on justice and ethics in tourism.

A pluralistic and flexible notion of justice is also evident in the context of democratic participation and governance in Chapter 6. Redistribution is an important consideration here, along with recognition to enable empowerment and learning for cultural groups to participate effectively in policy and planning processes, and to establish their rights to fair use, access, and conservation of their environmental, social, and cultural goods. Comporting with Fainstein (2010), recent research by Avni (2018) and others lend support for a pluralistic notion of justice as a key principle for evaluating public policy, development and "equity planning." To reiterate, it is really important to note that justice is not a firm or rigid framework where the same set of values and principles apply to every context. The tension between the *particular* and the *general/universal*, for example, has to be negotiated in every instance from a relational, integrated and contextual perspective, so *different approaches to justice may inform different situations*. The next section discusses this and summarizes a few important principles that have been arisen in previous chapters in relation to justice and tourism.

Some Guiding Principles Along the Journey to Justice

The interrelatedness of tourism with the social, political, and historical context may make it difficult to see how other influences (e.g., widespread political corruption) may be responsible for various injustices rather than tourism. A common criticism is that we might be blaming tourism for problems rooted elsewhere, such as in a failed state in which dictatorship has eliminated rights to free speech, free media, democratic voting, and the rule of law, etc. An important principle to address this has been raised in previous chapters, which is to carefully *examine social processes and institutional structures* where social inequities and injustices can become sedimented (Young, 2011). It requires studying tourism and justice from a contextual perspective, examining the historical context from the past into the present and future, the social and institutional context of tourism, as well as the geopolitical context. It also requires a relational perspective, as noted earlier. The diverse groups and stakeholders in a destination exist in relations with each other and in particular social and cultural relationships with Nature and the physical environment (e.g., human-environmental relationships, human-animal bonds, diverse spiritual relationships, worldviews, and ethical perspectives ranging from biocentric to anthropocentric, etc.).

Overall, the study of justice and ethics in tourism also requires a holistic, *integrated* approach to in tourism. This includes examining micro and macro-level issues of tourism from an interrelated *local-global* perspective, being careful to understand the notion of "impacts" (Chapter 1) and seeing the *interrelatedness* of environmental, social, cultural, economic and political aspects of tourism. Interdependencies arise and systemic issues that are societally embedded in the wider domain can affect or be affected by what happens in the "tourism system." As discussed in Chapter 1, the phenomenon of tourism is not confined to a separate system of its own—the "tourism system" is deeply interrelated with other local to global systems. Issues like widespread political corruption or institutionalized racism in the broader social and political context, for instance, may be reproduced in the touristic context via the very same societal processes and institutional structures that constitute the wider domain. Tourism's possible role in reproducing these structures and related injustices needs to be traced through careful scrutiny and analysis of social processes and institutional structures in the historical, societal, and political context in which tourism plays out. It requires an *integrated* and holistic approach, incorporating the local-global scale and the complex scope of tourism (including the interrelated picture above).

An additional principle that arises in relation to the above is to incorporate not just easily definable and measurable issues, effects, outcomes and "solutions," but to also strive to understand, evaluate, monitor and address relationships and

242 Toward Good and Just Tourism?

practices that are hard to identify or quantify, e.g., *"intangible" spiritual and cultural relationships* to place and to people (both in the present and past, i.e., cultural heritage). Chapter 5 explores this with respect to sustainability and takes up various issues ranging from environmental justice to heritage conservation and cultural resilience. These show the need to better incorporate intangible relationships and cultural practices into the notion of tourism and sustainable development. The discussion on Uluṟu in Chapter 5 plus other examples illustrates how important it is to examine historically influenced structures and processes (*the past*), as well as human-environmental relationships with land, with humans and with nonhuman others. The approach to justice and ethics in tourism, then, is *integrated, contextual* and *relational*.

Given the early stage of research and study of justice and ethics in tourism, we won't attempt to "define" justice in the complex, interrelated tourism context, not even here in Chapter 7. What we can do is begin to summarize some principles and characteristics of justice as you see emerging above. To continue, the notion of justice arising in this book is a *pluralistic* and flexible approach to identify and redress injustices with care and attentiveness to *particular* ways of being and belonging, particular practices for well-being and sustainability in the "pluriverse." How do we address this without falling into a relativistic mode of "anything goes"? Well, for one, you might agree that *universal* ethical principles like respect for persons and human rights principles ought to guide justice through the general *and* the particular context. Secondly, take a closer look at the dominant liberal principles in John Rawls's justice as fairness. His is an ideal theory of social justice in a liberal (pluralist) society, focused on the distribution of basic goods and based on the notion of the liberal autonomous subject (see Chapter 2). Iris Marion Young argues that his approach is unable to identify and evaluate class relations, or the social relations of production, or other social relations and institutional structures (Young, 2011). Eschewing the atomistic view of the liberal subject, she presents an embodied, affective human being in relations with others and directs our attention to the *recognition of difference* between and within groups. It follows that a *dual system of rights* for the group and at the societal level may be needed to embrace the *particular* and attend to the *general*. The particular is related to the general, it is not a matter of anything goes.

Young also explains that fostering *democracy* and democratic institutions that facilitate *self-determination* and *inclusiveness* in social and political processes is immensely important if justice is to be served to diverse groups and vulnerable populations, including people with disabilities, ethnic and gendered minorities, women and children, low-income and the poor. Whyte (2011, pp. 204–205) argues that recognition justice in Indigenous Tourism "requires the development of creative participatory processes that will be employed in various cases and that aim as much as possible for the inclusion of tribal values and tribes' particular situations into policy and programs ...."[3] As discussed in Chapter 6, aside from well-established norms like transparency, accountability, etc., good governance and policy making in tourism must be collaborative, democratic, and inclusive.

Good governance is both a goal and a means in this sense, it necessitates democracy and facilitating democratic participation and inclusiveness (Rodrik, 2008). This is especially important when we think about the fact that many tourism impacts are ambiguous and difficult to assess, such as intangible cultural relationships and long-term cultural change through tourism. Informed participation to understand the implications of tourism development and change over time is vital. Moreover, as noted earlier, politics abound. Who has the authority to determine what "ought" to be conserved among a large diversity of cultural goods, ecological and heritage sites and ways of being when funds and resources are limited? Who has the "correct" interpretation of historical and "dark" tourism events? Shouldn't local, traditional, and scientific knowledge all be at the negotiating table *inclusively*, i.e., involve the diverse stakeholders in decision making?

Adopting justice as a key principle to evaluate tourism policy (as Susan Fainstein suggests in her context of urban planning) may be helpful in the complex domain of travel and tourism, but which approaches to justice to apply will depend on the situation, context, etc. Policy and planning initiatives must include a close examination of social processes and institutional structures and norms in order to:

1. Acknowledge and facilitate *respect for difference* in various spheres of public and social encounters and interactions (e.g., in public spaces shared by residents and tourists).
2. Identify and *involve in decision making and policy evaluation* those who stand to be most impacted by intended outcomes. Especially important is inclusiveness of diverse groups and vulnerable populations that have been historically marginalized or disempowered due to institutional racism, or discriminated against for reasons of gender, ethnicity, religious or sexual orientation, age (e.g., ageism) or disabilities.
3. Enable destination developers, managers and marketers (e.g., destination marketing organizations [DMOs]) to address not just "tangible" aspects in policy making, such as counting the number of jobs or dollars generated by tourism activities, but also *intangible* aspects such as cultural change through commodification of cultural practices and cultural relationships (including human-environmental relationships), the psychological "in-between" spaces of postcolonialism and other traumatic events, and the "virtual" spaces in which many opportunities for justice and injustice arise.

Onwards We Go Toward...?

This book is a preliminary exploration of a number of challenging issues that face us as we progress into the 21st century. Travel and tourism offer a powerful lens to understand the world around us, to see it differently through each journey away and each return home, to make the strange familiar *and* to make the familiar

244 Toward Good and Just Tourism?

strange, as Mills put it. We have undertaken this exploratory journey here with a little help from some theoretical approaches to justice and ethics (there are many to investigate!), complemented by stories and cases from contributors around the world. The hope is that this book offers encouragement to advance the study of justice and ethics in tourism, to create new approaches and guidelines for tourism, and to address some pressing issues facing tourism practice.

It is a world of mobilities. Goods, finance, knowledge and diseases flow across borders and hemispheres, people are on the move, including economic migrants, climate refugees and tourists, while burgeoning new technologies and a digital economy reshape places and practices in everyday life and in travel. It is also the era of the Anthropocene. The chapters in the book highlight the need to understand tourism's contributions to challenges such as (but not limited to): (i) Global environmental issues like climate change and biodiversity loss (think of Jenna and the reef in Chapter 4); (ii) Conservation and justice issues related to environmental heritage and cultural heritage of diasporic, disadvantaged and marginalized groups; (iii) Structural injustices related to capitalist-colonial expansion and underdevelopment created by neoliberal programs (e.g., Structural Adjustment Programs); (iv) Social rights and responsibilities of residents and travelers (including second-home owners and long-haul international tourists) in an interrelated local-global domain. Let us look at a couple of the challenges awaiting us and hope that justice will be served through ongoing research and practice:

1. Borders have been slamming shut while this book project was being undertaken (consider those travel bans discussed earlier). Ethnic and cultural minority groups seek safety and livelihoods in the Global North after colonialism and neoliberal structural adjustment programs, etc., have facilitated major dislocation, dependency, underdevelopment, and poverty in their homeland. Their human rights and safety are also at risk, but so are their cultural rights. These involve, among other things, the right to "cultural recognition and expression and ownership...respect for diversity and otherness as well as the rights of minorities to have ethnic rights...," which would depend on the cultural and religious needs and values of specific groups (Bianchi & Stephenson, 2014, p. 68). As these authors discuss, the rights to travel freely without danger, harassment or discrimination, are not equally distributed—cultural factors along with distribution of wealth and power play a significant role. A closer look at tourists' rights and responsibilities is needed with respect to the liberal values of freedom that appear to be enshrined in discourses of travel and tourist mobilities, as they point out. Meanwhile, carry your passport when you're traveling elsewhere, you never know when you'll need it! Questions about hospitality and human rights (and the role of governments!) arise within and across borders as you jog along the beach, enjoying your holiday—if you're curious, read Hernandez's news article (Hernandez, 2018).

2. New technologies, including new information and communication technologies (ICTs), are reshaping everyday life in many good ways, but also presenting new challenges. Ethical issues abound in the domain of augmented reality and "virtual" travel. Global platforms like Airbnb have arisen in the sharing economy to establish dominant roles that are altering neighborhood characteristics, contributing to *overtourism* in already popular destinations like Amsterdam (Case 1.1, Chapter 1), and raising regulatory concerns (see Dredge & Gyimóthy, 2017). On the one hand, the rise of ICTs is providing new ways to resist structural injustices and culturally institutionalized forms of oppression and domination (patriarchy, gender inequalities, systematically entrenched sexual abuse, etc.), with social media playing an important role in rapid information communication, mobilizing and organizing social movements, etc. (see Chapter 4). On the other hand, ICTs also help to further the ability for increased corporate and state surveillance and intrusion into everyday life, (re-)shaping commodity consumption, consumer tastes, societal values and socioeconomic rights (see Hollinshead & Suleman, 2018 on *worldmaking*). What governance mechanisms within and across borders are required to ensure responsibility and accountability in these "virtual" in-between space for the safety and well-being of travelers and residents, the rights of workers, small businesses, and artisans, etc.? How best to ensure fair wages, labor rights, representation and voice for those most impacted, and fair use of cultural products (think, for example, of representation of cultural goods and groups in destination marketing and destination image)?

3. The 21st-century landscape of the Anthropocene ushers in immense responsibilities for sustainability, biodiversity conservation and cultural survival, as species, languages and cultural traditions and practices continue to disappear rapidly. The losses to current and future generations (using the future-oriented discourse of sustainable development) are not merely ones that can be easily measured and quantified, and they are not equitably distributed. Deadly heatwaves are forecast to increase across the globe, disproportionately affecting vulnerable groups, the elderly and the poor (see Leahy, 2017). And when biodiversity declines, like those majestic cedars of Lebanon that are dying due to human impacts and climate change, it is not just the loss of ancient trees (some more than 1,000 years old), it is a loss of symbolic meaning, the immensely rich stories and cultural beliefs that have been woven into the memory-laden setting from which they have watched civilizations come and go (Barnard, 2018). Cross-disciplinary collaboration is needed to develop approaches to justice that can inform theory and practice, including shaping specific laws and policies, e.g., on the well-being of vulnerable populations facing the effects of climate change; including them in adaptation processes, disaster planning and post-disaster recovery; on the social and cultural rights of diverse stakeholders including women and children, people with disabilities, LGBT+ groups, communities of color,

Indigenous and ethnic minorities; on labor rights in the virtual (and non-virtual) collaborative economies, etc.

Managing rampant tourism growth and consumption for sustainability in the 21st century becomes an even greater responsibility, e.g., managing cumulative stressors on social-ecological systems that in turn increase vulnerability to climate change. Degrowth (and demarketing in some instances) is an important 21st-century agenda item. Governments have started to take notice of the adverse effects of growth in various European cities, even if only from an instrumental perspective, but let us take hope from that (see Abend, 2018). And children and youth, too, are exercising democratic voice in climate change. There is hope for them to protect their future. Further to Case 6.1 in Chapter 6 (contributed by Dawn Jourdan), on July 30, 2018, and yet again on November 2, 2018, the US Supreme Court rejected the Trump Administration's requests to delay or block the constitutional climate change lawsuit filed by 21 youth plaintiffs against the federal government. Previously scheduled to go to trial on October 29, 2018, in Eugene, Oregon, the case will now proceed on this rocky road to trial unless the high court or the 9th US Circuit Court of Appeals intervenes (Hurley, 2018). These young people want the constitutional right to a "climate system capable of sustaining human life" (Our Children's Trust, 2018).

Perhaps what we need is not simply justice, but justice combined with an ethic of care *for* others (humans and other living beings) and an ethic of care *about* the places and things that sustain them (there is a role for democratic participation to address the political questions involved here, what to conserve, why, etc.). In relation to climate change, for example, an ethic of care *for* those who stand to inequitably bear the severest brunt of climate change and human injustices (consider, too, other living beings in addition to human beings!) plus an ethic of care *about* places like the Cedars of God reserve in Arz, where just 2,100 trees remain (Barnard, 2018). They represent the storied landscapes and cultural heritage of planet Earth. Like many other places torn apart by violence, war, climate change and other human induced crises, their habitats need conservation and they, too, deserve ecological justice.

Toward Good Tourism

Our journey culminates here but will hopefully stimulate many new adventures in theory and practice for justice and ethics in tourism. The journey has really just begun. Among the justice related approaches that help inform the way ahead are ones discussed in this book: distributive justice and equity, building capabilities, recognition, representation, and democratic processes (participating in decision making, inclusiveness, etc.). However, as noted earlier, they do not form a rigid framework of *pluralistic justice* to apply everywhere—which approaches are appropriate depend on the situation. Insights from various chapters indicate that an integrated and relational approach situated in history and context is helpful to identify and address injustices and to tackle the tension between the *general/ universal* and the *particular* (e.g., striving for justice at the societal level versus recognition of difference among cultural groups within a destination). Much needs to be done to explore other approaches that can help to frame just laws and policies for tourism within and beyond borders.

It would be remiss to end without revisiting the notion of "good tourism" also mentioned in Chapter 1 (this book's journey is a round trip home!). The challenging landscape of travel and tourism in the 21st century will need greater attention to justice and ethics to guide good tourism in the 21st century, it was said in Chapter 1. Good tourism is tourism that is based on *justice* plus an *ethic of care* and *responsibility* for a flourishing planet and the well-being of human and nonhuman others. An important consideration here is enabling "good" experiences (for both visitors and hosts!). The local-global scale and scope of tourism makes it a powerful pedagogic medium for facilitating local and global citizenship, thoughtful (sustainable!) consumption, and social-political action through learning and enjoyment, gaining ecological and cultural literacy and reflexivity (see Holden, 2018 on ecological reflexivity).[4] In addition, we need new understandings and new designs for the pluriverse (Escobar, 2018). In the tourism pluriverse, much greater responsibility and action is needed by academics, says Bernard Lane in Case 7.2 below. Without good actions based on justice *and* an ethic of care and responsibility, will the railway heritage in the case he describes be saved and shared for the present and the future, enabling others to learn about the values of freedom and democracy it represents? So, onwards we go, marvelous journeys await those who dare to venture forth…and those whose care!

Questions for Further Reflection

1. What are the characteristics of justice as being presented here in the context of tourism?
2. What does it mean for justice to "flexible"?
3. How do you reconcile justice and an ethic of care?
4. Based on the discussion in this chapter, what is the difference between "Just Tourism" and "Good Tourism"? See if you can describe these two concepts first and then identify some differences between them.

Case 7.2: Tourism and Conserving the Past: Addressing Ethical and Justice Issues in Heritage Tourism

Bernard Lane

Bramwell & Lane (1993) introduced the concept of intergenerational equity to tourism management. Tourism should leave a destination fit for future

248 Toward Good and Just Tourism?

generations. This note extends that idea and explores tourism's need to also offer equity to past generations, their stories, artefacts and creations, as well as to today's and tomorrow's communities and environments.

Heritage tourism is growing. The UNESCO's World Heritage Site system, and iconic sites, such as the Eiffel Tower, Beijing's Forbidden City, or Peru's Machu Picchu are well known and heavily visited, but these are rare, special sites. To bring equity, and justice, into heritage tourism, we need to examine how the "normal" world's local heritage, and often relatively modern heritage, can become known, enjoyed, understood, valued and conserved. Specifically, this note concentrates on the 19th century's Industrial Archaeology. It looks at the opportunities that tourism can bring to industrial archaeology's conservation, while at the same time bring opportunities for both visitors and local areas (Xie, 2015).

North Devon (UK) is a declining remote rural area, with low and static tourist numbers. Its tiny late-19th-century resorts have many problems. Their futures could be helped, and their heritage conserved, if that heritage was recognized and valorized. This case looks at the ethical and practical issues and opportunities surrounding a group working to reopen a heritage railway line in North Devon. The line (and its volunteer supporters) are typical of many hundreds in Europe and many more worldwide. They need visitors to ensure financial stability. But visitors need more than just a railway journey; they need an experience, somewhere to eat, somewhere to stay. The host areas need jobs, marketing, and revenue to spill over into their economies. The stories which the areas and their railways have can create—if truthfully and well told—strong experiences for visitors, and a valuable brand name for both region and railway.

This case covers the proposed reopening of a 19-mile railway between Barnstaple (population 25,000), running through land in protected areas to the late-19th-century seaside resorts of Lynton and Lynmouth (population 2,400). The railway opened in 1898, and closed in 1935, as competition from cars and buses grew. In 1979, a few local railway enthusiasts formed an action group to begin purchasing land, carriages and steam engines to reopen the railway. A charitable trust was formed, which became a social enterprise, largely staffed by volunteers. The first trains ran over one mile of track in 2004. Approximately 50,000 passengers are now carried annually (see Photos 7.2.1 and 7.2.2). Plans have been approved to extend the line to 9 miles, and eventually reinstate the entire route. The charitable trust now has a membership of 5,000 worldwide (see: https://en.wikipedia.org/wiki/Lynton_and_Barnstaple_Railway; www.lynton-rail.co.uk/).

But What Are the Justice and Ethical Issues?

At first glance, none. The project appears admirable. There is no remote developer taking profits out of the area; it is a social enterprise. Growth will

PHOTO 7.2.1 The Lynton and Barnstaple Railway: a southbound train prepares to start behind a restored 1915 UK built locomotive which began its life hauling First World War military trains to the front line in France. The locomotive you can see was one of 70 built in Stoke on Trent to a French design and sold to the French government for war service. In 1919 it was bought for use in a French quarry. It was dumped in the quarry in 1962, found in 1982, brought— as a rusty wreck—back to the UK and restored in c. 2010

be slow, small scale and organic. Heritage will be conserved. Handled well, this project could form a model of good sustainable tourism practice. But there are questions to ask.

The project is largely controlled by railway enthusiasts. Experience shows that railway (and other enthusiasts) rarely understand tourism, or how best to help their local area's conservation or economy (Lane et al., 2013). By accident or default, the failure of tourism and railway interests to work together means that justice or fairness for the area and its heritage may not be deliberately denied but may not be achieved. Lack of knowledge amongst the railway enthusiasts—of history, of communities, and of tourism management—can be a serious problem. Equally, neither side seems to understand low cost marketing, niche marketing and social media. The problems go further: should the reopened railway succeed, it could accidentally bring about the loss of the parallel bus service—a low cost alternative for many residents.

PHOTO 7.2.2 The Lynton and Barnstaple Railway: a northbound train climbs the gradient towards Woody Bay station, with Exmoor National Park's landscape in the background

There are ways to avoid all these issues. Most depend on creating local and *informed* partnerships to work out ways to pool resources and seek and use best practice. Here tourism academics could have a central role. But, while tourism academics have many ideas, they are rarely involved in working with communities, business and governance organizations (Lane, 2018). They should be. That way they could test and better understand such concepts as heritage regions, and slow tourism, and explore how to achieve justice for the local economy, its people and environment, while devising a thriving future for the past. The railway could become the spine of a slow

Toward Good and Just Tourism? **251**

tourism corridor, bringing together rail, bus, cycle and walking routes, reducing car use, bringing trade to village shops, pubs and restaurants en route, while creating an "Edwardian" brand, celebrating the special period 1900–1914, when this area flourished. The corridor could benefit from the new developments in interpretation now available to tell its story, including both the colorful, wealthy backers of the railway, and the equally fascinating lives of local working people, on and off the railway. Telling railway workers' stories was beautifully pioneered in Ireland, by Michael Barry (2014). And new techniques of telling are now available, including audio, smart phones, and festivals using low cost chamber opera/music theatre. The line runs through a national park. Getzner et al. (2014) and Eagles (2014) discuss contrasting and evolving developments in park management, many of which wrestle with positive and negative ethical approaches to tourism. Here, a positive approach would use the railway as a park-and-ride instrument, reducing car traffic, acting as bike carrier and rolling interpretation platform: a negative approach would banish trains as non-naturals, preventing the sound and visuals of small steam trains, concentrating on the traditional, noncontroversial interpretation of geology and biodiversity, and the silent archaeology of prehistory.

In tourism, justice and ethics can be more complex issues than they at first seem—even when small and local appear beautiful, there are often controversial decisions to be made, and risks taken. A valuable real-world learning ground could, however, emerge for academics (including postgraduates), and local stakeholders, if independent academic researchers became involved. Perhaps only academics can intervene to see a fair and socially just outcome: most other stakeholders have the overriding aims of making maximum money or obtaining maximum pleasure with minimum effort. The academic community should have a special role and above all, responsibility.

References

Barry, M. (2014). *Tales of the permanent way: Stories from the heart of Ireland's railways.* Dublin, Ireland: Andalus Press. Retrieved from https://www.amazon.com/Tales-Permanent-Way-Irelands-Railways-ebook/dp/B00I3KSHVI#reader_B00I3KSHVI

Bramwell, B., & Lane, B. (1993). Sustainable tourism: An evolving global approach. *Journal of Sustainable Tourism, 1*(1), 1–5. https://doi.org/10.1080/09669589309514792

Eagles, P. F. J. (2014). Research priorities in park tourism. *Journal of Sustainable Tourism, 22*(4), 528–549. https://doi.org/10.1080/09669582.2013.785554

Getzner, M., Vik, M. L., Brendehaug, E., & Lane, B. (2014). Governance and management strategies in national parks: Implications for sustainable regional development. *International Journal of Sustainable Society, 6*(1/2), 82. https://doi.org/10.1504/ijssoc.2014.057891

252 Toward Good and Just Tourism?

Lane, B. (2018). Will sustainable tourism research be sustainable in the future? An opinion piece. *Tourism Management Perspectives, 25*, 161–164. https://doi.org/10.1016/j.tmp.2017.12.001

Lane, B., Weston, R., Davies, N., Kastenholz, E., Lima, J., & Majewsjki, J. (2013). *Industrial heritage and agri/rural tourism in Europe: A review of their development, socio-economic systems and future policy issues* (Vol. 53). Brussels: European Union. https://doi.org/10.1017/CBO9781107415324.004

Xie, P. F. (2015). *Industrial heritage tourism.* Bristol, UK: Channel View Publications.

Notes

1 Note, too, that the notion of justice tourism that their study drew on is described somewhat differently by its various proponents (e.g, Higgins-Desbiolles, 2008; Scheyvens, 2002).

2 As noted throughout the book, these scholars and others like Mowforth and Munt (2016) have provided valuable insights on justice related issues. Higgins-Desbiolles (2011, p. 200) suggests viewing "justice tourism as a continuum of activities focused on fostering more just relationships and outcomes in tourism" ranging from responsible tourism to transnational solidarity activism. Her continuum is based on depth of solidarity and differs from Scheyvens (2002). The pluralistic approaches discussed here are on a conceptual level that may hopefully help to inform notions of "justice tourism" as well.

3 He argues, too, for compensation justice in the *particular* context of Indigenous Tourism (Whyte, 2010).

4 See Jamal (2004) for a virtue ethics perspective on good actions in tourism that is not discussed here. Jamal and Smith (2017) refer to Aldo Leopold and John Dewey to situate tourism and the tourist experience in relation to enjoyment and democratic pedagogy, facilitating experiential learning, care, responsibility and civic action toward conservation.

References

Abend, L. (2018, July 26). Europe made billions from tourists. Now it's rejecting them. Retrieved July 29, 2018, from http://time.com/5349533/europe-against-tourists/

Avni, N. (2018). Bridging equity? Washington D.C.'s new elevated park as a test case for just planning. *Urban Geography.* Advanced online publication. https://doi.org/10.1080/02723638.2018.1500252

Barnard, A. (2018, July 18). Climate change is killing the Cedars of Lebanon. Retrieved July 29, 2018, from https://www.nytimes.com/interactive/2018/07/18/climate/lebanon-climate-change-environment-cedars.html

Bianchi, R. B., & Stephenson, M. L. (2014). *Tourism and citizenship: Rights, freedoms and responsibilities in the global order.* New York: Routledge.

Dredge, D., & Gyimóthy, S. (Eds.). (2017). *Collaborative economy and tourism: Perspectives, politics, policies and prospects.* Cham, Switzerland: Springer.

Escobar, A. (2018). *Designs for the pluriverse: Radical interdependence, autonomy, and the making of worlds.* Durham, NC: Duke University Press.

Fainstein, S. S. (2010). *The just city.* Ithaca, NY: Cornell University Press.

Fennell, D. A. (2017). *Tourism ethics* (2nd ed.). Bristol, United Kingdom: Channel View Publications. Retrieved from https://www.world-of-digitals.com/en/fennell-tourism-ethics-ebook-pdf

Hernandez, J. (2018, June 22). Jogger who accidentally crossed U.S. border from B.C. detained for 2 weeks. Retrieved June 25, 2018, from https://www.cbc.ca/news/canada/british-columbia/jogger-accidentally-crosses-u-s-border-from-b-c-gets-detained-for-2-weeks-1.4717060

Higgins-Desbiolles, F. (2008). Justice tourism and alternative globalisation. *Journal of Sustainable Tourism, 16*(3), 345–364. https://doi.org/10.1080/09669580802154132

Higgins-Desboilles, F. (2011). Justifying tourism: Justice through tourism. In S. Cole & N. Morgan (Eds.), *Tourism and inequality: Problems and prospects* (pp. 194–211).

Holden, A. (2018). Environmental ethics for tourism–The state of the art. *Tourism Review,* TR-03-2017-0066. https://doi.org/10.1108/TR-03-2017-0066

Hollinshead, K., & Suleman, R. (2018). The everyday instillations of worldmaking: New Vistas of understanding on the declarative reach of tourism. *Tourism Analysis, 23*(2), 201–213. https://doi.org/10.3727/108354218X15210313504553

Hurley, L. (2018, November 2). U.S. top court rejects Trump administration bid to halt climate trial. Retrieved November 2, 2018, from https://www.reuters.com/article/us-usa-court-climate/u-s-top-court-rejects-trump-administration-bid-to-halt-climate-trial-idUSKCN1N72MK

Isaac, R. K., & Hodge, D. (2011). An exploratory study: Justice tourism in controversial areas. The case of Palestine. *Tourism Planning and Development.* https://doi.org/10.1080/21568316.2011.554048

Jamal, T. B. (2004). Virtue ethics and sustainable tourism pedagogy: Phronesis, principles and practice. *Journal of Sustainable Tourism, 12*(6), 530–545. https://doi.org/10.1080/09669580408667252

Jamal, T., & Smith, B. (2017). Tourism pedagogy and visitor responsibilities in destinations of local-global significance: Climate change and social-political action. *Sustainability (Switzerland), 9*(6). https://doi.org/10.3390/su9061082

Leahy, S. (2017, June 19). By 2100, deadly heat may threaten majority of humankind. Retrieved July 29, 2018, from https://news.nationalgeographic.com/2017/06/heat waves-climate-change-global-warming/

Mills, C. W. (1959). *The sociological imagination: Fortieth anniversary edition.* New York, NY: Oxford University Press.

Mowforth, M., & Munt, I. (2016). *Tourism and sustainability: Development, globalisation and new tourism in the Third World* (4th ed.). New York, NY: Routledge.

Our Children's Trust. (2018). Juliana v. U.S.–Climate Lawsuit. Retrieved August 2, 2018, from https://www.ourchildrenstrust.org/us/federal-lawsuit/

Rodrik, D. (2008). Thinking about governance. In *Governance, growth, and development decision-making* (pp. 17–24). Washington, DC: The International Bank for Reconstruction and Development/The World Bank. Retrieved from http://siteresources.world bank.org/EXTPUBLICSECTORANDGOVERNANCE/Resources/governanceand growth.pdf

Scheyvens, R. (2002). *Tourism for development: Empowering communities.* Harlow, UK: Prentice Hall. https://doi.org/10.1016/j.tourman.2005.07.013

Schlosberg, D. (2007). *Defining environmental justice.* Oxford: Oxford University Press.

Selsky, A. (2018, November 8). Appeals court puts youth climate change lawsuit on hold. Retrieved November 8, 2018, from https://apnews.com/06625c4352da47c3a80cc 31e4c482c98

Smith, M., & Duffy, R. (2003). *The ethics of tourism development*. New York, NY: Routledge.

Whyte, K. P. (2010). An environmental justice framework for Indigenous tourism. *Environmental Philosophy, 7*(2), 75–92.

Whyte, K. P. (2011). The recognition dimensions of environmental justice in Indian country. *Environmental Justice, 4*(4), 199–205. https://doi.org/10.1089/env.2011.0036

Young, I. M. (2011). *Justice and the politics of difference* (Paperback). Princeton, NJ: Princeton University Press.

INDEX

adaptation planning 155–156, 174, 217–218
African American 108, 113, 122–128
Airbnb 4, 6, 245
Alcatraz Island 149, 175, 182–188; *see also* impacts
Amsterdam 5–7, 10, 15
Anangu 157–158, 181; *see also* Uluru
Anthropocene 8, 21, 174, 181, 236, 244–245
Apo, P. *see* community tourism; Hawai'i
Arctic tourism 236–238
Aristotle 28
Australia 80–81, 103–105, 157–158, 222
Avni, N. 196, 211–212, 214, 230n8

Bhutan 10–11
Basarwa 158–159
Brazos Valley African American Museum 127–128; *see also* museum: community museum
Brundtland Commission 10, 148
Bruner, E. 91, 123–124
Buen Vivir 163; *see also* ontology, pluriverse
Burma/Myanmar 12, 22n3, 111

Camargo, B. 51, 72, 79, 230n7
Canada: Canmore 195–197, 209–211, 221
Capabilities Approach 29, 37, 67–71, 78; *see also* Capability Approach; Nussbaum, M.; Sen, A.
Capability Approach 33–34, 37, 67; *see also* Capabilities Approach; Nussbaum, M.; Sen, A.

care: ethic of care 20, 66–71, 78, 129, 132–134, 181, 220, 234–235, 246–247
Cartagena 72–75
Categorical Imperative 29, 38; *see also* Kant, I.
Chickasaw Nation 217
Children's University Tasmania 222–228
China 12, 78, 175–176, 178–179, 188; Beijing 175–176, 178, 180
Choi, J. 204–205
citizenship: global 102, 133, 222, 235, 247
climate change 8–9, 20, 105–106, 148–152, 154–155, 174, 181, 198, 200, 217–219, 221
climate justice 149, 162, 174; air travel 149–152; youth 155, 198–200, 246; *see also* emissions: greenhouse gas (GHG)
climate refugees 149–150
collaboration 196, 201–202, 208–214
collaborative planning 97, 155, 196, 198, 201–203, 208–211, 215; *see also* planning: public participation
Colombia: San Basilio de Palenque 72
colonialism 65, 80–83, 90, 107, 122, 134, 159, 162, 236, 240, 243–244; *see also* imperialism; neocolonialism
commemorative justice 97
commodification 17, 38, 75, 79, 159, 169, 243
community development 139, 206, 228; *see also* Capabilities Approach; community tourism; community-based tourism
community tourism 53, 65–67, 71, 90; *see also* community-based tourism; community development; Hawai'i

256 Index

community-based tourism 64, 66, 134–136, 140, 230n2; *see also* community development, community tourism
consensus 209–211, 224
conservation 70, 78, 148, 178; *see also* heritage conservation
control 17, 20, 49, 66, 68–69, 107, 128, 135–136, 140
Copenhagen: Street Voices 128–134
Corporate Social Responsibility (CSR) 47, 109, 129, 171
cosmopolitanism 102, 106, 203–204; ethical cosmopolitanism 102, 105–106
Cozumel 17, 25–26, 48–49, 52–53, 55–56; *see also* Maya; Quintana Roo
cruising 7, 26
cultural capital 223
cultural heritage 78, 89, 93, 123, 128, 178, 182–183, 188
cultural justice 147, 175, 181, 191n5, 235–236
cultural survival 12, 31, 55, 83, 175, 245

degrowth 163, 181, 246
democracy 12, 34, 47, 140, 204–206, 208, 210, 213, 215–216, 230n4, 230n9, 242; deliberative democracy 161, 209, 230n2
Destination Marketing Organization (DMO) 38, 130, 243
difference 37, 50, 71–72, 83, 85–87, 163–164, 214–217, 220–221, 242–243, 247; *see also* recognition; Young, I.M.
disability 33, 37, 67, 86, 211
disaster 116–117, 119, 122, 174, 191n8
discrimination 128, 148–149, 158–160, 198, 211, 240, 244
dispossession 66, 81–82, 93, 157–160, 175, 181
distributive justice 31–32, 34–35, 38, 47–50, 63, 84–85, 161, 181, 211, 240; *see also* Fainstein, S.; Fraser, N.; principles; Rawls, J.; redistribution
diversity 62–63, 66–67, 70, 85, 175–176, 178, 197, 210–211, 214; *see also* difference; Fainstein, S.; inclusiveness
Djabugay 80–81; *see also* Tjapukai Aboriginal Cultural Park
domination 79–80, 85–86, 90, 216
Dredge, D. 128–129, 230n2

dual system of rights 86, 147, 220
Earth Day 146, 160
ecological justice 19, 161, 165, 235, 240, 246

ecotourism 106, 142n1, 164–167, 169; *see also* Galápagos Islands
Edelheim, J. 27, 41
education: public education 175, 180, 186, 188
emissions: greenhouse gas (GHG) 149–152, 154, 174; *see also* climate justice: air travel
empowerment 12, 78, 115, 128–129, 164, 202, 208, 214; of women 39, 46, 67, 75, 78–79, 81–83, 86
endogenous development 65–66, 90, 164
energy justice 152
Enoh, L.L. 121–123
environmental heritage 157, 160–161; *see also* relational approach; Whyte, K.
environmental justice 151, 155, 157–162, 164, 181, 191n5, 236, 240, 242
equality 31–33, 35–37, 39–40, 47, 50; *see also* inequality
equity 18–19, 25, 35–36, 39, 50, 57, 148, 155, 169–170, 181, 210–211, 214, 220, 230n7, 230n8; social 45–46, 129, 152, 155, 191n8; *see also* inequity
Escobar, A. 147, 162–163, 174, 181; *see also* pluriverse; postdevelopment
ethnocentrism 64, 72
everyday life: everyday colonialism 83
exploitation 32, 34, 40, 46, 79–81, 83–84, 86, 107, 158, 166

Fainstein, S. 210–211, 213, 221, 239, 240, 243
Fennell, D. 19, 30, 98n6, 161, 239
Finland: trade unions 41–42, 45
Fraser, N. 84–86, 121–122, 128, 203, 215, 230n2, 235; *see also* Honneth, A.; recognition; redistribution; representation; Young, I.M.
freedom 22n3, 30, 32–33, 36, 47, 68, 98n4, 114, 203, 216
Friebele, J. 165

Galápagos Islands 164–168; *see also* impacts
gender *see* discrimination; empowerment of women; equity; exploitation; LGBT+
Ghana: Elmina Castle 121, 123
Global North 148, 154, 164, 181, 239, 244
Global South 154, 164, 181
globalization 7, 10, 12, 20, 26, 50, 197, 202, 236, 239
good tourism 1, 2, 19, 20, 50, 79, 234–235, 246–247
governance 17, 20, 106, 196–199, 201–204, 208, 221–222, 239–240, 243, 245

Great Barrier Reef 62, 103–104, 106, 112
greenwashing 10, 167, 170
Gross National Happiness (GNH) 10–11
groups: diasporic 89, 121, 123, 133, 239;
    group conscious policies 86, 211, 216, 220
growth 4–6, 11, 20, 38, 129, 133–135, 148,
    152, 167, 210, 221–223, 236

Hawai'i 64–67, 71, 90, 106, 159
Healy, N. 147, 149
heritage conservation 63, 78, 116, 128,
    174–176, 180, 182–183, 188; see also
    historic preservation
heritage tourism 184, 247–248
Higgins-Desbiolles, F. 115, 170, 252n1
historic preservation 174, 184; see also
    heritage conservation
Höckert, E. 134–135, 236
Holden, A. 19, 115, 247
Honneth, A. 84, 235; see also Fraser, N.
hospitality 30, 32, 41–46, 65–67, 71, 107,
    109, 128, 134, 138–141, 142n4, 158–159
housing: affordable housing 196–197,
    210–211, 221
human dignity 32, 68, 78, 163
human rights 12, 32, 39–40, 45, 69, 111,
    114, 128, 142n4, 188, 242, 244

impacts 5, 8, 13, 15–18, 20–21, 39, 64, 154,
    241; see also Alcatraz; Galápagos Islands
imperialism: cultural imperialism 80, 82,
    86, 90
inclusiveness 63, 80, 92, 148, 175, 242–243,
    246
India: Agra 87–89; Taj Mahal 87–89
Indigenous people see Anangu; Basarwa;
    Chickasaw Nation; Djabugay; Maya;
    Native Americans; Native Hawaiians;
    Palenquero
Indigenous women see Raibmon
inequality 33, 36, 38–39, 69, 75, 79, 114,
    141, 148, 150, 152, 154, 159, 173, 215,
    223; see also equality
inequity 49, 51, 57, 75, 92, 197; see also
    equity
information and communication
    technologies (ICTs) 20, 201, 245
injustice: land 80–83, 93, 108–109; see also
    Basarwa; Uluru
intangible heritage 62, 72, 75, 119, 128, 147,
    174, 182–183, 188, 206–207, 235, 242
international tourism 4, 8, 26. 53, 72, 91,
    98n7, 106, 135, 149, 151–152, 236

Jaffa Port: redevelopment 211–214
Jamal, T. 3, 5, 10, 20, 51, 87, 104, 182, 183,
    195, 210
Japan: war memorials 117–119, 128
Jourdan, D. 155, 199, 217–218
just tourism 19, 46, 233, 247
justice as fairness 29, 31–32, 34–38,
    40, 50, 59n4, 63, 67; see also distributive
    justice
justice tourism 30, 115, 170, 252n1,
    252n2
justice tourist 115, 235

Kant, I. 29, 38, 117, 142n4, 203–204; see also
    Categorical Imperative; cosmopolitanism
Kim, S. 204–205

land rights 66, 157, 160, 175, 181
Lane, B. 147, 170, 247
law 20, 31, 40, 53, 155, 159, 199–200, 203
League of Nations 204
Levinas, E. 140–141
LGBT+ 63, 98n1, 128, 221
liberal pluralist see distributive justice;
    Rawls, J.
Little Bighorn Battlefield 85, 92–97
Liu, M. 175

Manrique, Carolina 116, 182
Marx, Karl 34–35
mass tourism 5–7, 10, 13, 65, 80, 83. 98n7,
    142n2, 147, 164
Maya 25–27, 38, 47–49, 51–53, 55–56; see
    also Cozumel; Quintana Roo; racism;
    representation; tourism policy
Meehan, E. 128–129, 131
Mexico 25–27, 48, 51, 202
mobilities 2, 4, 7–8, 20, 196, 201–202
modernist 147, 162–163, 181, 236;
    modernist principles 65, 147, 162
morality 28–30, 203
Mowforth, M. and Munt, I. 30, 79,
    98n7, 154
museum: community museum 127–128,
    147, 175–176, 178, 180; see also Brazos
    Valley African American Museum; Shijia
    Hutong Museum

Native Americans 93–97, 184–188
Native Hawaiians 64–66, 159
nature's rights 161, 163; see also justice:
    ecological; Schlosberg, D.
neocolonialism 65, 83, 90, 98n7, 162

258 Index

neoliberal globalization 20, 26, 133, 164, 202, 236, 239; *see also* neoliberalism
neoliberalism 7, 19, 49, 106, 148, 154, 181, 201–202, 244; *see also* neoliberal globalization
New Zealand 197
Nussbaum, M. 28–29, 34, 37, 48, 67–69, 71, 78–79, 90–91, 234, 239; *see also* Capabilities Approach; community development

ontology: non-dualist 163, 174
ontology: relational 18–19, 129, 132, 140, 162–163, 174; *see also* Buen Vivir; pluriverse
Ooi, C.-S. 222
oppression 32, 85–86, 107, 216; *see also* Young, I.M.

Palenquera 72–76, 79, 81, 91–92; *see also* Palenquero; racism
Palenquero 72–75, 79; *see also* Palenquera
parity of participation 84–85, 122; *see also* participation; planning: public participation
participation 45, 53, 63, 69, 86–87, 133, 183, 199, 239–240, 243, 246; *see also* democracy; procedural justice; planning: public participation
planning: public participation 31, 80, 95, 213–214, 230n8; *see also* collaborative planning; parity of participation; participation; public sphere
Playa del Carmen 25, 52–53
pluralism 36, 50, 86, 210, 215, 220
pluralistic justice 147, 159–162, 175, 181–182, 210, 214, 222, 239–240
pluriverse 162–164, 174, 181–182, 236, 242, 247; *see also* Buen Vivir; Escobar, A.; ontology; postdevelopment
policy 29, 55, 67, 69, 152, 178, 201–203, 215; *see also* Children's University Tasmania; Fainstein, S.; Jaffa port: redevelopment; power; South Korea; tourism policy
pollution: toxic waste 159–160
postdevelopment 147, 162–164, 181–182; *see also* Escobar, A.
power 17, 26, 33, 35, 49, 90, 112–113, 141, 188, 201, 203, 208, 210–211, 213, 215; *see also* policy
principles 27, 32, 38–39, 45, 129, 181, 183, 202–203, 210–211, 214, 227, 240–241;

see also Alcatraz; community tourism; distributive justice
procedural justice 31, 49, 69, 160–161, 230n9, 240; *see also* participation
progress 147, 162, 236
Pro-Poor Tourism 27, 32, 38, 69, 91
public sphere 201, 203–204; *see also* planning: public participation

Quintana Roo: as part of Mayan culture 25, 38, 47–48, 51–57, 240; *see also* Maya; racism

racism 38, 49, 56, 73, 81, 91, 108–109, 151, 159–160; *see also* Maya; Palenquero; Quintana Roo; Starbucks
Raibmon, P. 82–83, 98n8
Rawls, J. 31, 34–39, 59n1, 67, 69, 220, 239; justice as fairness 29, 31–32, 34–38, 40, 50, 59n4, 63, 67; *see also* distributive justice; redistribution; rights
recognition 62–64, 72, 74, 77–87, 91, 95, 121, 126, 160, 161, 164, 186, 215–216, 221; psychological 122, 128; *see also* Fraser, N.; Honneth, A.; Young, I.M.
redistribution 32, 63, 79–80, 84–85, 122, 128, 133, 160, 240; *see also* Fraser, N.; Rawls, J.; recognition; redistribution; representation
relational approach 18–19, 129, 132–135, 140–141, 158–165, 181–182, 211, 234–236, 240–242, 246; *see also* Buen Vivir; environmental heritage; Escobar, A.; pluriverse
representation 56, 73, 79, 85, 92, 97, 122, 133, 160, 164, 178, 198, 212, 240; *see also* Fraser, N.; Maya
resilience 5, 9, 116–117, 163, 173, 235, 242; cultural resilience 174–175, 181–183, 188; ecological resilience 167, 169, 174; social resilience 174; *see also* Alcatraz
respect 28–29, 35, 40, 46, 67–70, 78, 80, 142n4, 158, 215, 235, 242–244
responsibility 47, 102, 104–116, 128–130, 132, 134, 140, 146, 182, 247; *see also* responsible tourism
responsibility for justice: political responsibility 103, 109–115, 133, 146, 235
responsible tourism 27–28, 70–71, 91; *see also* responsibility
restorative justice 81, 127, 133, 159, 186
retributive justice 31, 109

rights 27, 33, 36, 38, 47, 56, 186, 188, 220; *see also* dispossession; distributive justice; Rawls, J.

safety 121, 128
Sandel, M. 29–30
Scheyvens, R. 30, 252n1; *see also* justice tourism
Schlosberg, D. 161–162, 181, 240; *see also* nature's rights
sea level rise 147, 149–150, 155–157
self-determination 45, 79, 80, 86, 114, 128, 133, 242
Sen, A. 28–34, 37, 50, 234, 239; *see also* Capability Approach; Nussbaum, M.
settler colonialism 82, 90
sex trade 30, 33, 142n6
Shelley, B. 222–223
Shijia Hutong Museum 175–180; *see also* museum: community museum
Smith, M. and Duffy, R. 19, 30, 114, 148, 239
social enterprise 79, 128–131, 133, 248
social rights 47, 63, 67, 76, 196–198, 215, 220–222
solidarity 28, 41, 108, 114–116, 119, 127–128, 133, 136, 252; *see also* Higgins-Desbiolles, F.
South Africa 47, 70
South Korea: Gangneung Danoje Festival 197, 205–208; tourism governance and policy 204–208
Starbucks 107–110; *see also* racism
structural injustice 106–116, 122, 133, 146, 244–245; *see also* injustice; Young, I.M.
sustainable development 9–10, 39, 148, 173
sustainable tourism: 10–11, 70, 114, 148–149, 169–171

terrorism 7–8, 20–21
The International Ecotourism Society 142n1, 165
Tibet: cultural genocide 12–13
Tjapukai Aboriginal Cultural Park 80–81; *see also* Djabugay; heritage tourism
Tourism Concern 45–46, 51, 114

tourism policy 6, 11, 55, 196, 198, 210–211; *see also* policy
tourism system: local-global tourism system 13–15, 17–18, 20, 196, 198, 201, 222, 241
tourists rights 148, 154, 197
trade unions 27, 41–42, 45

UDHR 32–33, 39, 50
Uluru 157–158, 160, 175, 181, 234, 242; *see also* Anangu; Australia
UNESCO 62, 72, 81, 87, 103, 123, 158, 164, 207
United Nations 28, 32, 39–40, 50, 148
United Nations World Tourism Organization (UNWTO) 4–5, 13–15
USA 81–82, 92, 127–128, 155
utilitarianism 29, 31

value: instrumental 29; intrinsic 66, 68
values 39, 65, 68, 84, 116, 147–148, 182, 210, 220, 240, 242, 244; *see also* modernist; worldview
violence 26, 63–64, 86, 107, 159

Wahl, J. 64, 85, 91–92
water rights 38, 160
Weis, T. 147, 149
well-being 10–11, 17, 19–20, 28, 33, 50, 67–69, 71, 163, 165, 242, 245, 247
Whyte, K. 160–161, 181; *see also* environmental heritage
World Travel and Tourism Council (WTTC) 4, 201
worldmaking 21, 245
worldview 19, 21, 29, 50, 106, 162–165, 181, 236, 241; *see also* modernist; ontology; pluriverse
worth: self-worth 79; *see also* human dignity

Young, I.M. 49, 81, 85–87, 91, 142n4, 161, 215–216, 220, 222, 230n4, 235, 239, 241–242; responsibility for justice 103, 109–113, 133–134, 142n3, 146, 154; *see also* Fraser, N.; injustice; oppression; recognition
youth rights 155, 198–200, 246

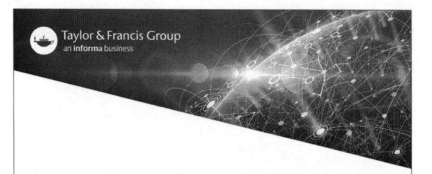

Taylor & Francis eBooks

www.taylorfrancis.com

A single destination for eBooks from Taylor & Francis with increased functionality and an improved user experience to meet the needs of our customers.

90,000+ eBooks of award-winning academic content in Humanities, Social Science, Science, Technology, Engineering, and Medical written by a global network of editors and authors.

TAYLOR & FRANCIS EBOOKS OFFERS:

A streamlined experience for our library customers

A single point of discovery for all of our eBook content

Improved search and discovery of content at both book and chapter level

REQUEST A FREE TRIAL
support@taylorfrancis.com